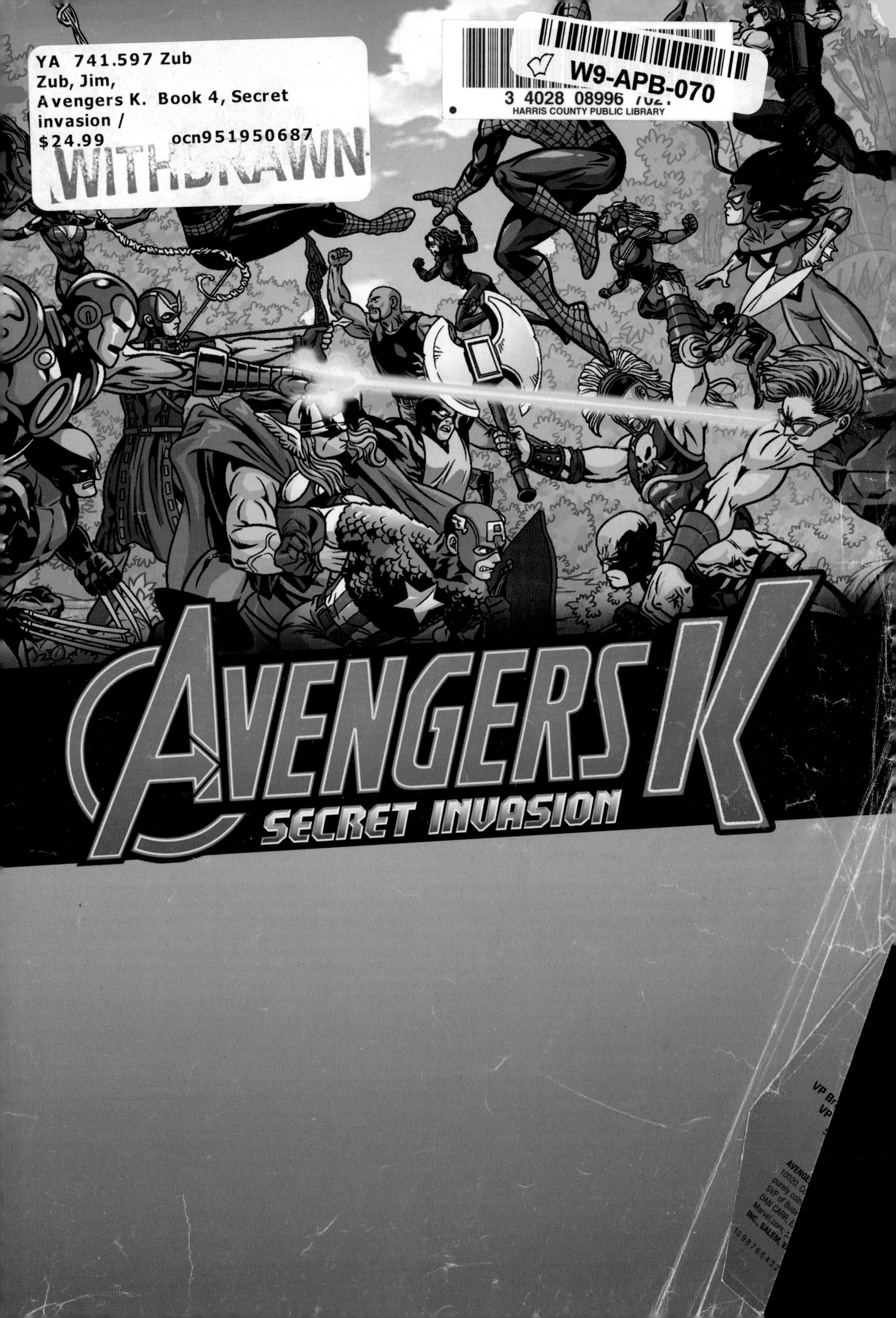
AVENGERS K
SECRET INVASION

VP Br
VP
AVENGE
10020, C
purely coin
SVP of Busi
DAN CARR, E
Marvel.com, p
INC., SALEM, V
10987654321

AVENGERS K
SECRET INVASION

JIM ZUB
SCRIPT

WOO BIN CHOI with **JAE SUNG LEE**
PENCILS

MIN JU LEE
INKS

JAE WOONG LEE & HEE YE CHO
COLORS

VC's CORY PETIT
LETTERS

WOO BIN CHOI with **JAE SUNG LEE, MIN JU LEE, JAE WOONG LEE & HEE YE CHO**
COVER ART

Adapted from *SECRET INVASION #1-8*

Original comics written by BRIAN MICHAEL BENDIS
and illustrated by LEINIL FRANCIS YU, MARK MORALES & LAURA MARTIN with EMILY WARREN and CHRISTINA STRAIN.

Adaptations written by SI YEON PARK and translated by JI EUN PARK

AVENGERS created by STAN LEE & JACK KIRBY

Editor SARAH BRUNSTAD
Manager, Licensed Publishing JEFF REINGOLD
and Management & Development, Asia C.B. CEBULSKI
Production & Special Projects JEFF YOUNGQUIST
SVP Print, Sales & Marketing DAVID GABRIEL

Associate Manager, Digital Assets JOE HOCHSTEIN
Associate Managing Editor KATERI WOODY
Senior Editor, Special Projects JENNIFER GRÜNWALD
Editor, Special Projects MARK D. BEAZLEY
Book Designer: ADAM DEL RE

Editor In Chief AXEL ALONSO
Chief Creative Officer JOE QUESADA
Publisher DAN BUCKLEY
Executive Producer ALAN FINE

RS K BOOK 4: SECRET INVASION. First printing 2017. ISBN# 978-1-302-90412-8. Published by MARVEL WORLDWIDE, INC., a subsidiary of MARVEL ENTERTAINMENT, LLC. OFFICE OF PUBLICATION: 135 West 50th Street, New York, NY

Printed in the U.S.A. ALAN FINE, President, Marvel Entertainment; DAN BUCKLEY, President, TV, Publishing & Brand Management; JOE QUESADA, Chief Creative Officer; TOM BREVOORT, SVP of Publishing; DAVID BOGART, ess Affairs & Operations, Publishing & Partnership; C.B. CEBULSKI, VP of Brand Management & Development, Asia; DAVID GABRIEL, SVP of Sales & Marketing, Publishing; JEFF YOUNGQUIST, VP of Production & Special Projects; xecutive Director of Publishing Technology; ALEX MORALES, Director of Publishing Operations; SUSAN CRESPI, Production Manager; STAN LEE, Chairman Emeritus. For information regarding advertising in Marvel Comics or on ease contact Vit DeBellis, Integrated Sales Manager, at vdebellis@marvel.com. For Marvel subscription inquiries, please call 888-511-5480. **Manufactured between 12/16/2016 and 1/23/2017 by LSC COMMUNICATIONS , USA.**

1

AVENGERS ACTIVE ROST

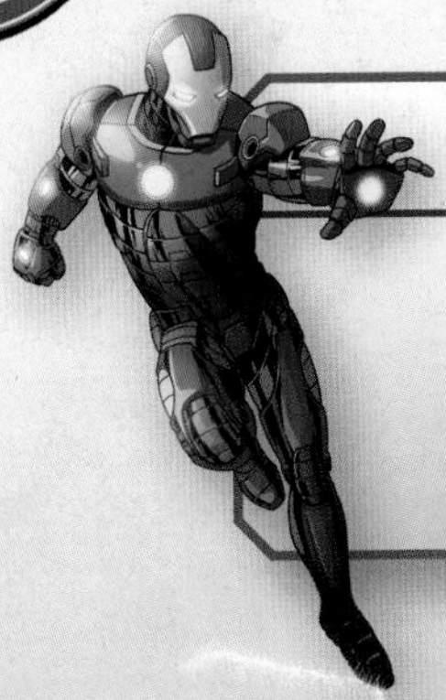

IRON MAN | Real Name: ANTHONY EDWARD STARK

Billionaire playboy and genius industrialist Tony Stark was kidnapped during a routine weapons test. His captors attempted to force him to build a weapon of mass destruction. Instead, he created a powerful suit of armor that saved his life. From that day on, he has used the suit to protect the world as the invincible Avenger Iron Man.

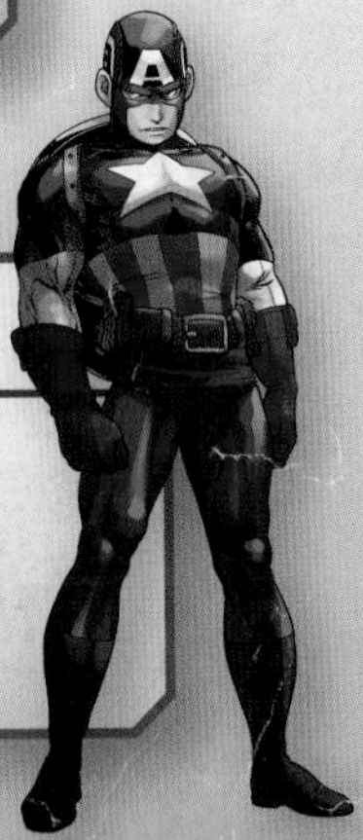

Real Name: STEVEN ROGERS | CAPTAIN AMERICA

During World War II, a secret military experiment turned scrawny Steve Rogers into America's first Super-Soldier, Captain America. Near the end of the war, Rogers was presumed dead in an explosion over the English Channel. Decades later, Cap was found frozen in ice and was revived. Steve Rogers awakened to a world he never imagined—a man out of time. He again took up the mantle of Captain America, defending the United States and the world from threats of all kinds.

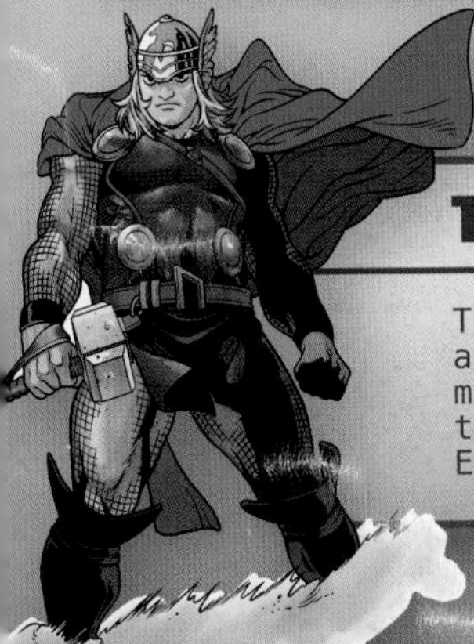

THOR | Real Name: THOR ODINSON

Thor is the Asgardian God of Thunder and an Avenger. Wielding Mjolnir, a mystical uru hammer of immense power, the son of Odin fights to protect Earth and all the Nine Realms.

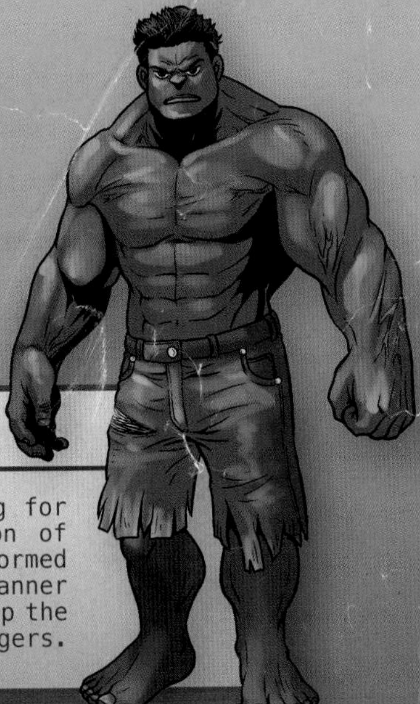

Real Name: ROBERT BRUCE BANNER | HULK

Bruce Banner was a brilliant scientist working for the Army when he was caught in the explosion of a gamma bomb of his own creation and transformed into the nearly indestructible Hulk. Now, Dr. Banner struggles to control his anger and anxiety to keep the Hulk in check while he fights alongside the Avengers.

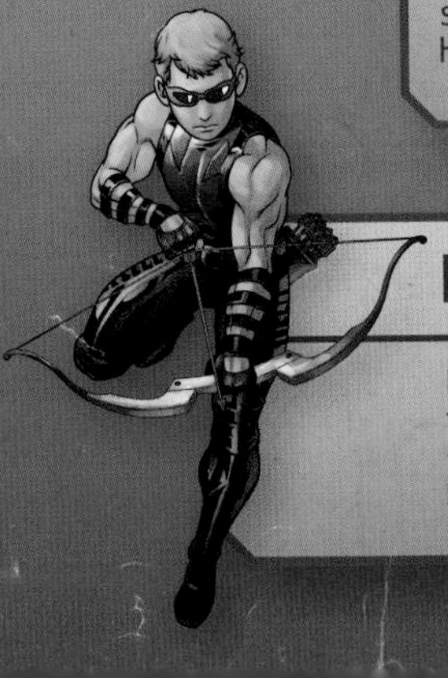

HAWKEYE | Real Name: CLINT BARTON

Former criminal Clint Barton used his circus training to become the greatest sharpshooter the world has ever seen. He reformed and joined the Avengers, quickly becoming one of the team's most stalwart members.

BLACK WIDOW | Real Name: NATASHA ROMANOFF

Natasha Romanoff is a deadly operative equipped with state-of-the-art weaponry and extensive hand-to-hand combat training. Before joining S.H.I.E.L.D. and the Avengers, she was an enemy spy; now, she uses her unique skills to atone for her past.

WASP | Real Name: JANET VAN DYNE

Janet van Dyne was a flighty socialite until she met brilliant biochemist Hank Pym. When Hank shared his size-altering Pym Particles with her, she gained not only the ability to manipulate her size, but also bioelectric stings and wings that manifest when she shrinks to insect-size. Calling herself the Wasp, Janet soon helped form the Avengers.

ANT-MAN | Real Name: HANK PYM

Scientific genius Henry "Hank" Pym invented a serum that could change the size of his body at will, and a helmet that allowed him to communicate with and control insects. Along with his partner, the Wasp, he helped found the Avengers and rescue Captain America. But in a stroke of arrogance, he accidentally created his own worst enemy and one of the Avengers' deadliest villains: the artificial intelligence known as Ultron.

QUICKSILVER & SCARLET WITCH
Real Names: PIETRO & WANDA MAXIMOFF

Twins Pietro and Wanda Maximoff were normal children kidnapped by the High Evolutionary, who experimented on them. As a result, Pietro gained the ability to travel at extremely high speeds, able to run across the entire Earth in a matter of minutes; and Wanda gained the ability to manipulate chaos magic. The twins' powers are still barely understood. For years, they believed Magneto was their father, though they later discovered their true parentage.

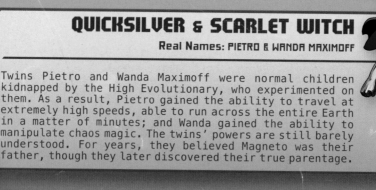

CAPTAIN MARVEL | Real Name: CAROL DANVERS

Thanks to an infusion of Kree DNA via the Psyche-Magnitron device, former Air Force pilot Carol Danvers gained the powers of flight, superhuman strength, and energy projection. She used the name "Ms. Marvel" until her friend and mentor Mar-Vell died; after his passing, Carol took his title to honor his legacy. She's an expert strategist and a heavy hitter in the field.

EXTRAORDINARY ALLIES

BLACK PANTHER
T'Challa is the king of Wakanda and is endowed with the powers of the Panther God, Bast.

SPIDER-MAN
After a bite from an irradiated spider, the young Peter Parker gained powers to become Spider-Man. When he's not guarding his home city of New York, he often assists the Avengers.

SPIDER-WOMAN
Jessica Drew was poisoned with radiation as a child. Attempting to cure her, Jessica's dad accidentally gave her spider-like super-powers, including lethal venom blasts and pheromone secretions that allow her to influence the moods of people around her. Jessica's always fought for the good guys, but lately, she's been acting a little weird…

THE FANTASTIC FOUR
The Fantastic Four got their powers from cosmic rays in space. Super-genius Reed Richards—a.k.a. Mr. Fantastic—can stretch his body to impossible lengths; his wife Sue Richards—a.k.a. Invisible Woman—can turn invisible and project force fields; Sue's brother Johnny Storm—The Human Torch—can light his entire body on fire and fly; and their best friend Ben Grimm—a.k.a. the Thing—is a lovable-but-not-huggable man with a rocky hide and a powerful punch. Reed Richards discovered the Negative Zone, a parallel dimension composed entirely of antimatter. It's a dangerous place, full of warlike races and explosive booby traps…

ABIGAIL BRAND
Abigail Brand is a half-alien with the power to burn through metal. She's the head of S.W.O.R.D., the Sentient World Observation and Response Department—a subdivision of S.H.I.E.L.D. that protects Earth from extraterrestrial threats.

NICK FURY AND HIS HOWLING COMMANDOS
Over years of fighting to protect the United States and the world, former soldier Nick Fury has made a few friends. Sometimes they work together in a team called the Howling Commandos. The team roster is always changing based on who's needed, but one friend Nick's always been able to count on is Dum Dum Dugan, a cunning strategist who's fought at Nick's side since World War II. Dum Dum is the one man Nick knows he can trust… Right?

LUKE CAGE
Luke Cage went to prison for a crime he didn't commit. Forced into illegal experiments there, he gained impenetrable skin and super-strength. Despite all the ways the world has wronged him, Luke always fights on the side of good.

WOLVERINE
James "Logan" Howlett is a mutant with a super-powerful healing factor and Adamantium claws that burst through his knuckles. He's got a fierce temper, but it's usually pointed at the bad guys.

JARVIS
Edwin Jarvis has been the Avengers' butler since their inception. He takes care of everything around the Mansion, and the Avengers trust him with their lives.

AVENGERS MOST WANTED:

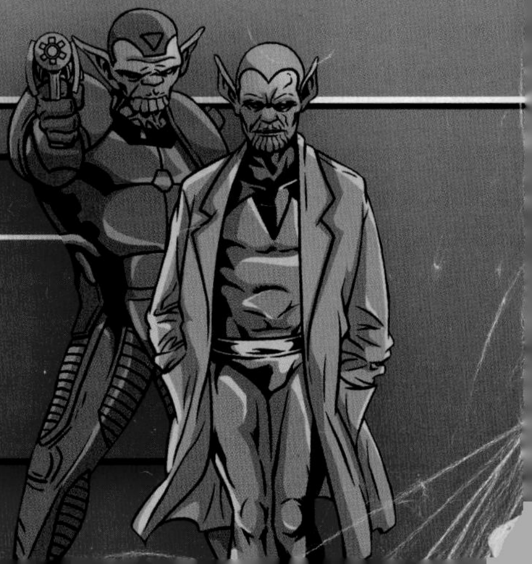

THE SKRULL EMPIRE

The Skrulls are a fierce, warlike race of shape-shifters from the Andromeda Galaxy. They can look like any species in the Multiverse, and some Skrulls can even mimic the super-powers of the heroes they're imitating. Over millions of years, the Skrulls conquered large parts of space, but after much of their empire was destroyed during an intergalactic war, they grew desperate for more territory—and set their sights on Earth!

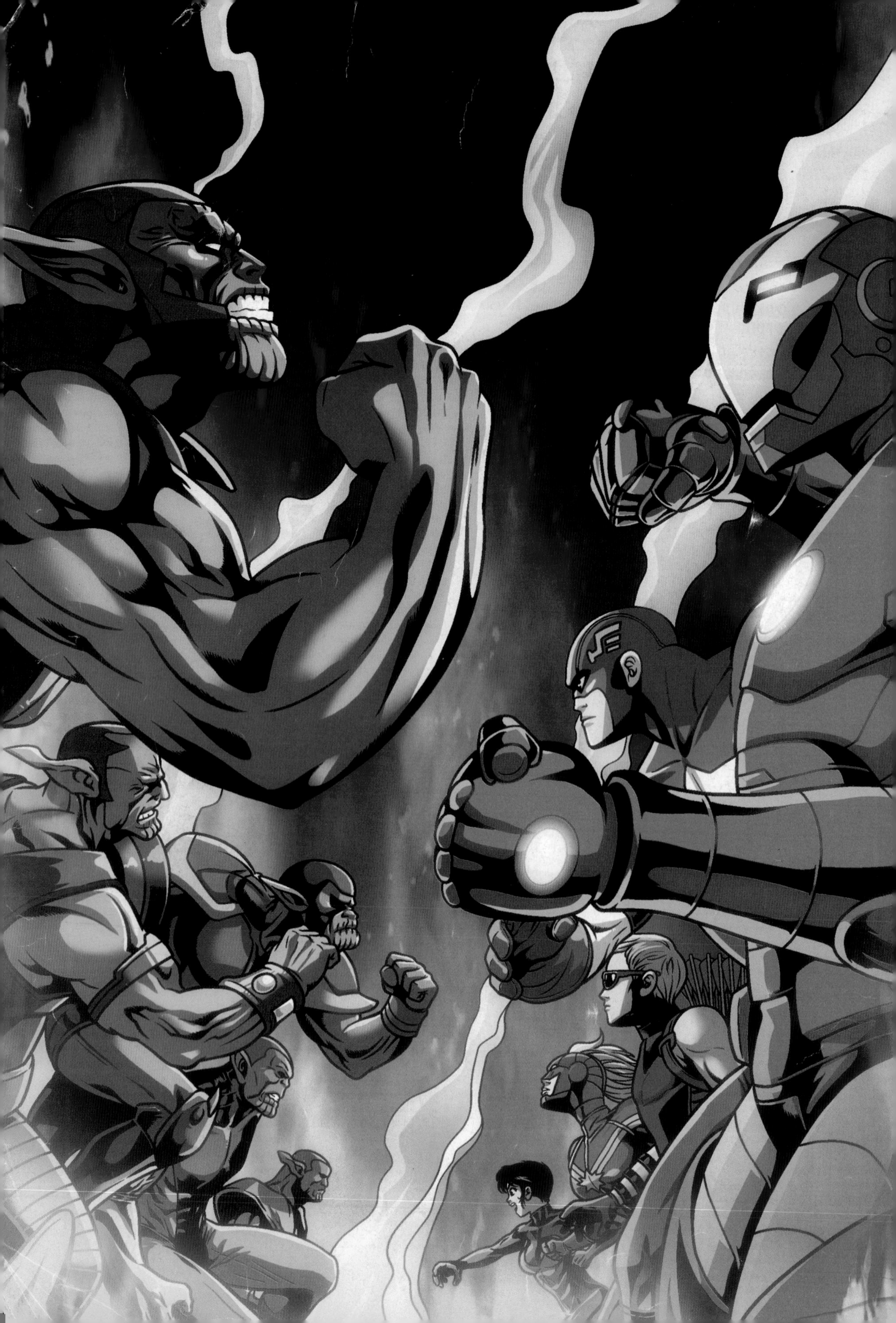

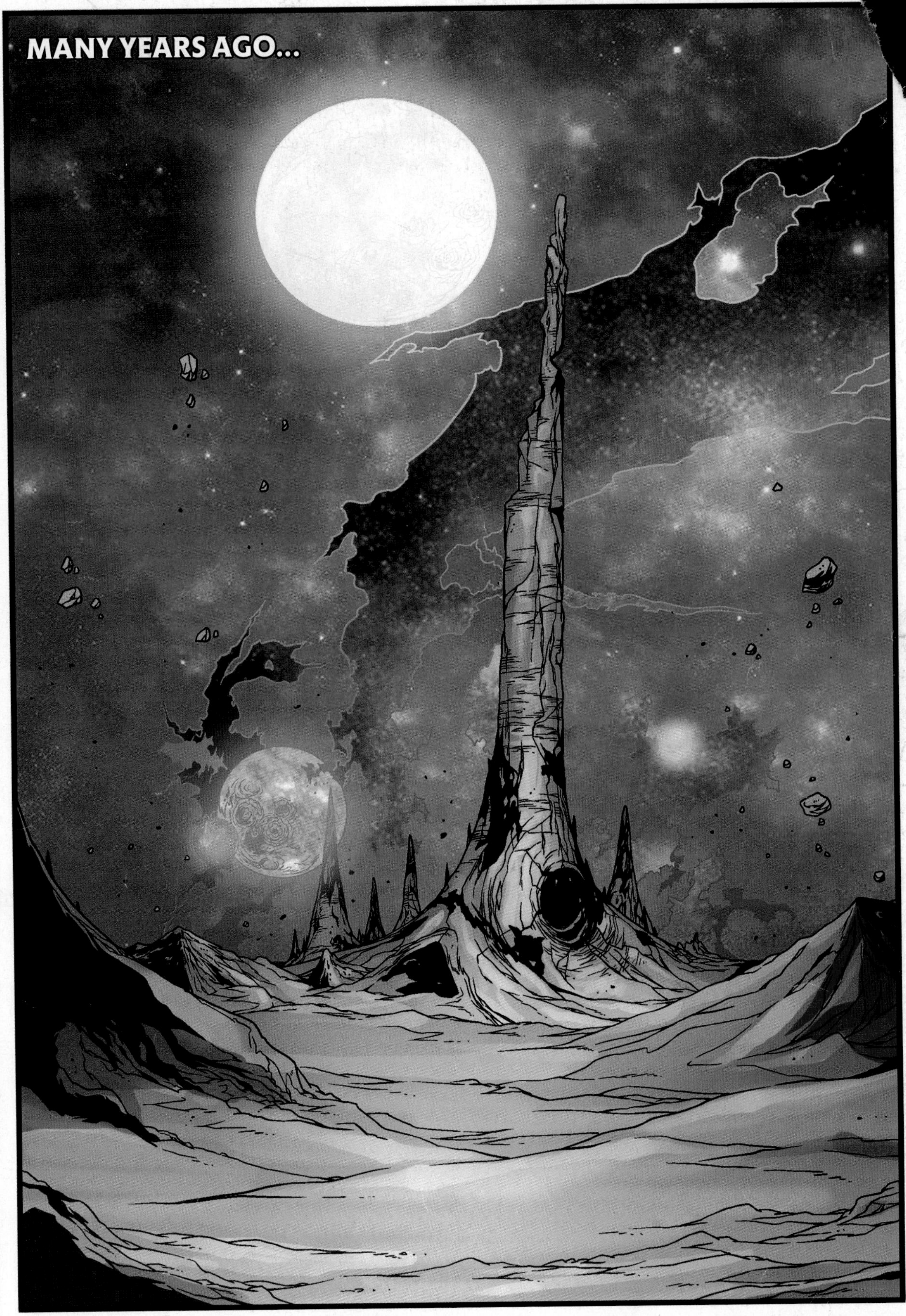
MANY YEARS AGO...

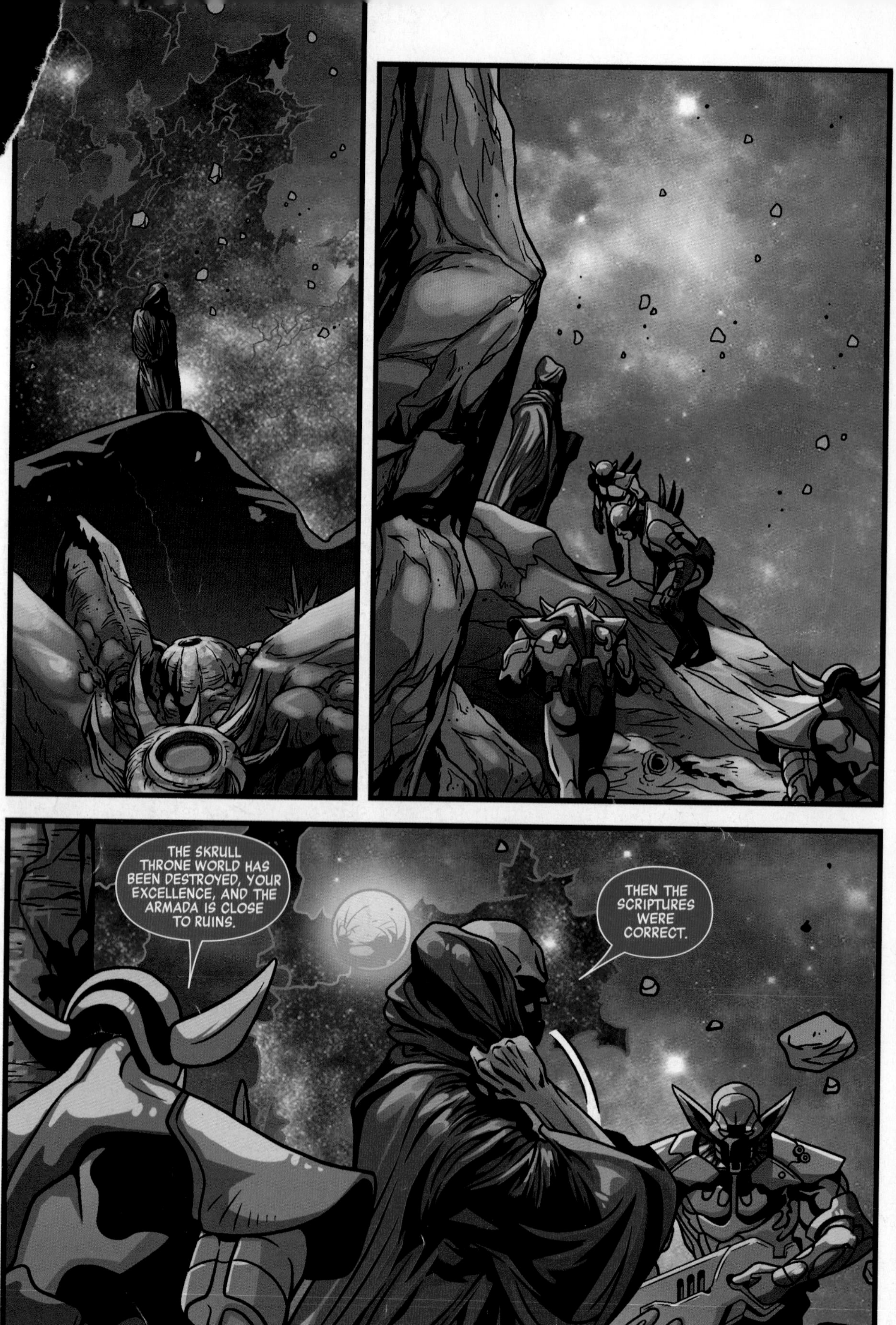
THE SKRULL THRONE WORLD HAS BEEN DESTROYED, YOUR EXCELLENCE, AND THE ARMADA IS CLOSE TO RUINS.
THEN THE SCRIPTURES WERE CORRECT.

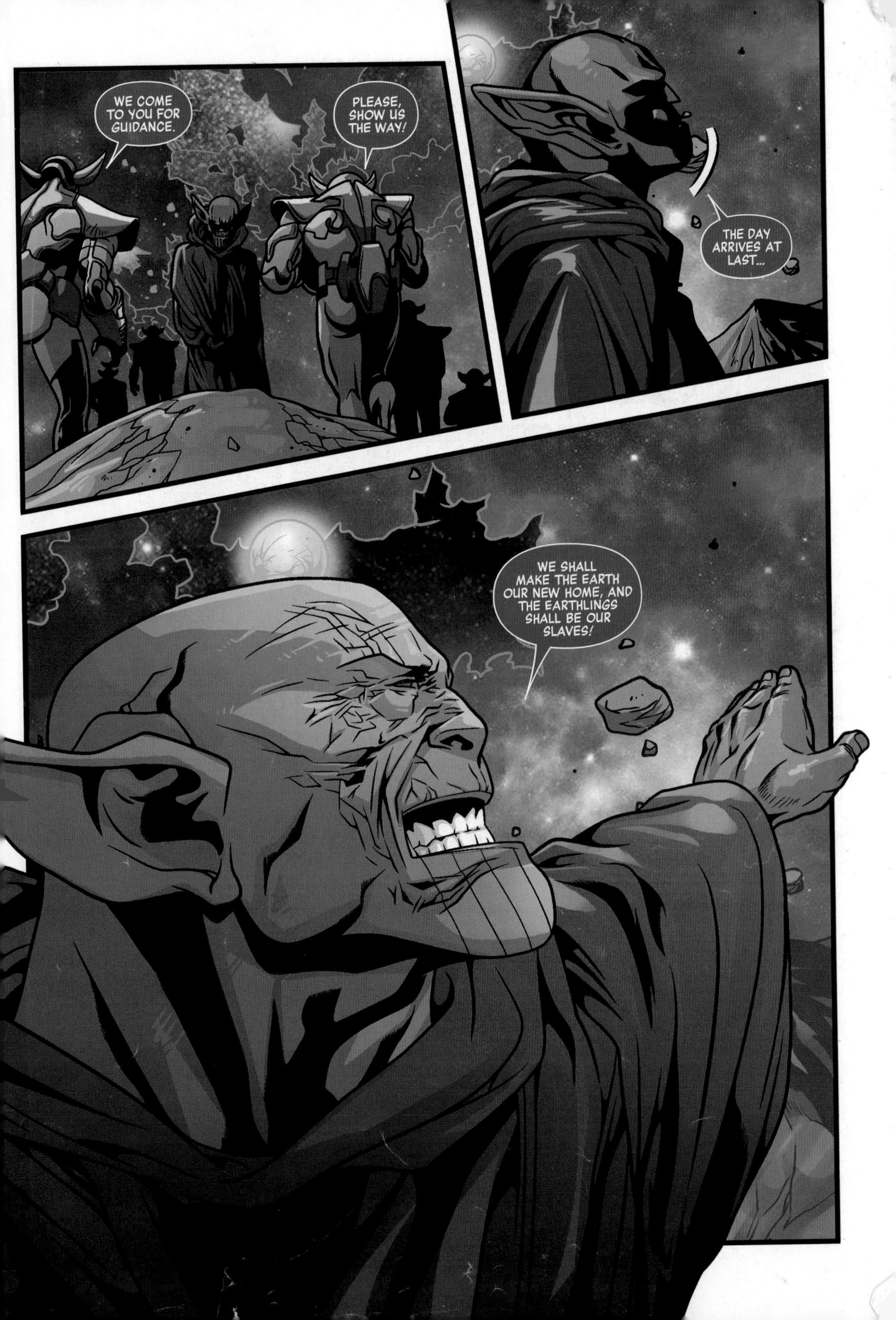
WE COME TO YOU FOR GUIDANCE.
PLEASE, SHOW US THE WAY!
THE DAY ARRIVES AT LAST...
WE SHALL MAKE THE EARTH OUR NEW HOME, AND THE EARTHLINGS SHALL BE OUR SLAVES!

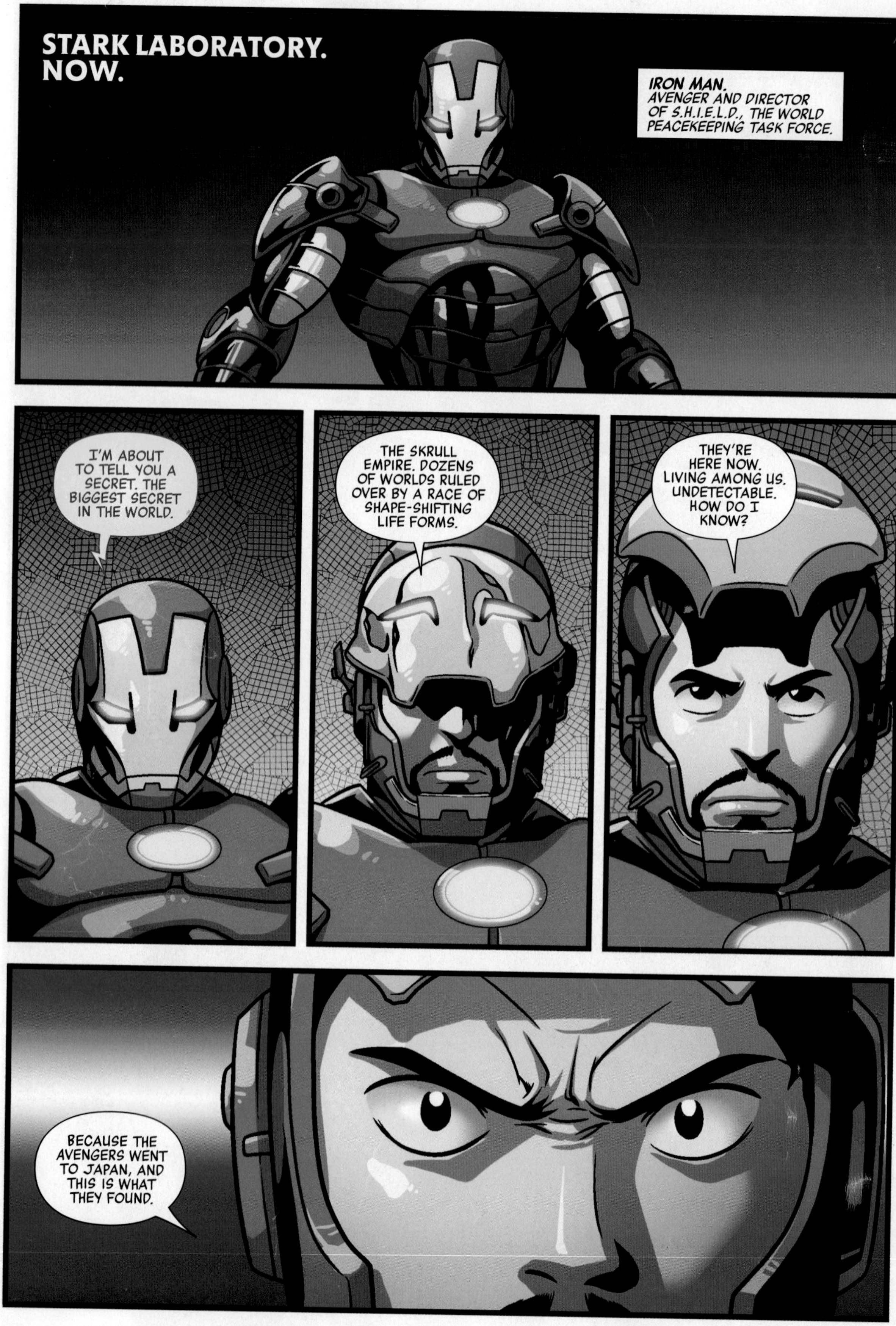
STARK LABORATORY. NOW.
IRON MAN. AVENGER AND DIRECTOR OF S.H.I.E.L.D., THE WORLD PEACEKEEPING TASK FORCE.
I'M ABOUT TO TELL YOU A SECRET. THE BIGGEST SECRET IN THE WORLD.
THE SKRULL EMPIRE. DOZENS OF WORLDS RULED OVER BY A RACE OF SHAPE-SHIFTING LIFE FORMS.
THEY'RE HERE NOW. LIVING AMONG US. UNDETECTABLE. HOW DO I KNOW?
BECAUSE THE AVENGERS WENT TO JAPAN, AND THIS IS WHAT THEY FOUND.

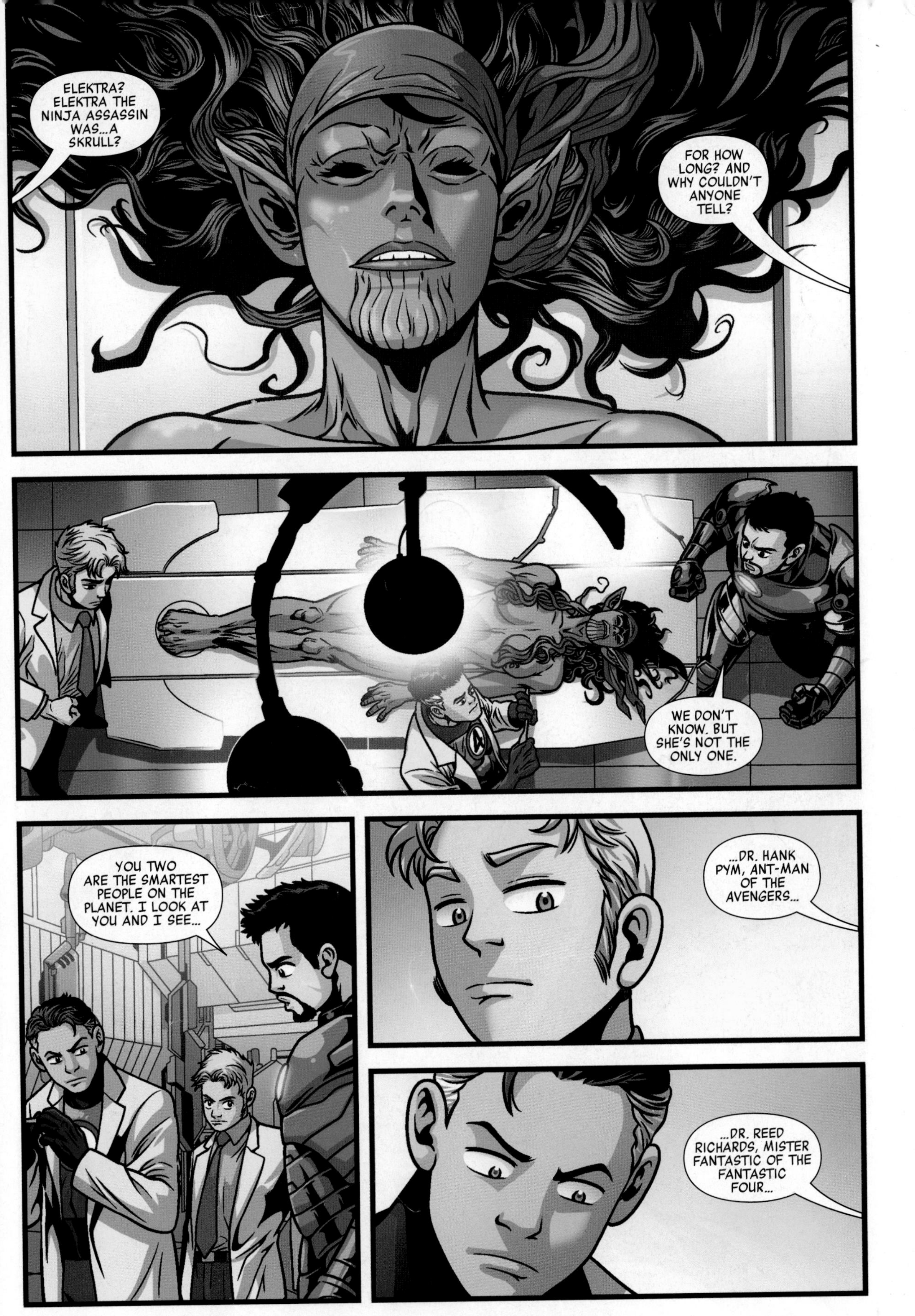
ELEKTRA? ELEKTRA THE NINJA ASSASSIN WAS...A SKRULL?
FOR HOW LONG? AND WHY COULDN'T ANYONE TELL?
WE DON'T KNOW. BUT SHE'S NOT THE ONLY ONE.
YOU TWO ARE THE SMARTEST PEOPLE ON THE PLANET. I LOOK AT YOU AND I SEE...
...DR. HANK PYM, ANT-MAN OF THE AVENGERS...
...DR. REED RICHARDS, MISTER FANTASTIC OF THE FANTASTIC FOUR...

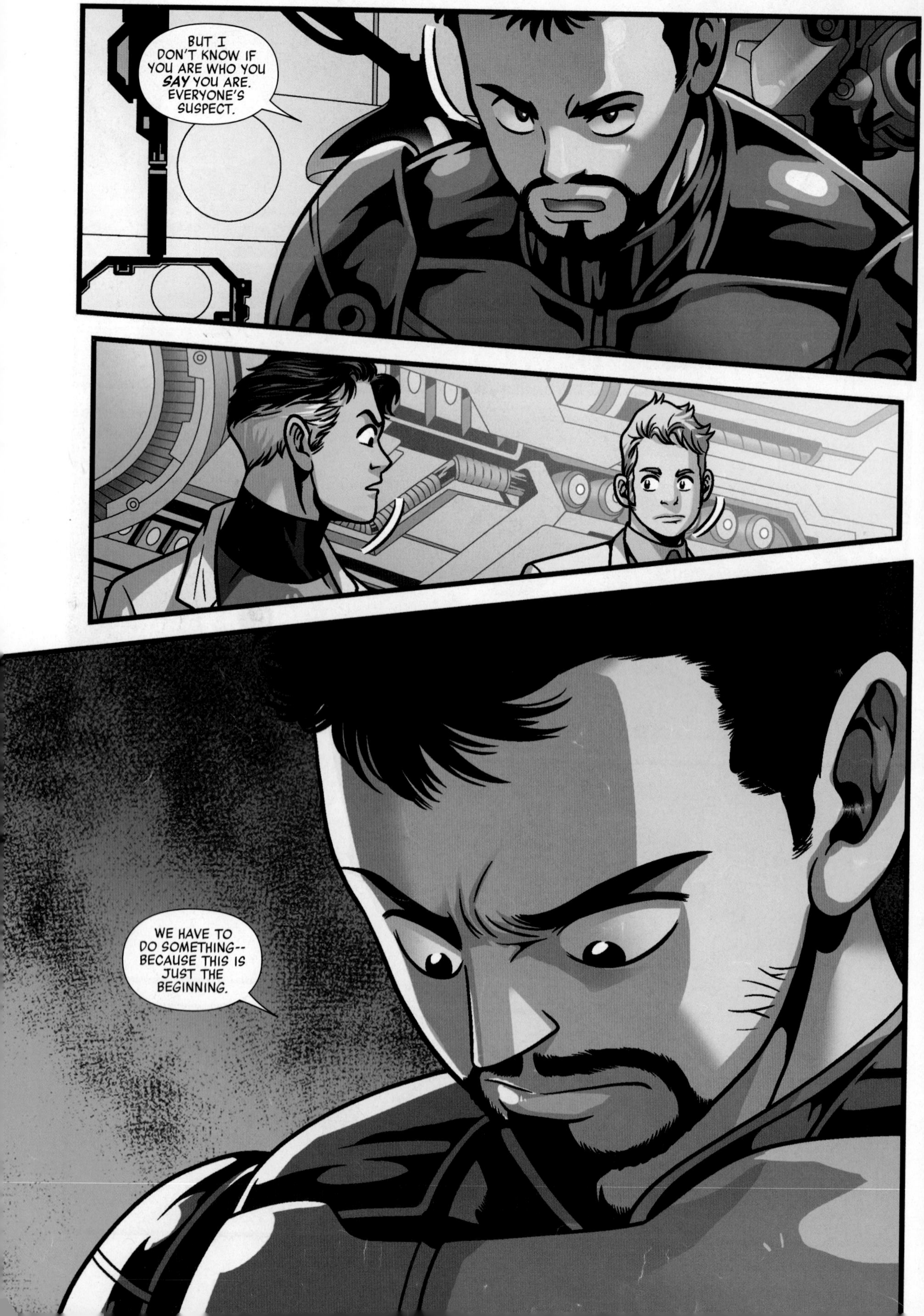
BUT I DON'T KNOW IF YOU ARE WHO YOU **SAY** YOU ARE. EVERYONE'S SUSPECT.
WE HAVE TO DO SOMETHING-- BECAUSE THIS IS JUST THE BEGINNING.

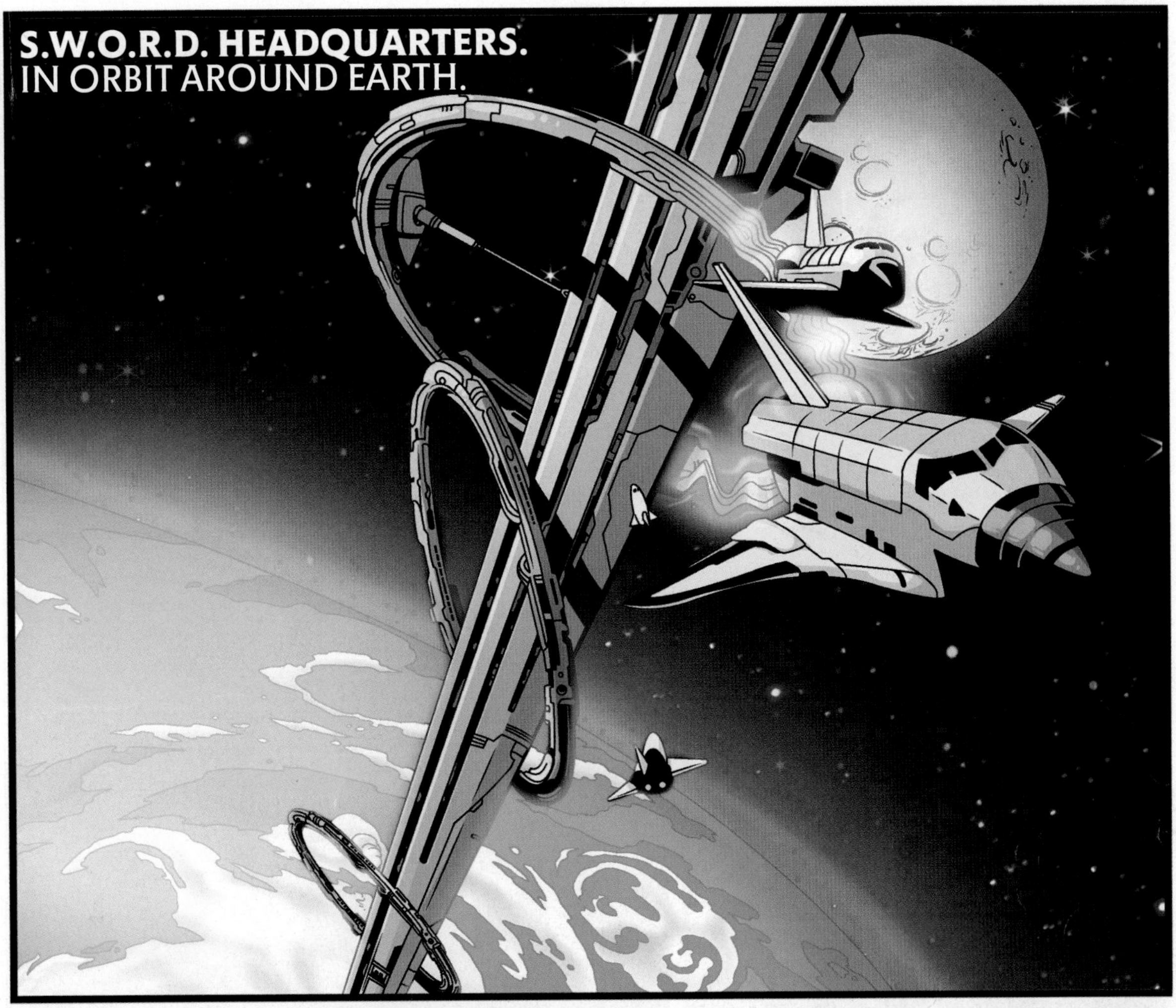

S.W.O.R.D. HEADQUARTERS.
IN ORBIT AROUND EARTH.

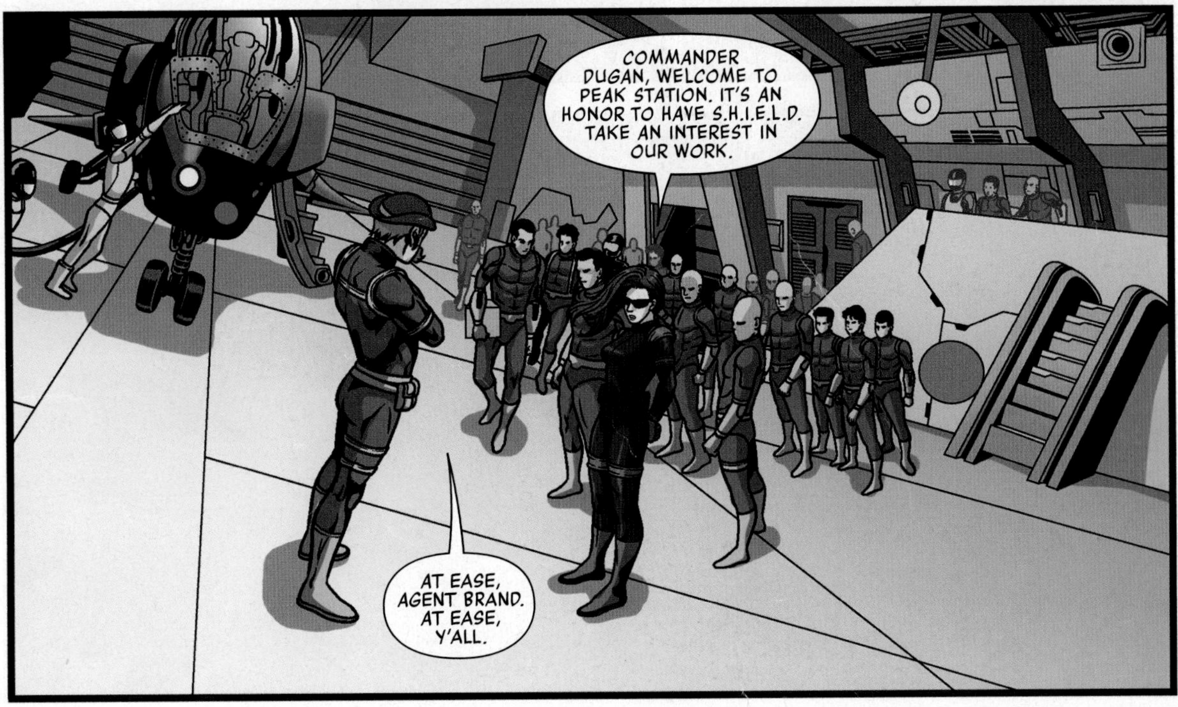

COMMANDER DUGAN, WELCOME TO PEAK STATION. IT'S AN HONOR TO HAVE S.H.I.E.L.D. TAKE AN INTEREST IN OUR WORK.
AT EASE, AGENT BRAND. AT EASE, Y'ALL.

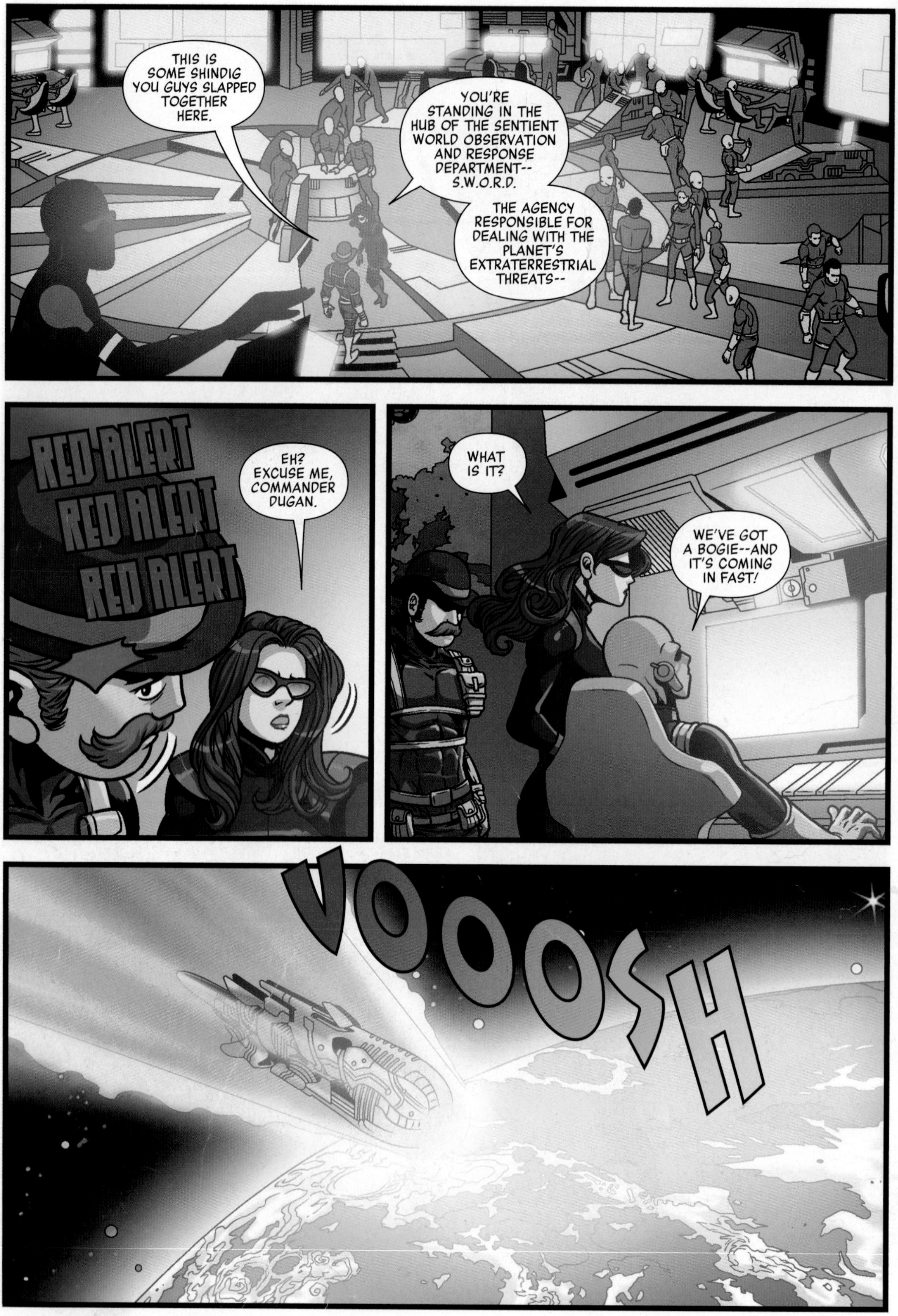
THIS IS SOME SHINDIG YOU GUYS SLAPPED TOGETHER HERE.
YOU'RE STANDING IN THE HUB OF THE SENTIENT WORLD OBSERVATION AND RESPONSE DEPARTMENT-- S.W.O.R.D.
THE AGENCY RESPONSIBLE FOR DEALING WITH THE PLANET'S EXTRATERRESTRIAL THREATS--
RED ALERT
RED ALERT
RED ALERT
EH? EXCUSE ME, COMMANDER DUGAN.
WHAT IS IT?
WE'VE GOT A BOGIE--AND IT'S COMING IN FAST!
VOOOSH

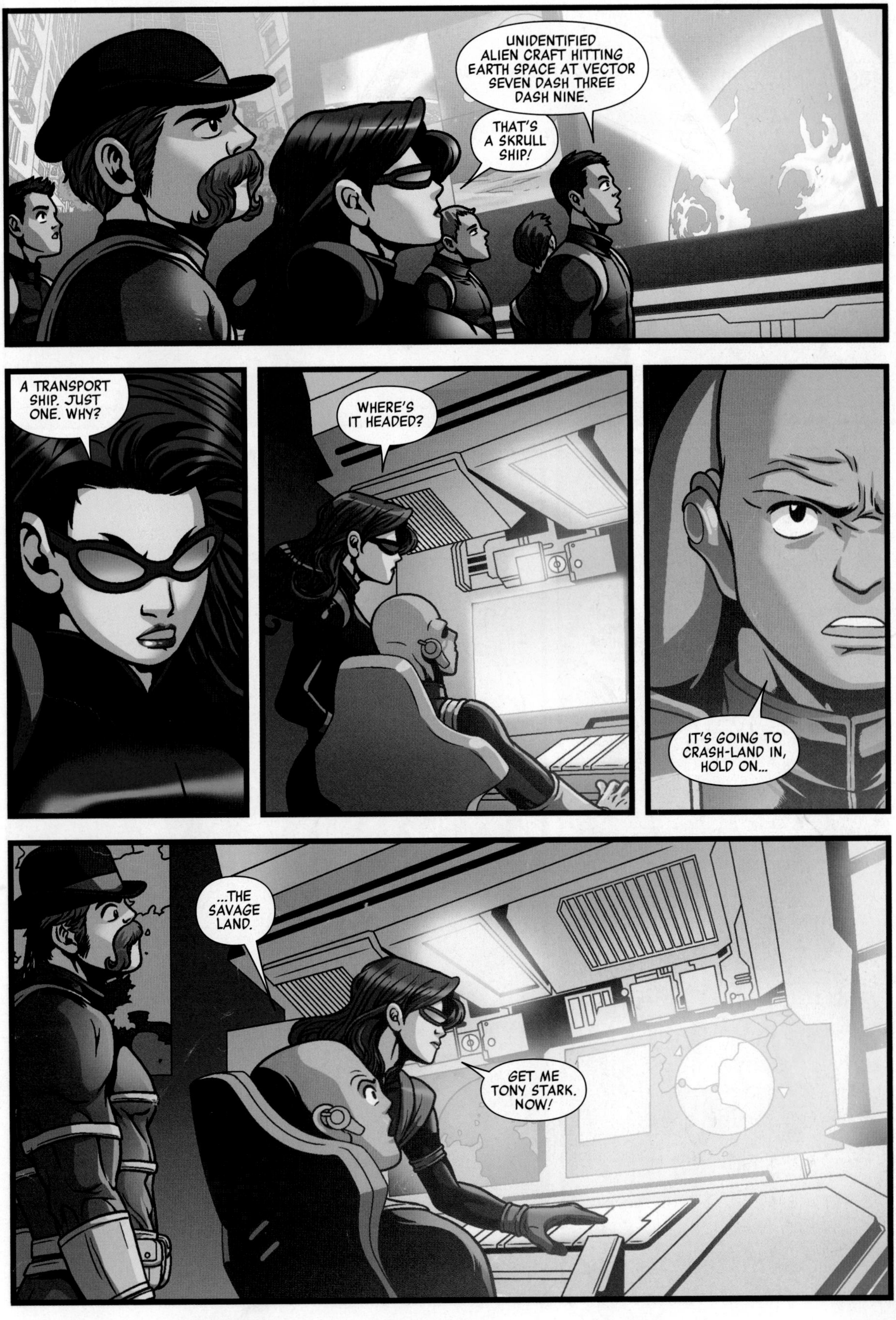
UNIDENTIFIED ALIEN CRAFT HITTING EARTH SPACE AT VECTOR SEVEN DASH THREE DASH NINE.
THAT'S A SKRULL SHIP!
A TRANSPORT SHIP. JUST ONE. WHY?
WHERE'S IT HEADED?
IT'S GOING TO CRASH-LAND IN, HOLD ON...
...THE SAVAGE LAND.
GET ME TONY STARK. NOW!

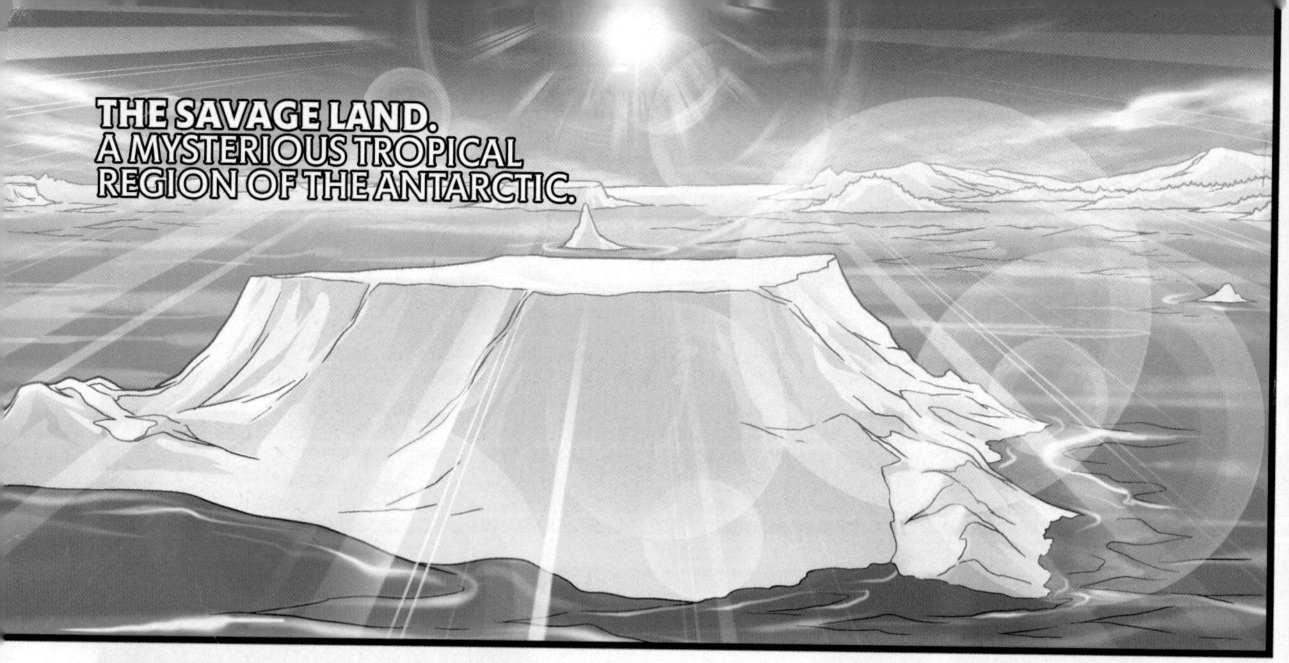
THE SAVAGE LAND.
A MYSTERIOUS TROPICAL REGION OF THE ANTARCTIC.

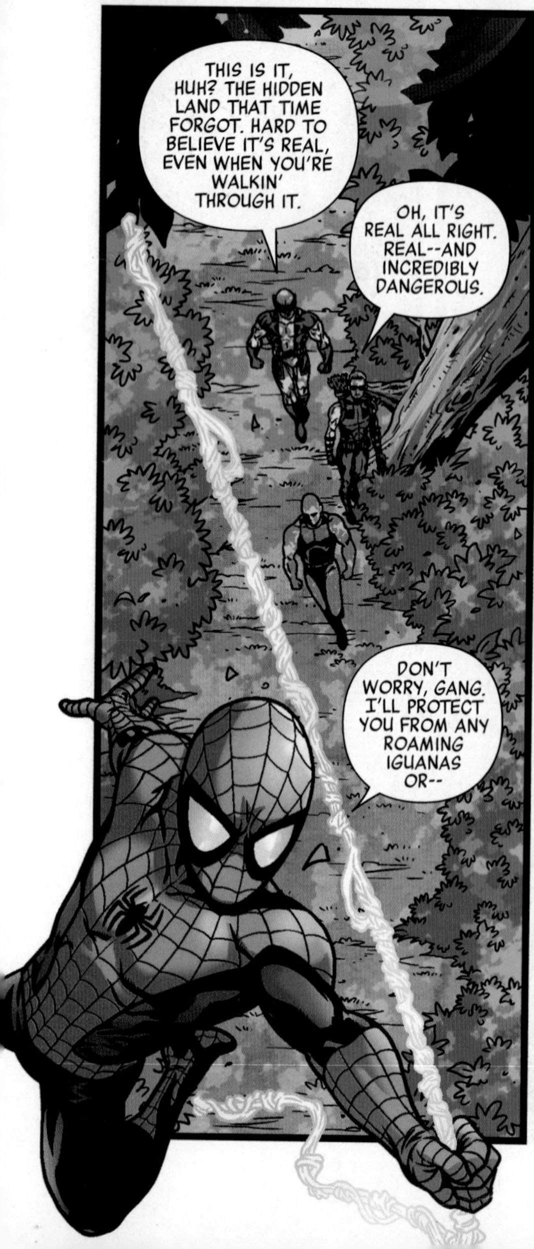
THIS IS IT, HUH? THE HIDDEN LAND THAT TIME FORGOT. HARD TO BELIEVE IT'S REAL, EVEN WHEN YOU'RE WALKIN' THROUGH IT.
OH, IT'S REAL ALL RIGHT. REAL--AND INCREDIBLY DANGEROUS.
DON'T WORRY, GANG. I'LL PROTECT YOU FROM ANY ROAMING IGUANAS OR--

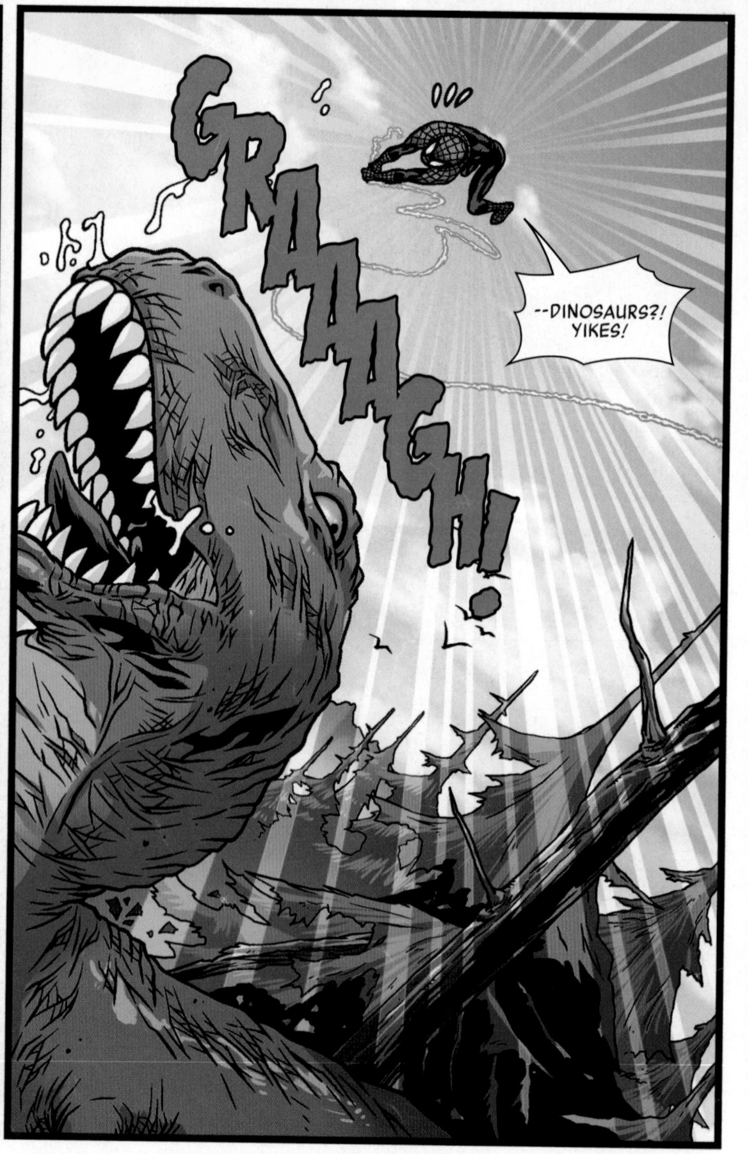
GRAAAAGH!
--DINOSAURS?! YIKES!

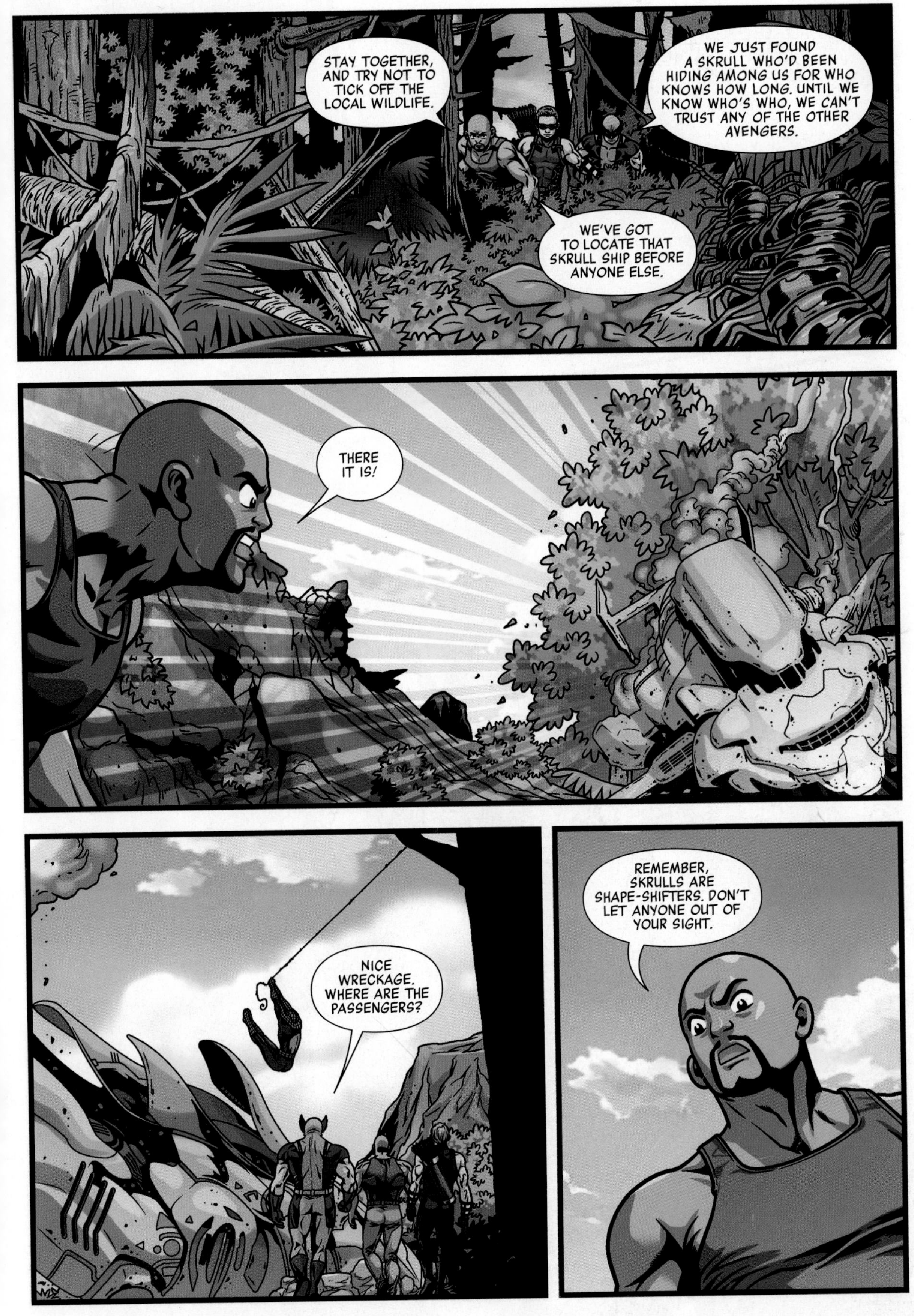
STAY TOGETHER, AND TRY NOT TO TICK OFF THE LOCAL WILDLIFE.
WE JUST FOUND A SKRULL WHO'D BEEN HIDING AMONG US FOR WHO KNOWS HOW LONG. UNTIL WE KNOW WHO'S WHO, WE CAN'T TRUST ANY OF THE OTHER AVENGERS.
WE'VE GOT TO LOCATE THAT SKRULL SHIP BEFORE ANYONE ELSE.
THERE IT IS!
NICE WRECKAGE. WHERE ARE THE PASSENGERS?
REMEMBER, SKRULLS ARE SHAPE-SHIFTERS. DON'T LET ANYONE OUT OF YOUR SIGHT.

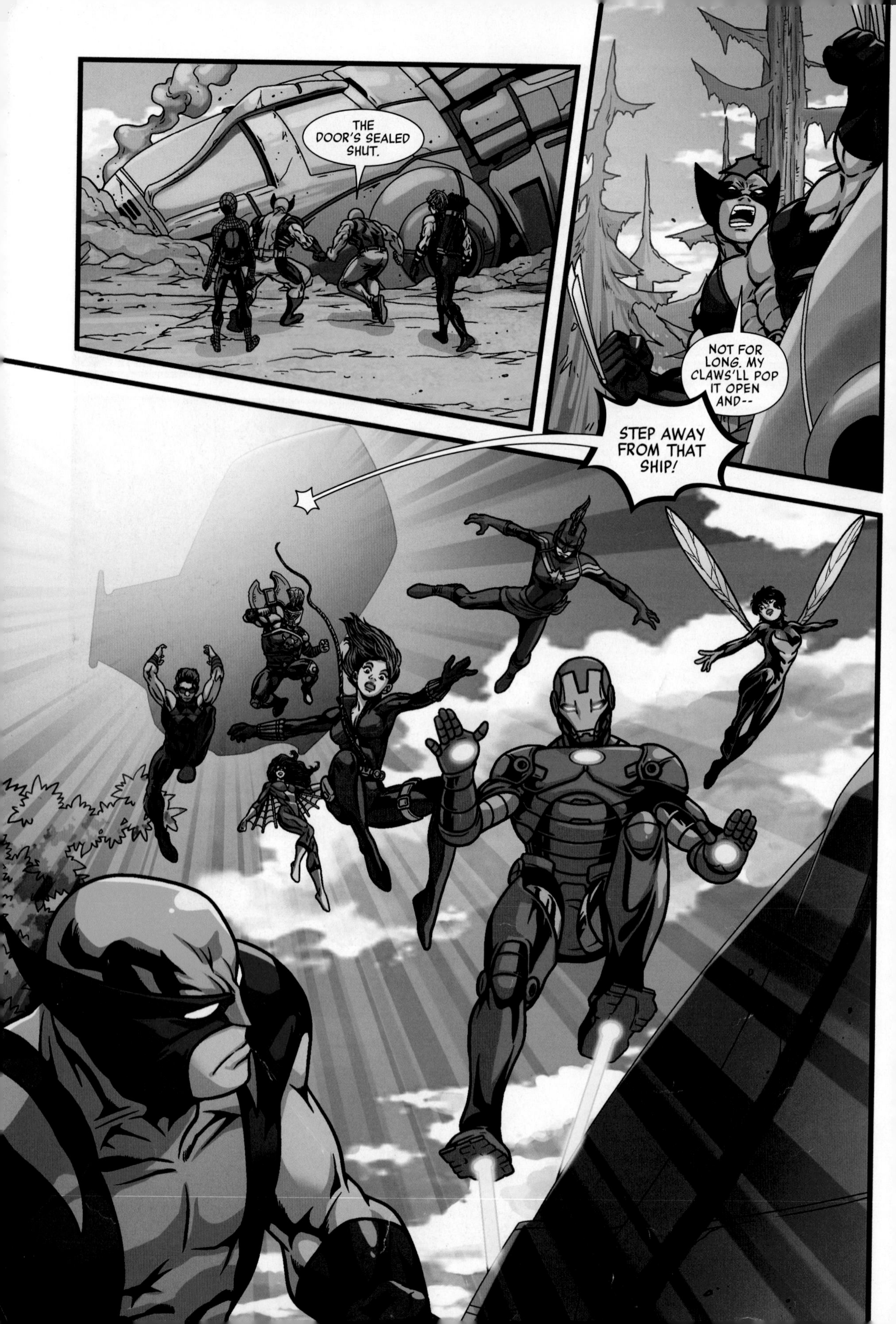
THE DOOR'S SEALED SHUT.
NOT FOR LONG. MY CLAWS'LL POP IT OPEN AND--
STEP AWAY FROM THAT SHIP!

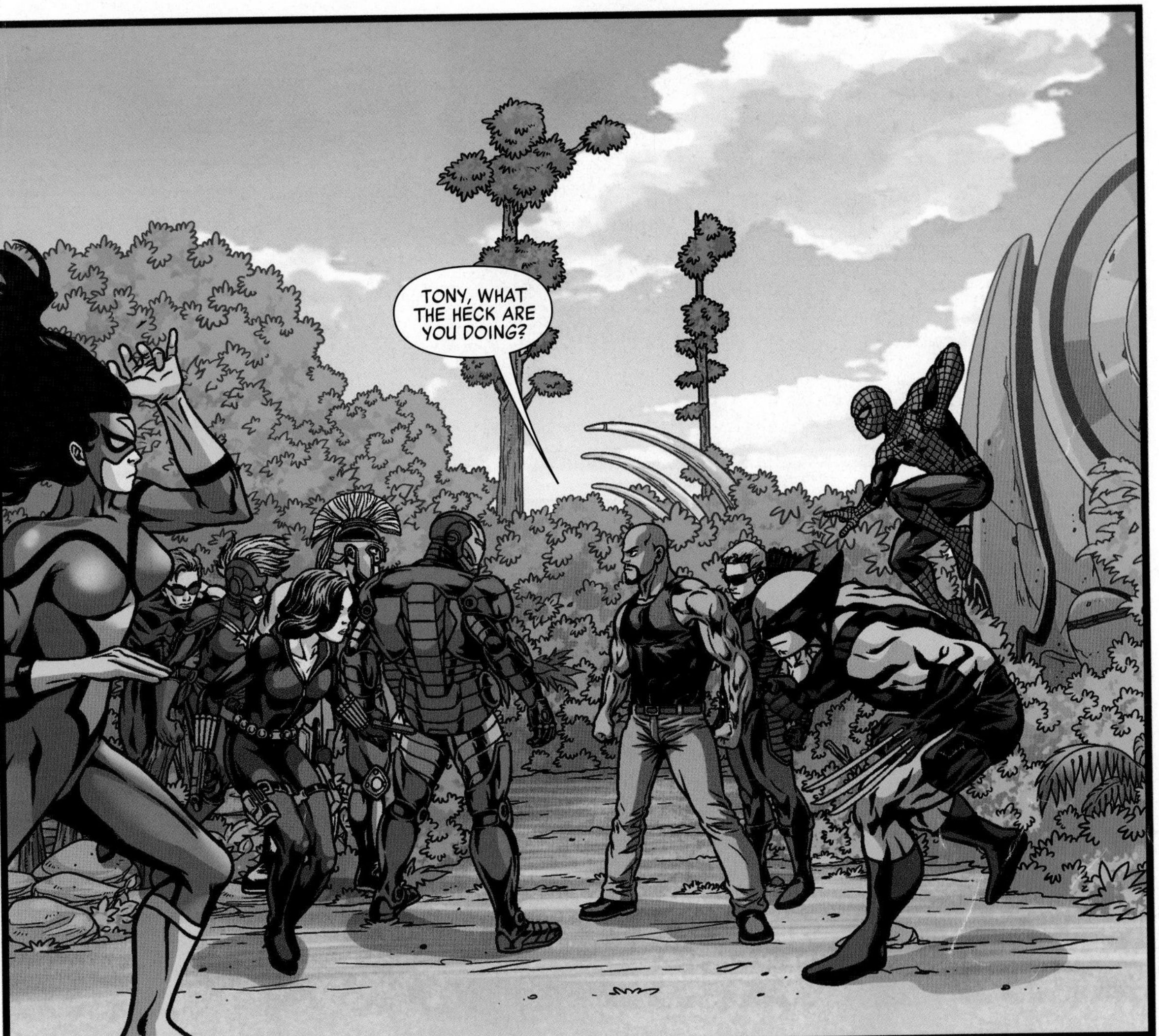
TONY, WHAT THE HECK ARE YOU DOING?

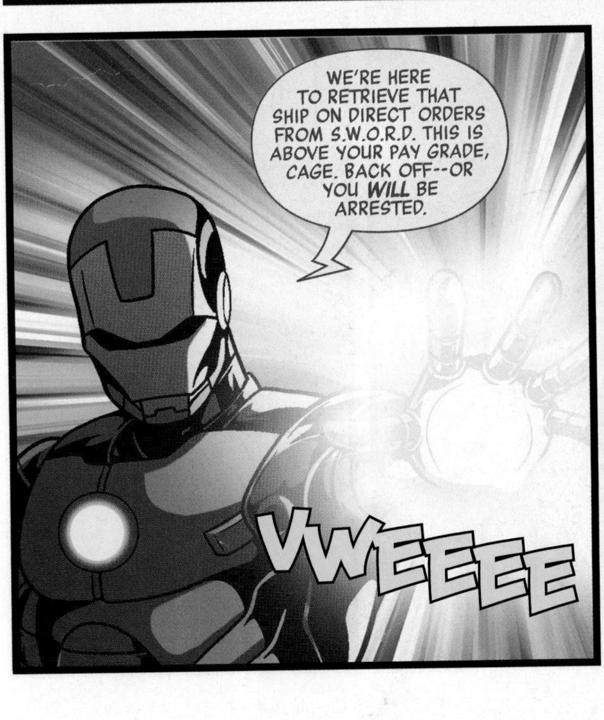
WE'RE HERE TO RETRIEVE THAT SHIP ON DIRECT ORDERS FROM S.W.O.R.D. THIS IS ABOVE YOUR PAY GRADE, CAGE. BACK OFF--OR YOU *WILL* BE ARRESTED.
VWEEEE

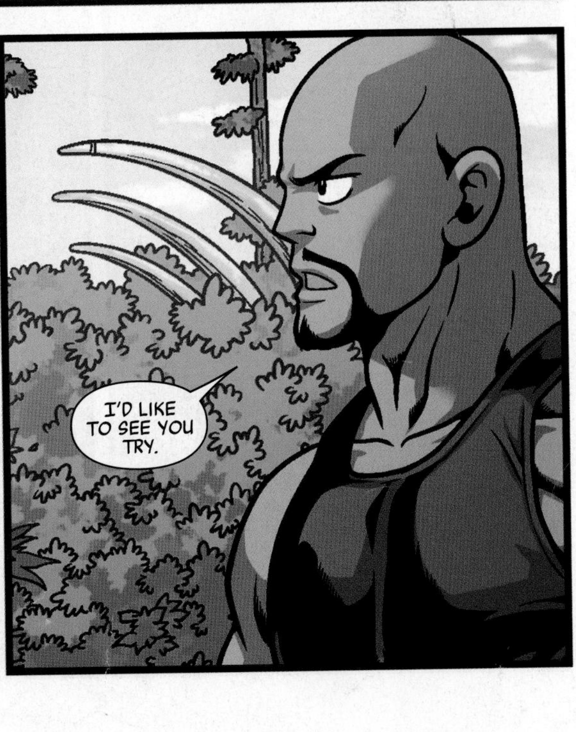
I'D LIKE TO SEE YOU TRY.

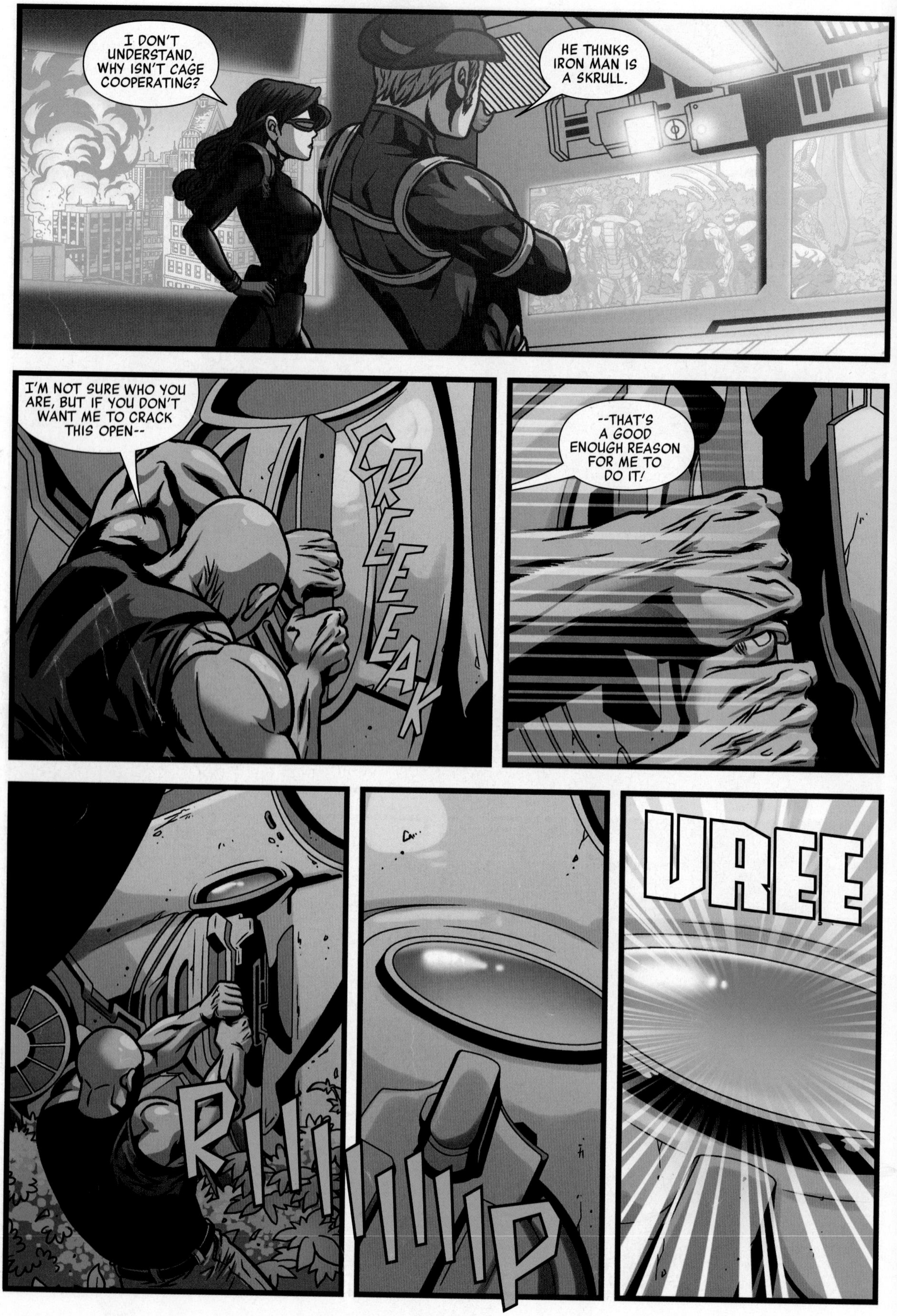
I DON'T UNDERSTAND. WHY ISN'T CAGE COOPERATING?
HE THINKS IRON MAN IS A SKRULL.
I'M NOT SURE WHO YOU ARE, BUT IF YOU DON'T WANT ME TO CRACK THIS OPEN--
CREEEEAK
--THAT'S A GOOD ENOUGH REASON FOR ME TO DO IT!
RIIIIIIIP
VREE

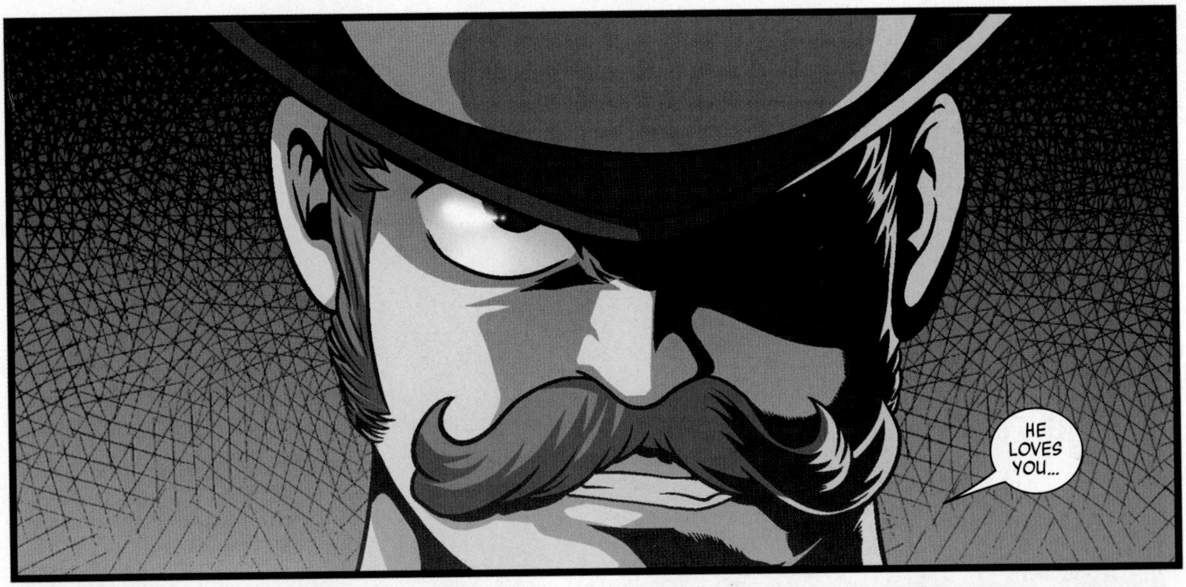
HE LOVES YOU...

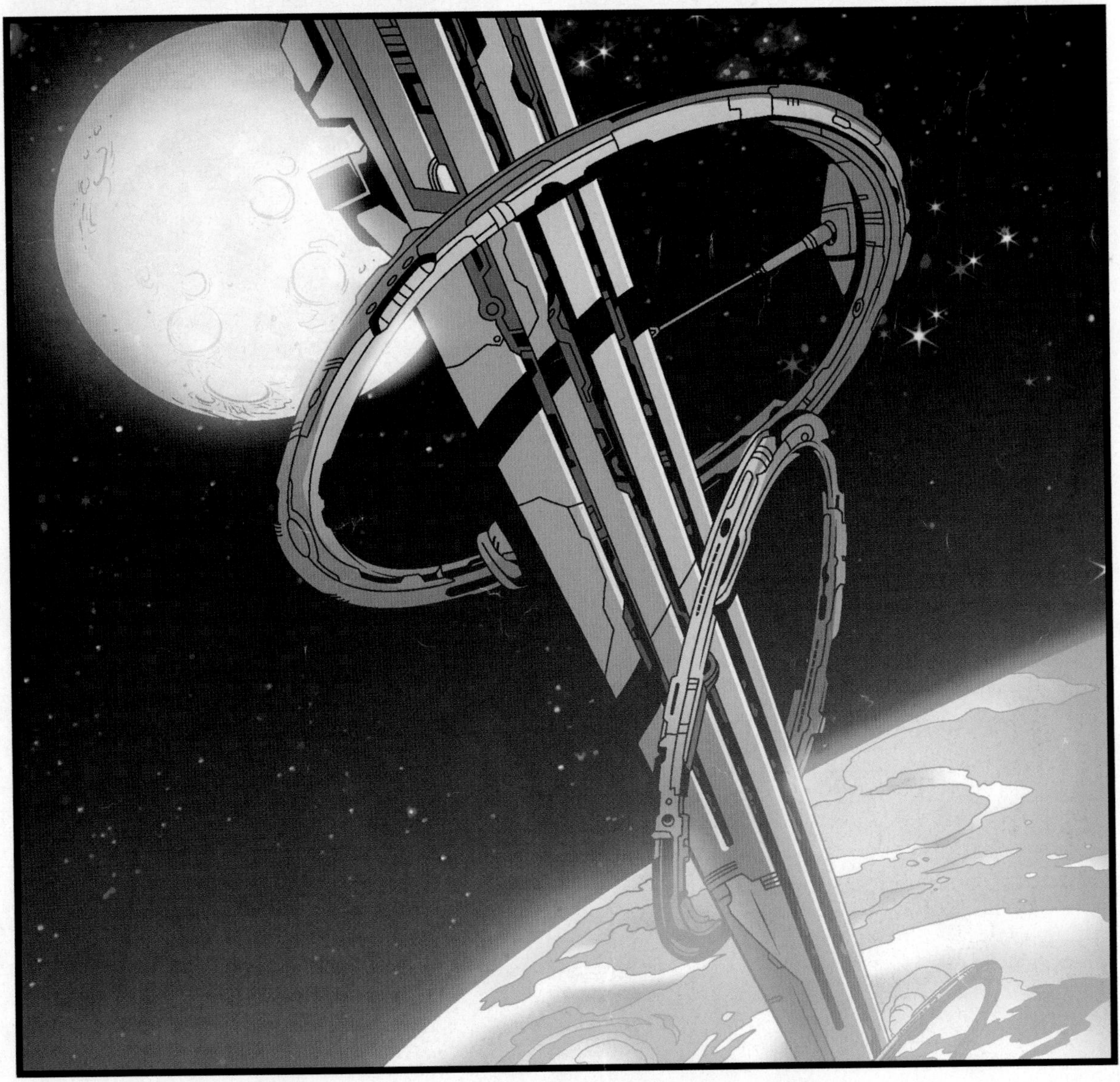

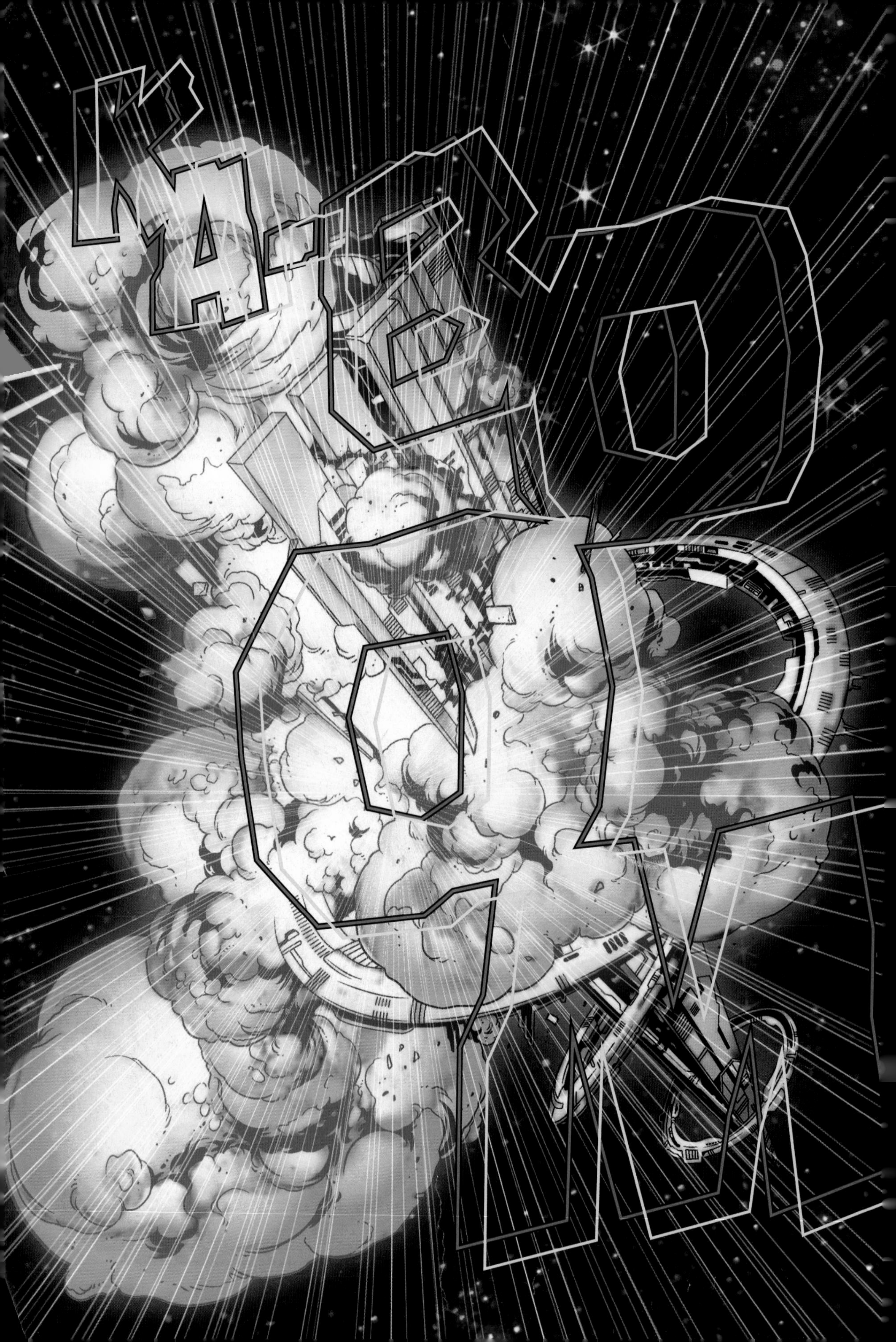

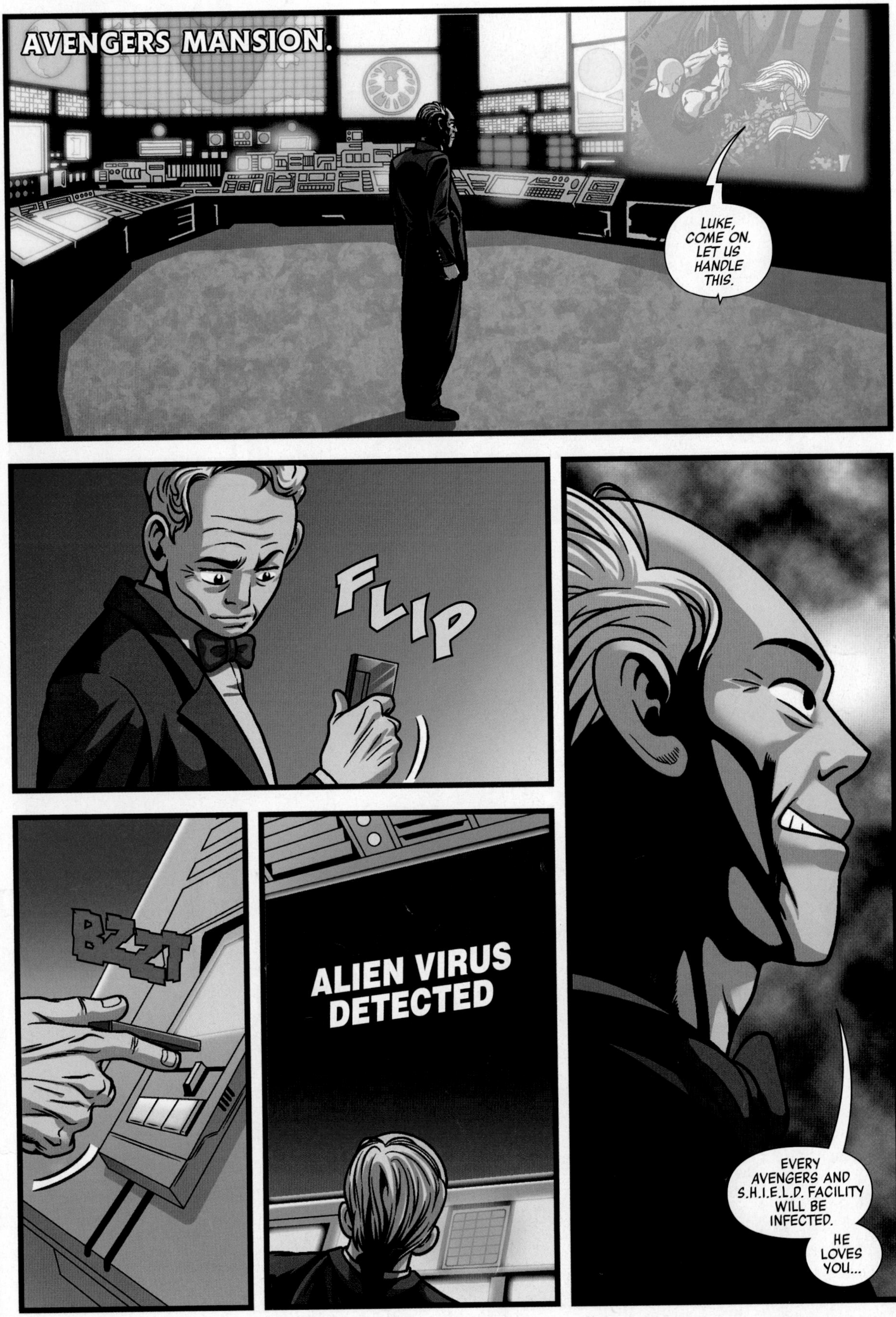
AVENGERS MANSION.
LUKE, COME ON. LET US HANDLE THIS.
FLIP
BZZT
ALIEN VIRUS DETECTED
EVERY AVENGERS AND S.H.I.E.L.D. FACILITY WILL BE INFECTED.
HE LOVES YOU...

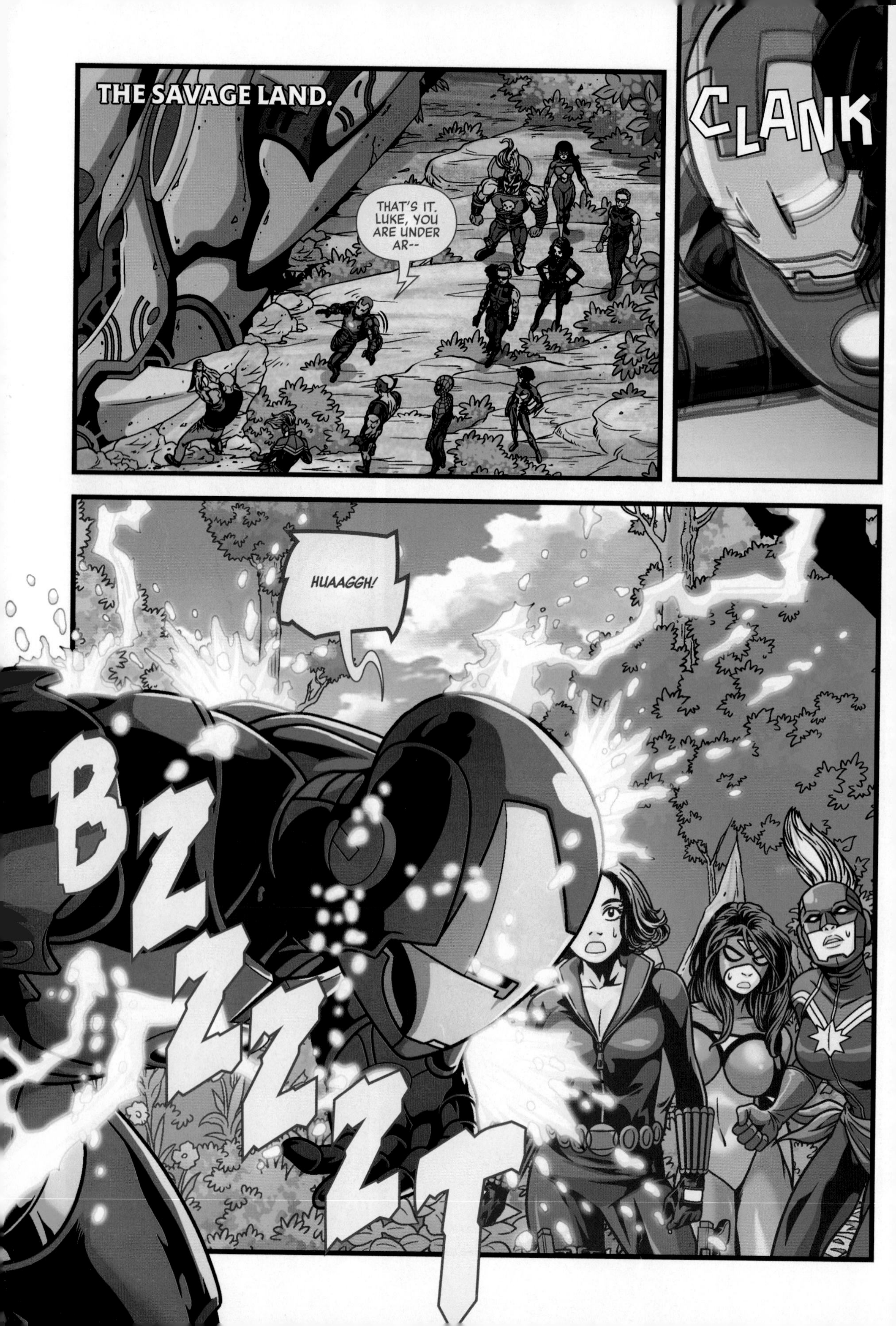
THE SAVAGE LAND.
THAT'S IT. LUKE, YOU ARE UNDER AR--
CLANK
HUAAGGH!
BZZZZT

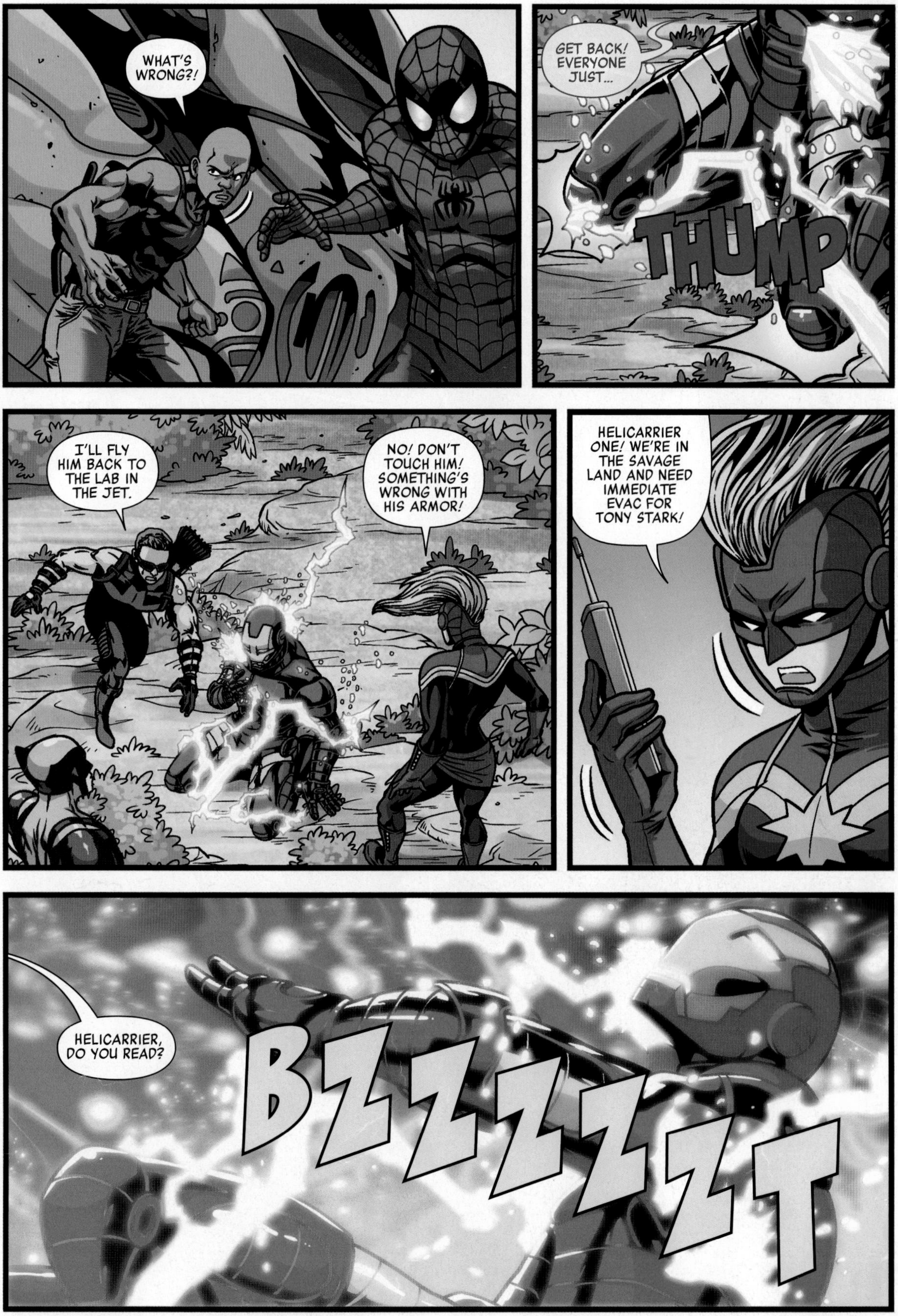
WHAT'S WRONG?!
GET BACK! EVERYONE JUST...
THUMP
I'LL FLY HIM BACK TO THE LAB IN THE JET.
NO! DON'T TOUCH HIM! SOMETHING'S WRONG WITH HIS ARMOR!
HELICARRIER ONE! WE'RE IN THE SAVAGE LAND AND NEED IMMEDIATE EVAC FOR TONY STARK!
HELICARRIER, DO YOU READ?
BZZZZZZT

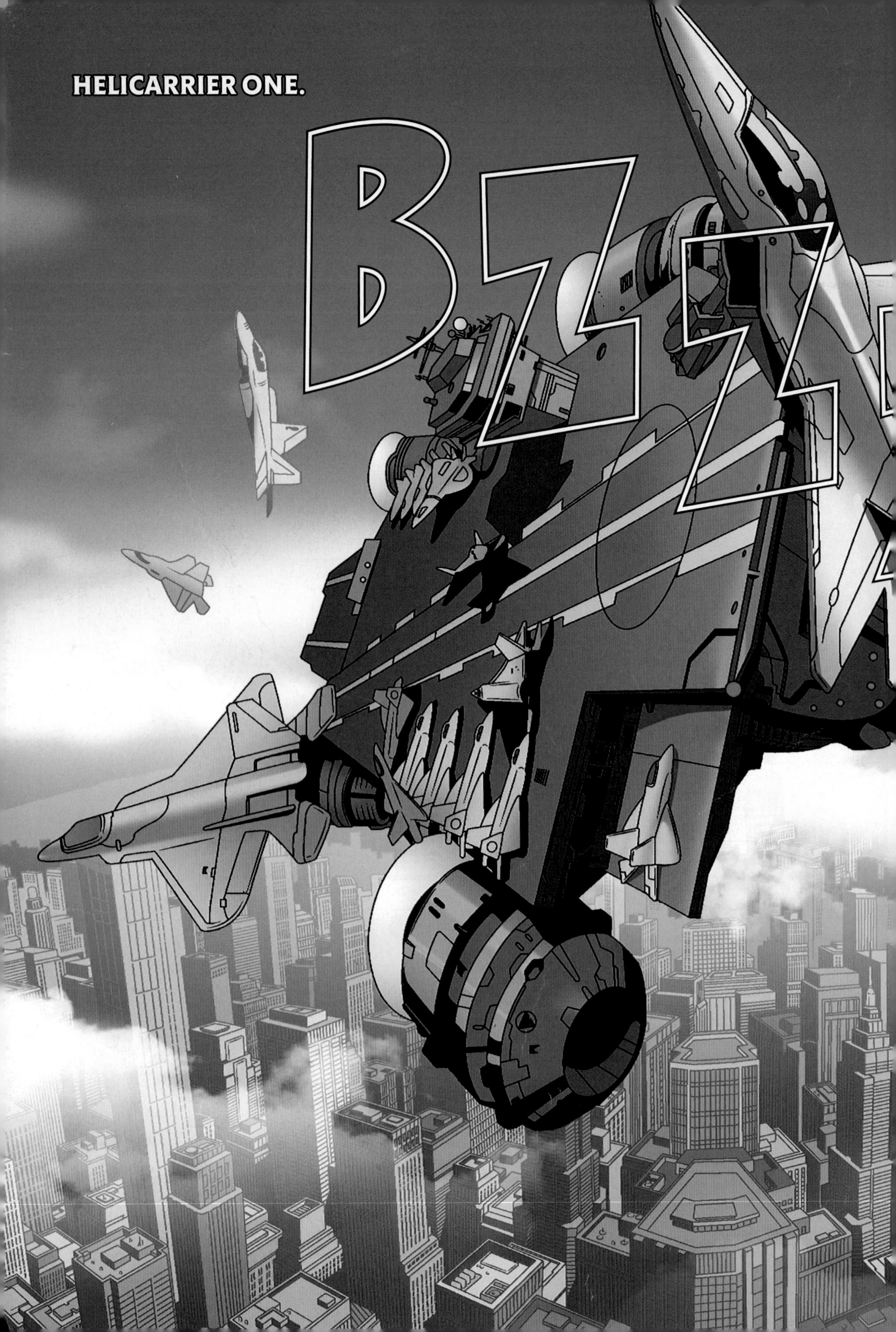
HELICARRIER ONE.
BZZZ

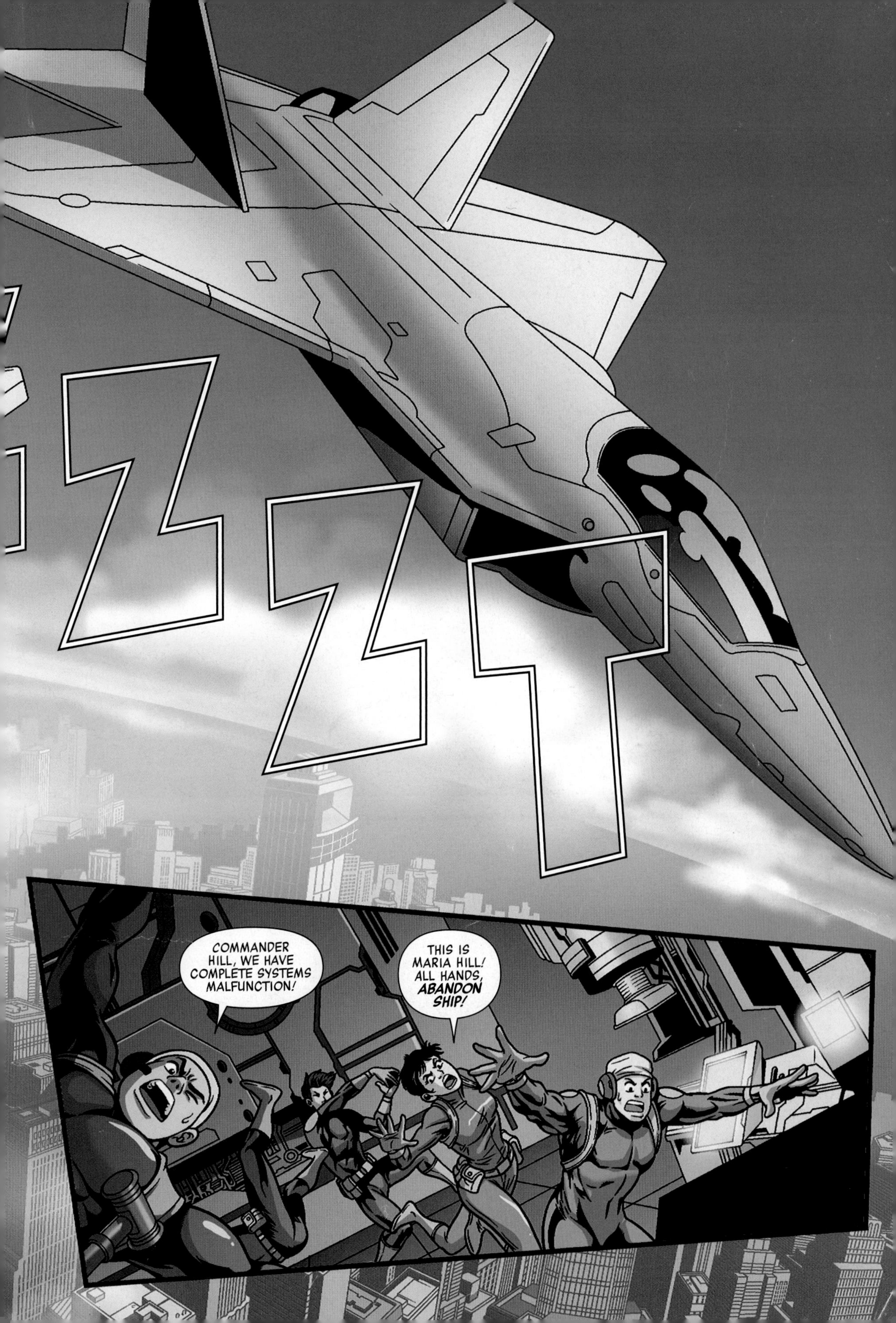
ZZZT
COMMANDER HILL, WE HAVE COMPLETE SYSTEMS MALFUNCTION!
THIS IS MARIA HILL! ALL HANDS, ABANDON SHIP!

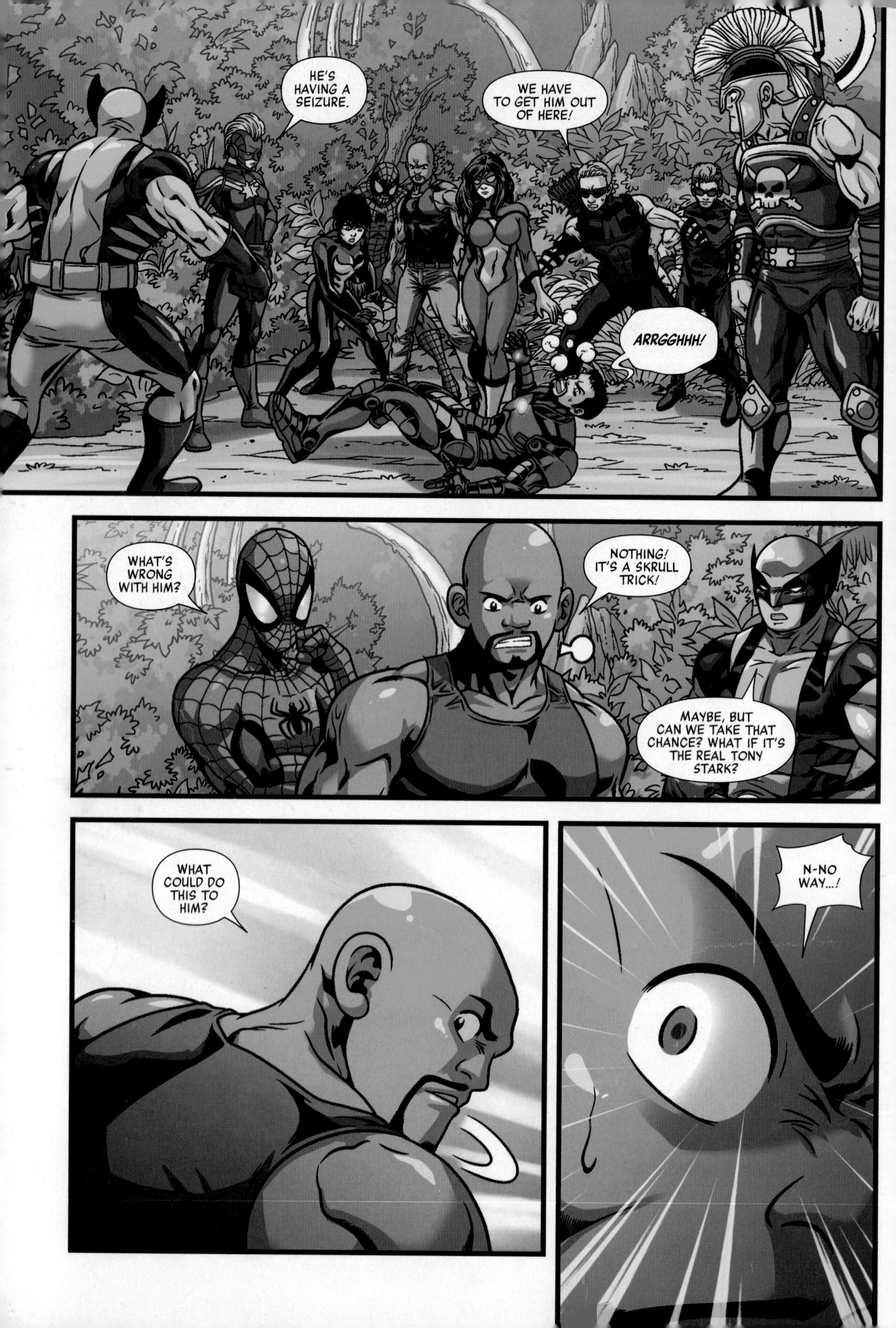
HE'S HAVING A SEIZURE.
WE HAVE TO GET HIM OUT OF HERE!
ARRGGHHH!
WHAT'S WRONG WITH HIM?
NOTHING! IT'S A SKRULL TRICK!
MAYBE, BUT CAN WE TAKE THAT CHANCE? WHAT IF IT'S THE REAL TONY STARK?
WHAT COULD DO THIS TO HIM?
N-NO WAY...!

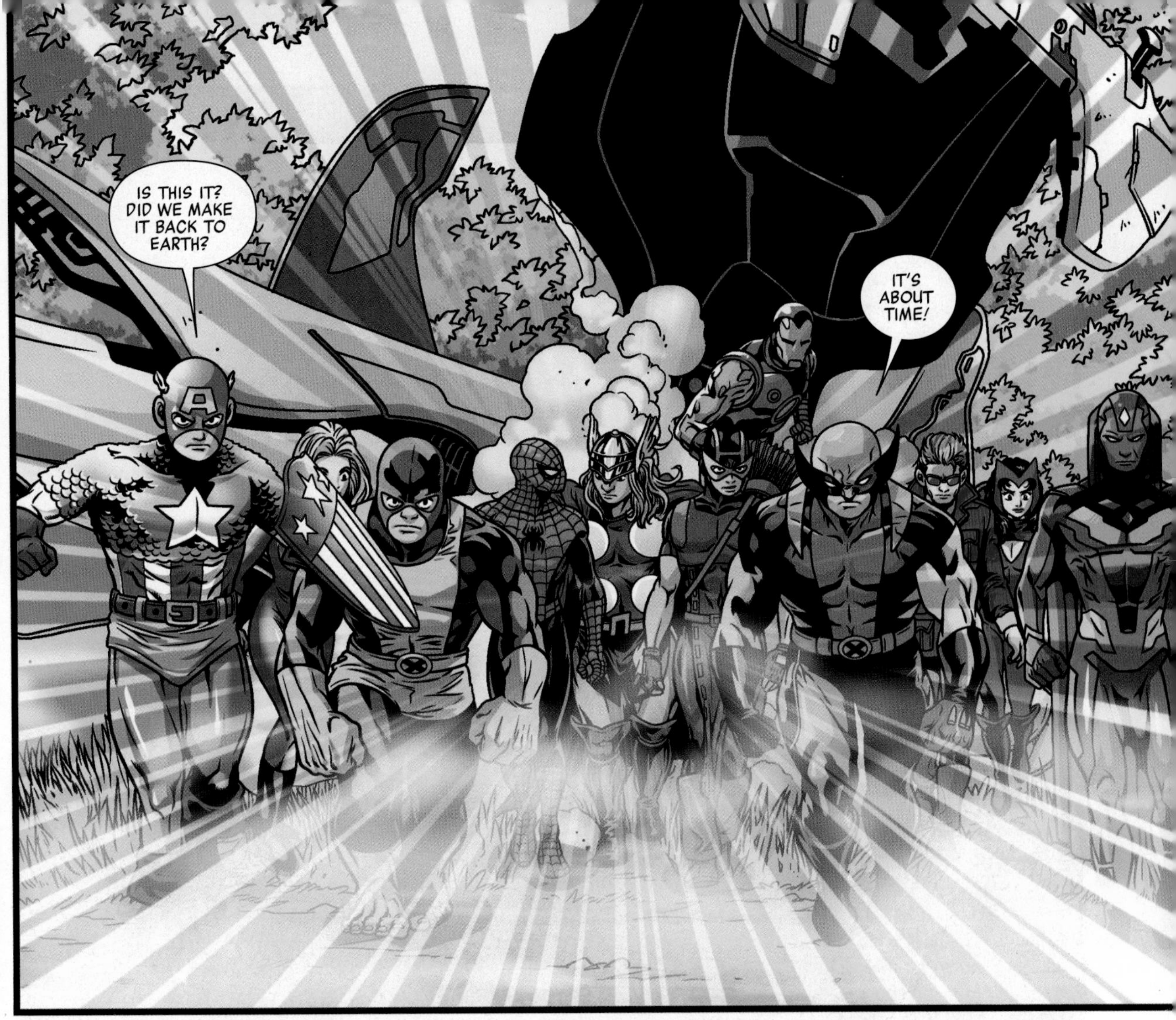
IS THIS IT? DID WE MAKE IT BACK TO EARTH?
IT'S ABOUT TIME!

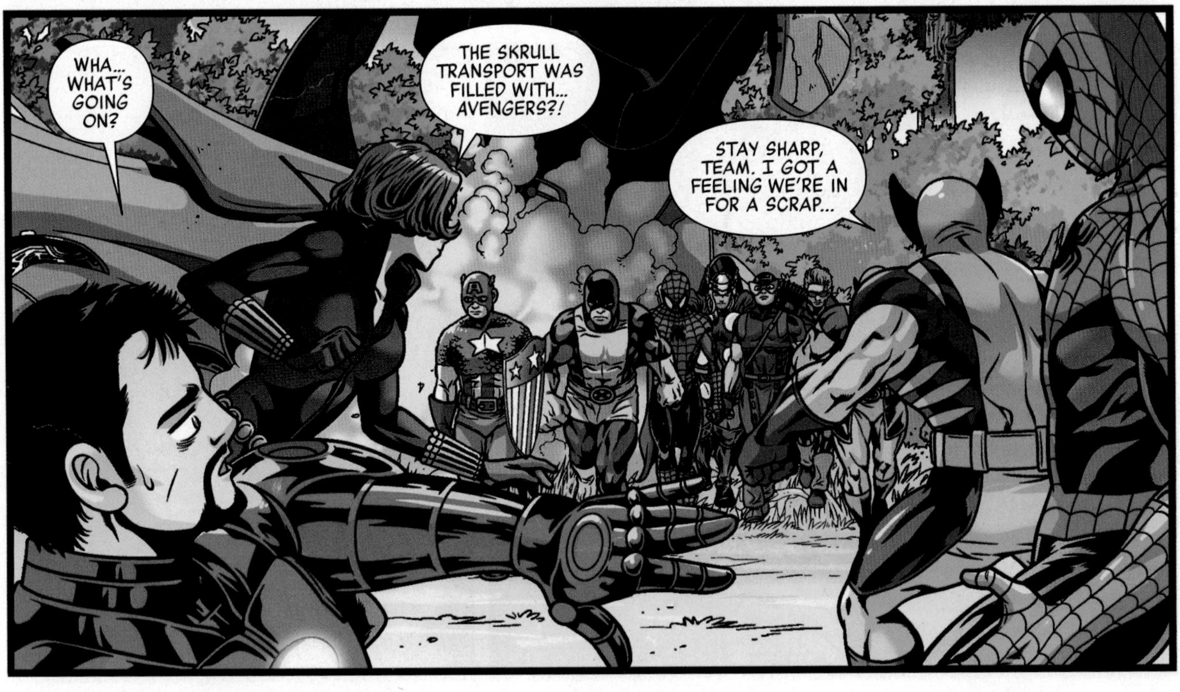
WHA... WHAT'S GOING ON?
THE SKRULL TRANSPORT WAS FILLED WITH... AVENGERS?!
STAY SHARP, TEAM. I GOT A FEELING WE'RE IN FOR A SCRAP...

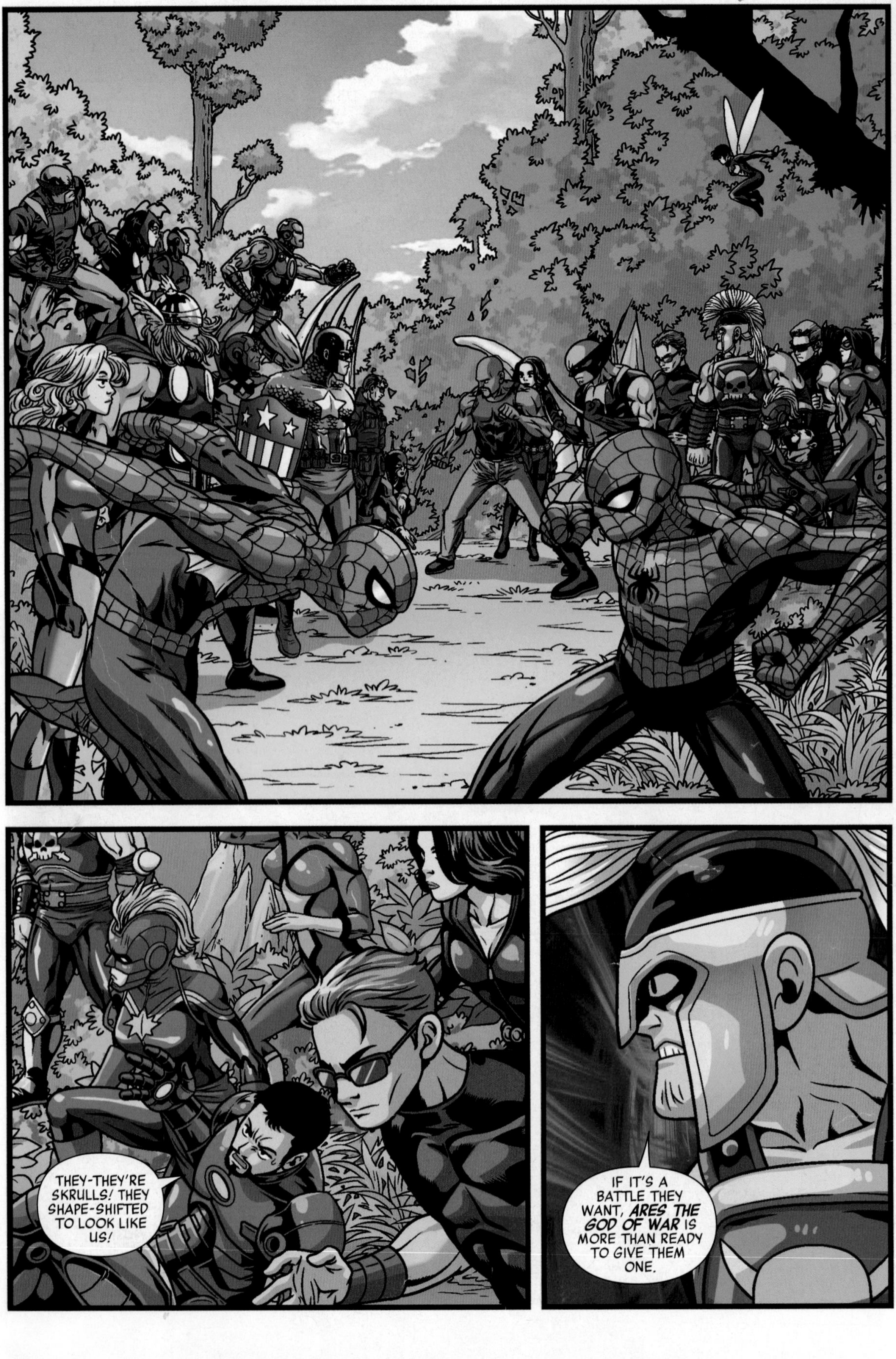
THEY-THEY'RE SKRULLS! THEY SHAPE-SHIFTED TO LOOK LIKE US!
IF IT'S A BATTLE THEY WANT, ***ARES THE GOD OF WAR*** IS MORE THAN READY TO GIVE THEM ONE.

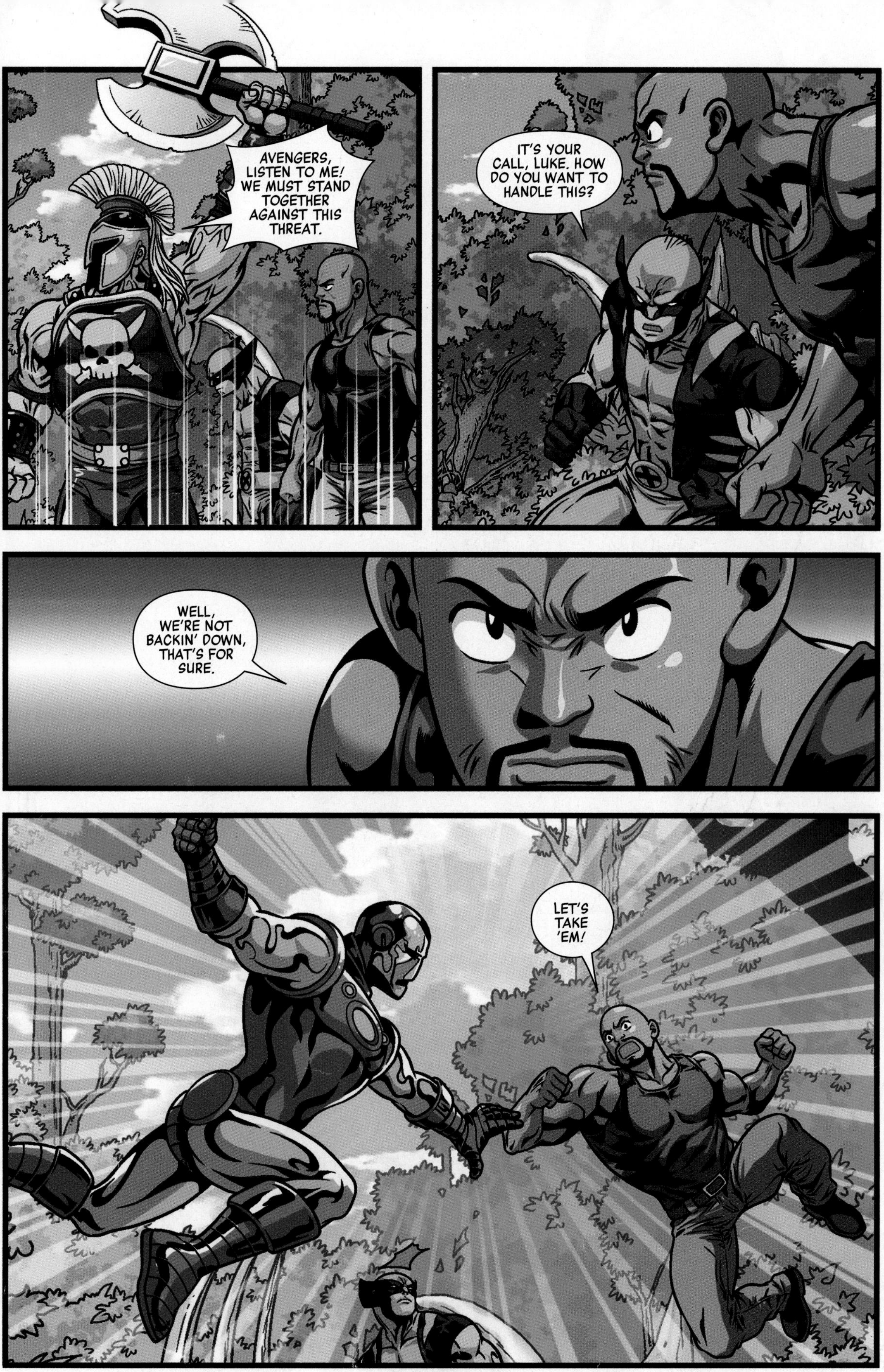
AVENGERS, LISTEN TO ME! WE MUST STAND TOGETHER AGAINST THIS THREAT.
IT'S YOUR CALL, LUKE. HOW DO YOU WANT TO HANDLE THIS?
WELL, WE'RE NOT BACKIN' DOWN, THAT'S FOR SURE.
LET'S TAKE 'EM!

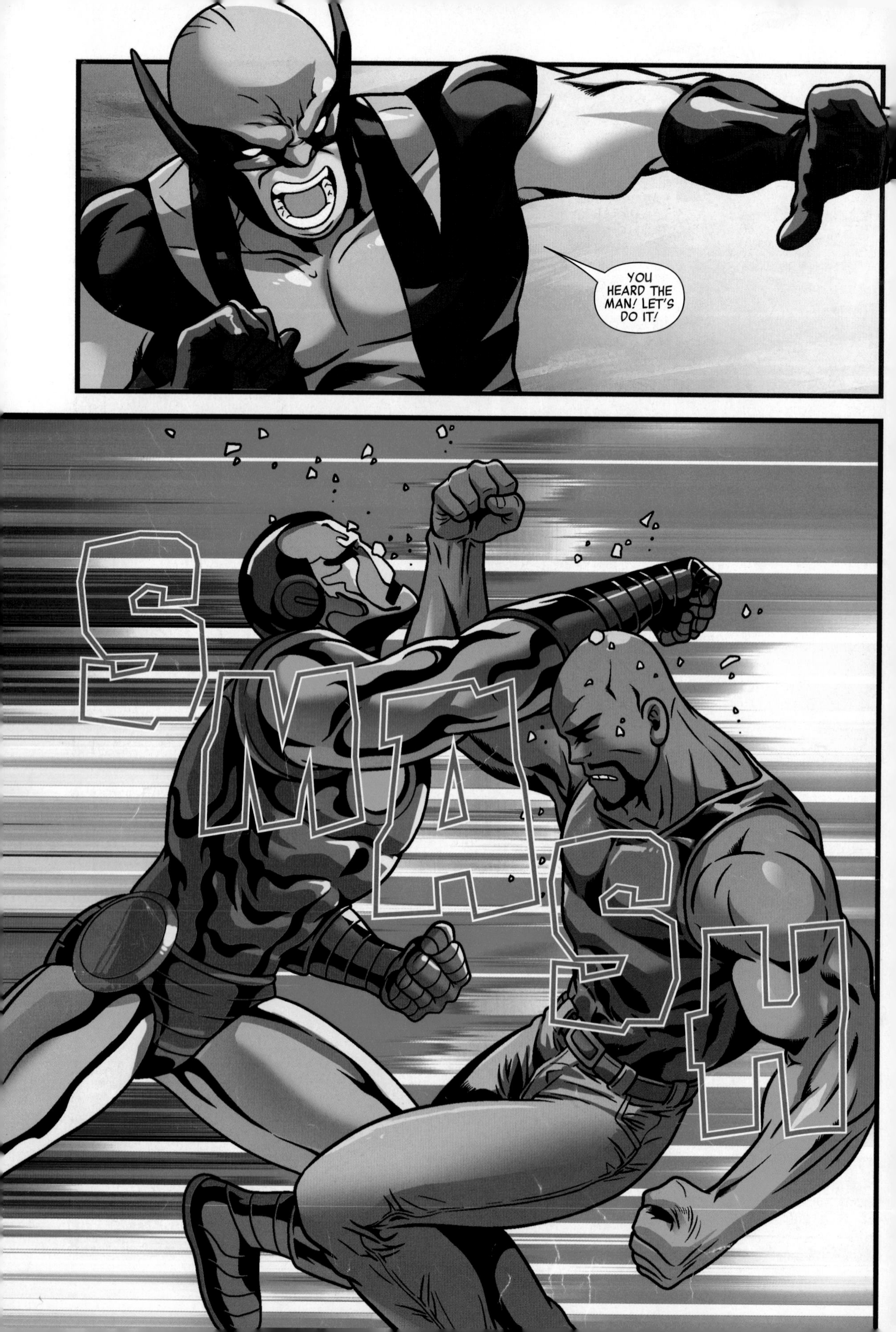
YOU HEARD THE MAN! LET'S DO IT!
SMASH

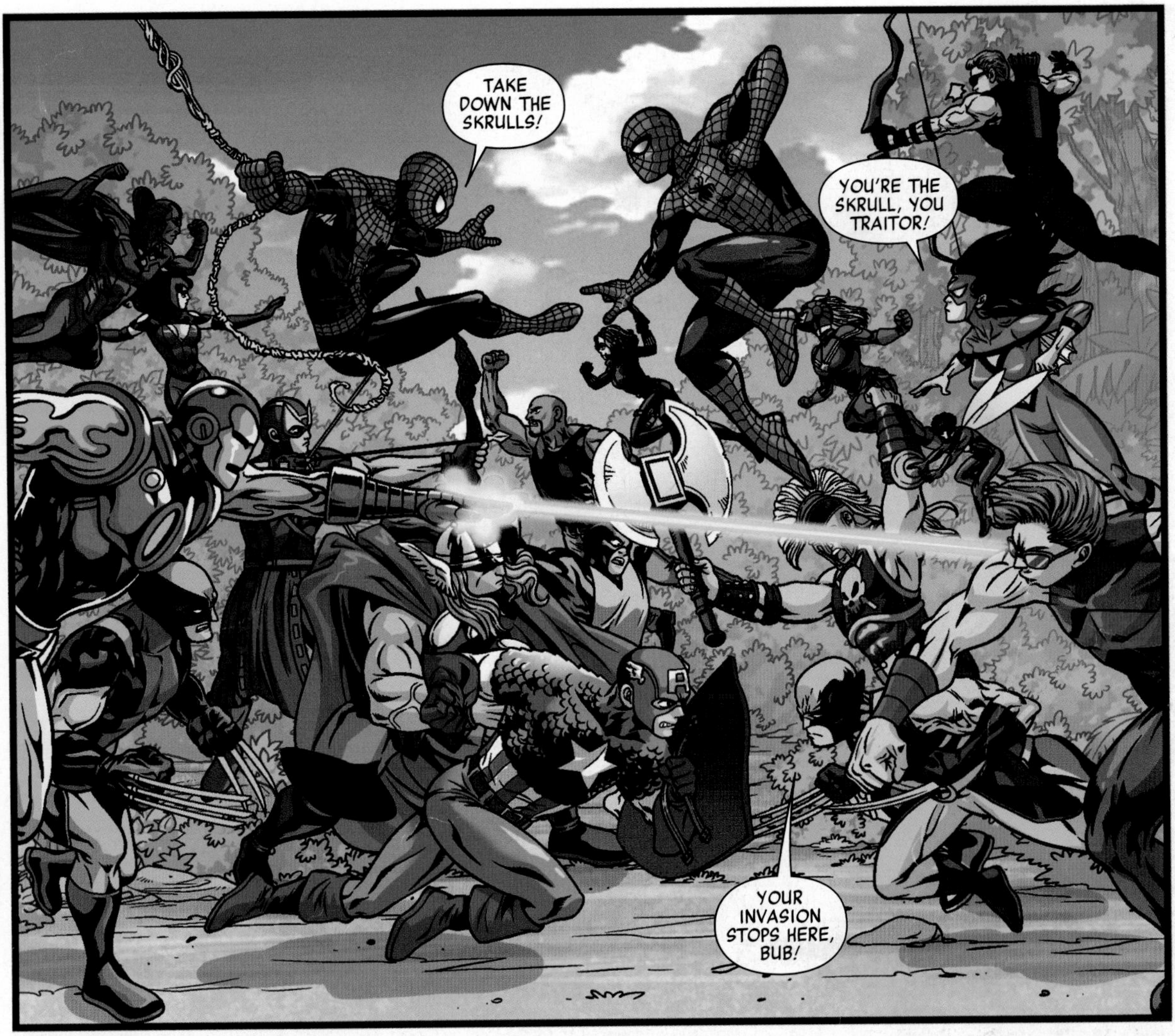
TAKE DOWN THE SKRULLS!
YOU'RE THE SKRULL, YOU TRAITOR!
YOUR INVASION STOPS HERE, BUB!

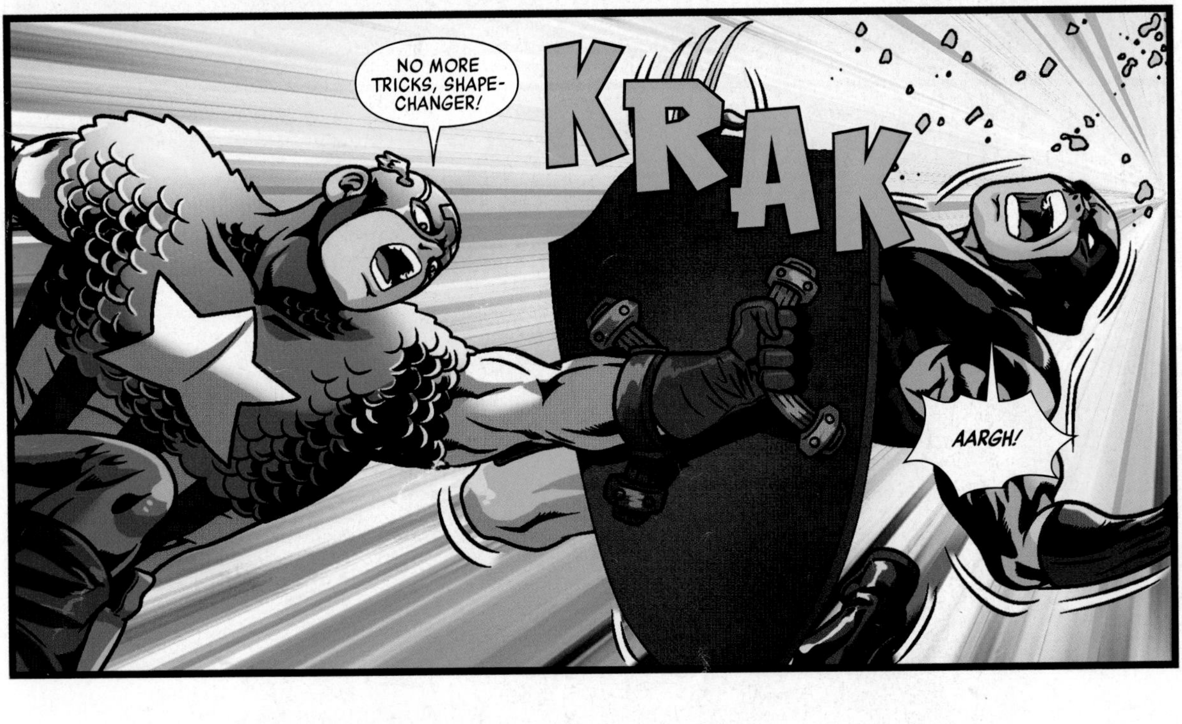
NO MORE TRICKS, SHAPE-CHANGER!
KRAK
AARGH!

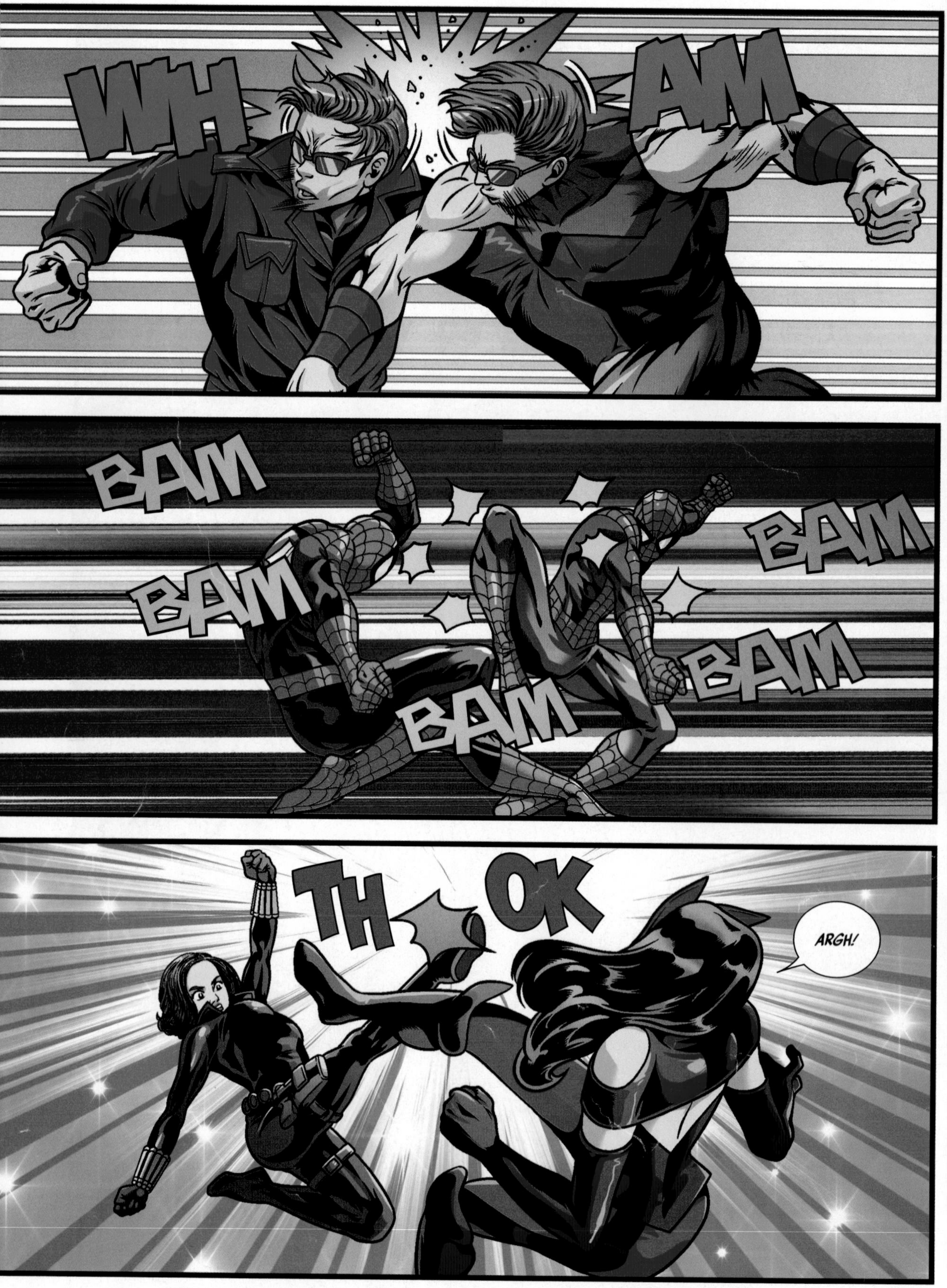
WH
AM
BAM
BAM
BAM
BAM
BAM
TH
OK
ARGH!

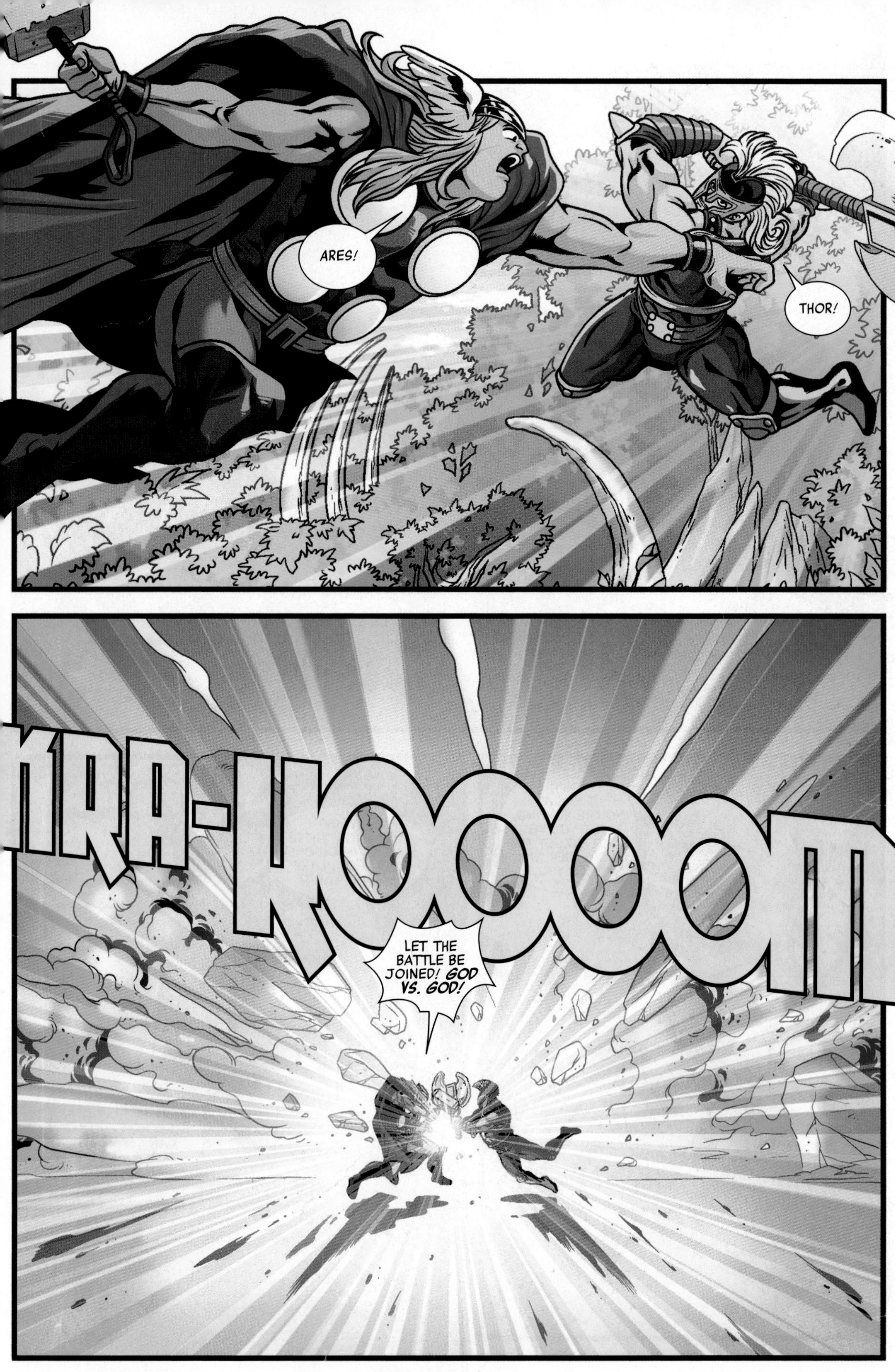
ARES!
THOR!
KRA-KOOOOM
LET THE BATTLE BE JOINED! GOD VS. GOD!

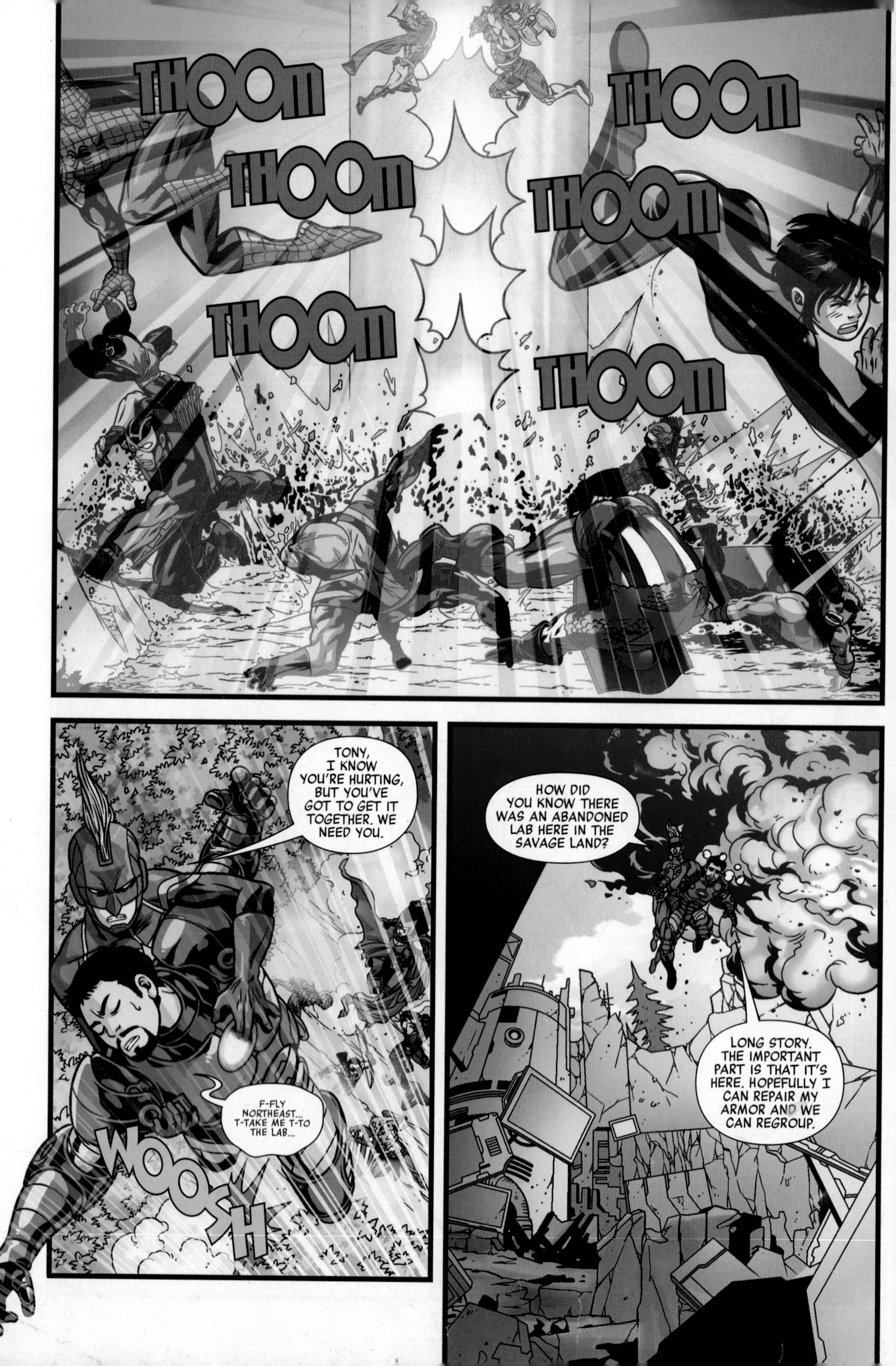
THOOM
THOOM
THOOM
THOOM
THOOM
THOOM
TONY, I KNOW YOU'RE HURTING, BUT YOU'VE GOT TO GET IT TOGETHER. WE NEED YOU.
F-FLY NORTHEAST... T-TAKE ME T-TO THE LAB...
WOOSH
HOW DID YOU KNOW THERE WAS AN ABANDONED LAB HERE IN THE SAVAGE LAND?
LONG STORY. THE IMPORTANT PART IS THAT IT'S HERE. HOPEFULLY I CAN REPAIR MY ARMOR AND WE CAN REGROUP.

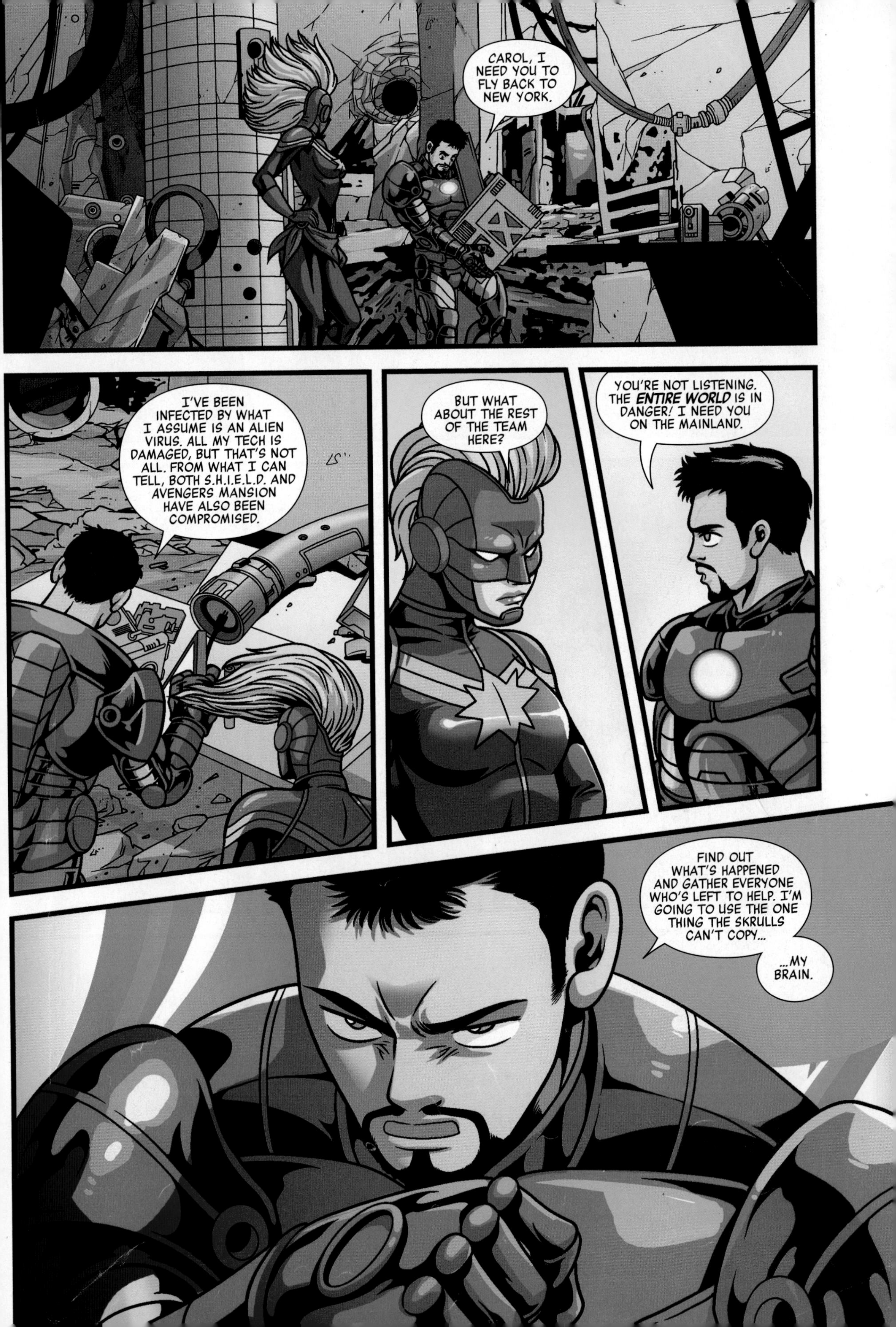
CAROL, I NEED YOU TO FLY BACK TO NEW YORK.
I'VE BEEN INFECTED BY WHAT I ASSUME IS AN ALIEN VIRUS. ALL MY TECH IS DAMAGED, BUT THAT'S NOT ALL. FROM WHAT I CAN TELL, BOTH S.H.I.E.L.D. AND AVENGERS MANSION HAVE ALSO BEEN COMPROMISED.
BUT WHAT ABOUT THE REST OF THE TEAM HERE?
YOU'RE NOT LISTENING. THE ***ENTIRE WORLD*** IS IN DANGER! I NEED YOU ON THE MAINLAND.
FIND OUT WHAT'S HAPPENED AND GATHER EVERYONE WHO'S LEFT TO HELP. I'M GOING TO USE THE ONE THING THE SKRULLS CAN'T COPY...
...MY BRAIN.

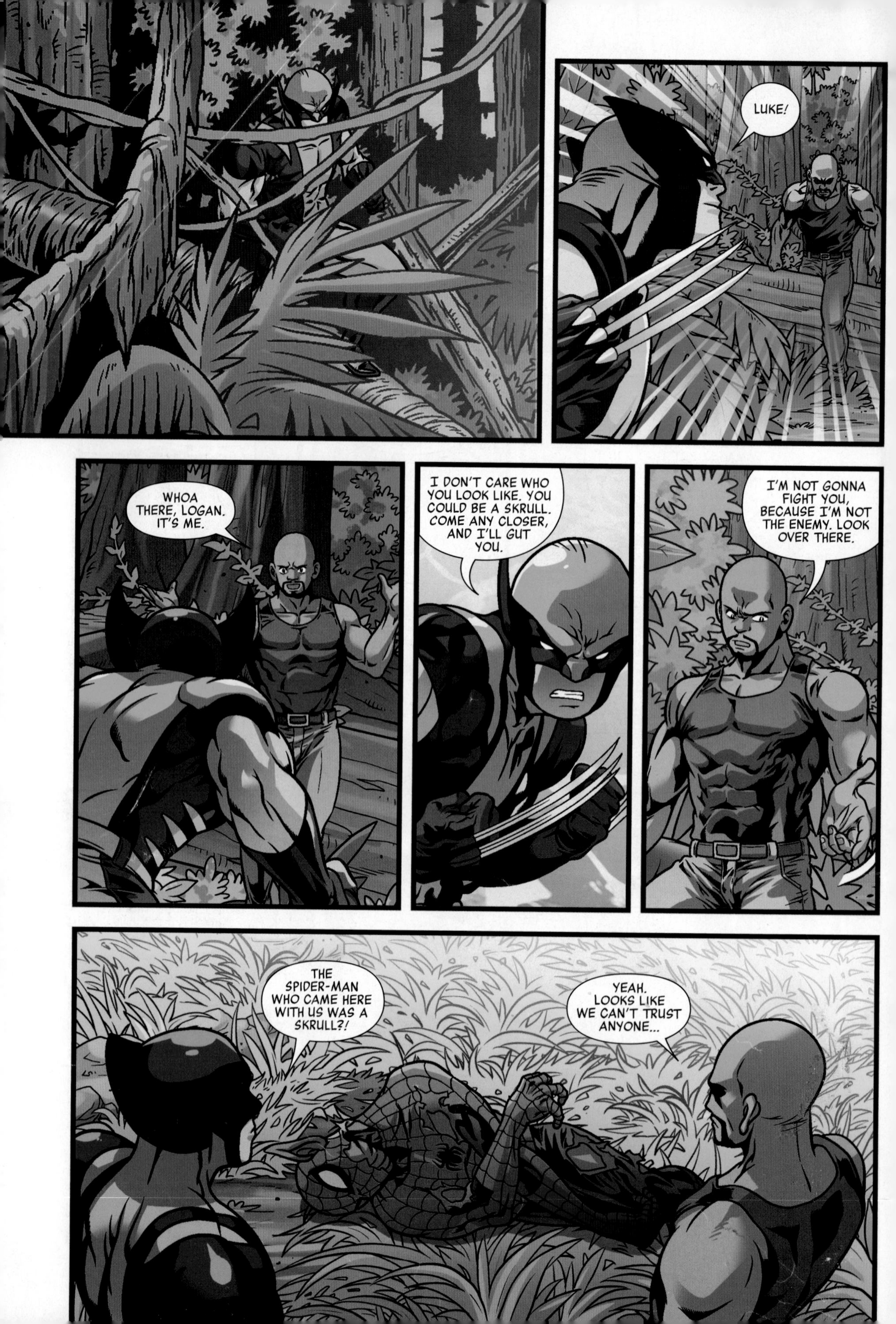
LUKE!
WHOA THERE, LOGAN. IT'S ME.
I DON'T CARE WHO YOU LOOK LIKE. YOU COULD BE A SKRULL. COME ANY CLOSER, AND I'LL GUT YOU.
I'M NOT GONNA FIGHT YOU, BECAUSE I'M NOT THE ENEMY. LOOK OVER THERE.
THE SPIDER-MAN WHO CAME HERE WITH US WAS A SKRULL?!
YEAH. LOOKS LIKE WE CAN'T TRUST ANYONE...

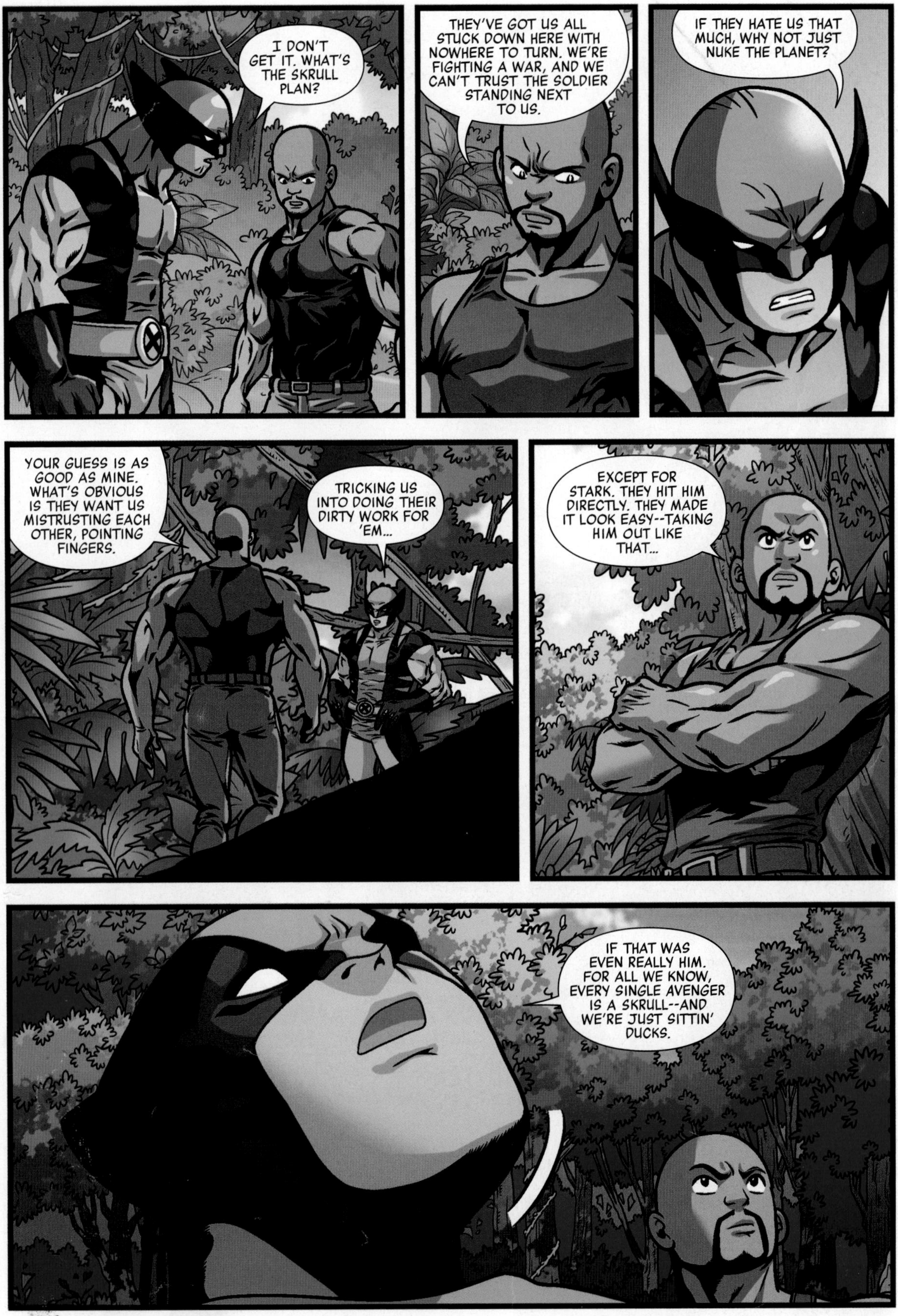
I DON'T GET IT. WHAT'S THE SKRULL PLAN?
THEY'VE GOT US ALL STUCK DOWN HERE WITH NOWHERE TO TURN. WE'RE FIGHTING A WAR, AND WE CAN'T TRUST THE SOLDIER STANDING NEXT TO US.
IF THEY HATE US THAT MUCH, WHY NOT JUST NUKE THE PLANET?
YOUR GUESS IS AS GOOD AS MINE. WHAT'S OBVIOUS IS THEY WANT US MISTRUSTING EACH OTHER, POINTING FINGERS.
TRICKING US INTO DOING THEIR DIRTY WORK FOR 'EM...
EXCEPT FOR STARK. THEY HIT HIM DIRECTLY. THEY MADE IT LOOK EASY--TAKING HIM OUT LIKE THAT...
IF THAT WAS EVEN REALLY HIM. FOR ALL WE KNOW, EVERY SINGLE AVENGER IS A SKRULL--AND WE'RE JUST SITTIN' DUCKS.

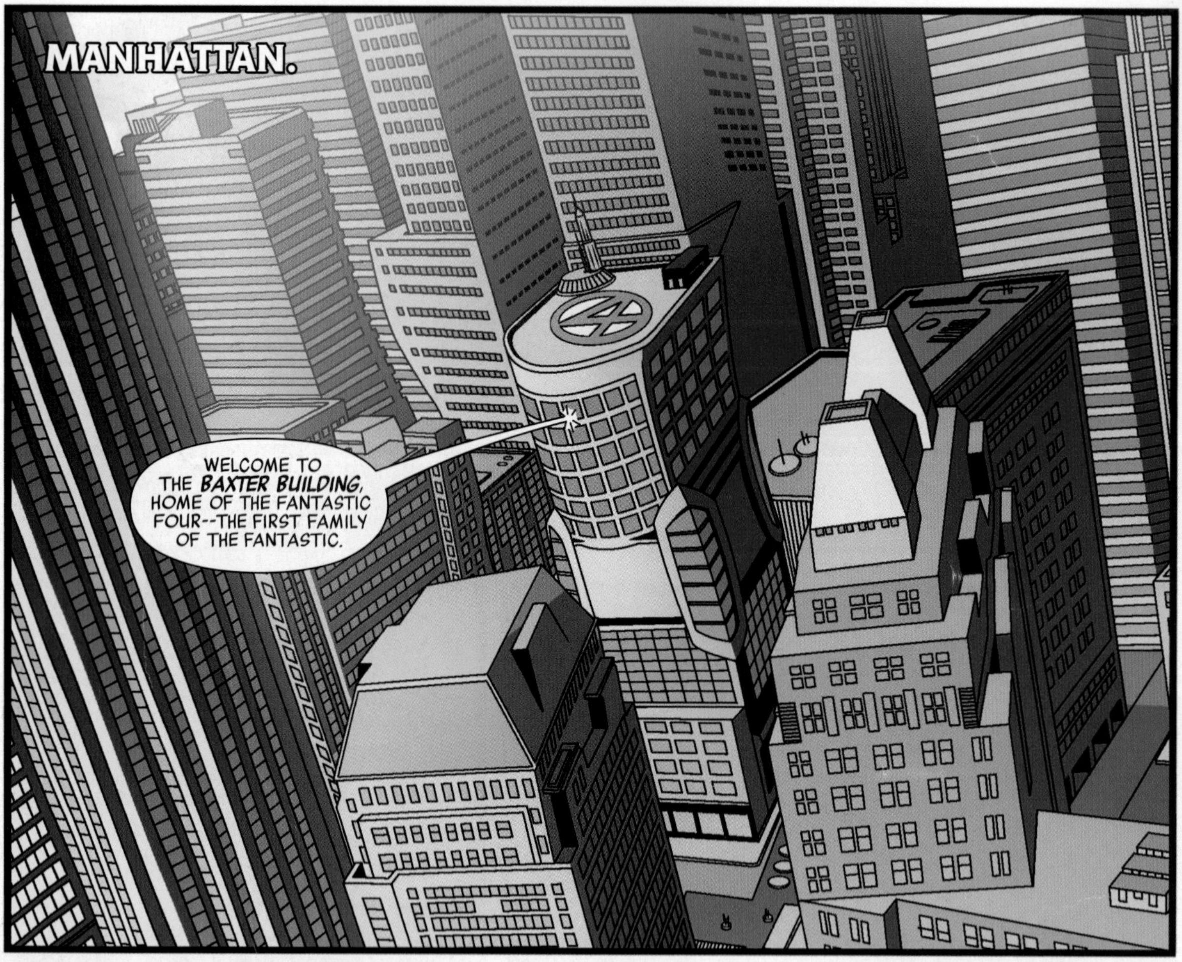
MANHATTAN.
WELCOME TO THE BAXTER BUILDING, HOME OF THE FANTASTIC FOUR--THE FIRST FAMILY OF THE FANTASTIC.

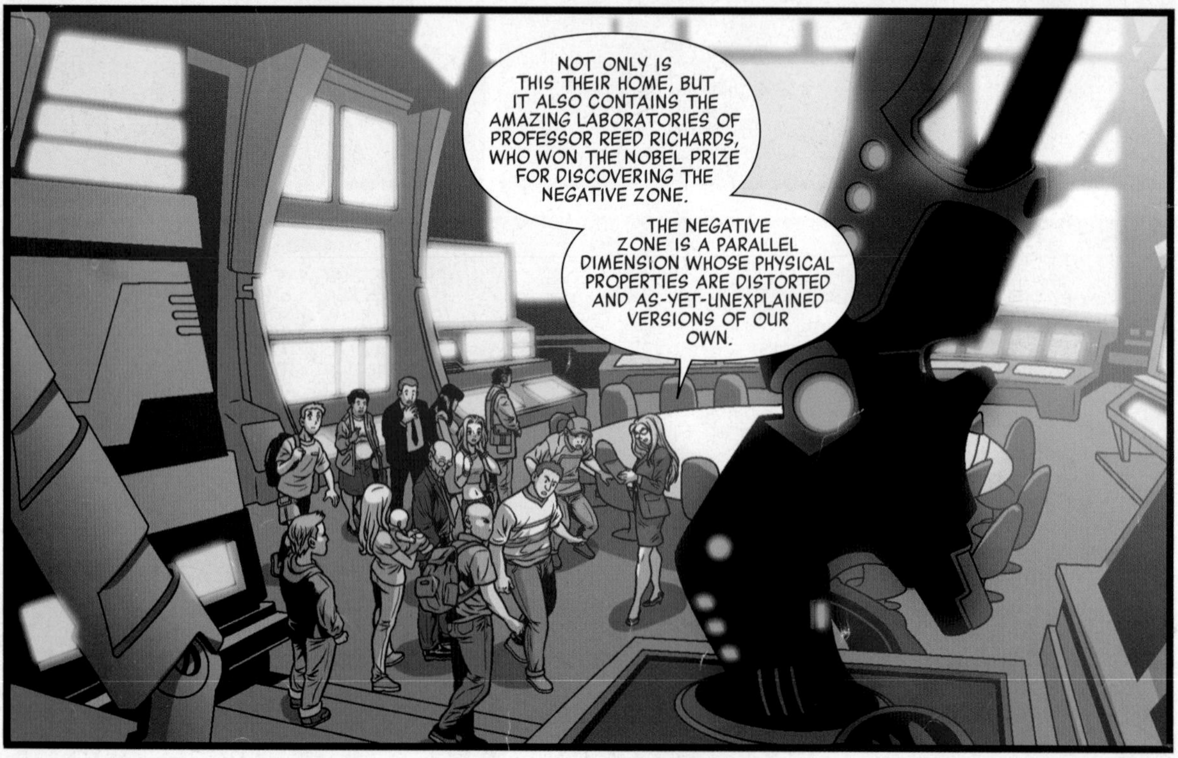
NOT ONLY IS THIS THEIR HOME, BUT IT ALSO CONTAINS THE AMAZING LABORATORIES OF PROFESSOR REED RICHARDS, WHO WON THE NOBEL PRIZE FOR DISCOVERING THE NEGATIVE ZONE.
THE NEGATIVE ZONE IS A PARALLEL DIMENSION WHOSE PHYSICAL PROPERTIES ARE DISTORTED AND AS-YET-UNEXPLAINED VERSIONS OF OUR OWN.

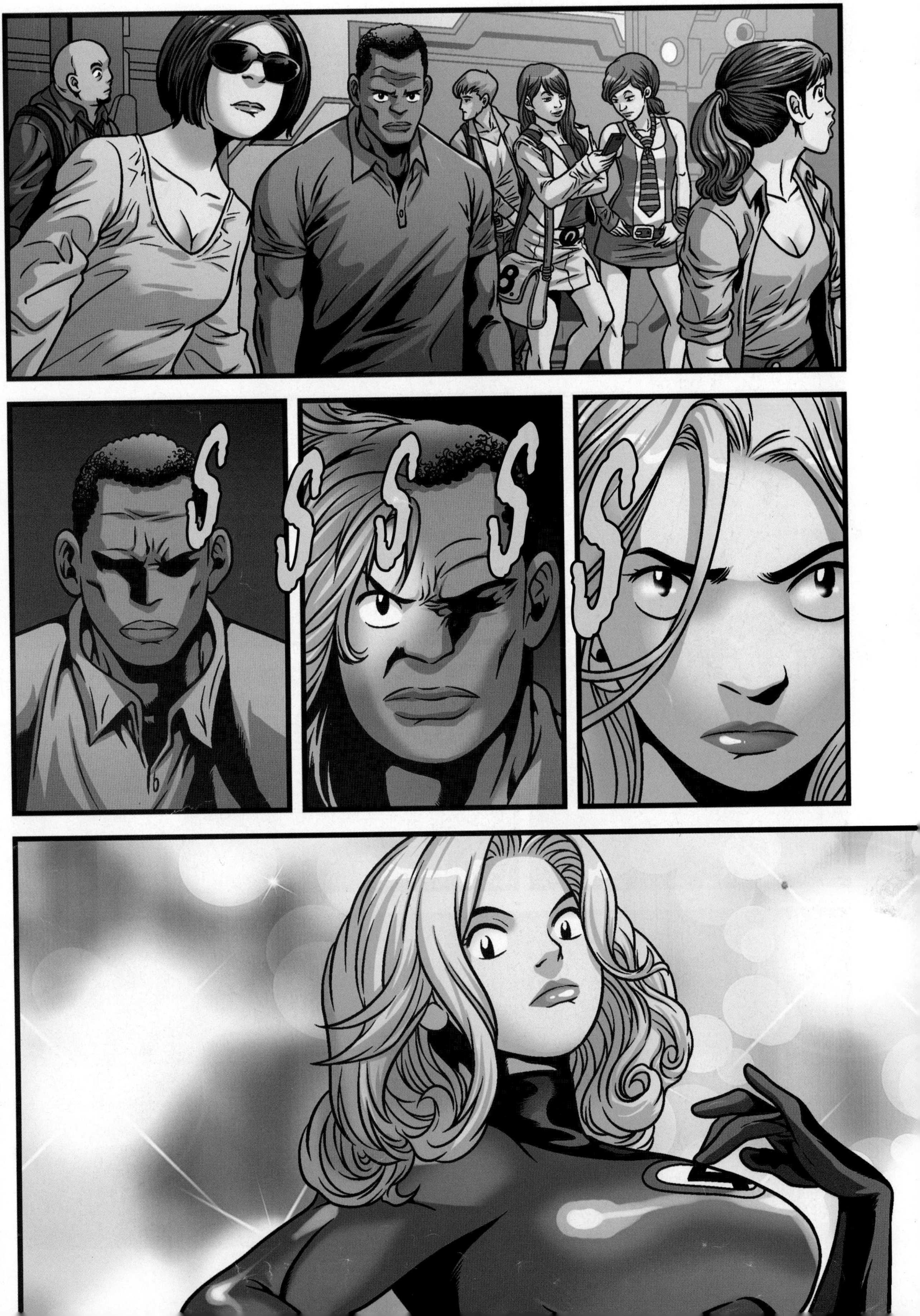
SSSSS

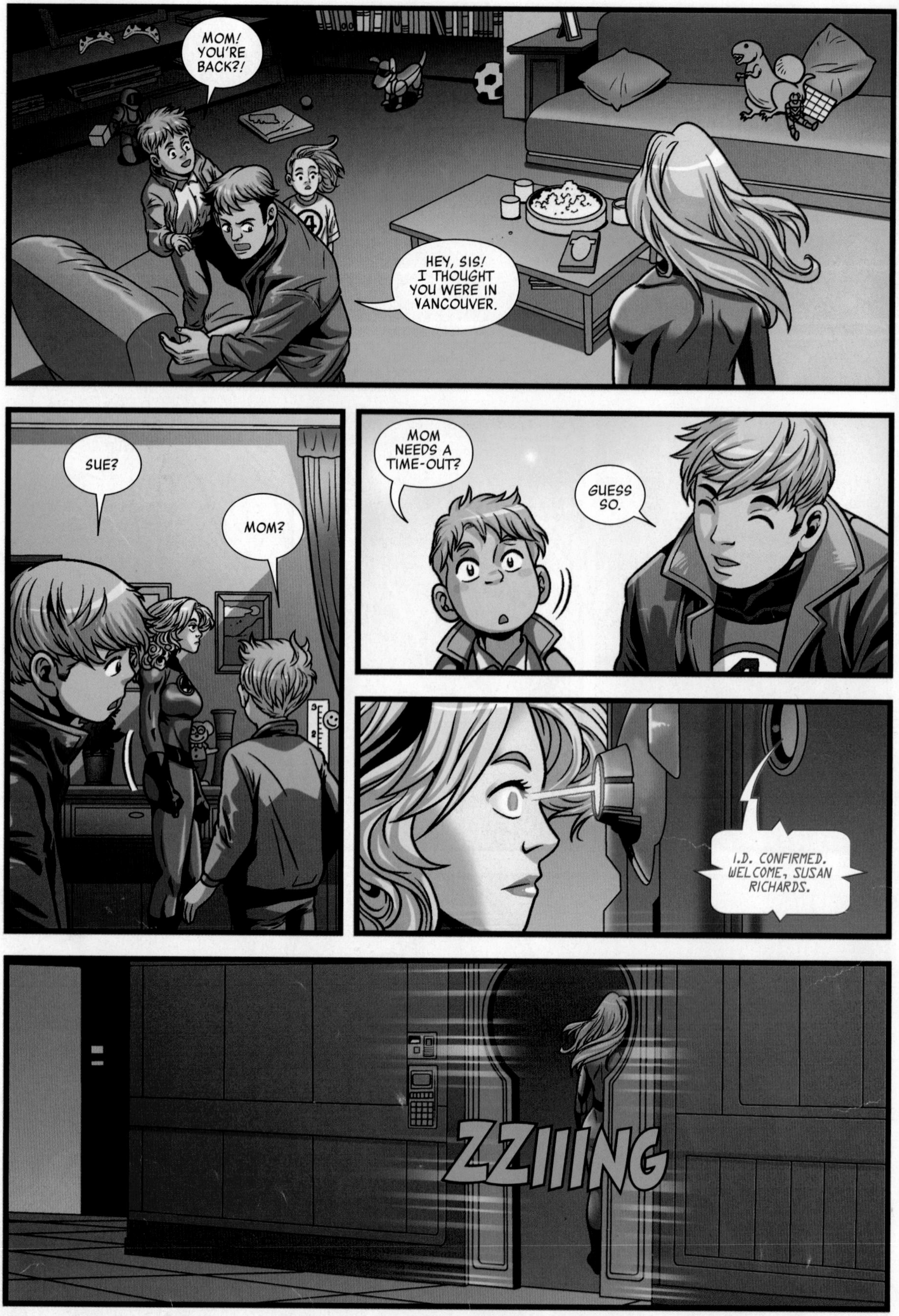
MOM! YOU'RE BACK?!
HEY, SIS! I THOUGHT YOU WERE IN VANCOUVER.
SUE?
MOM?
MOM NEEDS A TIME-OUT?
GUESS SO.
I.D. CONFIRMED. WELCOME, SUSAN RICHARDS.
ZZIIING

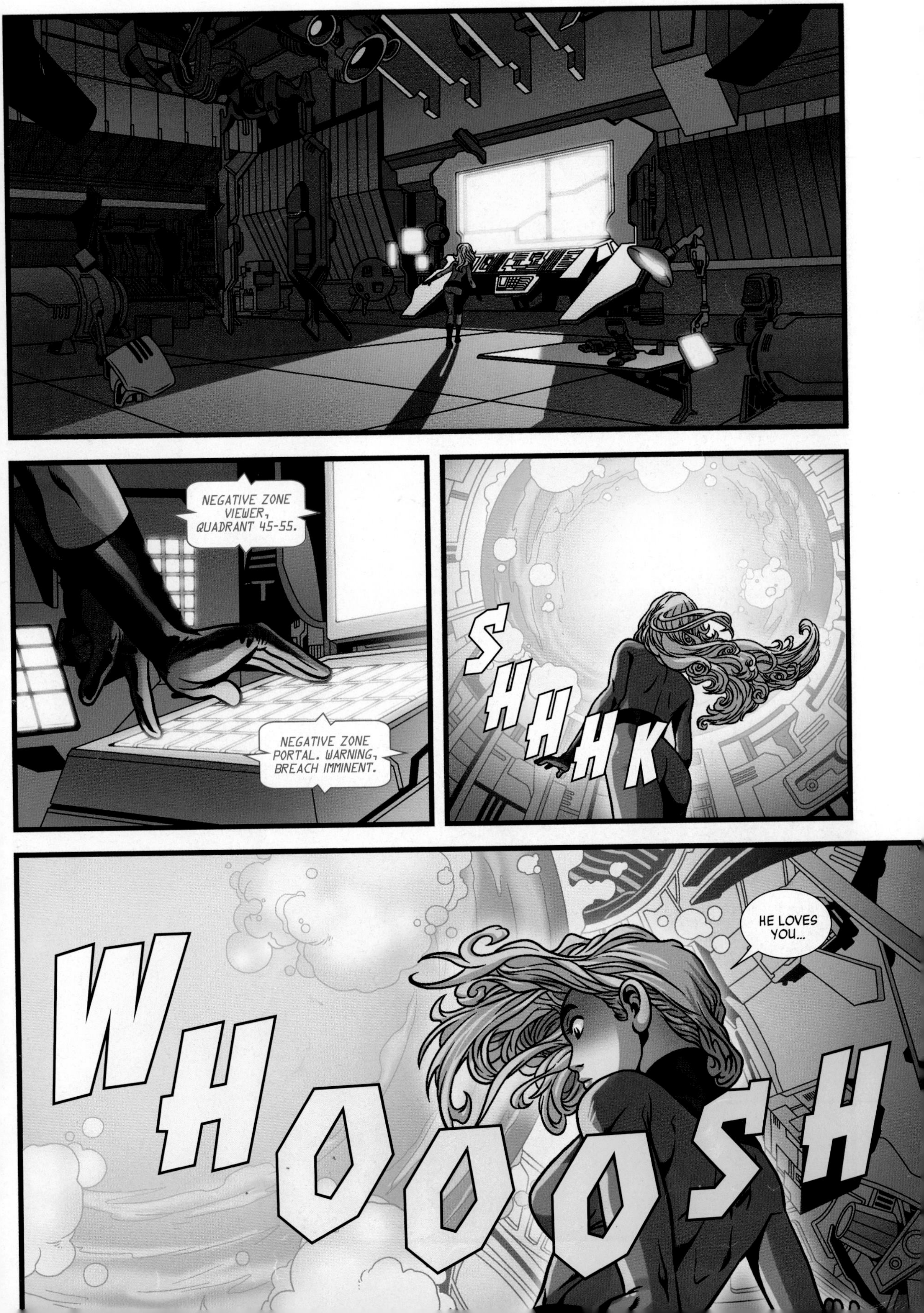
NEGATIVE ZONE VIEWER, QUADRANT 45-55.
NEGATIVE ZONE PORTAL. WARNING, BREACH IMMINENT.
SHHHHK
HE LOVES YOU...
WHOOOSH

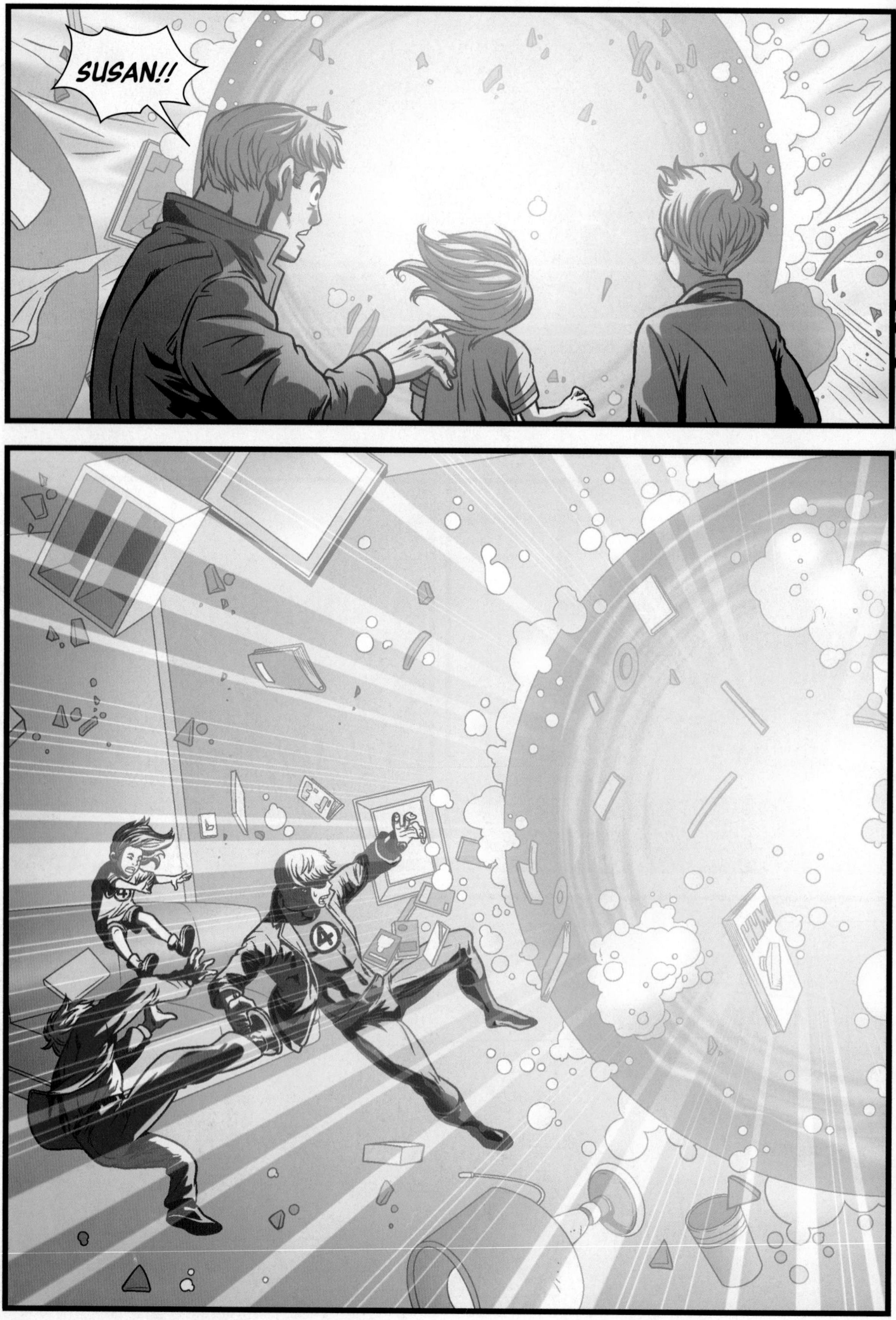
SUSAN!!

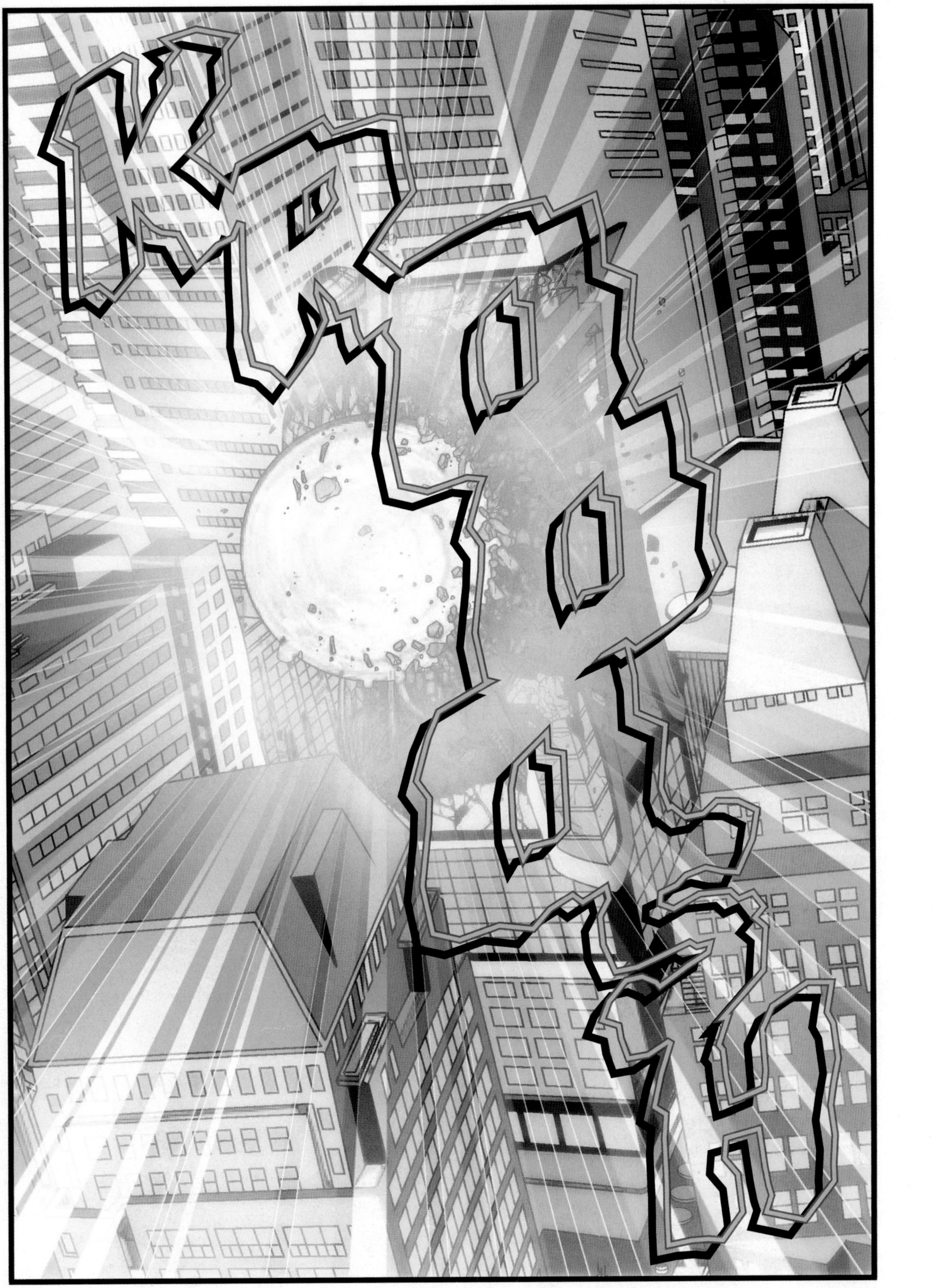
KROOOSH

STARK LABORATORY.

I-I THINK I GOT IT, HANK!

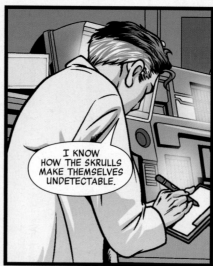

I KNOW HOW THE SKRULLS MAKE THEMSELVES UNDETECTABLE.

YOU KNOW WHAT THEY DID? THEY--

I DO, ACTUALLY.

H-HANK...?!

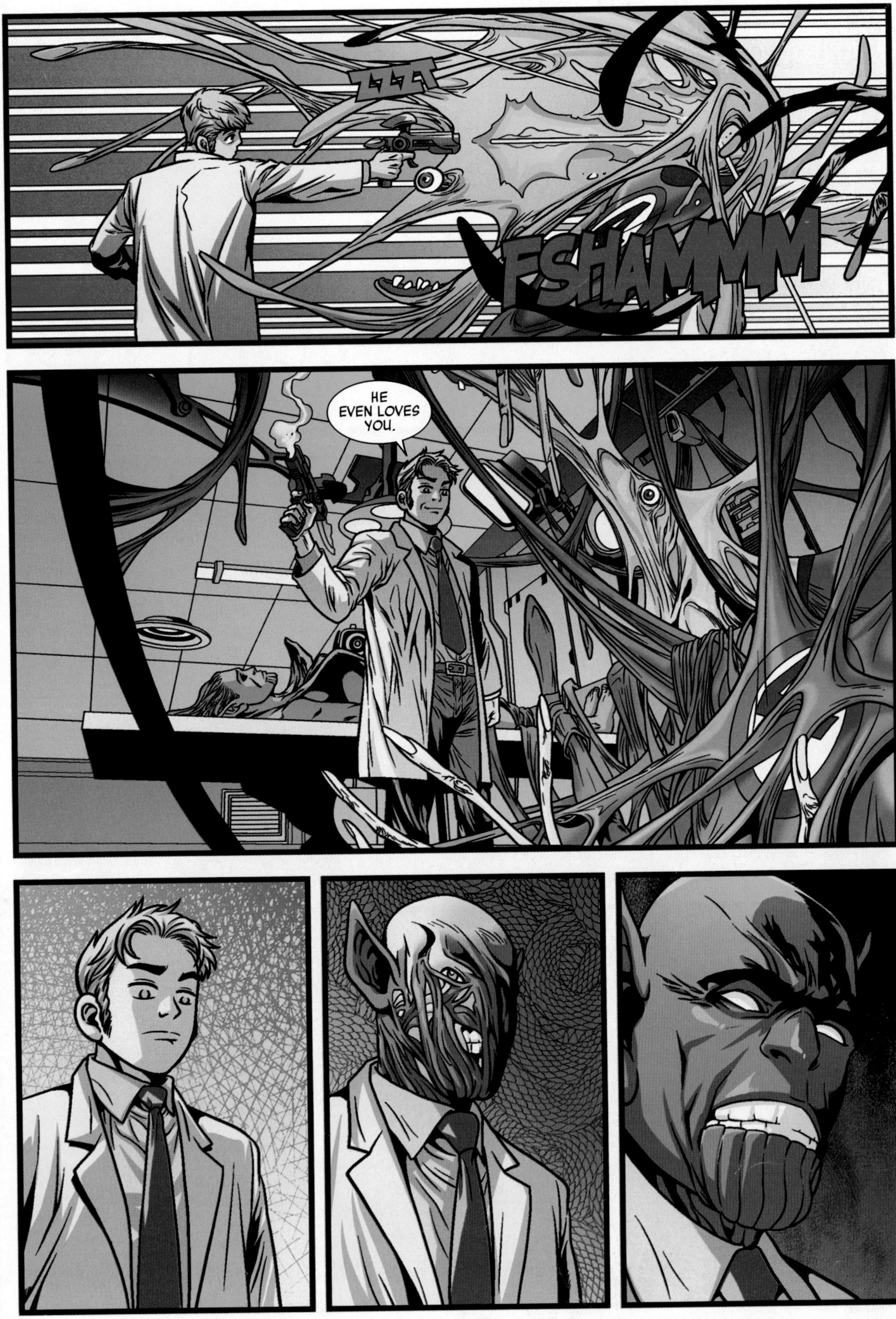
ZZZT
FSHAMMMM
HE EVEN LOVES YOU.

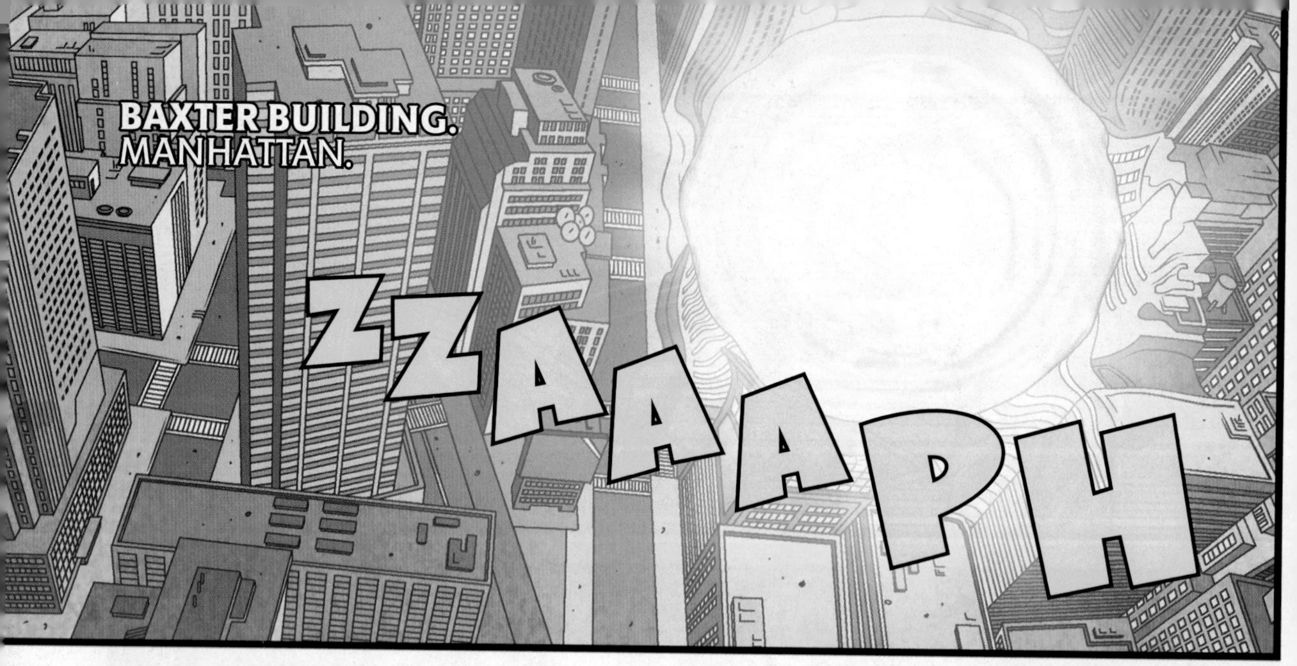
BAXTER BUILDING.
MANHATTAN.
ZZAAAAPH

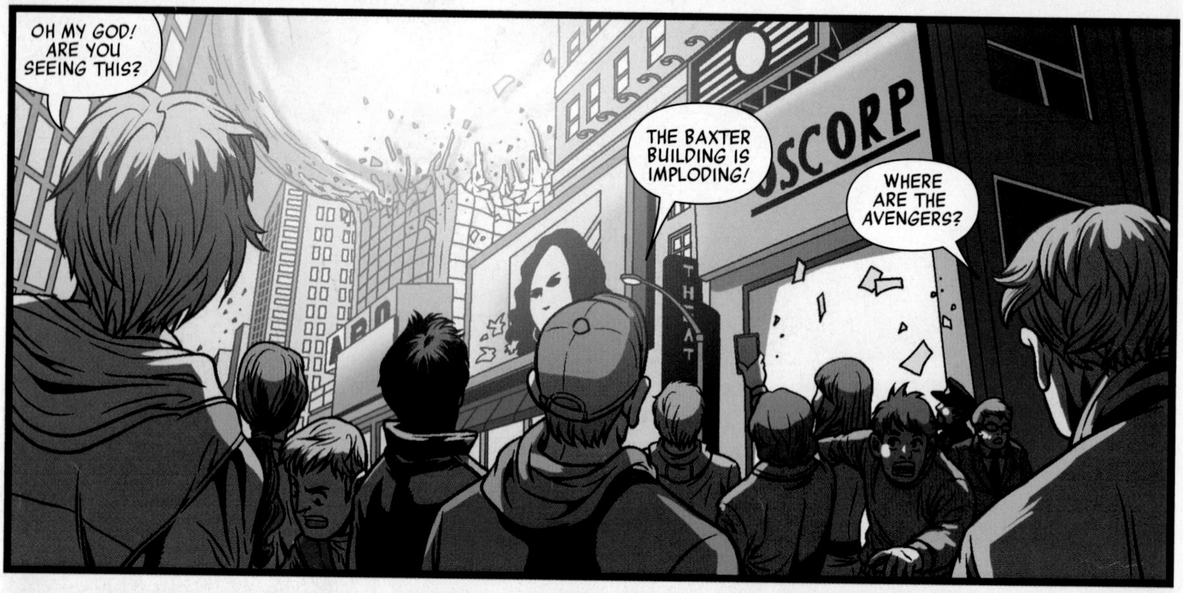
OH MY GOD! ARE YOU SEEING THIS?
THE BAXTER BUILDING IS IMPLODING!
WHERE ARE THE AVENGERS?
OSCORP

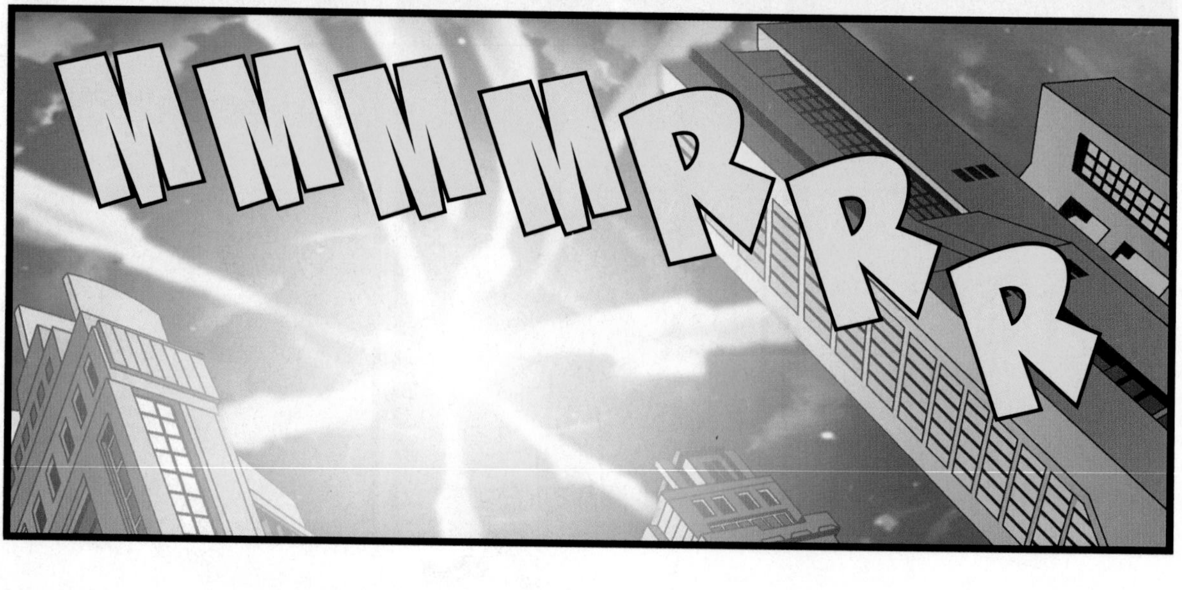
MMMMRRR

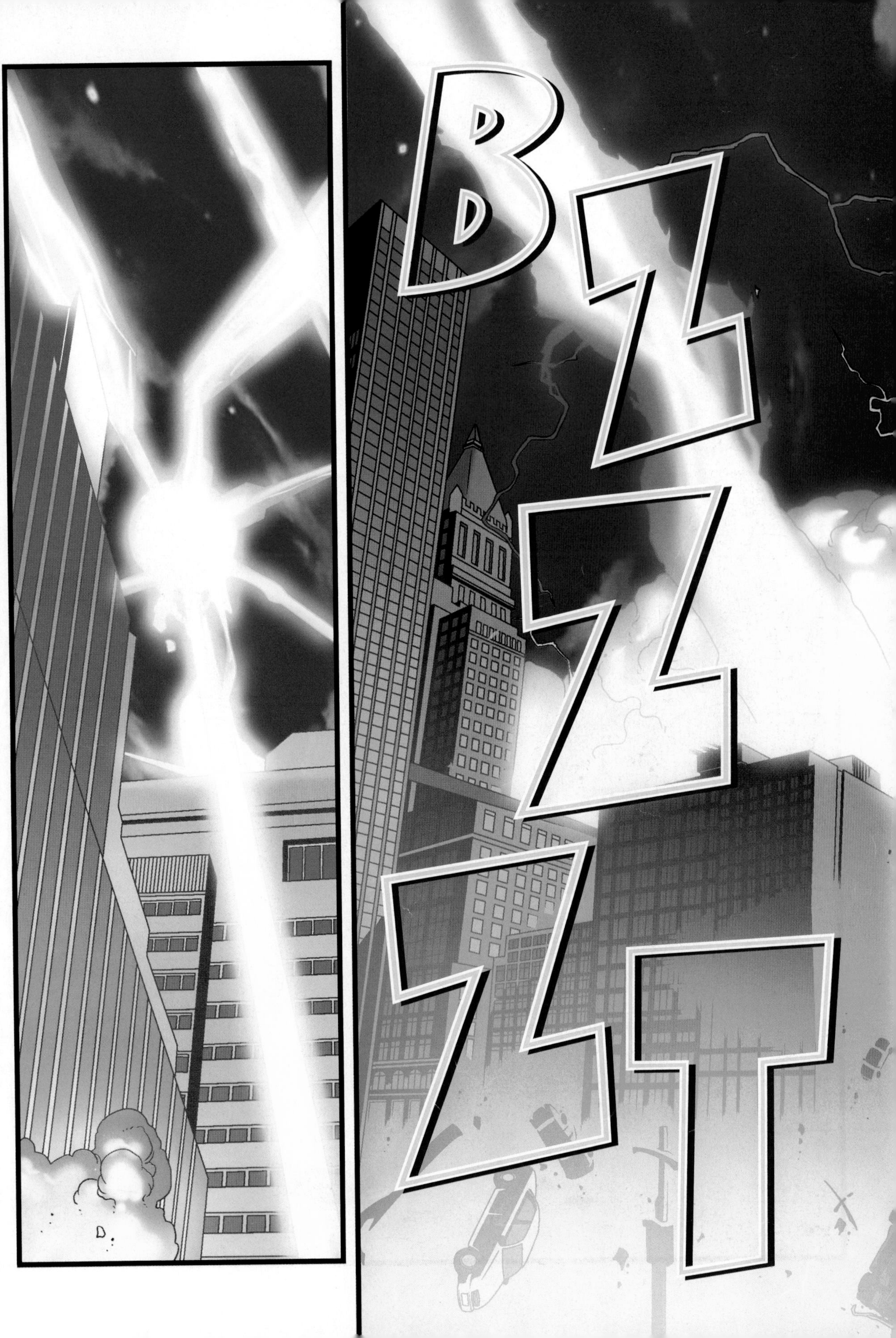
BZZZT

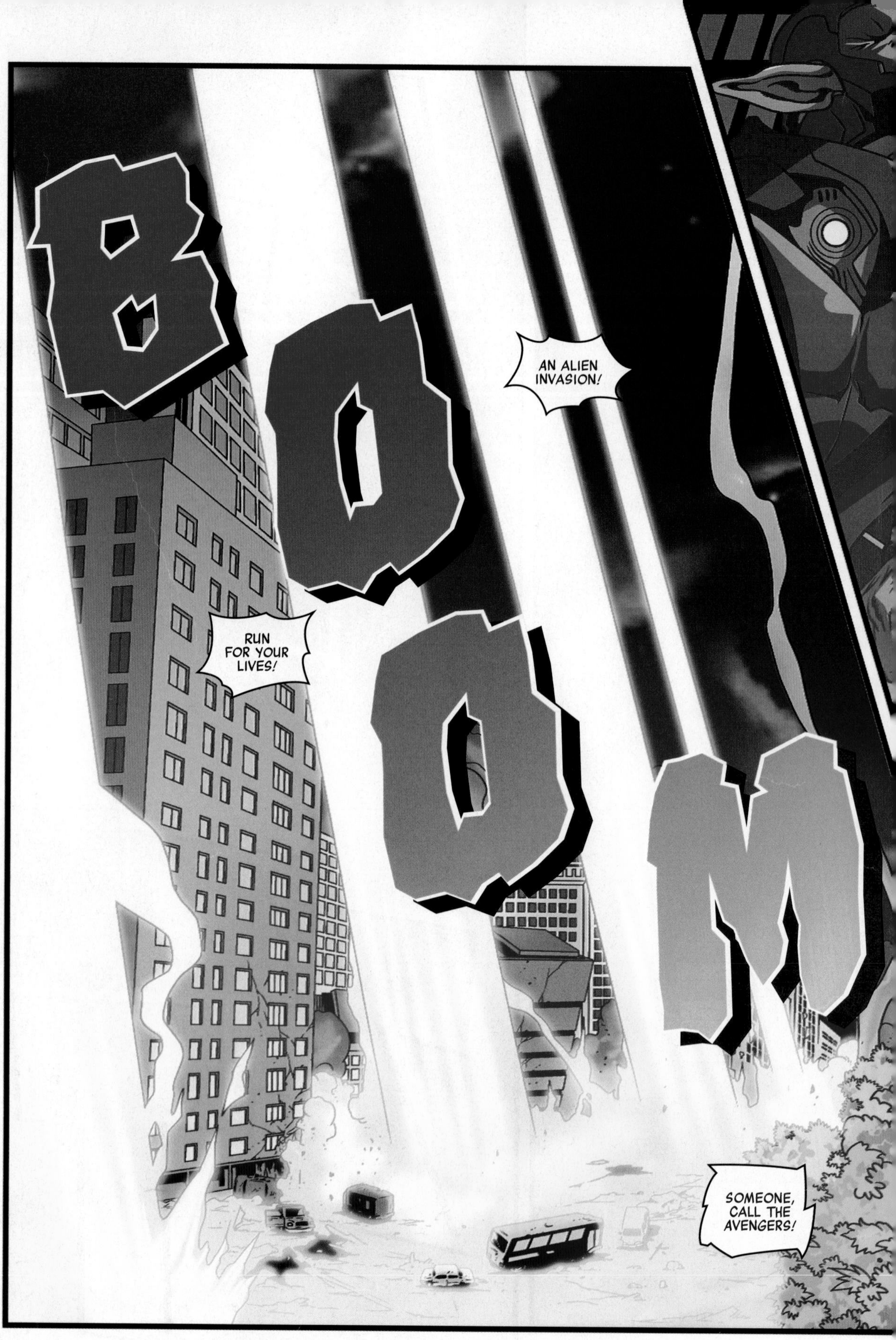
BOOM
AN ALIEN INVASION!
RUN FOR YOUR LIVES!
SOMEONE, CALL THE AVENGERS!

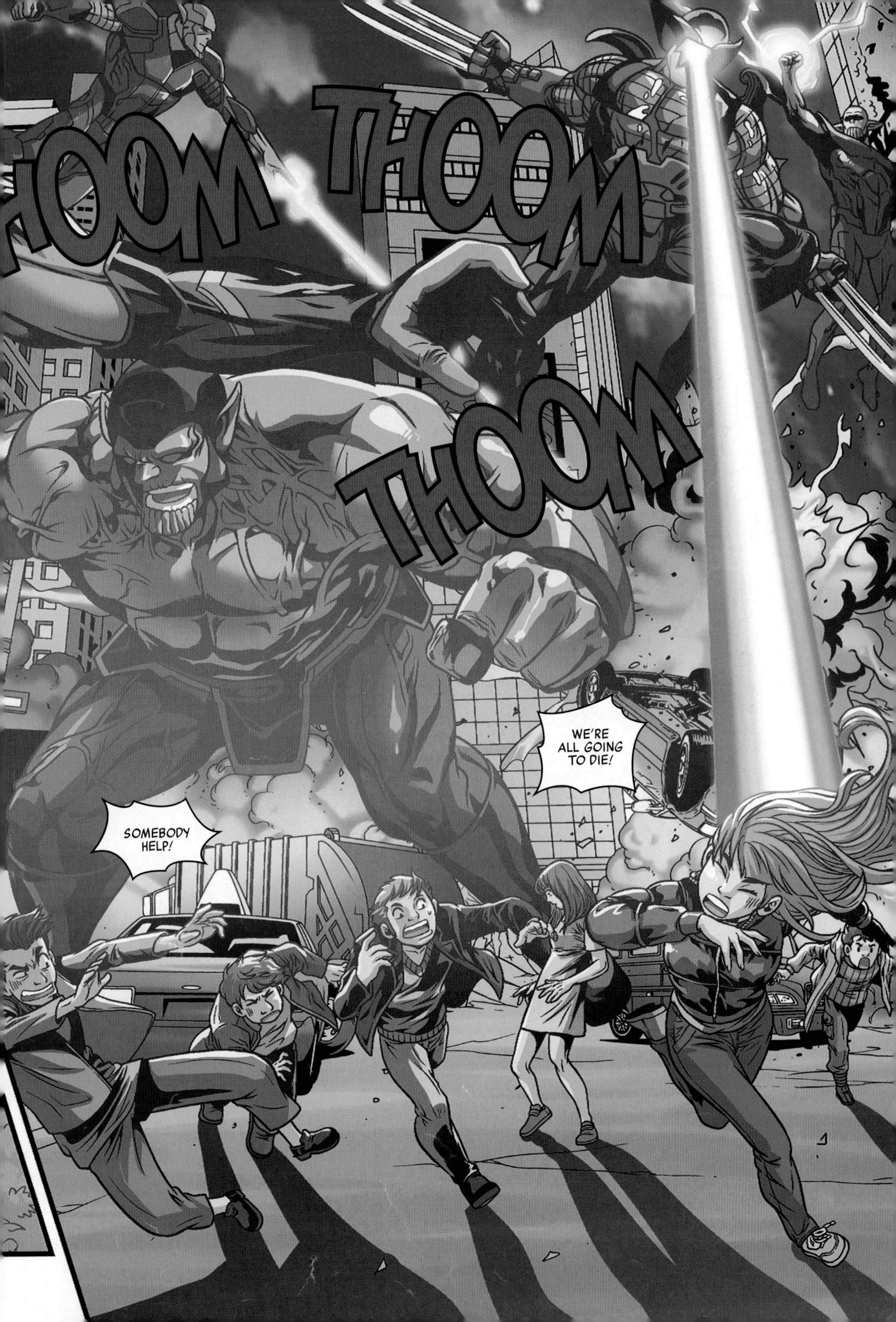
THOOM
THOOM
THOOM
WE'RE ALL GOING TO DIE!
SOMEBODY HELP!

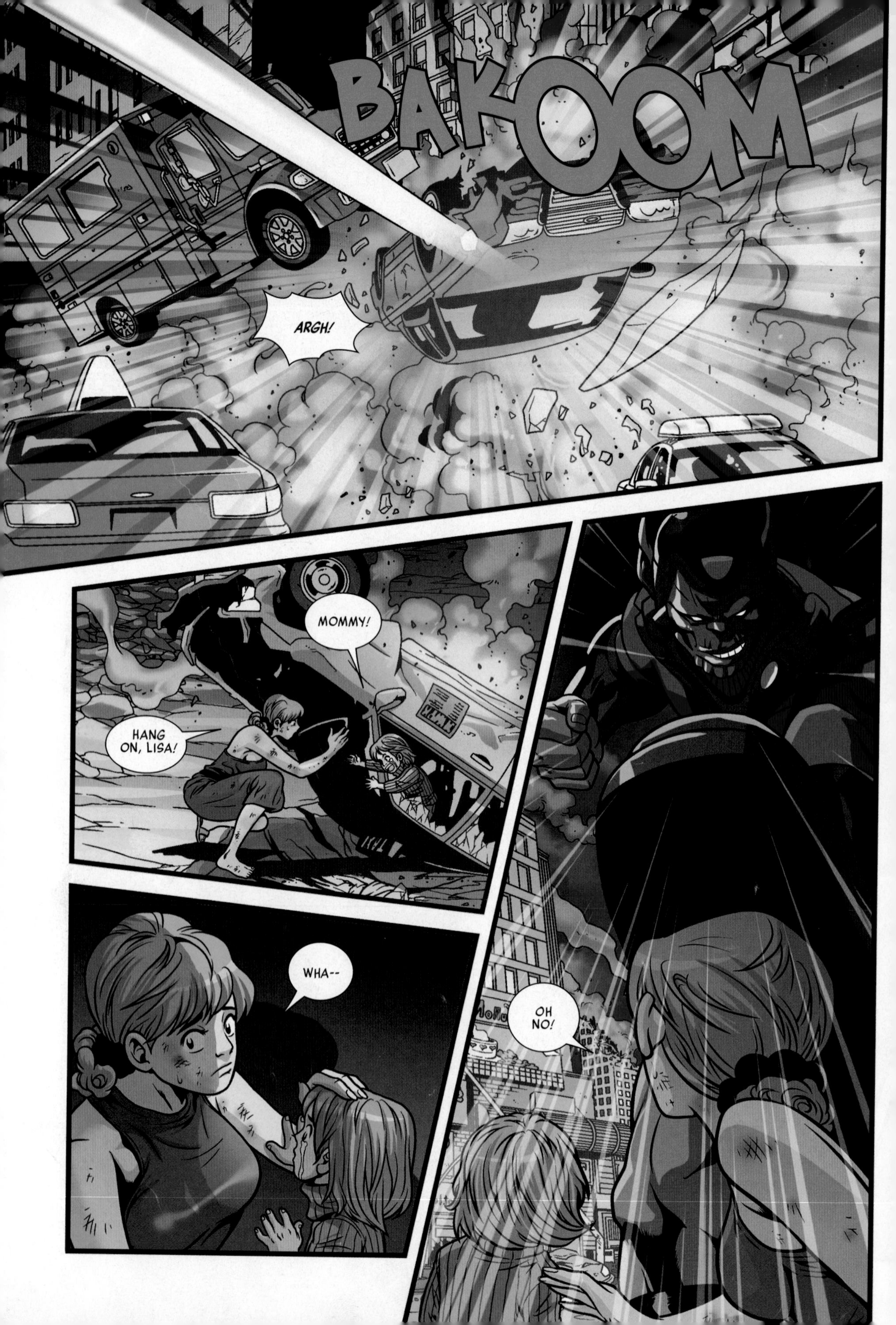
BAKOOM
ARGH!
MOMMY!
HANG ON, LISA!
WHA--
OH NO!

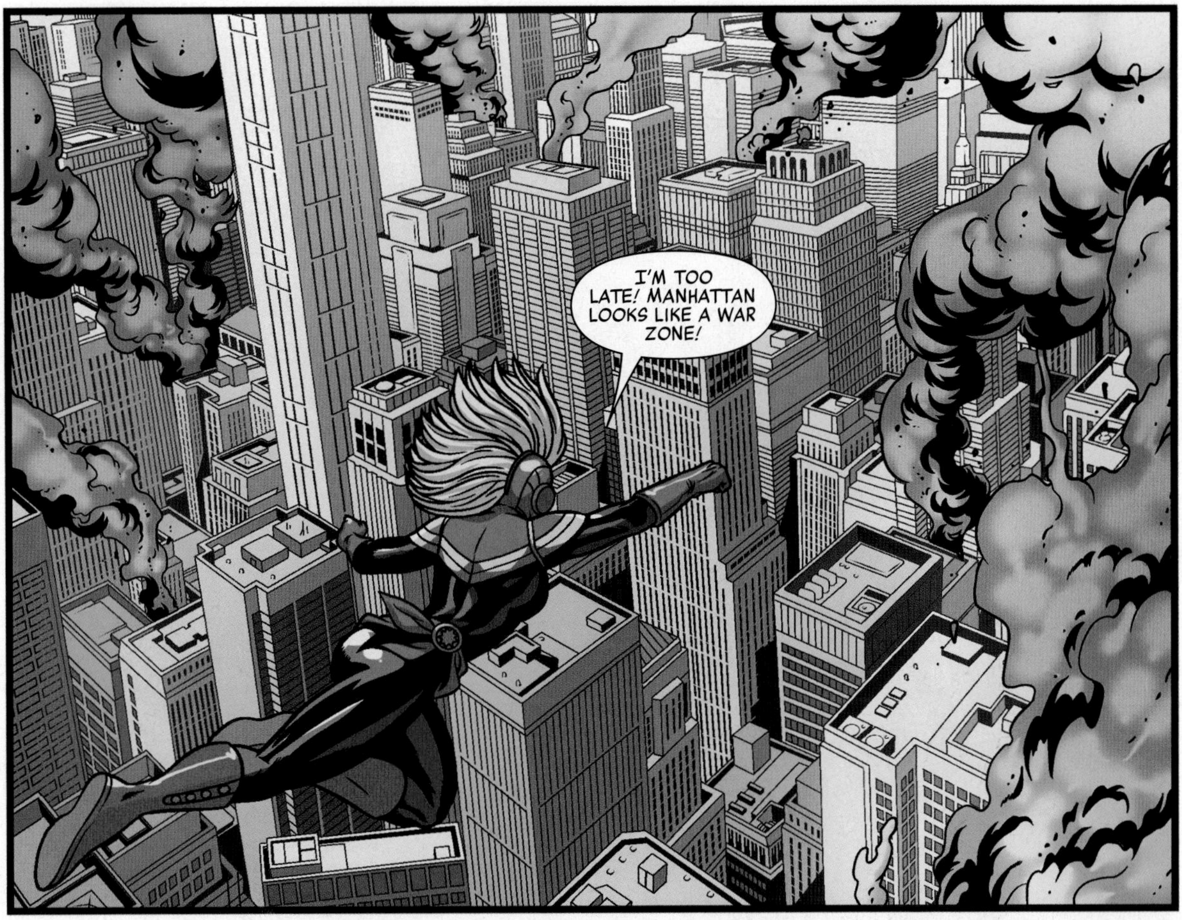
I'M TOO LATE! MANHATTAN LOOKS LIKE A WAR ZONE!

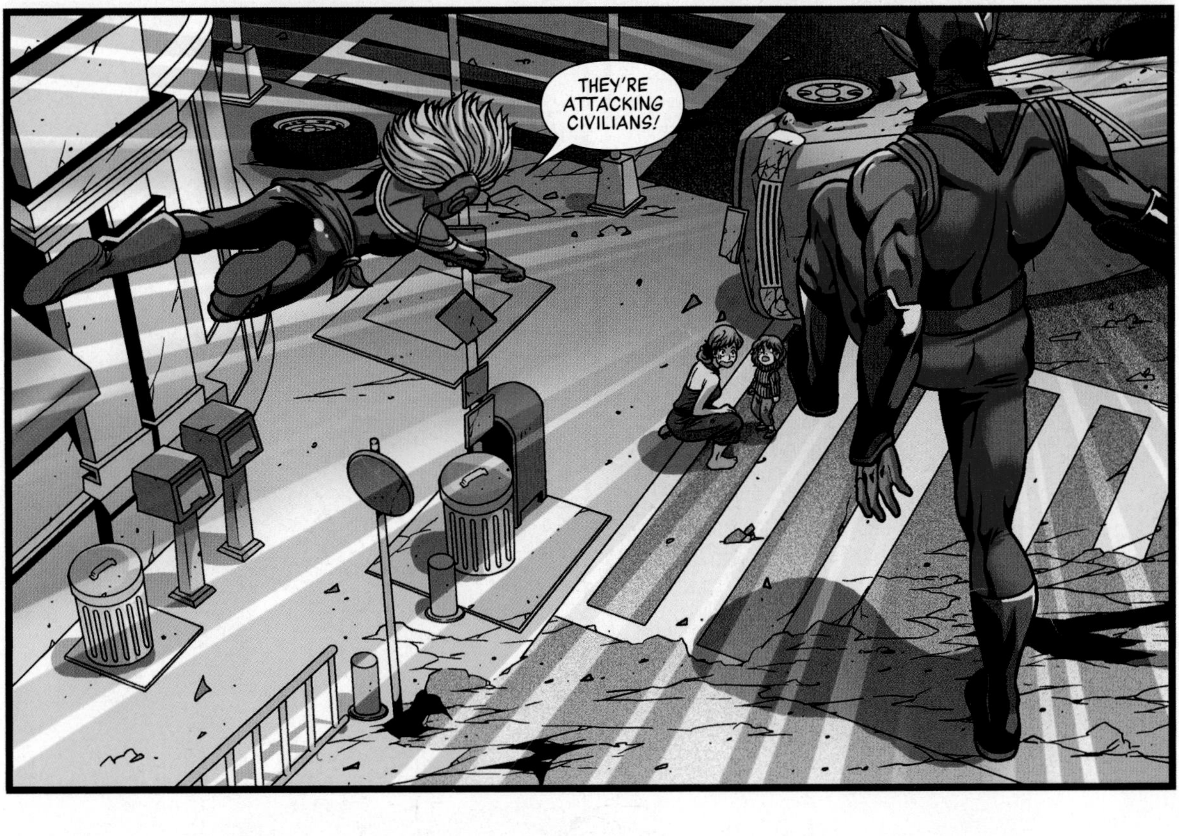
THEY'RE ATTACKING CIVILIANS!

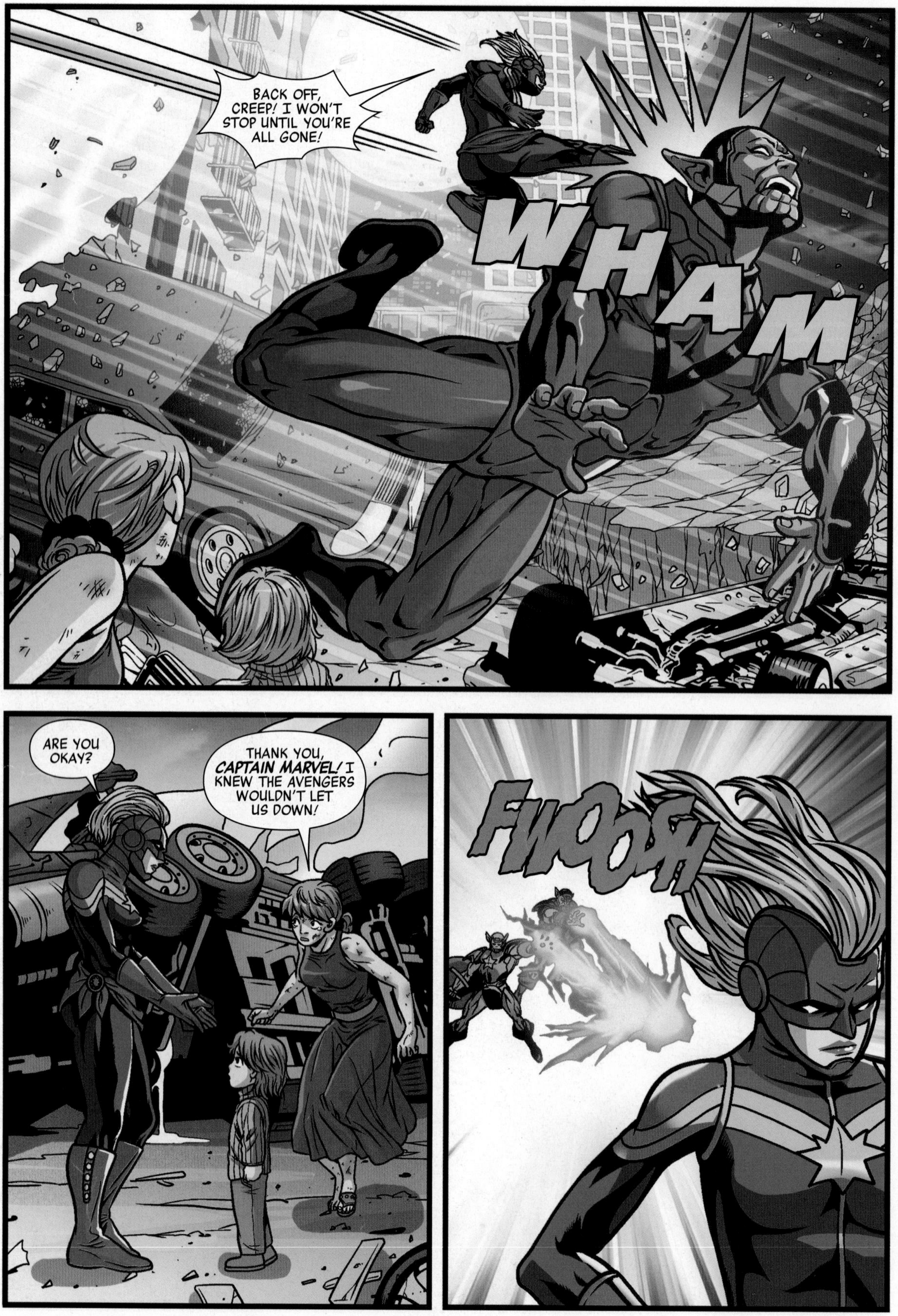
BACK OFF, CREEP! I WON'T STOP UNTIL YOU'RE ALL GONE!
WHAM
ARE YOU OKAY?
THANK YOU, CAPTAIN MARVEL! I KNEW THE AVENGERS WOULDN'T LET US DOWN!
FWOOSH

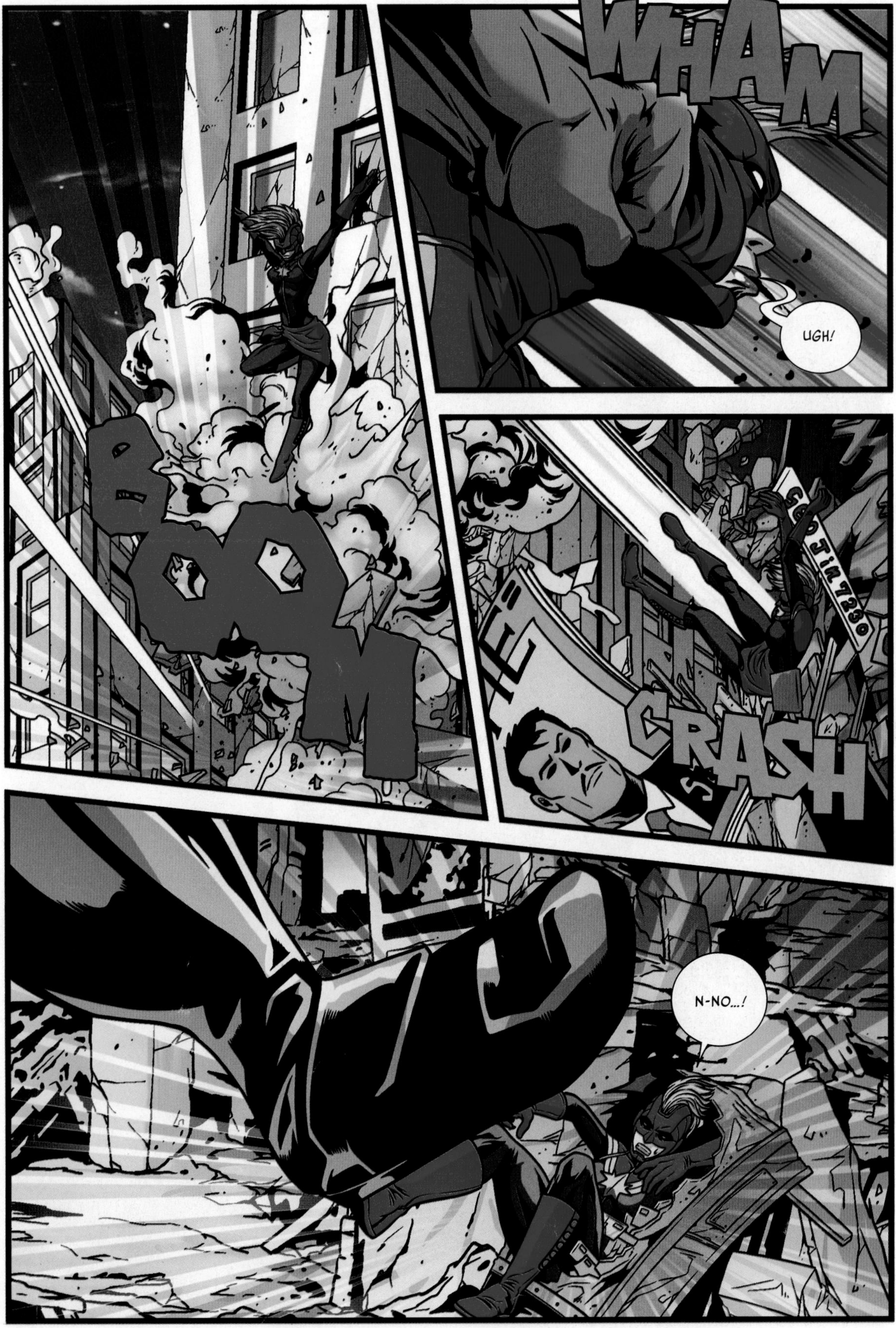
BOOM
WHAM
UGH!
CRASH
N-NO...!

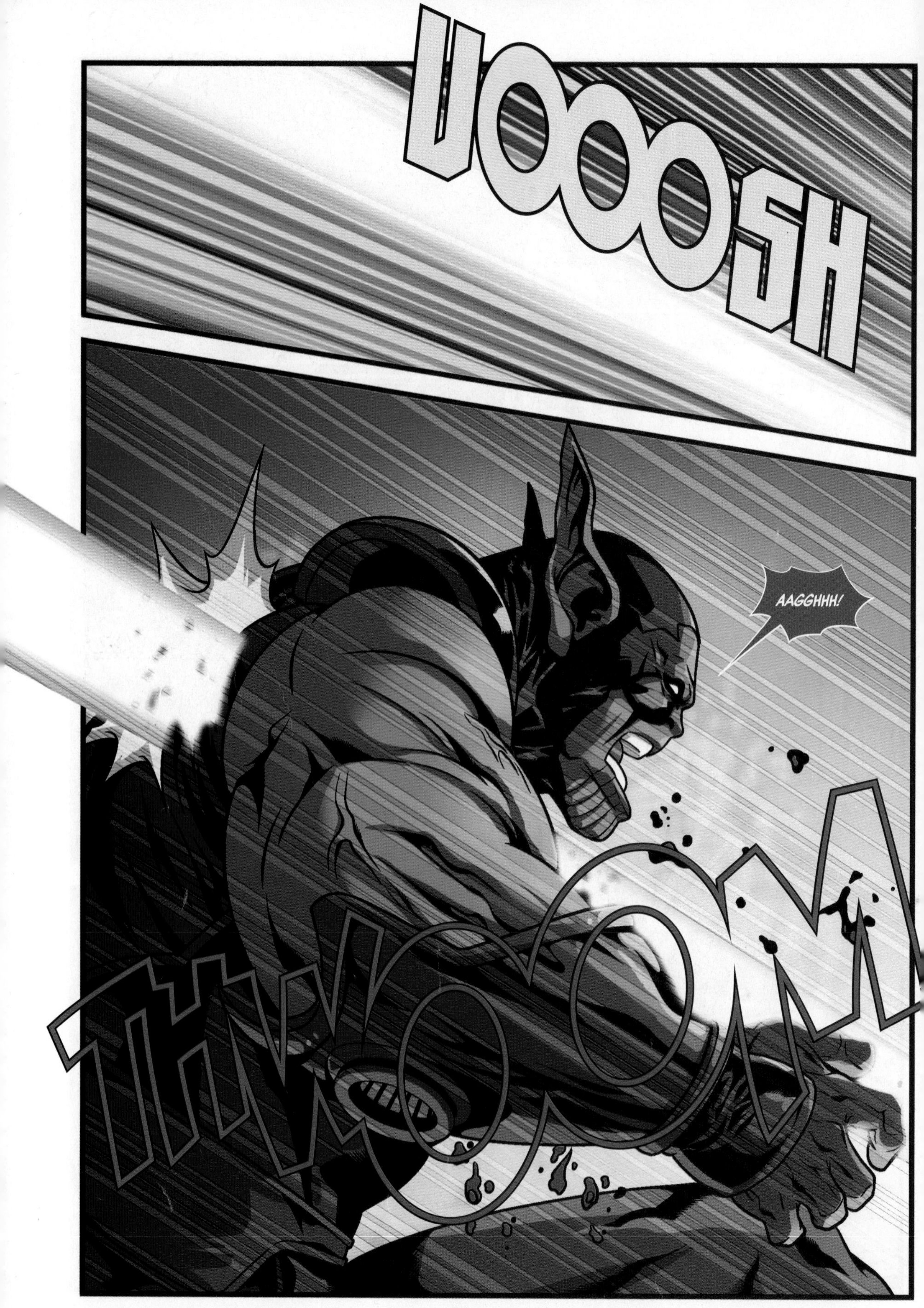
VOOOSH
AAGGHHH!
THWOOM

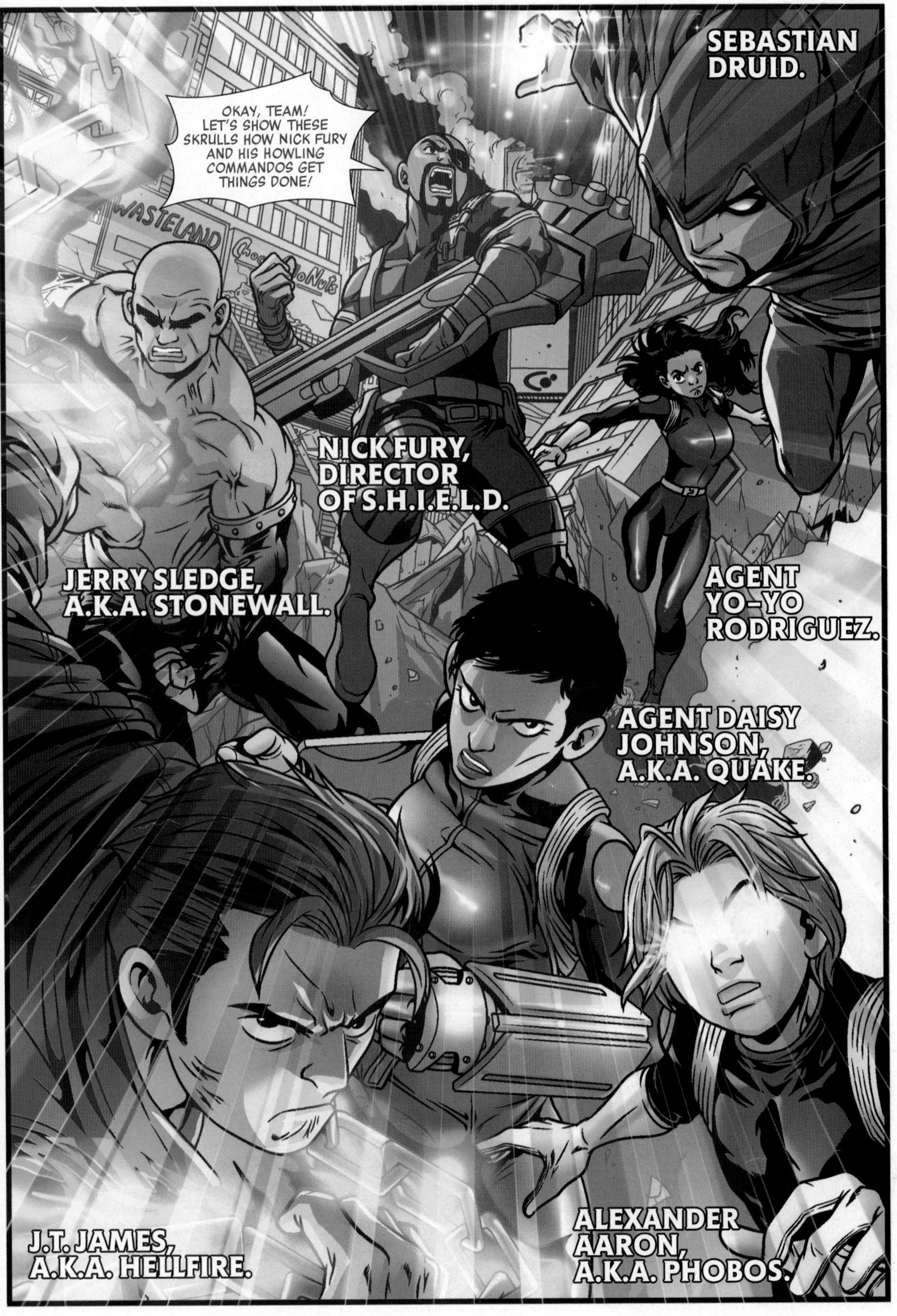
SEBASTIAN DRUID.
OKAY, TEAM! LET'S SHOW THESE SKRULLS HOW NICK FURY AND HIS HOWLING COMMANDOS GET THINGS DONE!
WASTELAND
NICK FURY, DIRECTOR OF S.H.I.E.L.D.
JERRY SLEDGE, A.K.A. STONEWALL.
AGENT YO-YO RODRIGUEZ.
AGENT DAISY JOHNSON, A.K.A. QUAKE.
J.T. JAMES, A.K.A. HELLFIRE.
ALEXANDER AARON, A.K.A. PHOBOS.

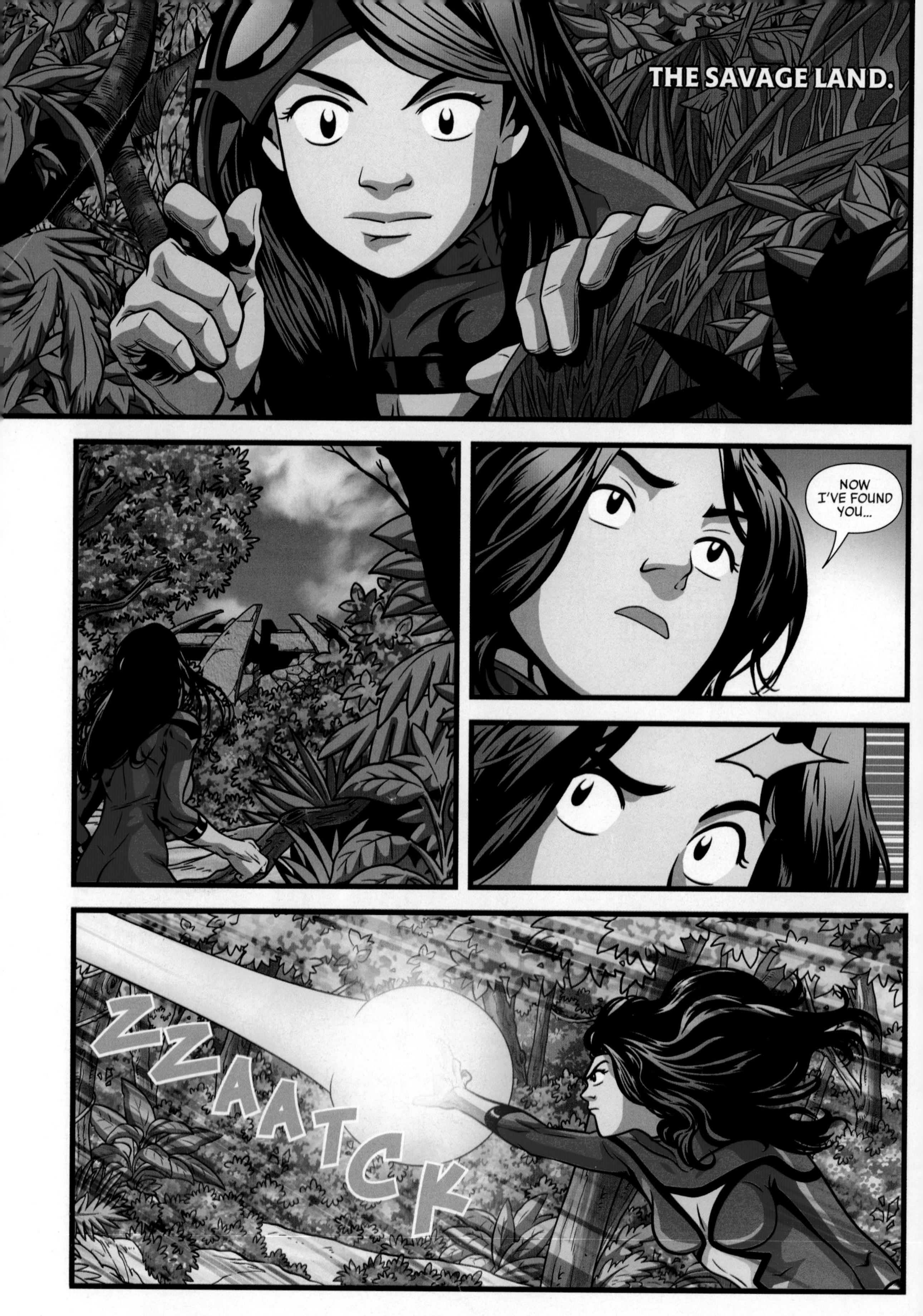
THE SAVAGE LAND.
NOW I'VE FOUND YOU...
ZZAATCK

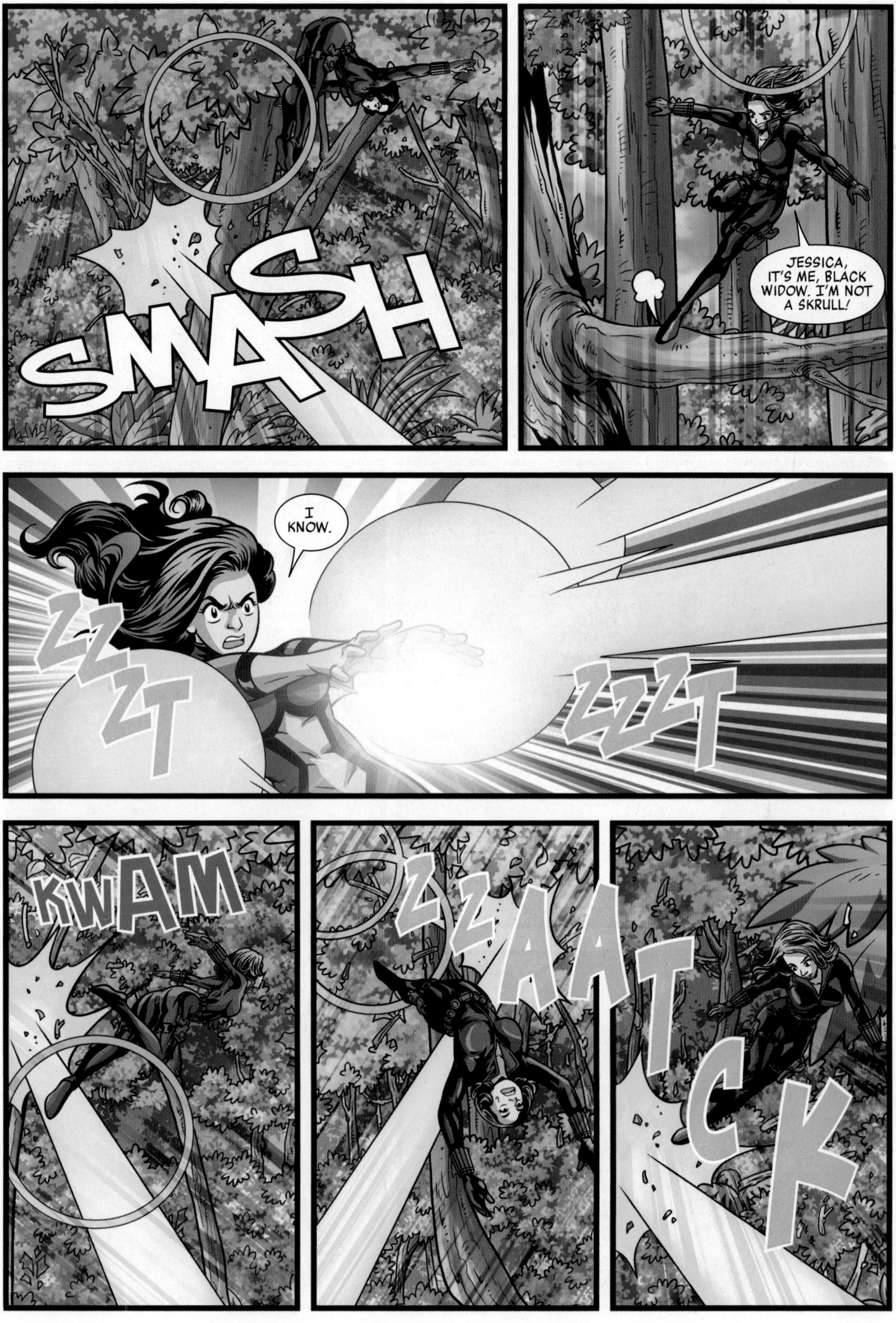
SMASH
JESSICA, IT'S ME, BLACK WIDOW. I'M NOT A SKRULL!
I KNOW.
ZZZT
ZZZT
KWAM
ZZAATCK

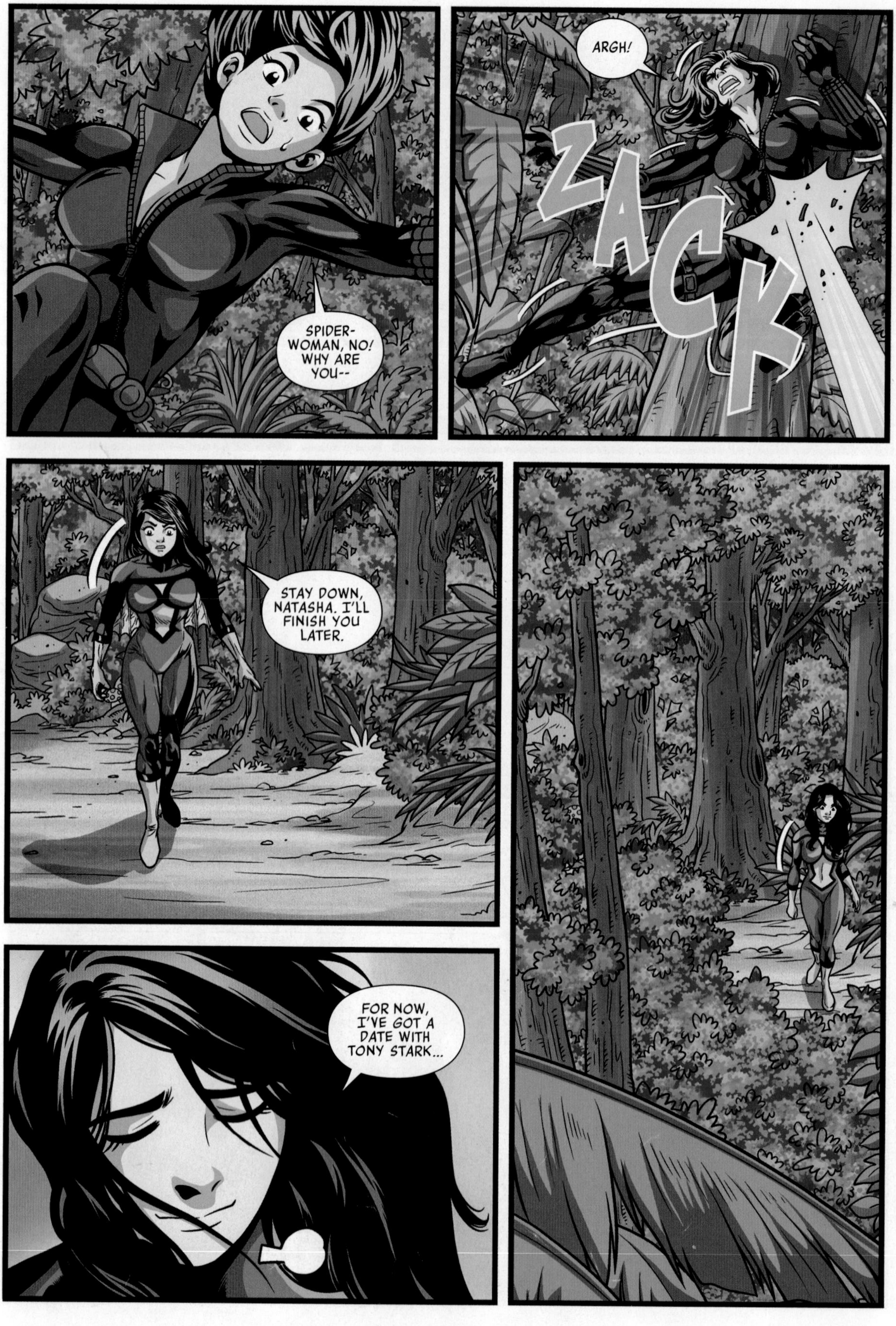
SPIDER-WOMAN, NO! WHY ARE YOU--
ARGH!
ZACK
STAY DOWN, NATASHA. I'LL FINISH YOU LATER.
FOR NOW, I'VE GOT A DATE WITH TONY STARK...

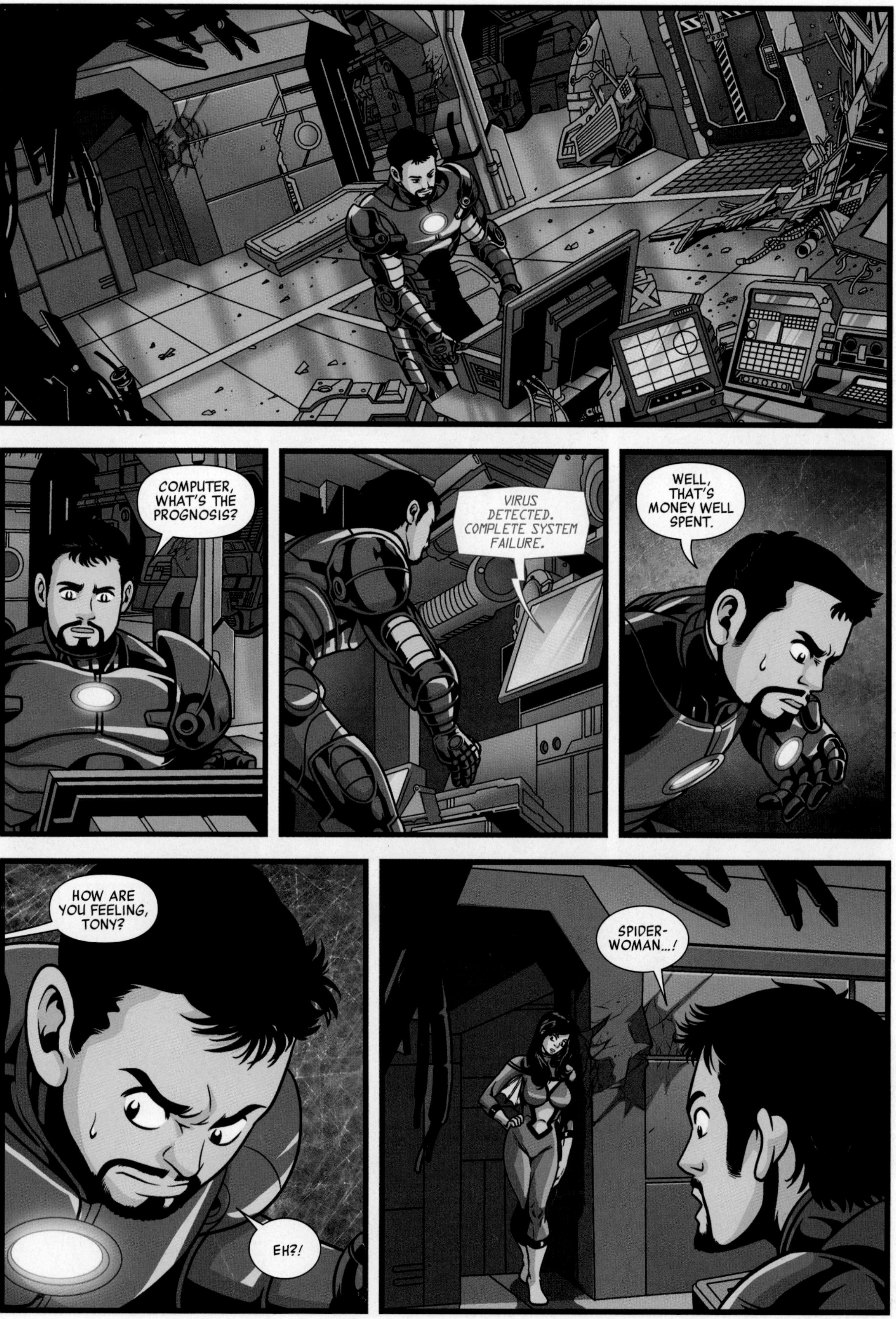
COMPUTER, WHAT'S THE PROGNOSIS?
VIRUS DETECTED. COMPLETE SYSTEM FAILURE.
WELL, THAT'S MONEY WELL SPENT.
HOW ARE YOU FEELING, TONY?
EH?!
SPIDER-WOMAN...!

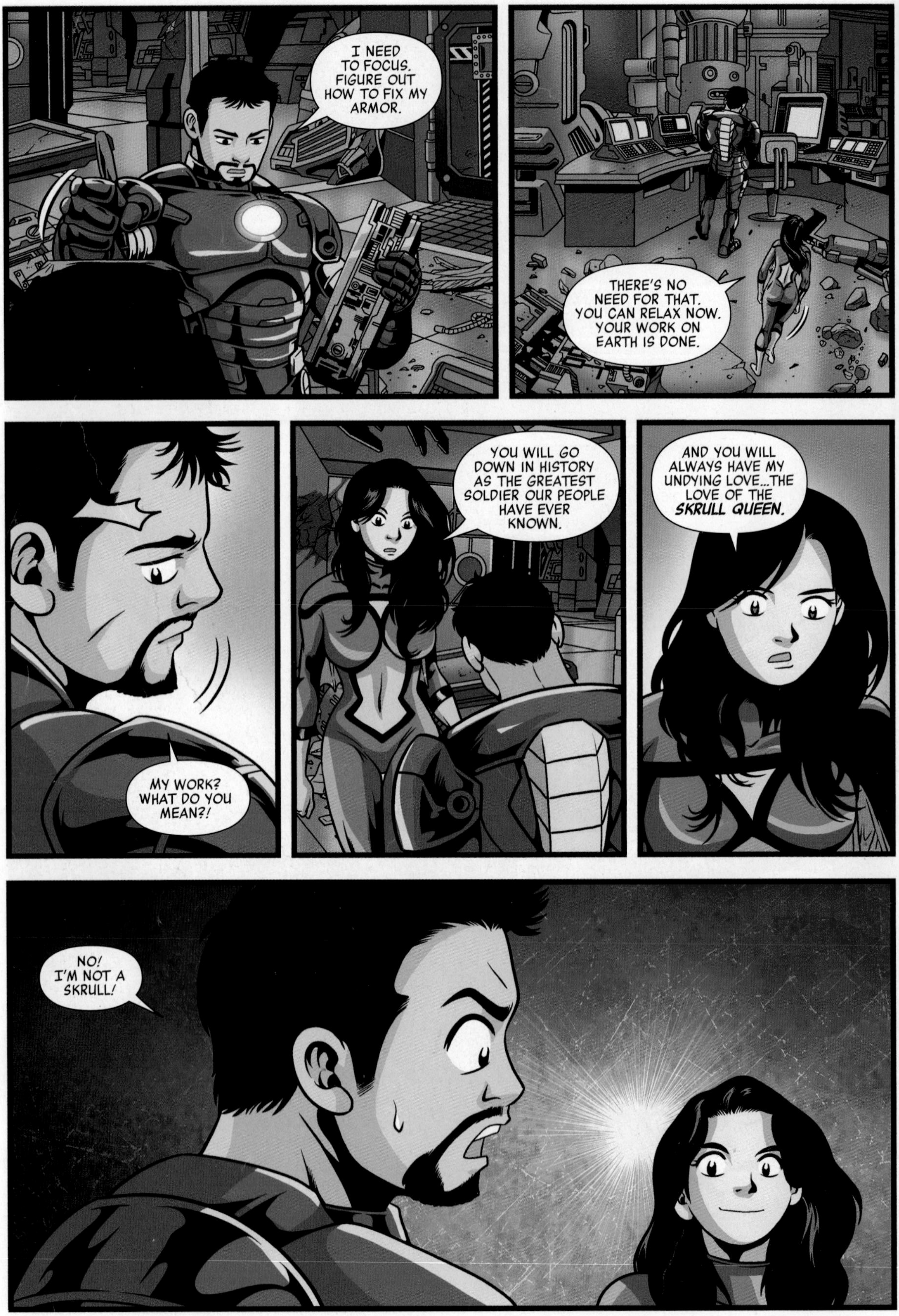
I NEED TO FOCUS. FIGURE OUT HOW TO FIX MY ARMOR.
THERE'S NO NEED FOR THAT. YOU CAN RELAX NOW. YOUR WORK ON EARTH IS DONE.
MY WORK? WHAT DO YOU MEAN?!
YOU WILL GO DOWN IN HISTORY AS THE GREATEST SOLDIER OUR PEOPLE HAVE EVER KNOWN.
AND YOU WILL ALWAYS HAVE MY UNDYING LOVE...THE LOVE OF THE SKRULL QUEEN.
NO! I'M NOT A SKRULL!

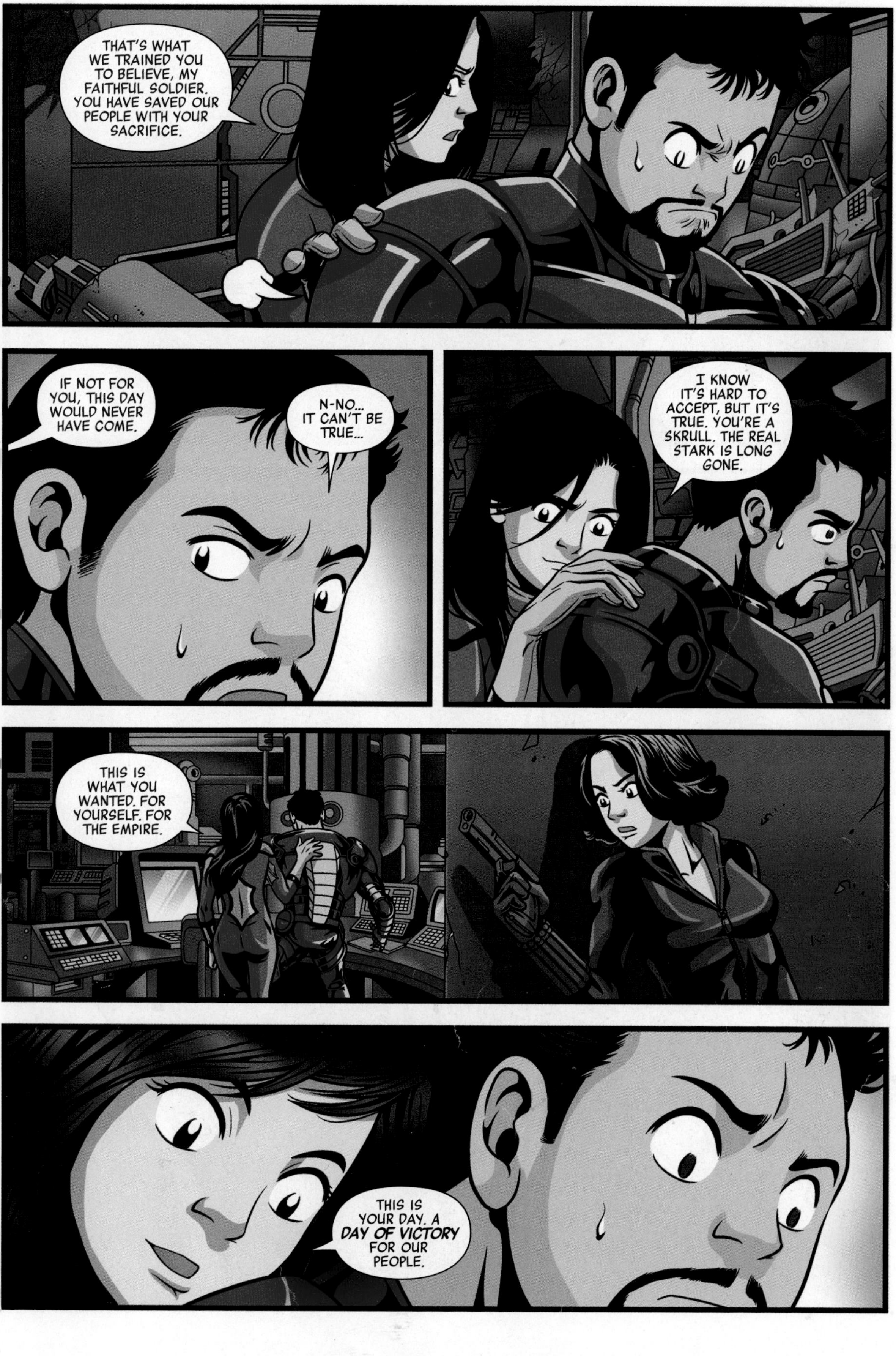
THAT'S WHAT WE TRAINED YOU TO BELIEVE, MY FAITHFUL SOLDIER. YOU HAVE SAVED OUR PEOPLE WITH YOUR SACRIFICE.
IF NOT FOR YOU, THIS DAY WOULD NEVER HAVE COME.
N-NO... IT CAN'T BE TRUE...
I KNOW IT'S HARD TO ACCEPT, BUT IT'S TRUE. YOU'RE A SKRULL. THE REAL STARK IS LONG GONE.
THIS IS WHAT YOU WANTED. FOR YOURSELF. FOR THE EMPIRE.
THIS IS YOUR DAY. A DAY OF VICTORY FOR OUR PEOPLE.

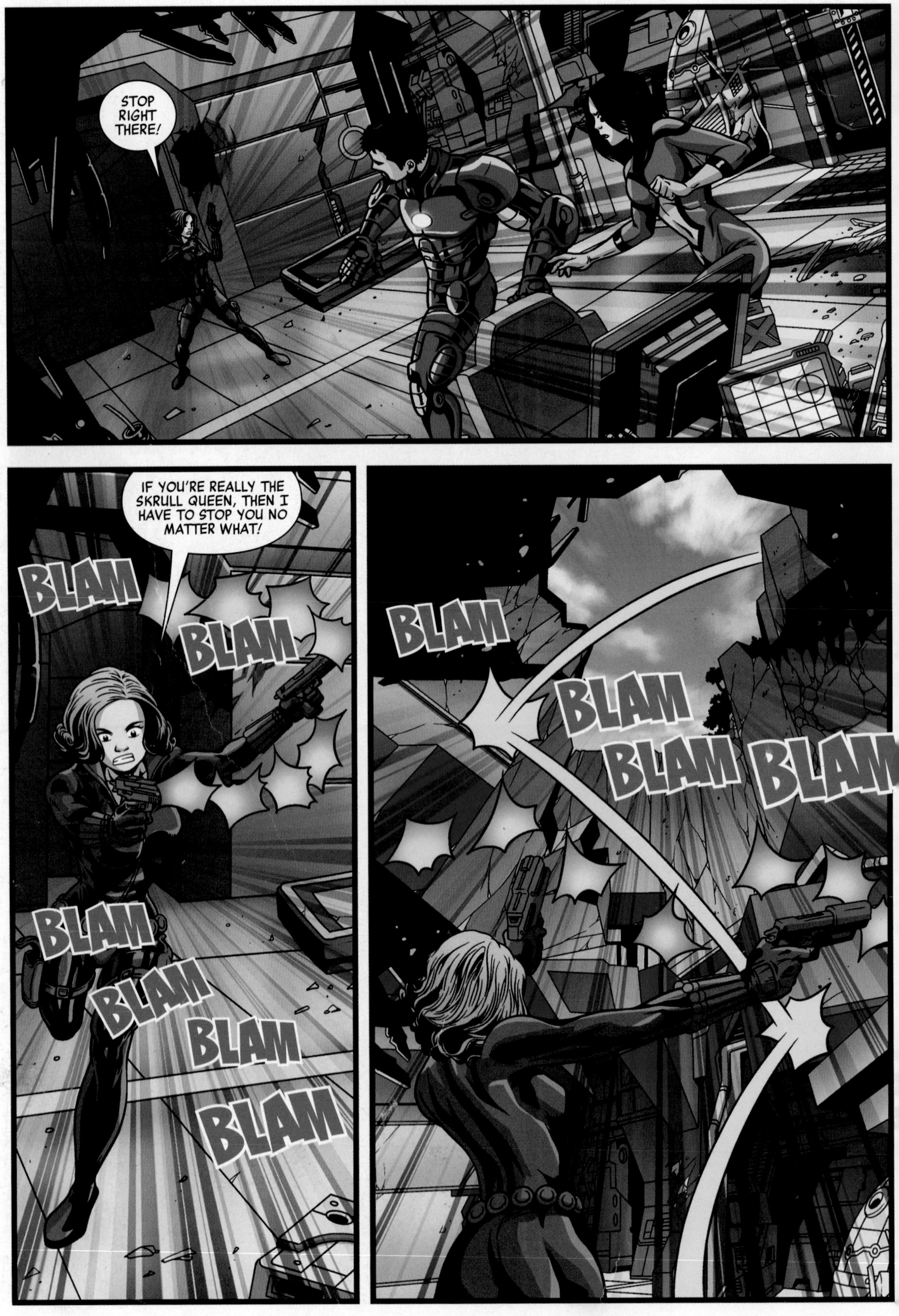
STOP RIGHT THERE!
IF YOU'RE REALLY THE SKRULL QUEEN, THEN I HAVE TO STOP YOU NO MATTER WHAT!
BLAM
BLAM
BLAM
BLAM
BLAM
BLAM
BLAM
BLAM
BLAM
BLAM

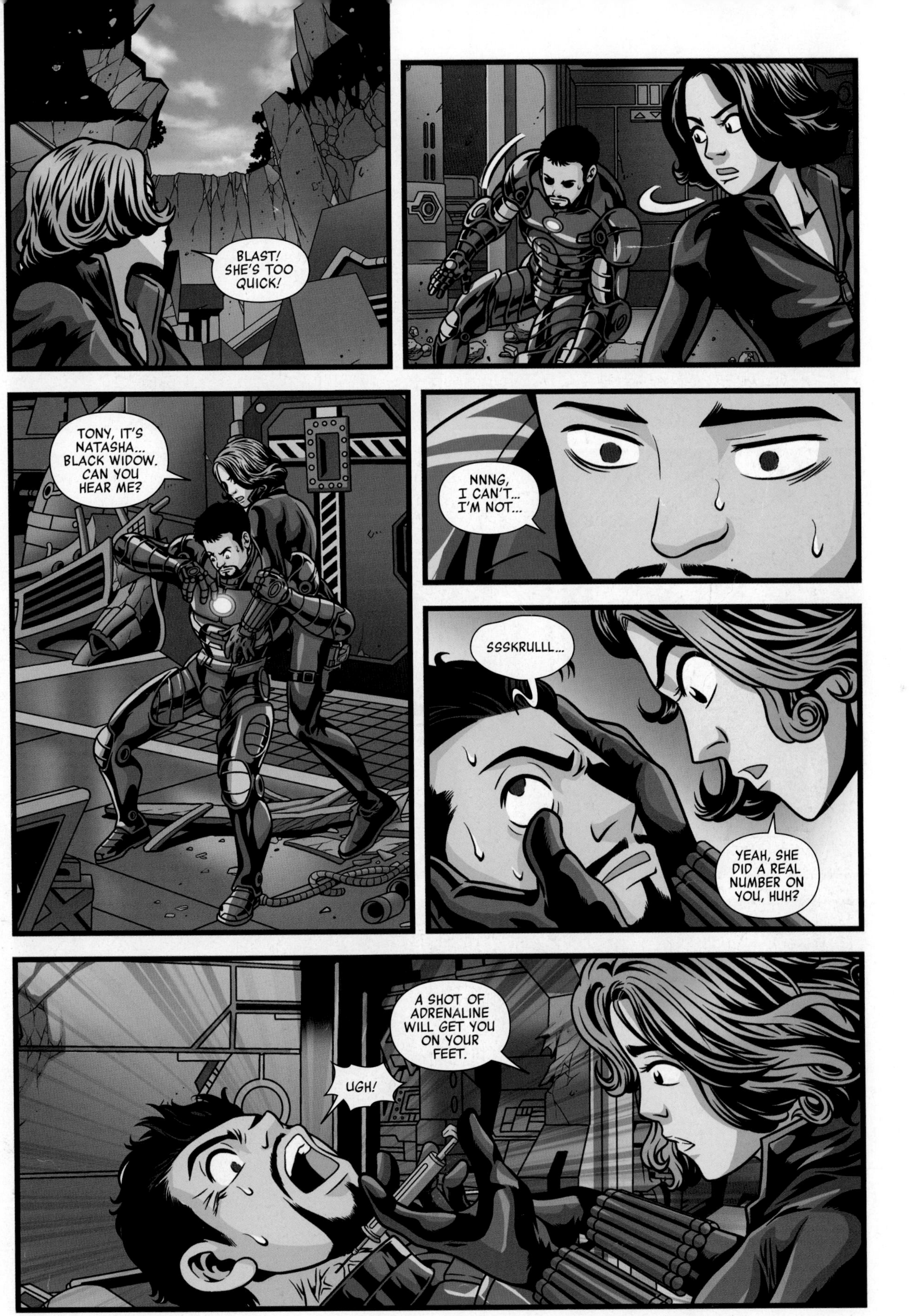
BLAST! SHE'S TOO QUICK!
TONY, IT'S NATASHA... BLACK WIDOW. CAN YOU HEAR ME?
NNNG, I CAN'T... I'M NOT...
SSSKRULLL...
YEAH, SHE DID A REAL NUMBER ON YOU, HUH?
A SHOT OF ADRENALINE WILL GET YOU ON YOUR FEET.
UGH!

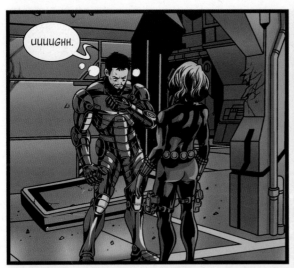

UUUUGHH.

FOCUS, TONY. WHAT EXACTLY DID SHE SAY TO YOU?

SHE SAID... SHE SAID I'M A SKRULL.

NOT A CHANCE. SHE WAS MESSING WITH YOU.

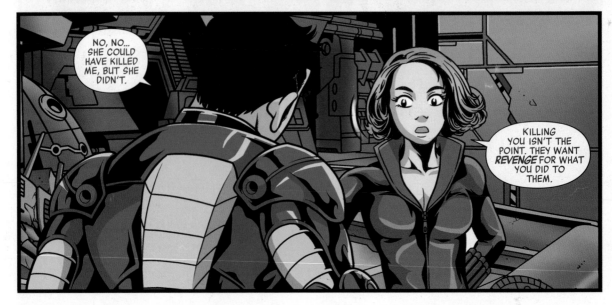

NO, NO... SHE COULD HAVE KILLED ME, BUT SHE DIDN'T.

KILLING YOU ISN'T THE POINT. THEY WANT *REVENGE* FOR WHAT YOU DID TO THEM.

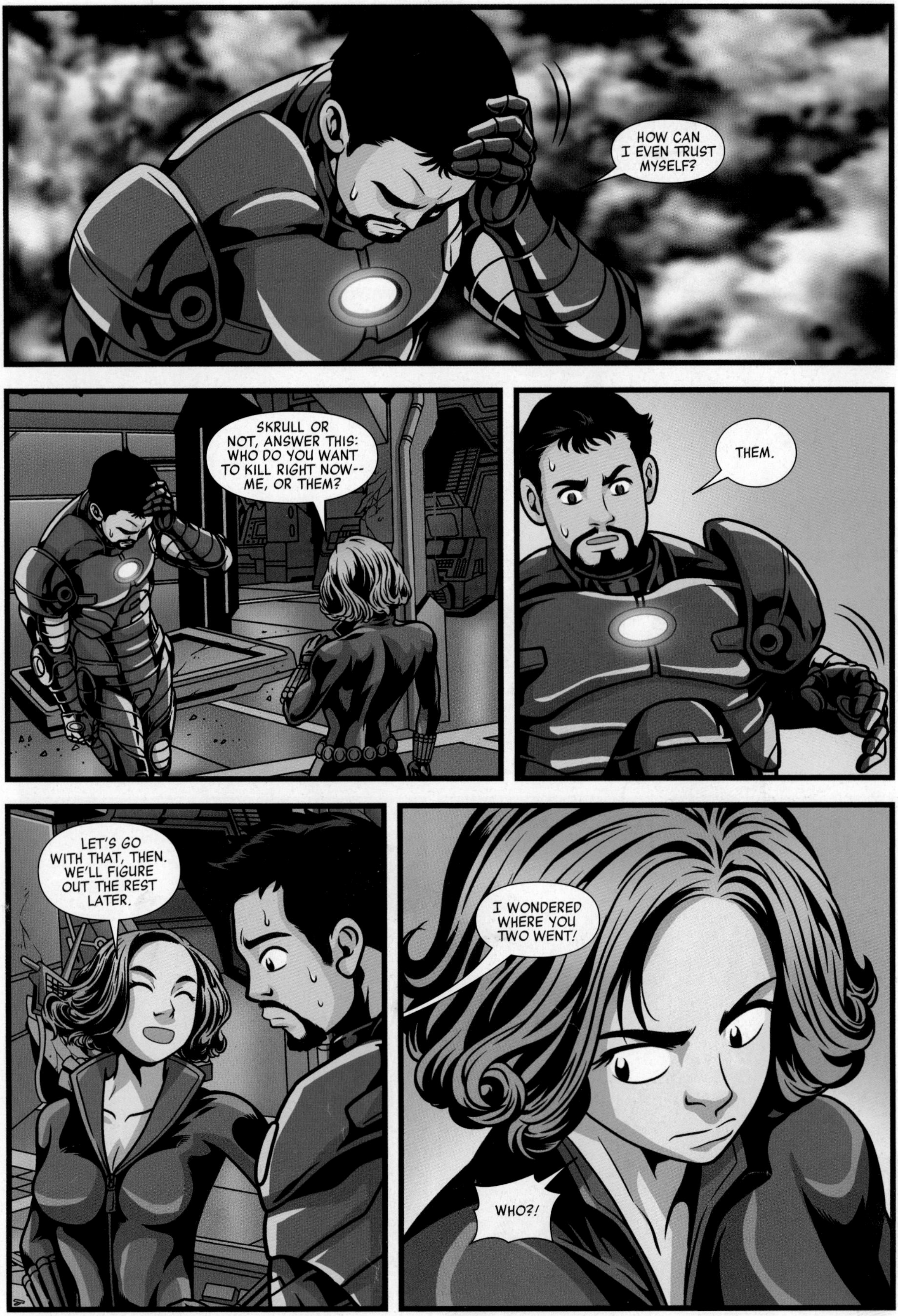
HOW CAN I EVEN TRUST MYSELF?
SKRULL OR NOT, ANSWER THIS: WHO DO YOU WANT TO KILL RIGHT NOW--ME, OR THEM?
THEM.
LET'S GO WITH THAT, THEN. WE'LL FIGURE OUT THE REST LATER.
I WONDERED WHERE YOU TWO WENT!
WHO?!

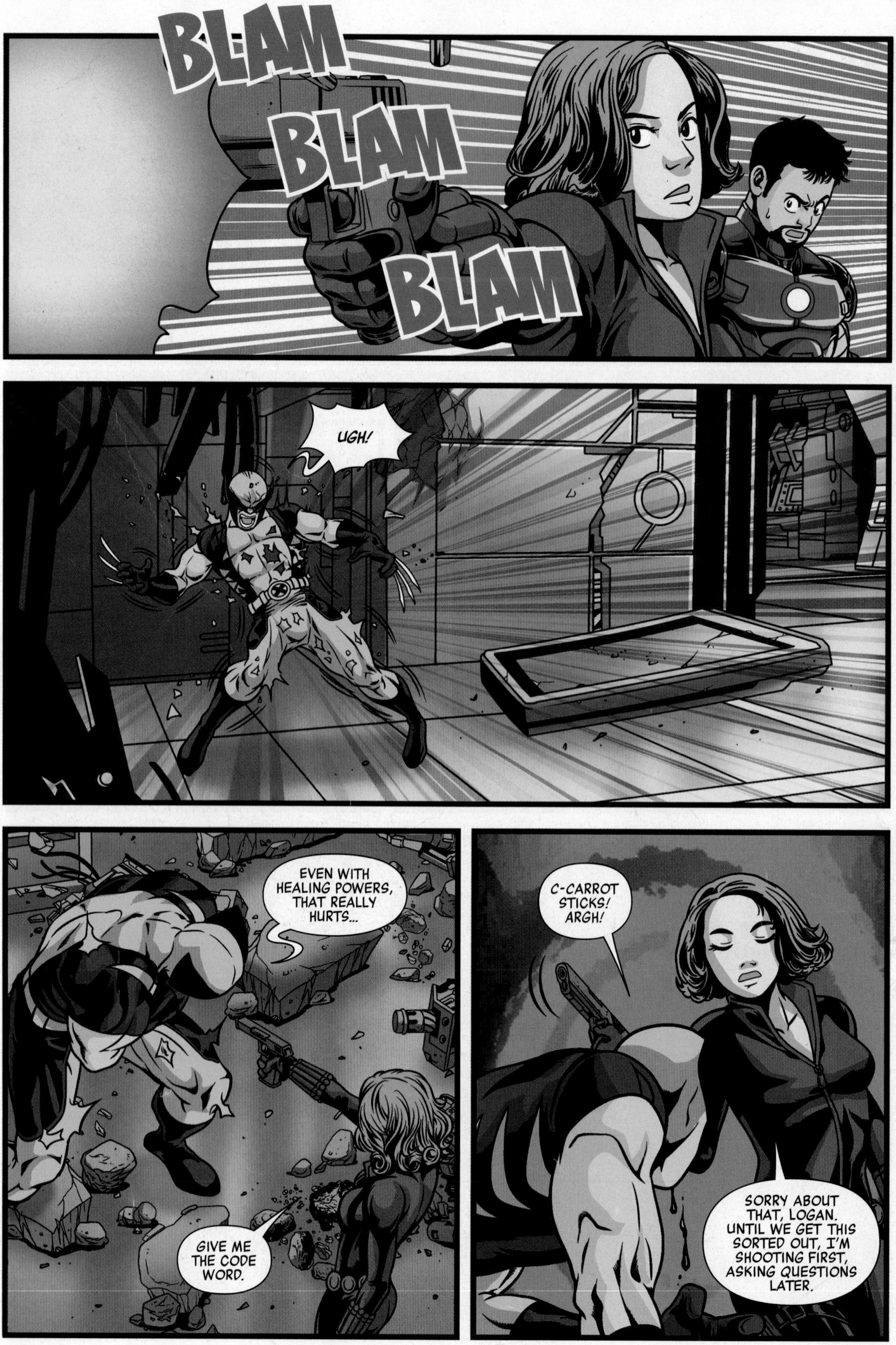
BLAM
BLAM
BLAM
UGH!
EVEN WITH HEALING POWERS, THAT REALLY HURTS...
GIVE ME THE CODE WORD.
C-CARROT STICKS! ARGH!
SORRY ABOUT THAT, LOGAN. UNTIL WE GET THIS SORTED OUT, I'M SHOOTING FIRST, ASKING QUESTIONS LATER.

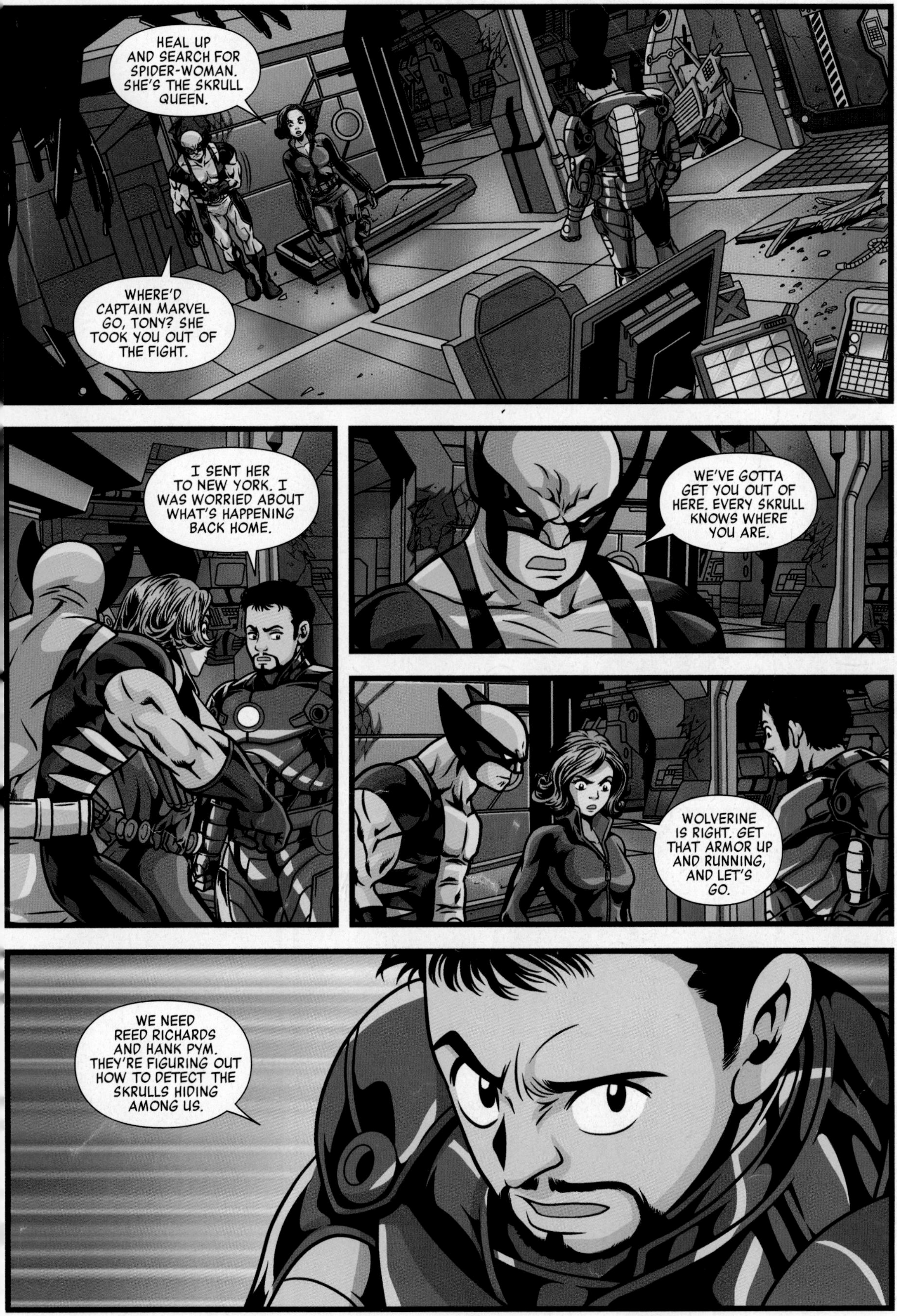
HEAL UP AND SEARCH FOR SPIDER-WOMAN. SHE'S THE SKRULL QUEEN.
WHERE'D CAPTAIN MARVEL GO, TONY? SHE TOOK YOU OUT OF THE FIGHT.
I SENT HER TO NEW YORK. I WAS WORRIED ABOUT WHAT'S HAPPENING BACK HOME.
WE'VE GOTTA GET YOU OUT OF HERE. EVERY SKRULL KNOWS WHERE YOU ARE.
WOLVERINE IS RIGHT. GET THAT ARMOR UP AND RUNNING, AND LET'S GO.
WE NEED REED RICHARDS AND HANK PYM. THEY'RE FIGURING OUT HOW TO DETECT THE SKRULLS HIDING AMONG US.

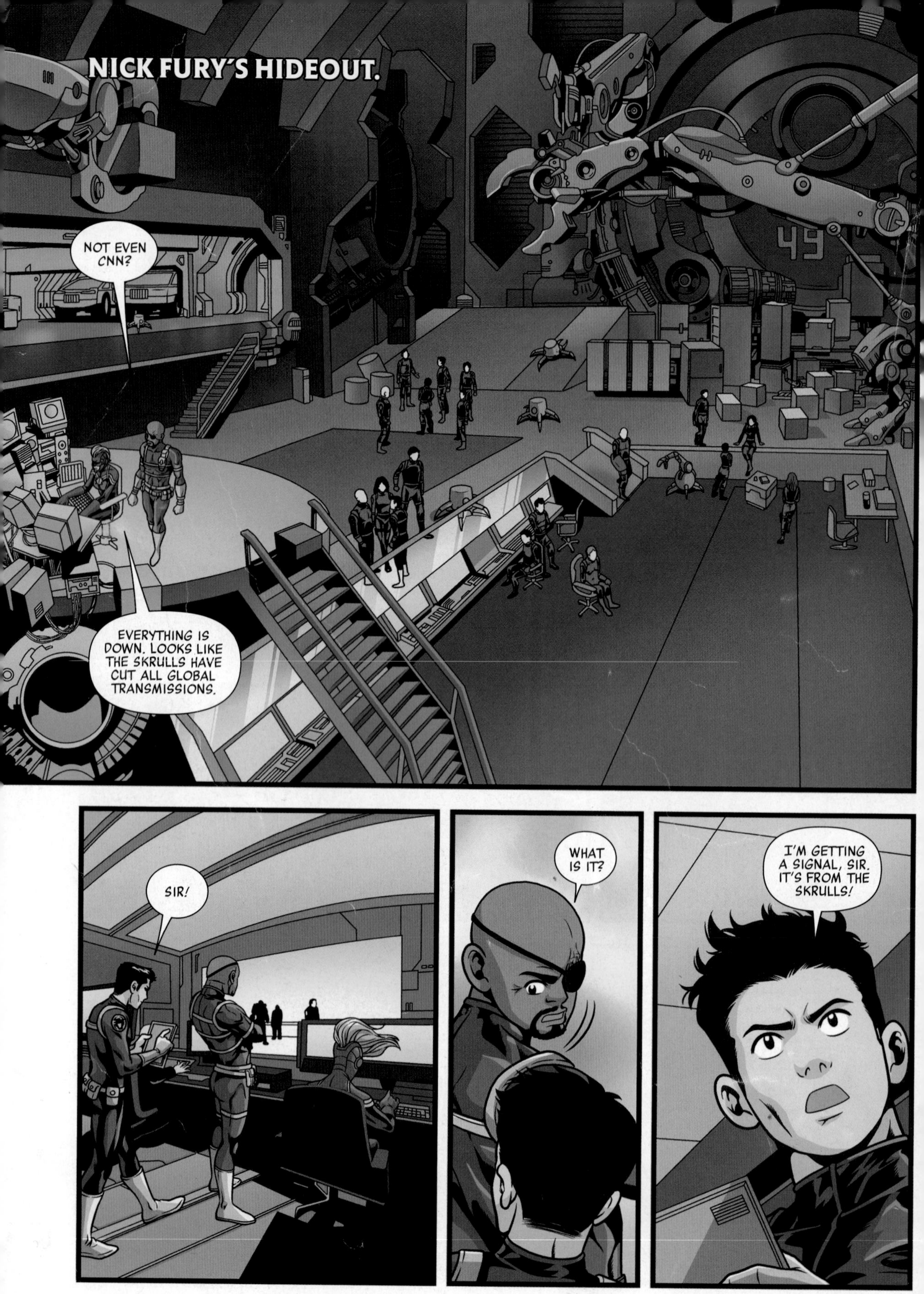

NICK FURY'S HIDEOUT.
NOT EVEN CNN?
EVERYTHING IS DOWN. LOOKS LIKE THE SKRULLS HAVE CUT ALL GLOBAL TRANSMISSIONS.
SIR!
WHAT IS IT?
I'M GETTING A SIGNAL, SIR. IT'S FROM THE SKRULLS!

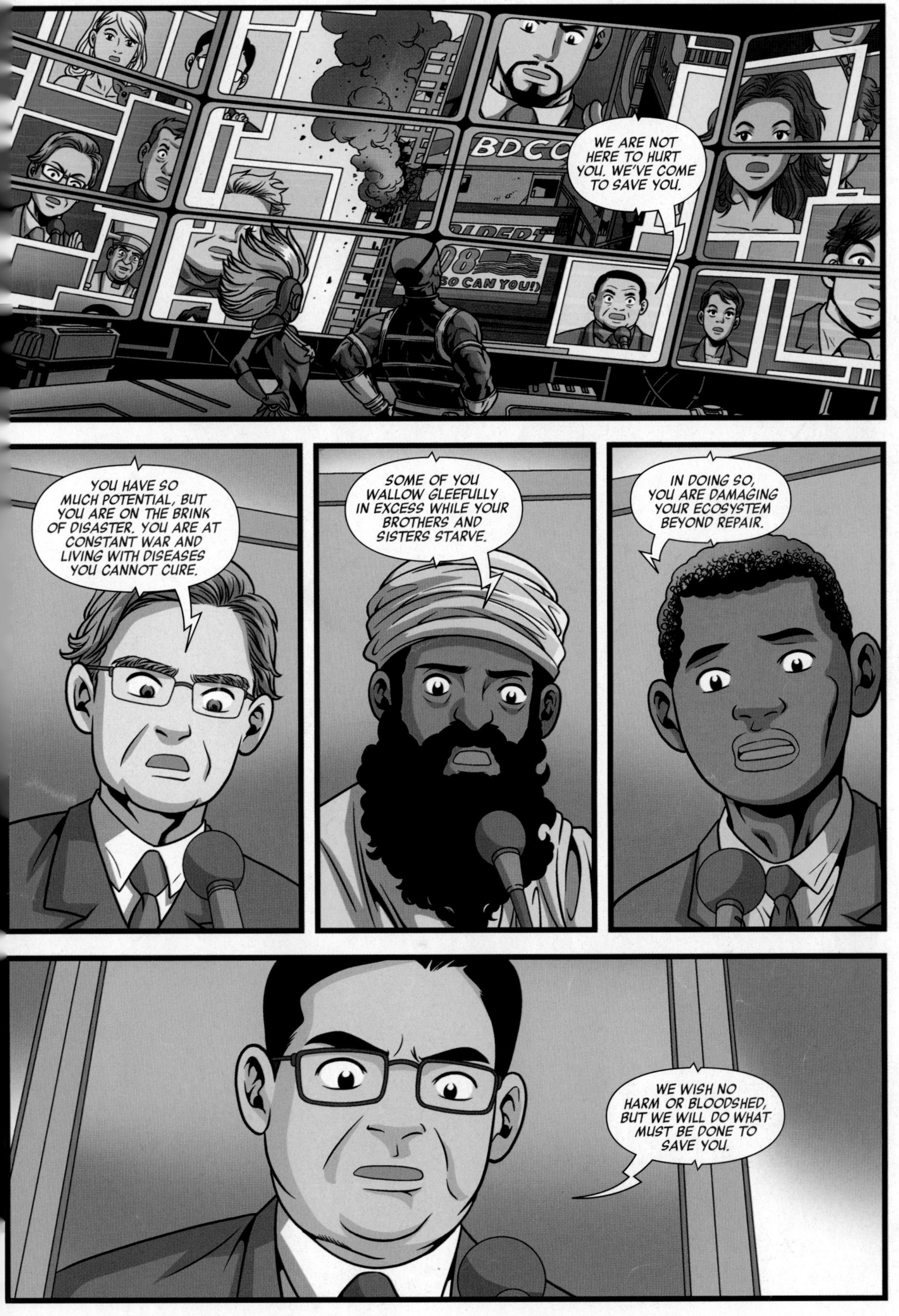
WE ARE NOT HERE TO HURT YOU. WE'VE COME TO SAVE YOU.
YOU HAVE SO MUCH POTENTIAL, BUT YOU ARE ON THE BRINK OF DISASTER. YOU ARE AT CONSTANT WAR AND LIVING WITH DISEASES YOU CANNOT CURE.
SOME OF YOU WALLOW GLEEFULLY IN EXCESS WHILE YOUR BROTHERS AND SISTERS STARVE.
IN DOING SO, YOU ARE DAMAGING YOUR ECOSYSTEM BEYOND REPAIR.
WE WISH NO HARM OR BLOODSHED, BUT WE WILL DO WHAT MUST BE DONE TO SAVE YOU.

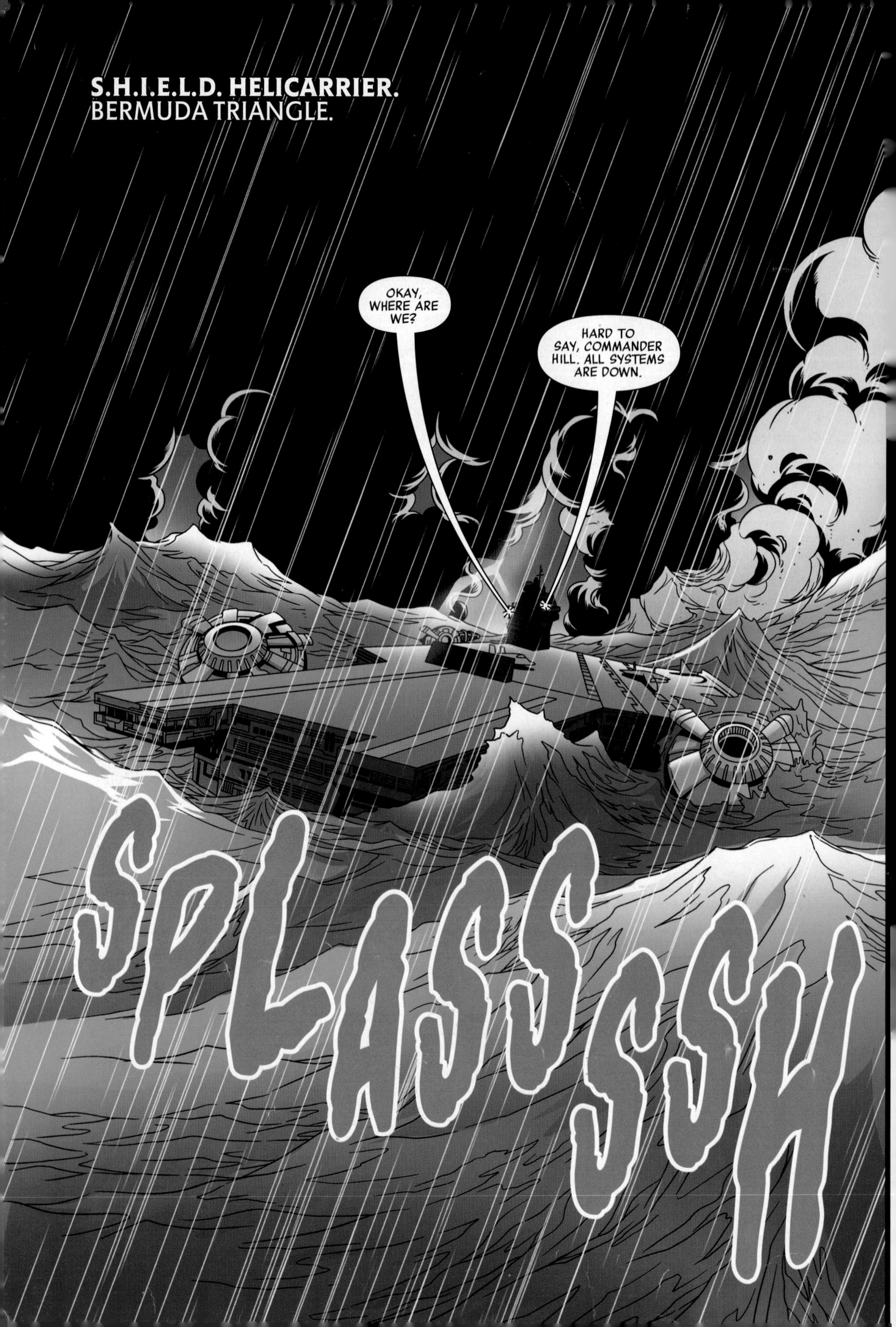
S.H.I.E.L.D. HELICARRIER.
BERMUDA TRIANGLE.
OKAY, WHERE ARE WE?
HARD TO SAY, COMMANDER HILL. ALL SYSTEMS ARE DOWN.
SPLASSSSH

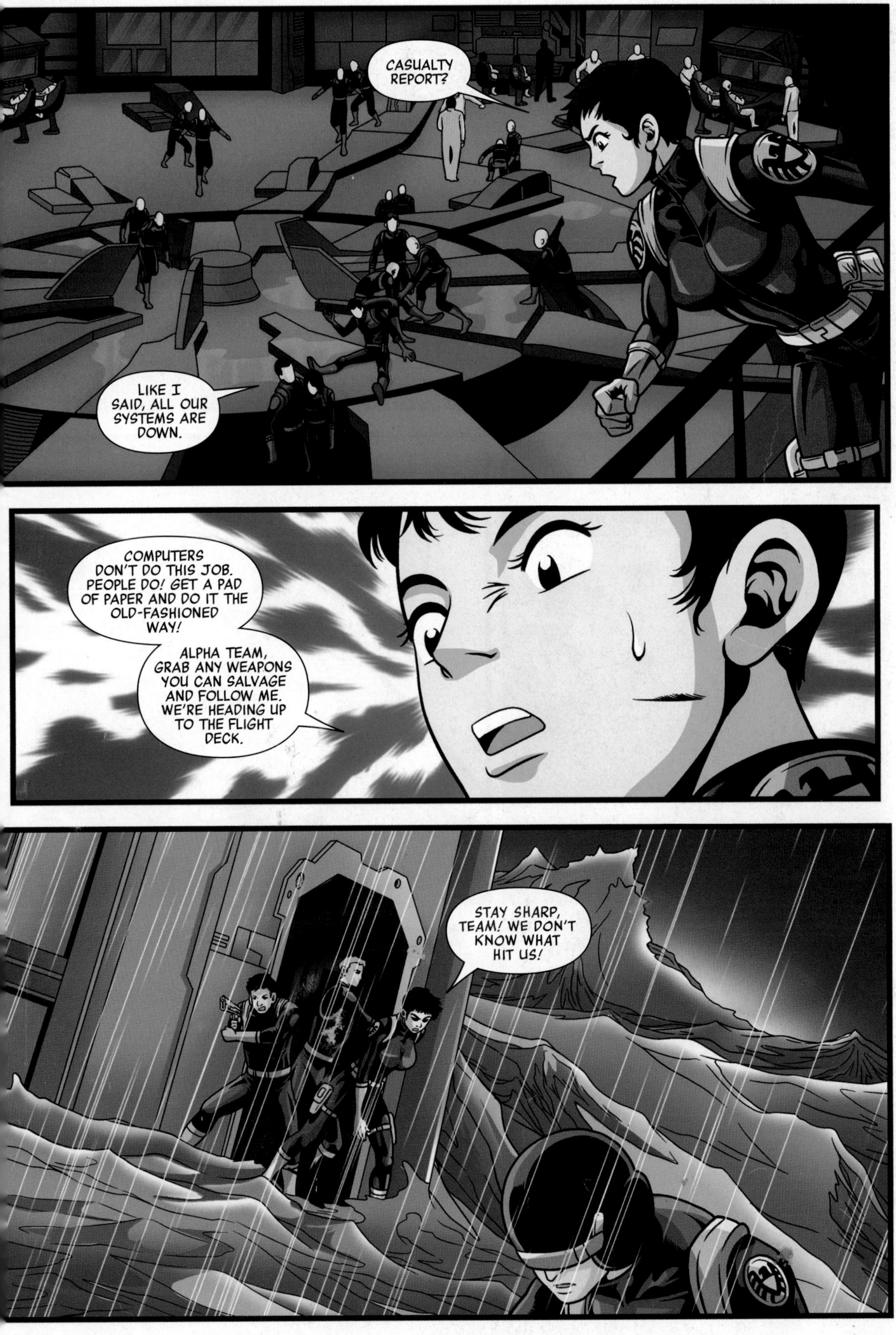
CASUALTY REPORT?
LIKE I SAID, ALL OUR SYSTEMS ARE DOWN.
COMPUTERS DON'T DO THIS JOB. PEOPLE DO! GET A PAD OF PAPER AND DO IT THE OLD-FASHIONED WAY!
ALPHA TEAM, GRAB ANY WEAPONS YOU CAN SALVAGE AND FOLLOW ME. WE'RE HEADING UP TO THE FLIGHT DECK.
STAY SHARP, TEAM! WE DON'T KNOW WHAT HIT US!

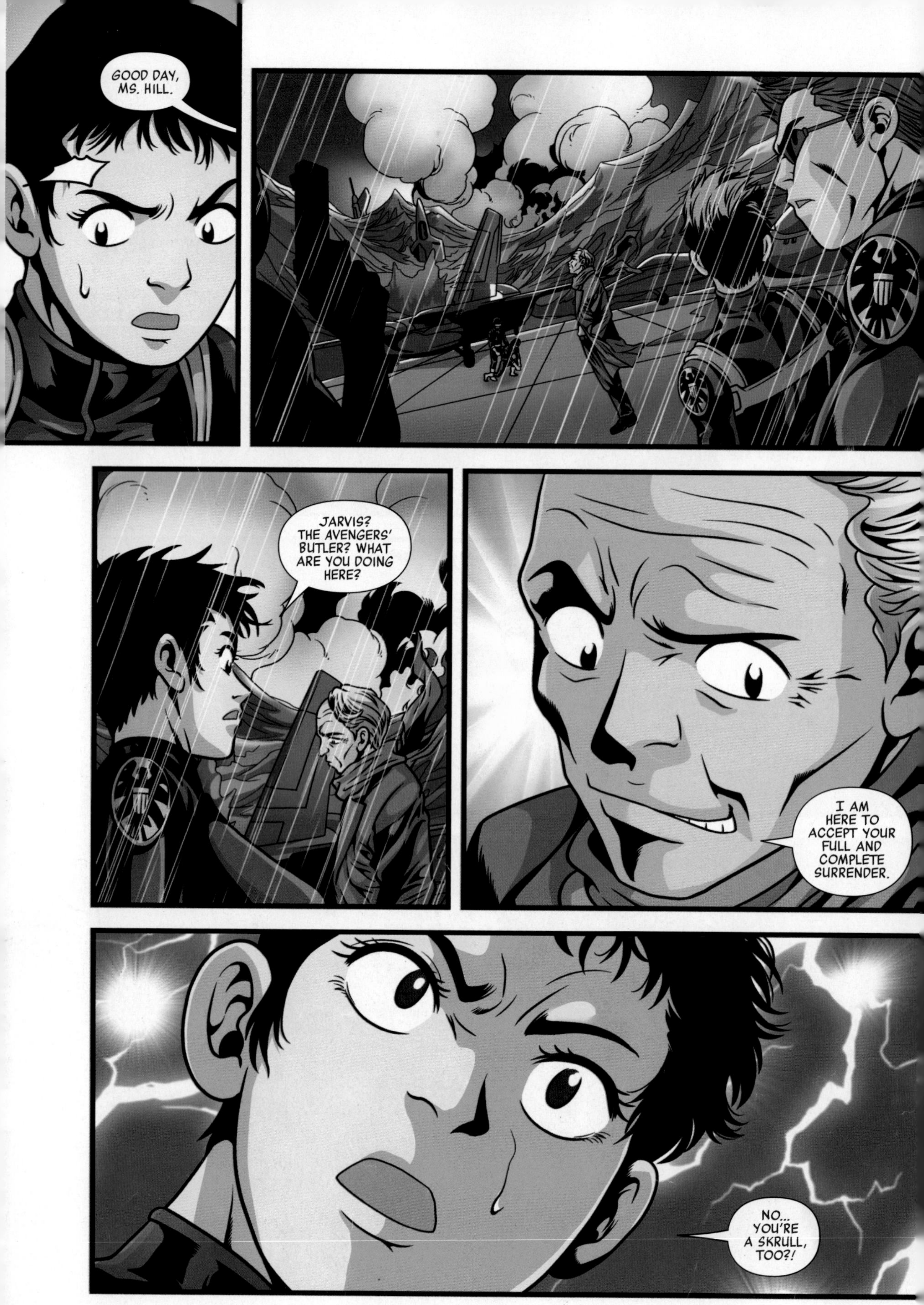
GOOD DAY, MS. HILL.
JARVIS? THE AVENGERS' BUTLER? WHAT ARE YOU DOING HERE?
I AM HERE TO ACCEPT YOUR FULL AND COMPLETE SURRENDER.
NO... YOU'RE A SKRULL, TOO?!

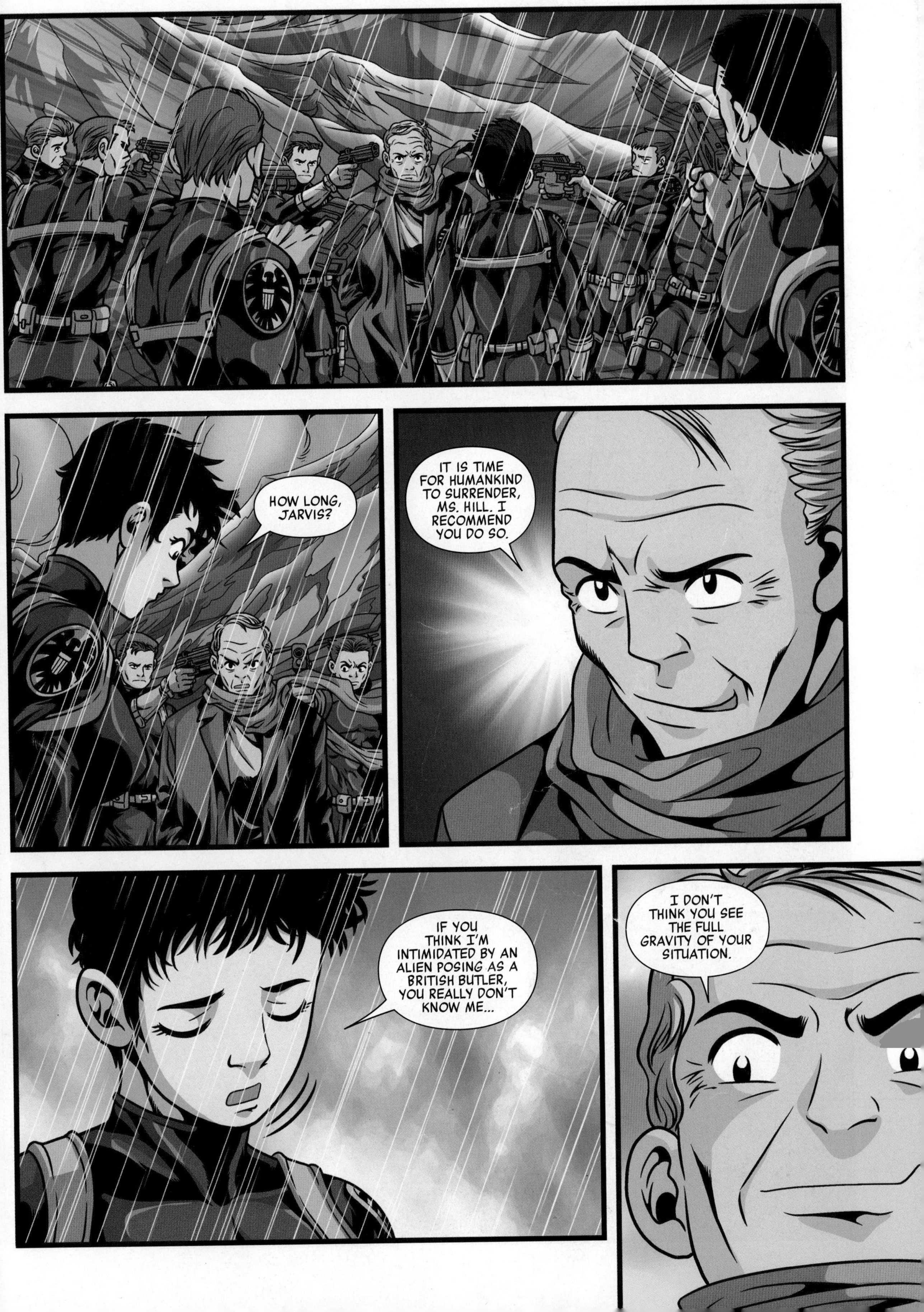
HOW LONG, JARVIS?
IT IS TIME FOR HUMANKIND TO SURRENDER, MS. HILL. I RECOMMEND YOU DO SO.
IF YOU THINK I'M INTIMIDATED BY AN ALIEN POSING AS A BRITISH BUTLER, YOU REALLY DON'T KNOW ME...
I DON'T THINK YOU SEE THE FULL GRAVITY OF YOUR SITUATION.

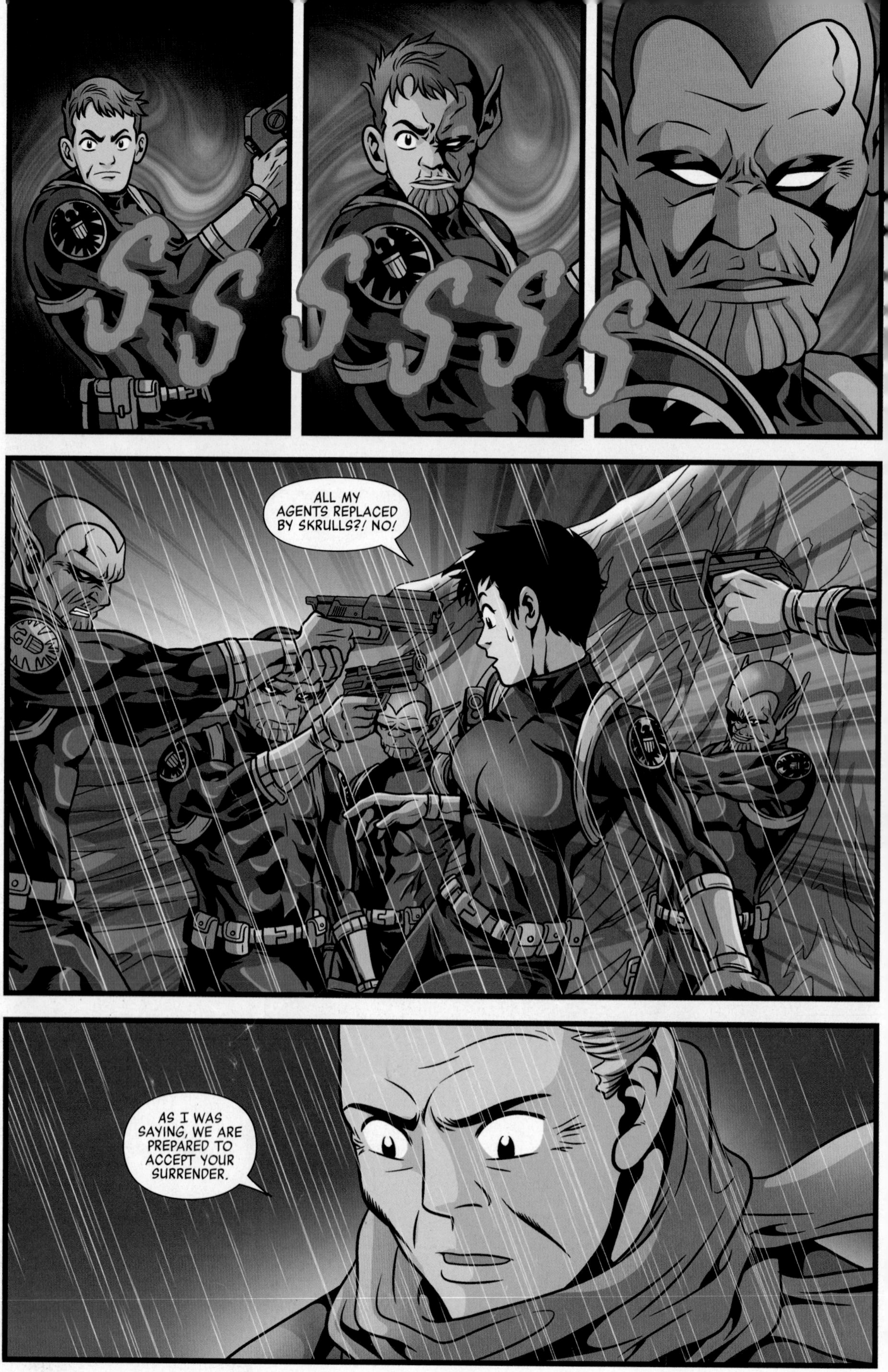
SSSSSS
ALL MY AGENTS REPLACED BY SKRULLS?! NO!
AS I WAS SAYING, WE ARE PREPARED TO ACCEPT YOUR SURRENDER.

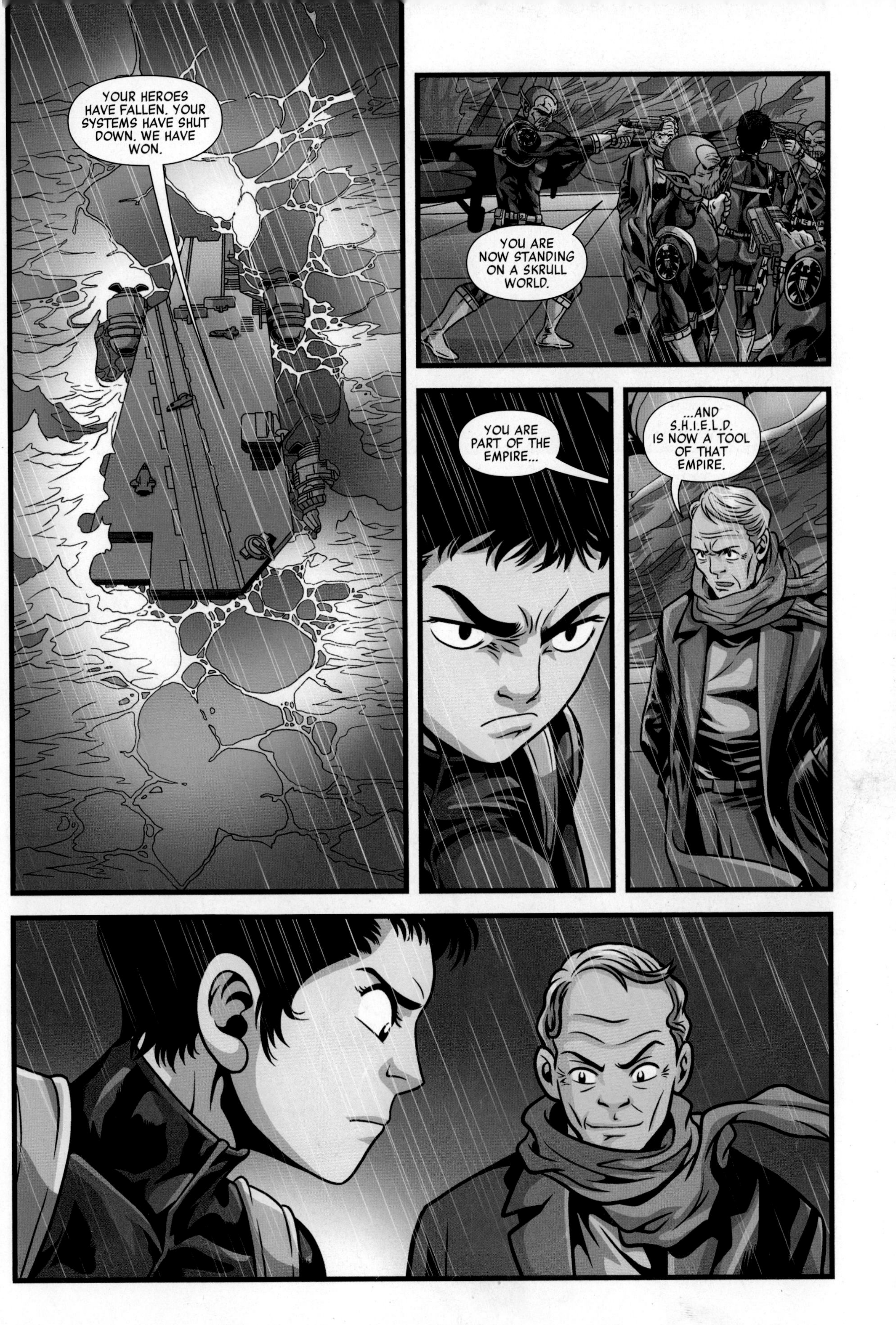
YOUR HEROES HAVE FALLEN. YOUR SYSTEMS HAVE SHUT DOWN. WE HAVE WON.
YOU ARE NOW STANDING ON A SKRULL WORLD.
YOU ARE PART OF THE EMPIRE...
...AND S.H.I.E.L.D. IS NOW A TOOL OF THAT EMPIRE.

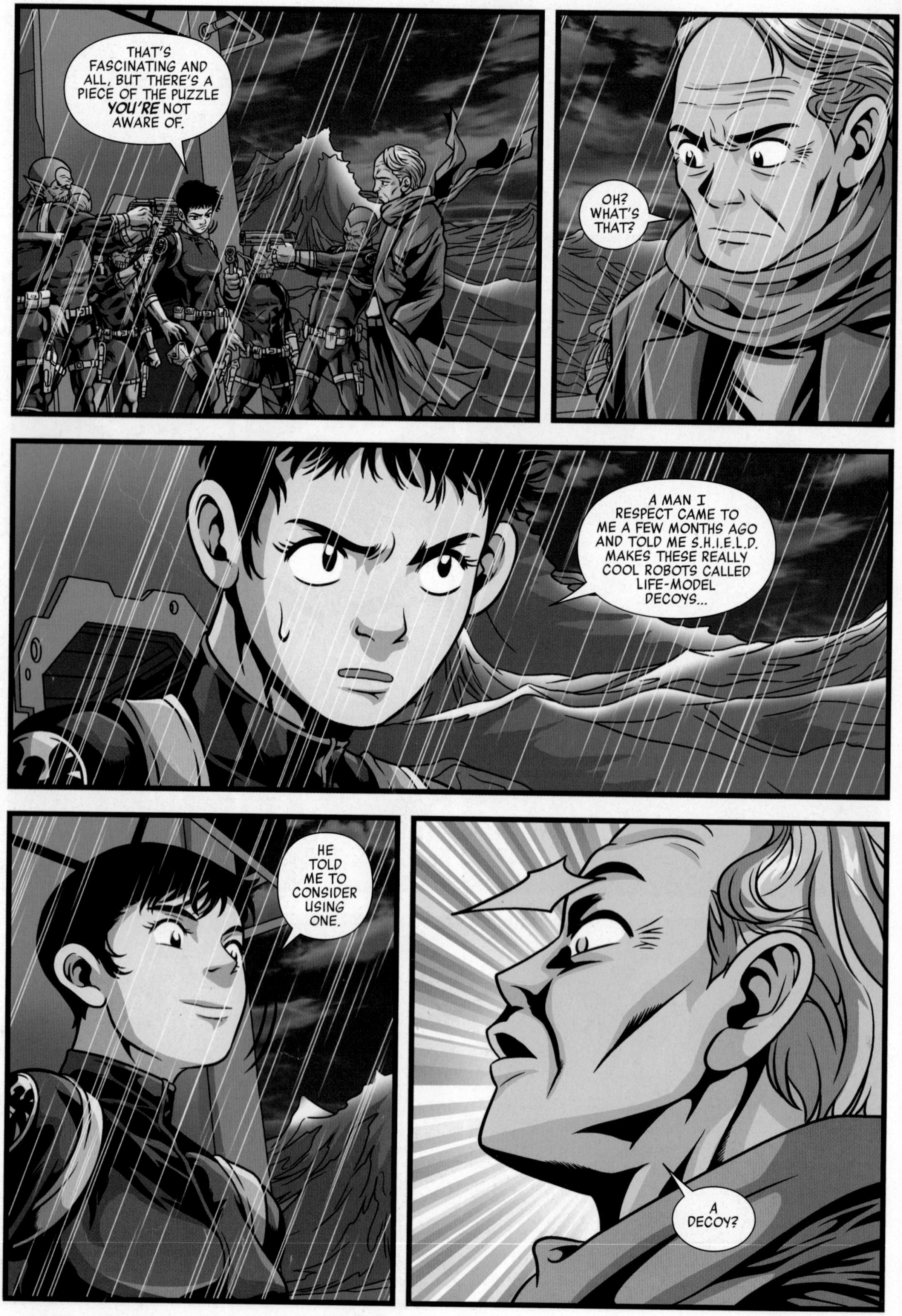
THAT'S FASCINATING AND ALL, BUT THERE'S A PIECE OF THE PUZZLE YOU'RE NOT AWARE OF.
OH? WHAT'S THAT?
A MAN I RESPECT CAME TO ME A FEW MONTHS AGO AND TOLD ME S.H.I.E.L.D. MAKES THESE REALLY COOL ROBOTS CALLED LIFE-MODEL DECOYS...
HE TOLD ME TO CONSIDER USING ONE.
A DECOY?

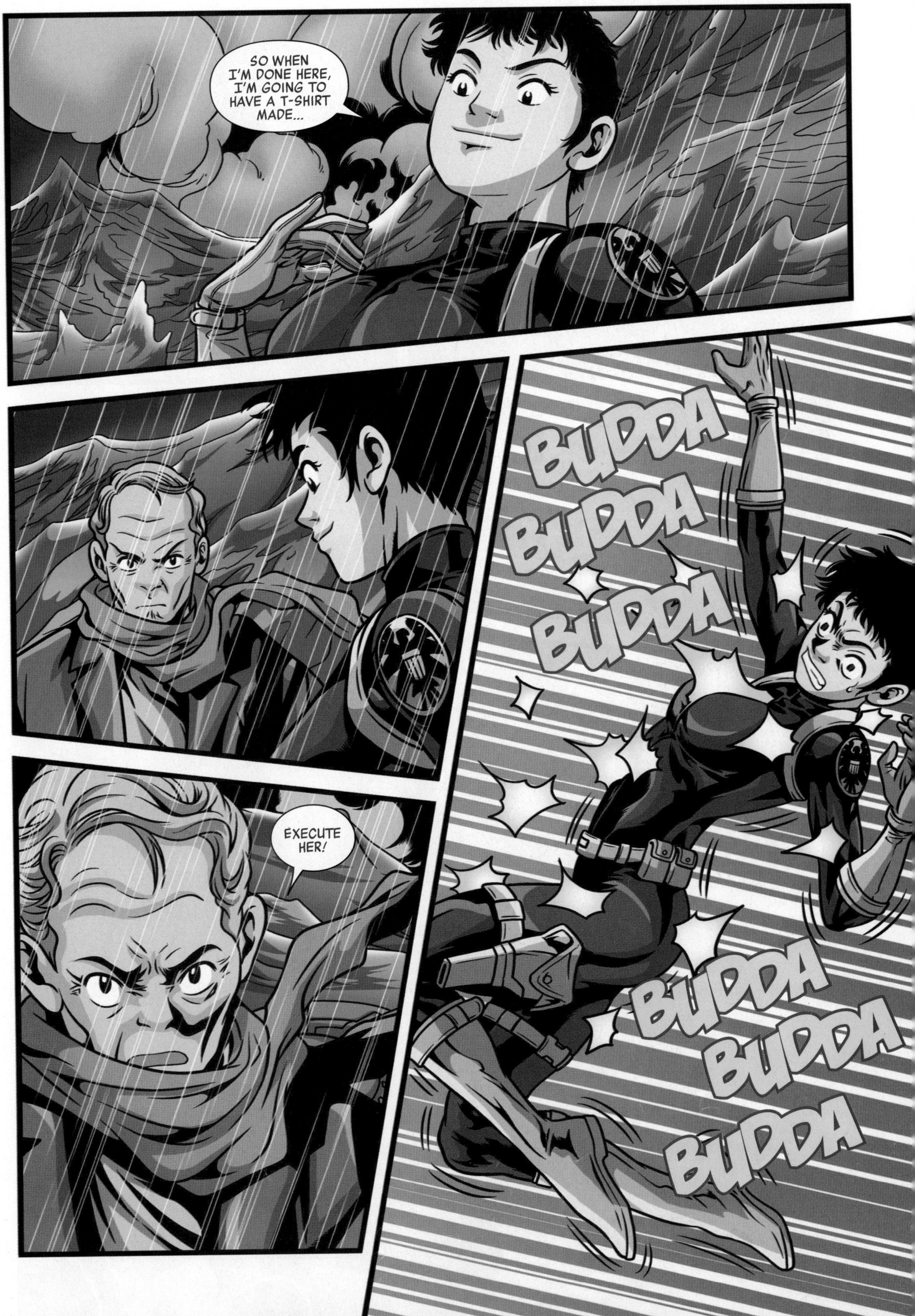
SO WHEN I'M DONE HERE, I'M GOING TO HAVE A T-SHIRT MADE...
EXECUTE HER!
BUDDA BUDDA BUDDA
BUDDA BUDDA BUDDA

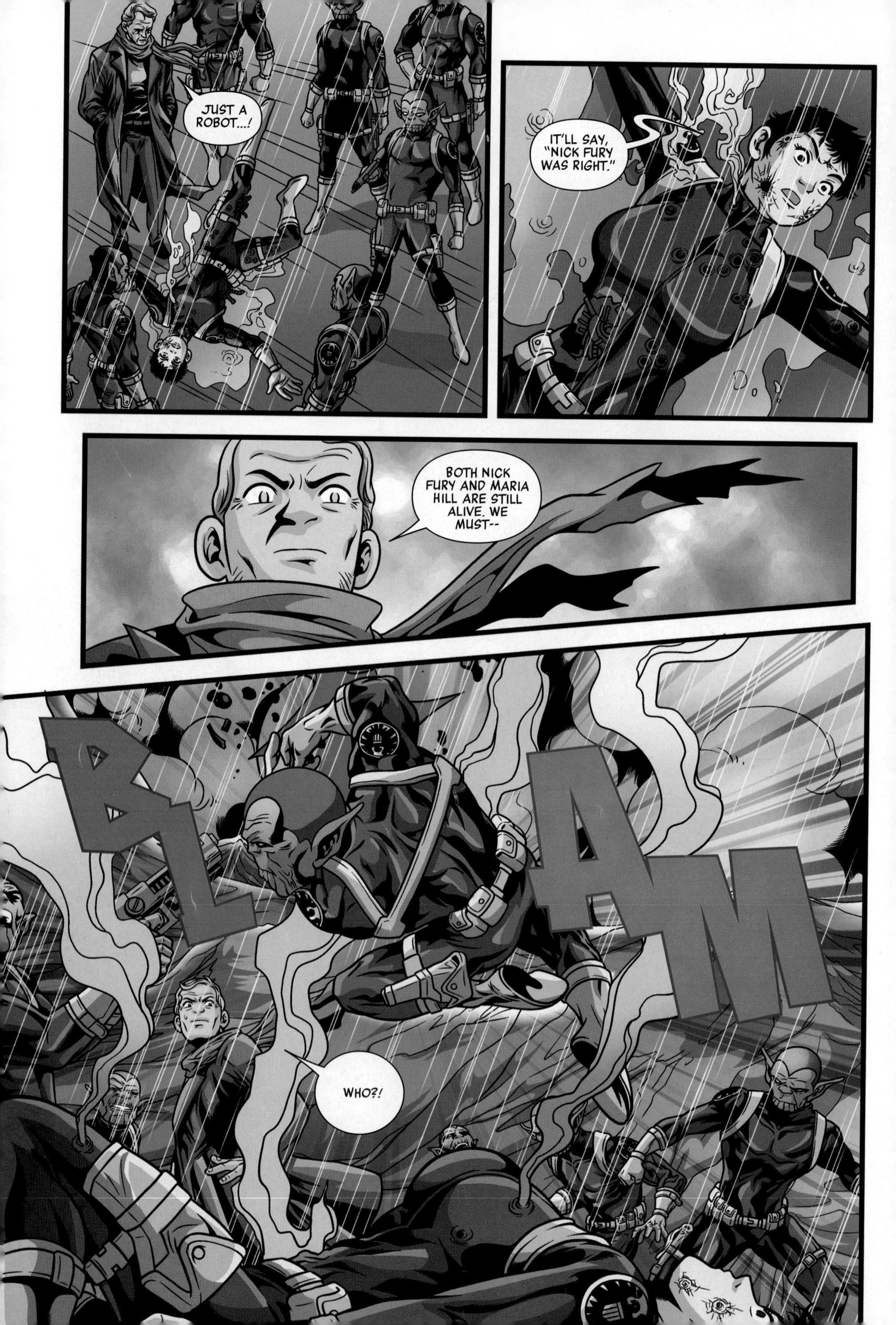
JUST A ROBOT...!
IT'LL SAY, "NICK FURY WAS RIGHT."
BOTH NICK FURY AND MARIA HILL ARE STILL ALIVE. WE MUST--
BLAM
WHO?!

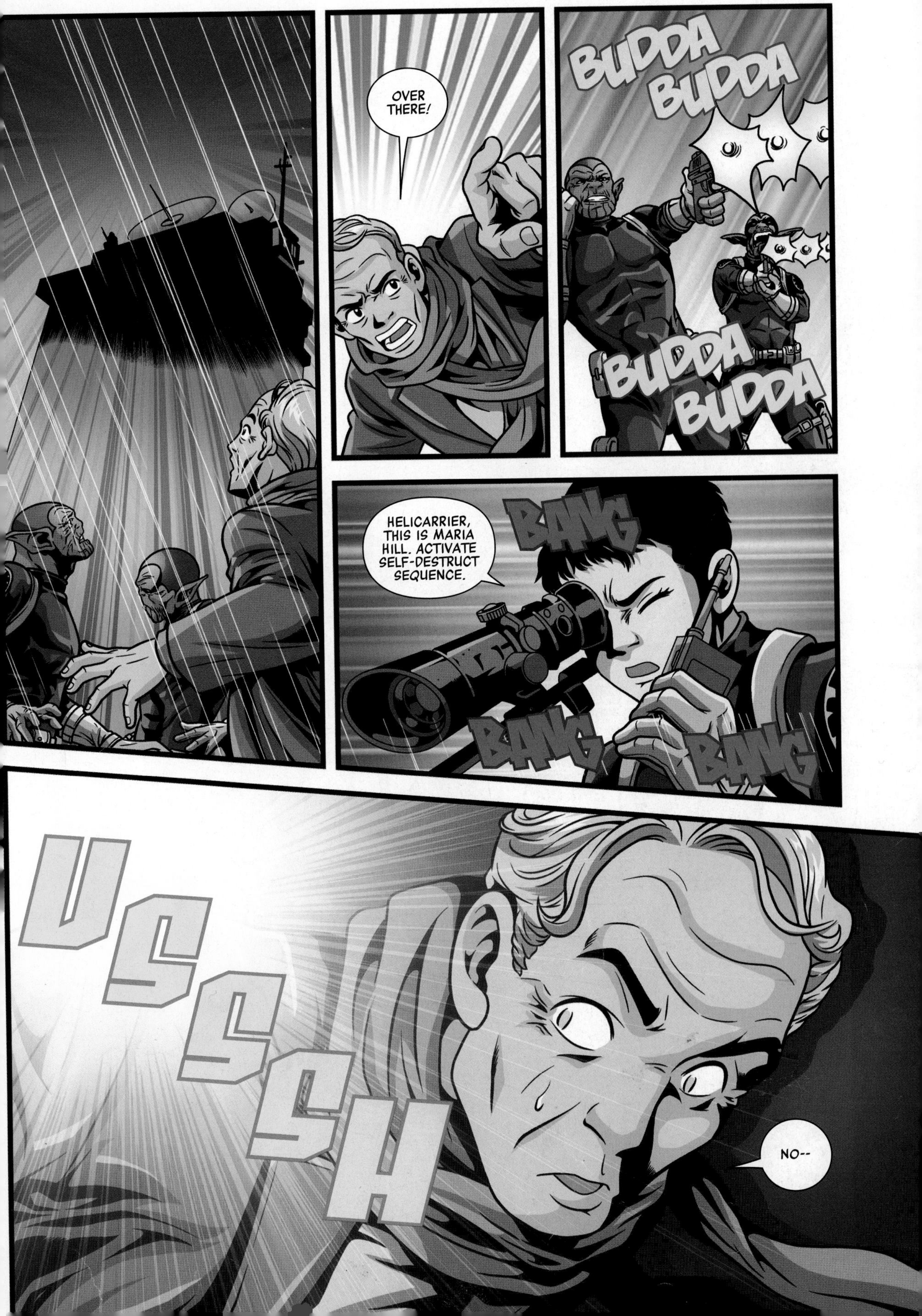
OVER THERE!
BUDDA BUDDA
BUDDA BUDDA
HELICARRIER, THIS IS MARIA HILL. ACTIVATE SELF-DESTRUCT SEQUENCE.
BANG
BANG
BANG
VSSSH
NO--

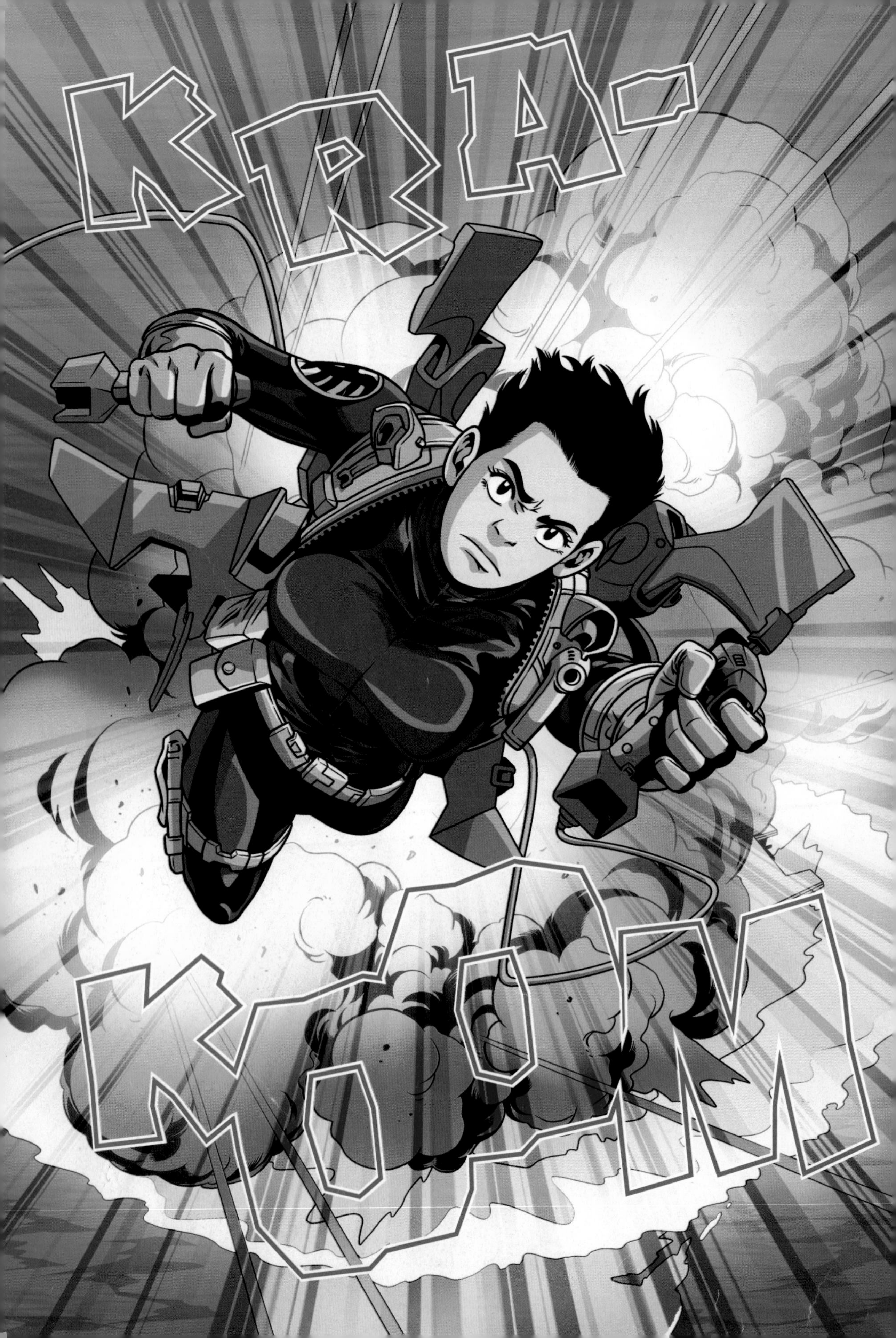
KRA-
KOOM

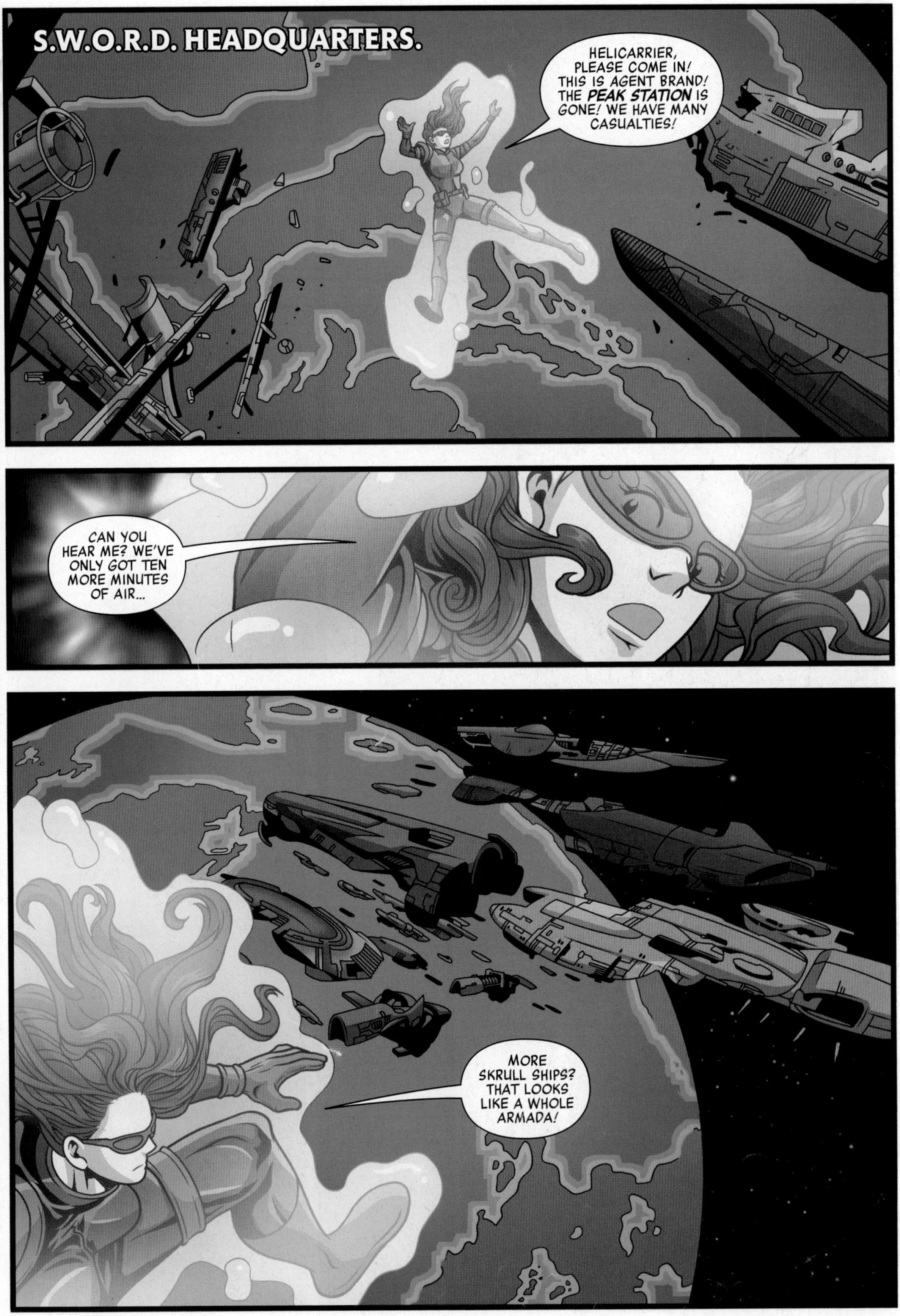
S.W.O.R.D. HEADQUARTERS.
HELICARRIER, PLEASE COME IN! THIS IS AGENT BRAND! THE PEAK STATION IS GONE! WE HAVE MANY CASUALTIES!
CAN YOU HEAR ME? WE'VE ONLY GOT TEN MORE MINUTES OF AIR...
MORE SKRULL SHIPS? THAT LOOKS LIKE A WHOLE ARMADA!

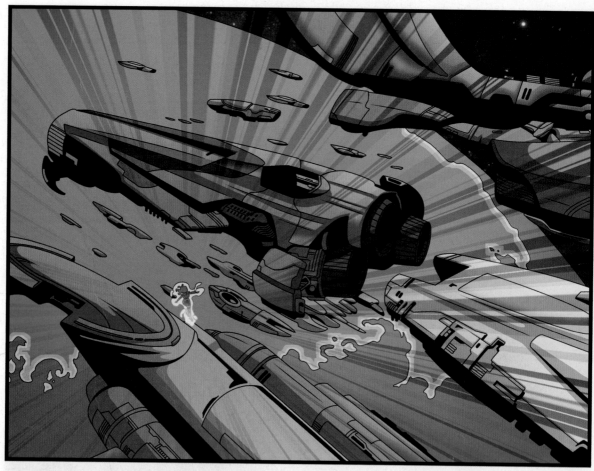

TAK

VOOSH

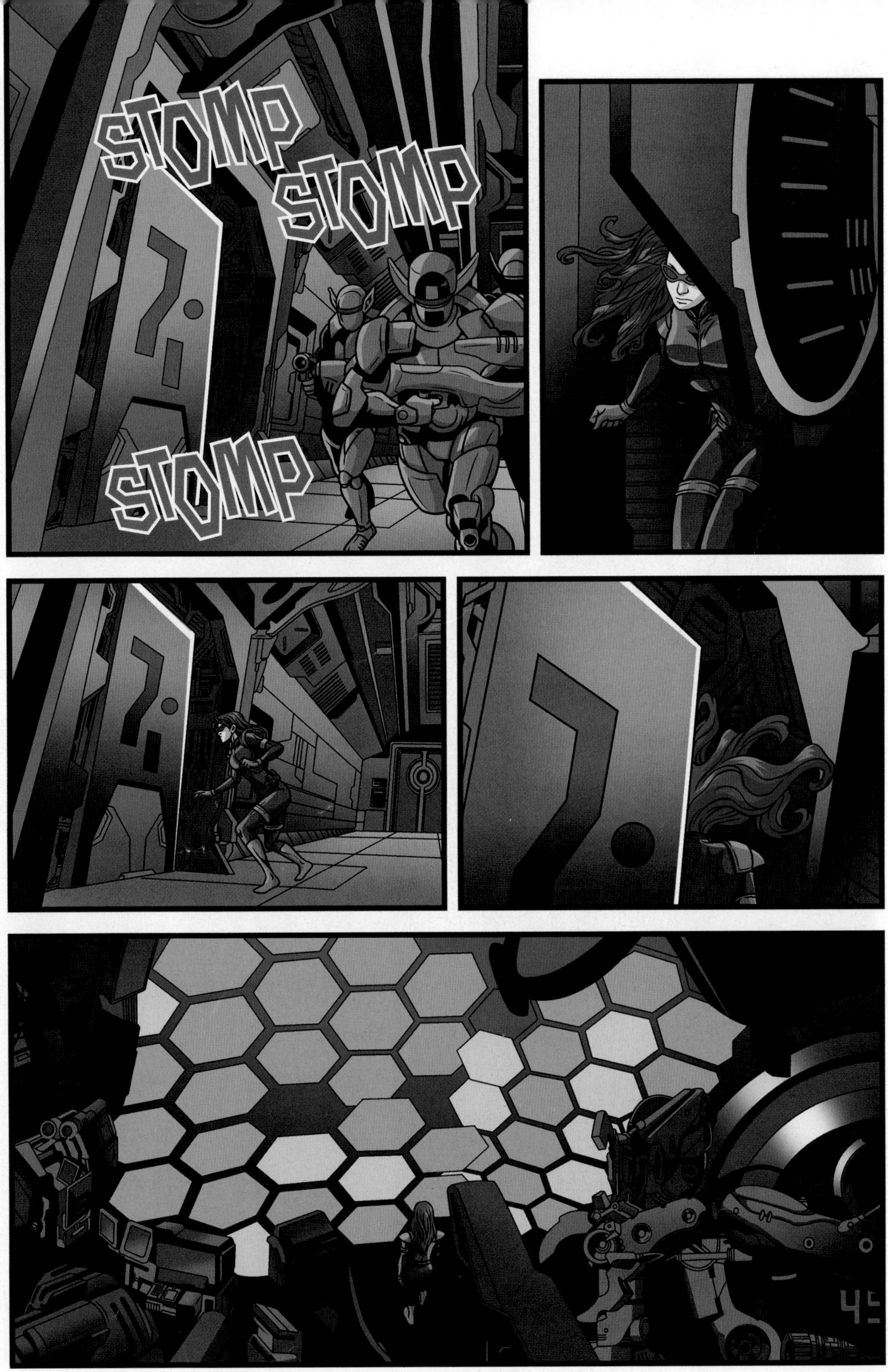
STOMP
STOMP
STOMP

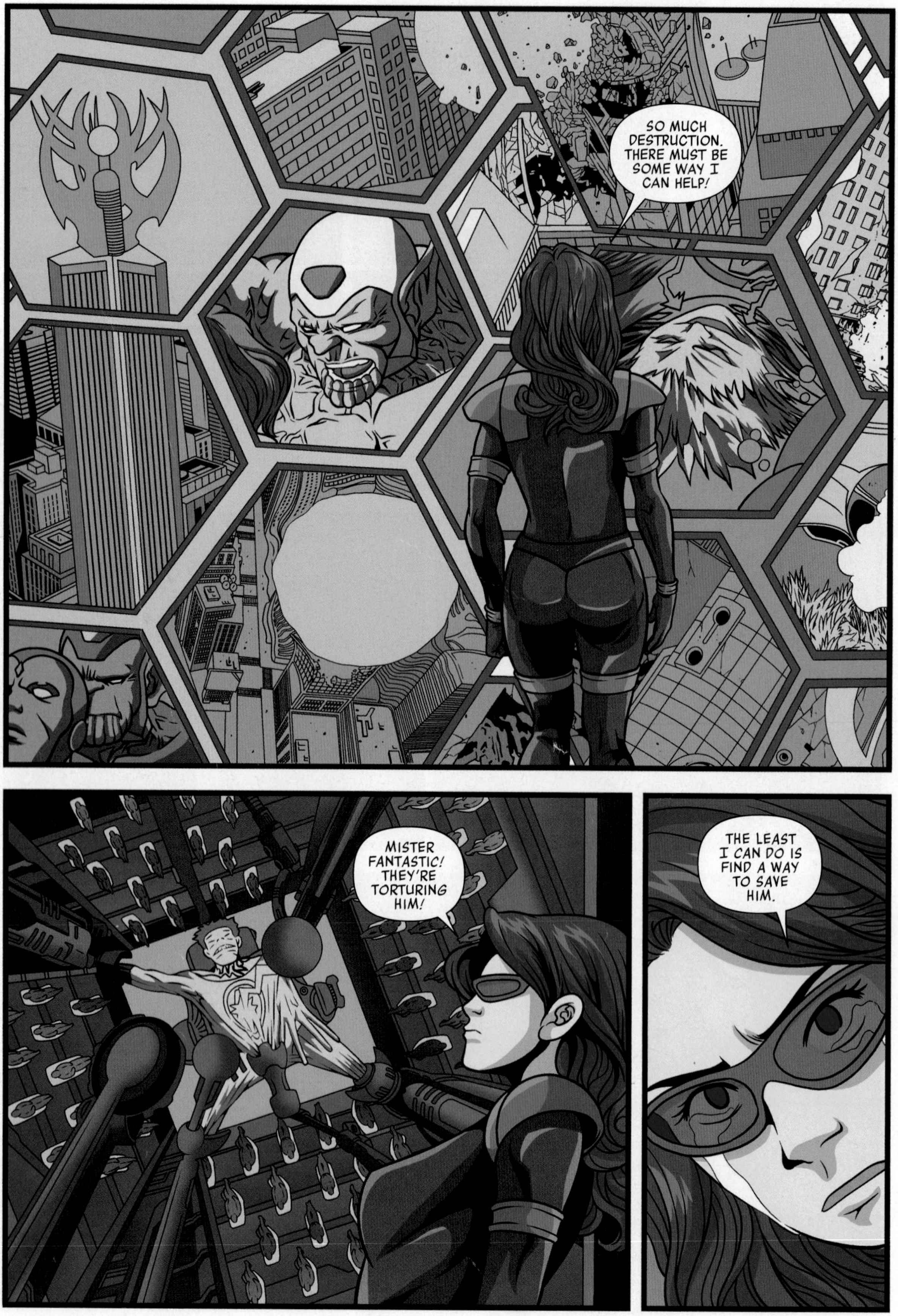
SO MUCH DESTRUCTION. THERE MUST BE SOME WAY I CAN HELP!
MISTER FANTASTIC! THEY'RE TORTURING HIM!
THE LEAST I CAN DO IS FIND A WAY TO SAVE HIM.

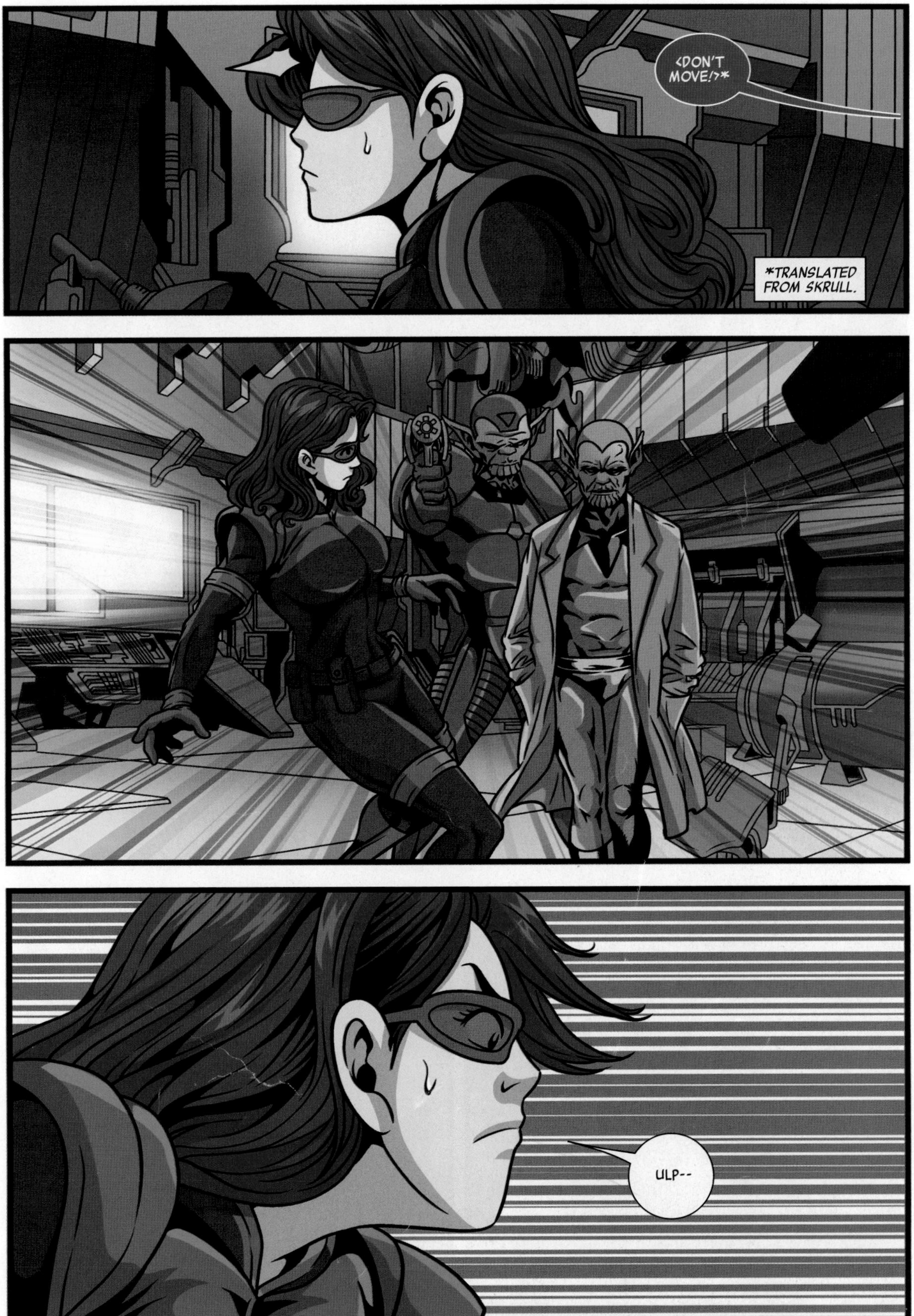
<DON'T MOVE!>*
*TRANSLATED FROM SKRULL.
ULP--

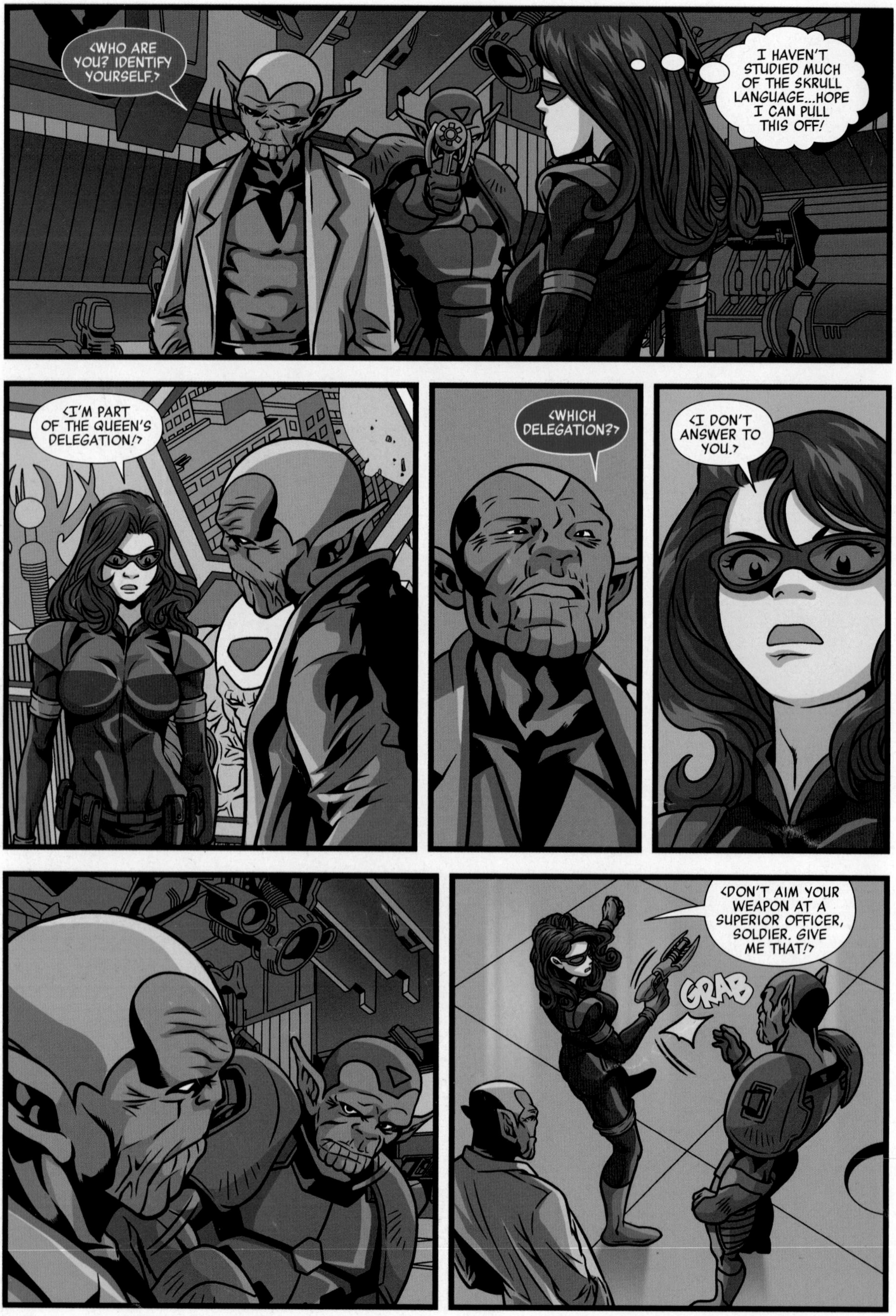
<WHO ARE YOU? IDENTIFY YOURSELF.>
I HAVEN'T STUDIED MUCH OF THE SKRULL LANGUAGE...HOPE I CAN PULL THIS OFF!
<I'M PART OF THE QUEEN'S DELEGATION!>
<WHICH DELEGATION?>
<I DON'T ANSWER TO YOU.>
<DON'T AIM YOUR WEAPON AT A SUPERIOR OFFICER, SOLDIER. GIVE ME THAT!>
GRAB

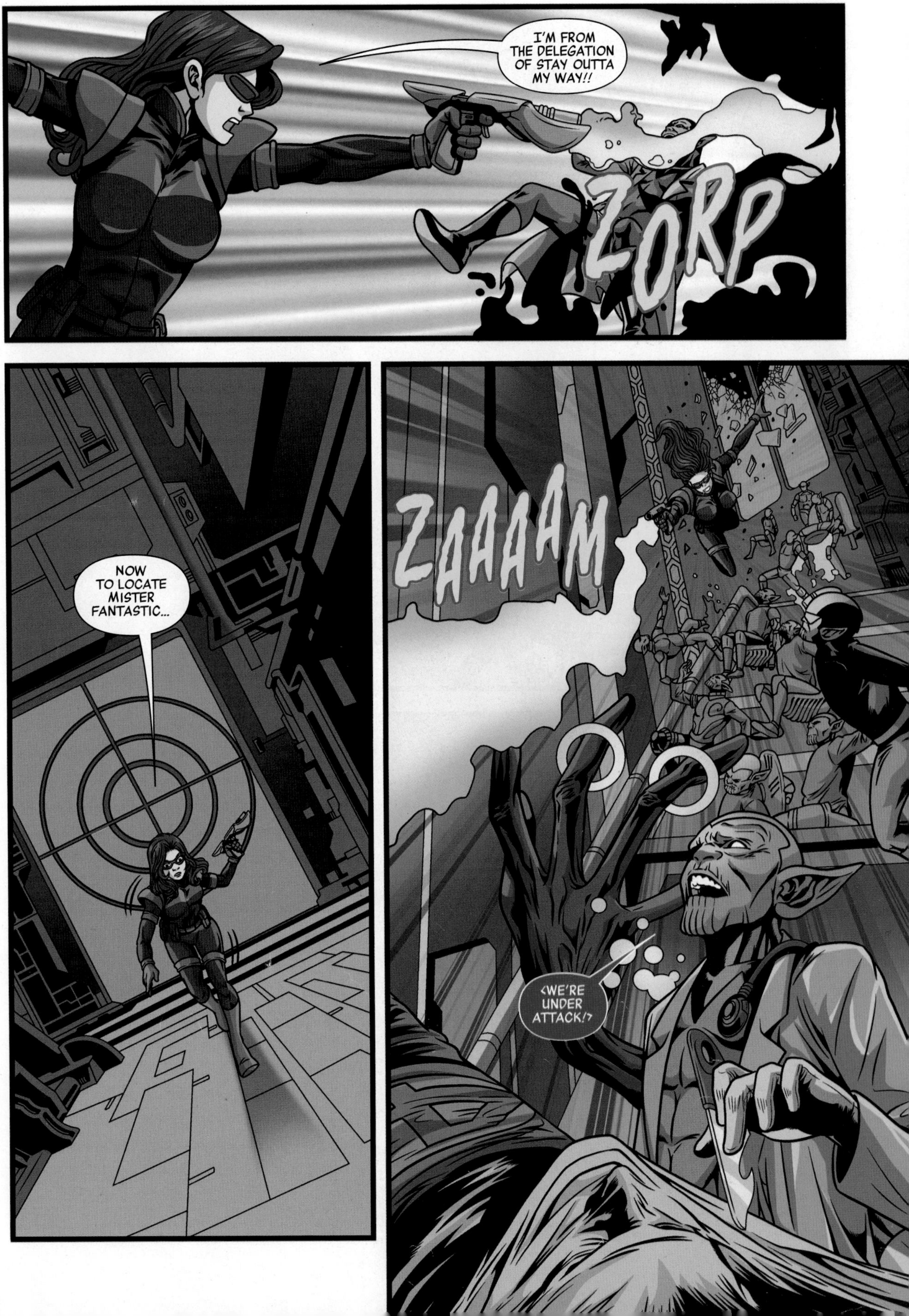
I'M FROM THE DELEGATION OF STAY OUTTA MY WAY!!
ZORP
NOW TO LOCATE MISTER FANTASTIC...
ZAAAAM
<WE'RE UNDER ATTACK!?

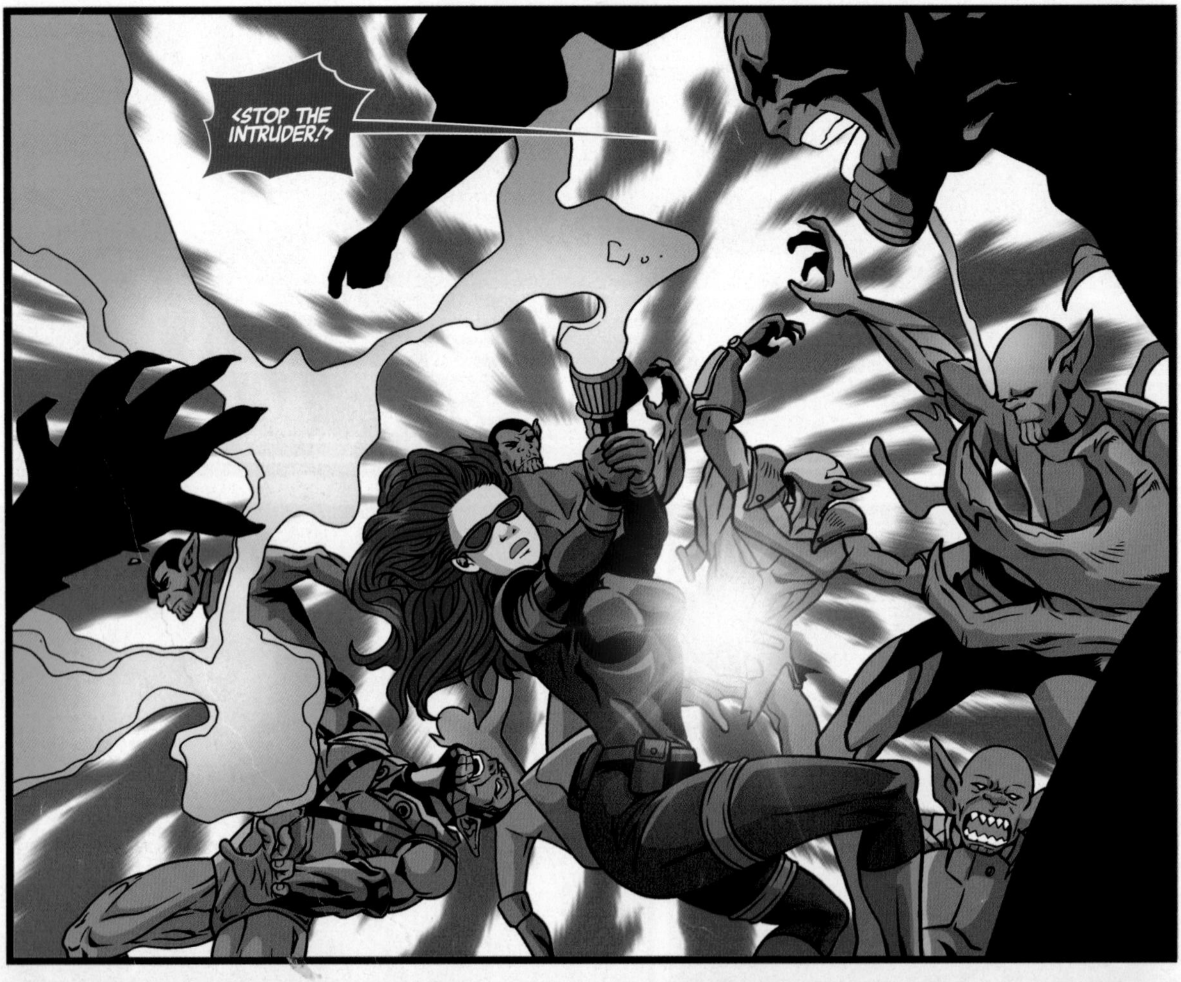
<STOP THE INTRUDER!>

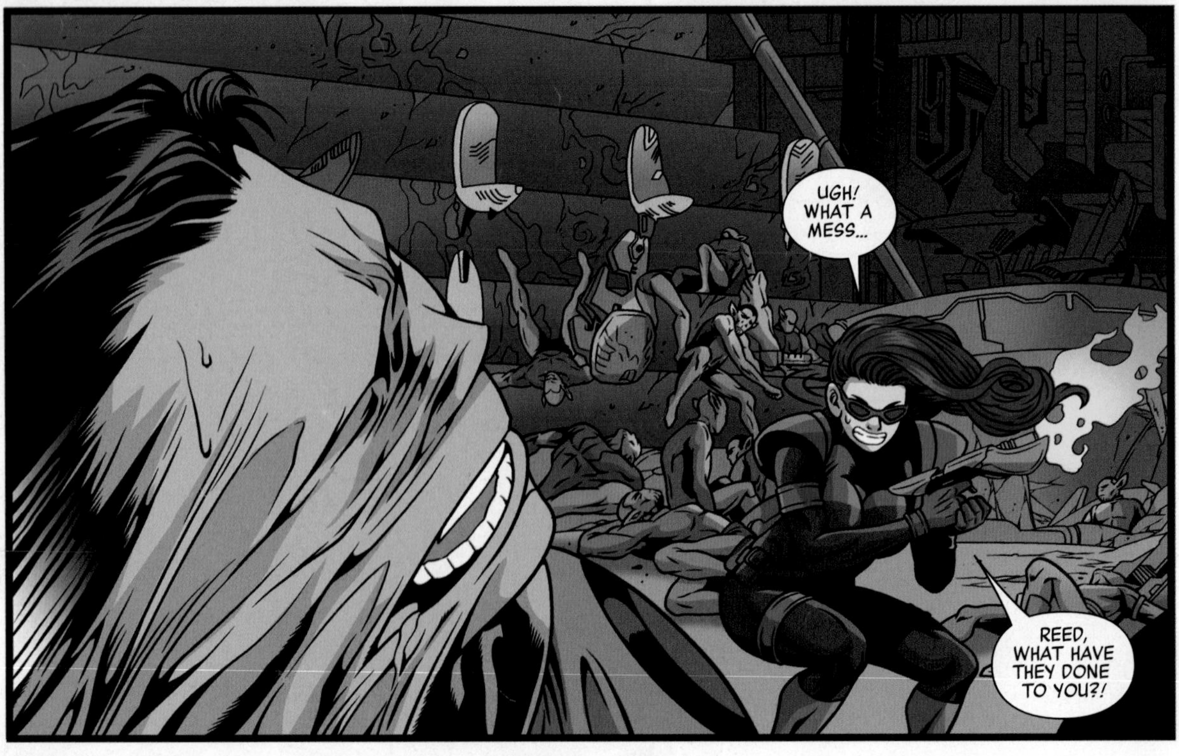
UGH! WHAT A MESS...
REED, WHAT HAVE THEY DONE TO YOU?!

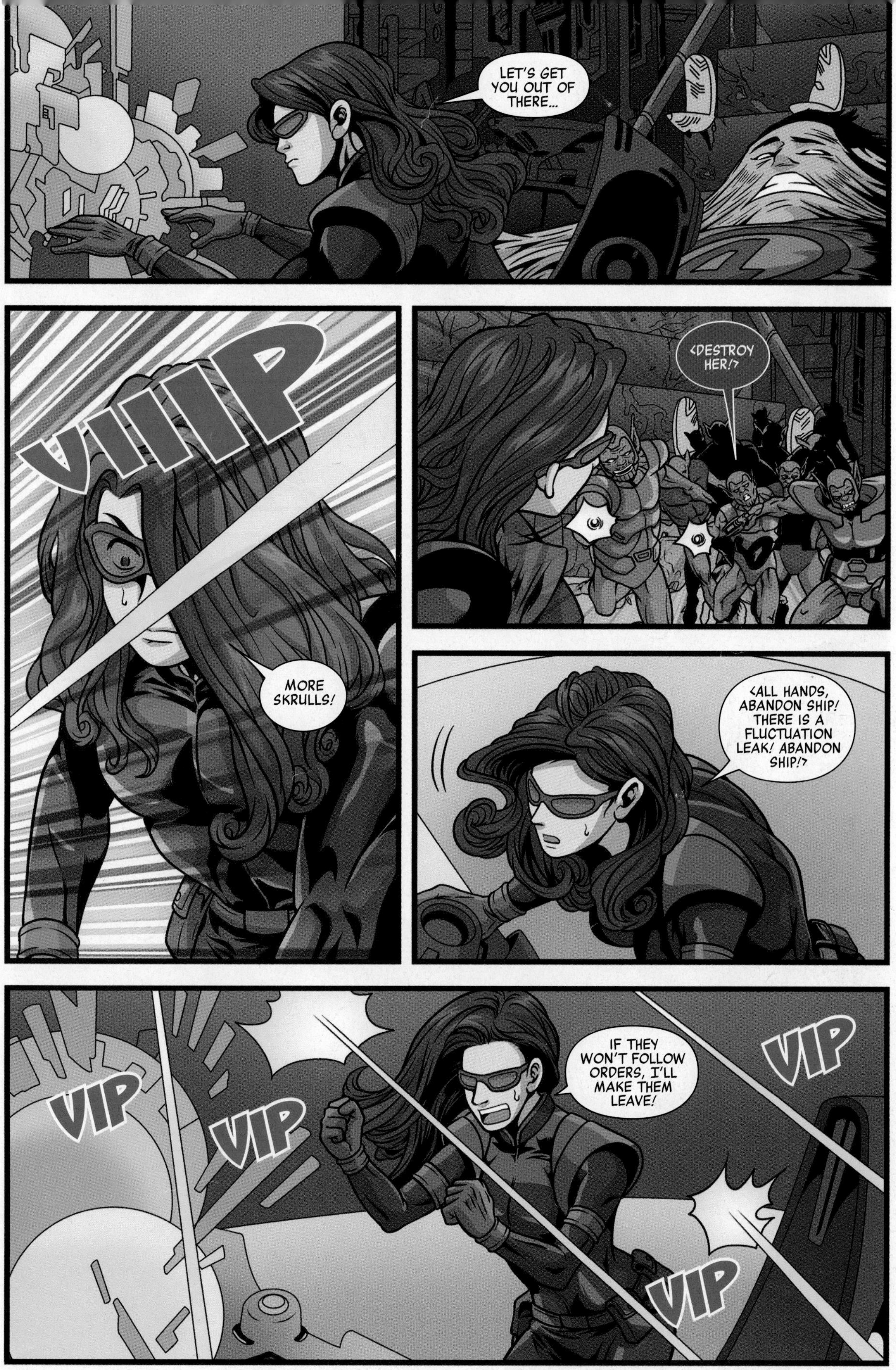
LET'S GET YOU OUT OF THERE...
VIIIP
MORE SKRULLS!
<DESTROY HER!>
<ALL HANDS, ABANDON SHIP! THERE IS A FLUCTUATION LEAK! ABANDON SHIP!>
VIP
VIP
IF THEY WON'T FOLLOW ORDERS, I'LL MAKE THEM LEAVE!
VIP
VIP

FFFFFF
WHOOSH
WHOOOOOOOSH
AAAGH!

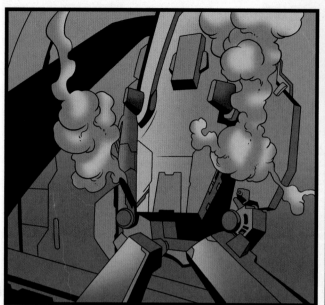

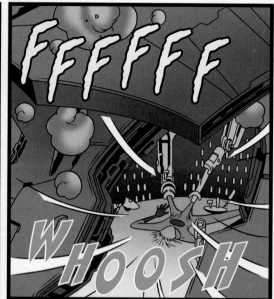

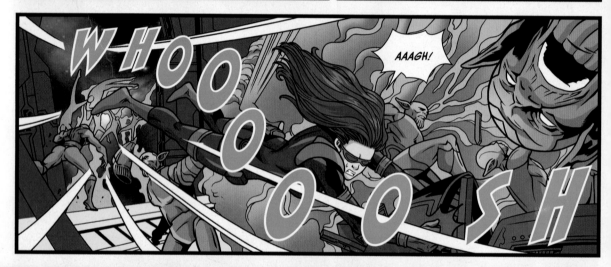

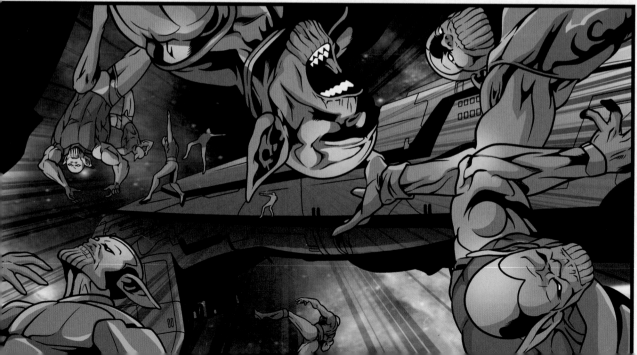

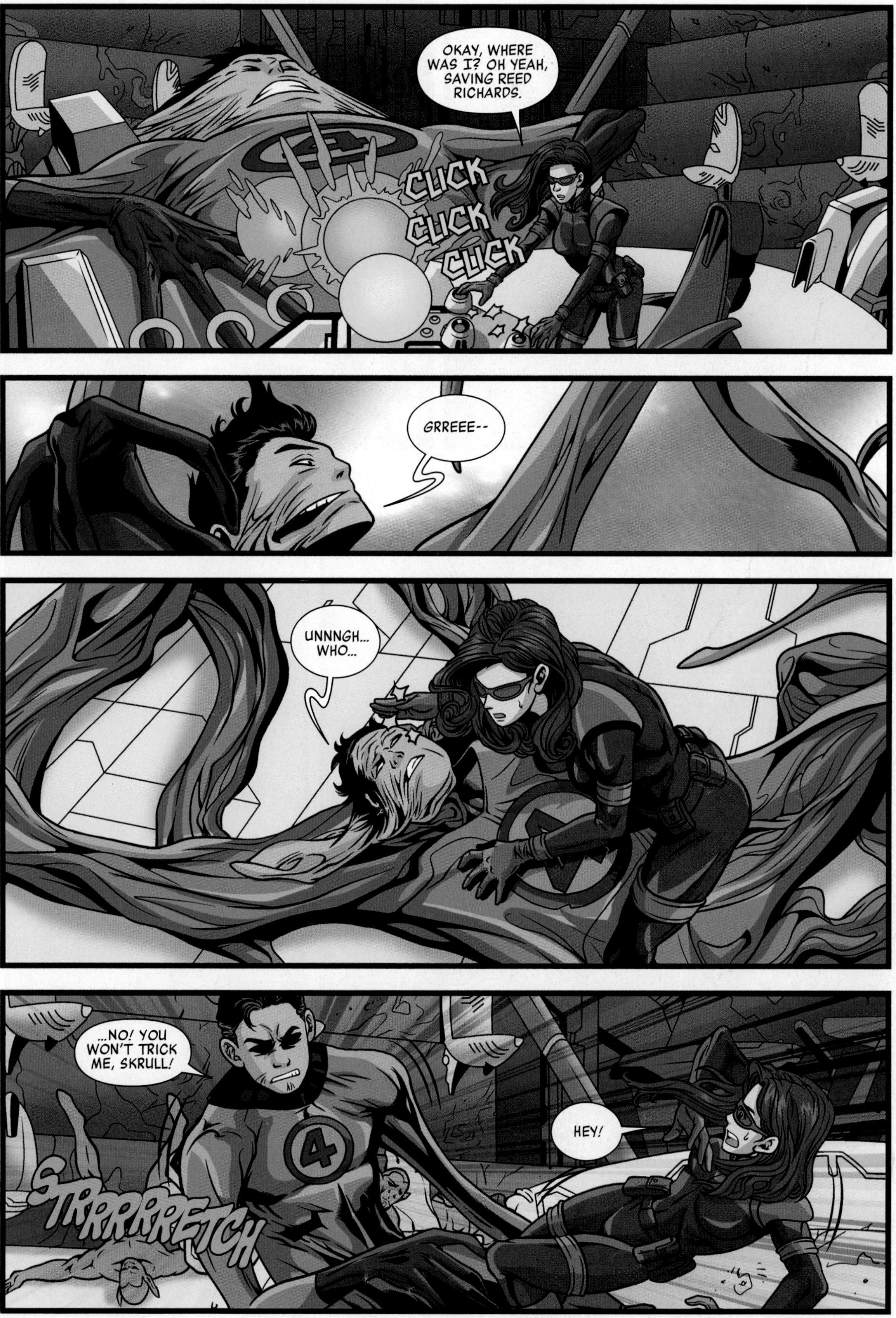
OKAY, WHERE WAS I? OH YEAH, SAVING REED RICHARDS.
CLICK CLICK CLICK
GRREEE--
UNNNGH... WHO...
...NO! YOU WON'T TRICK ME, SKRULL!
HEY!
STRRRRRETCH

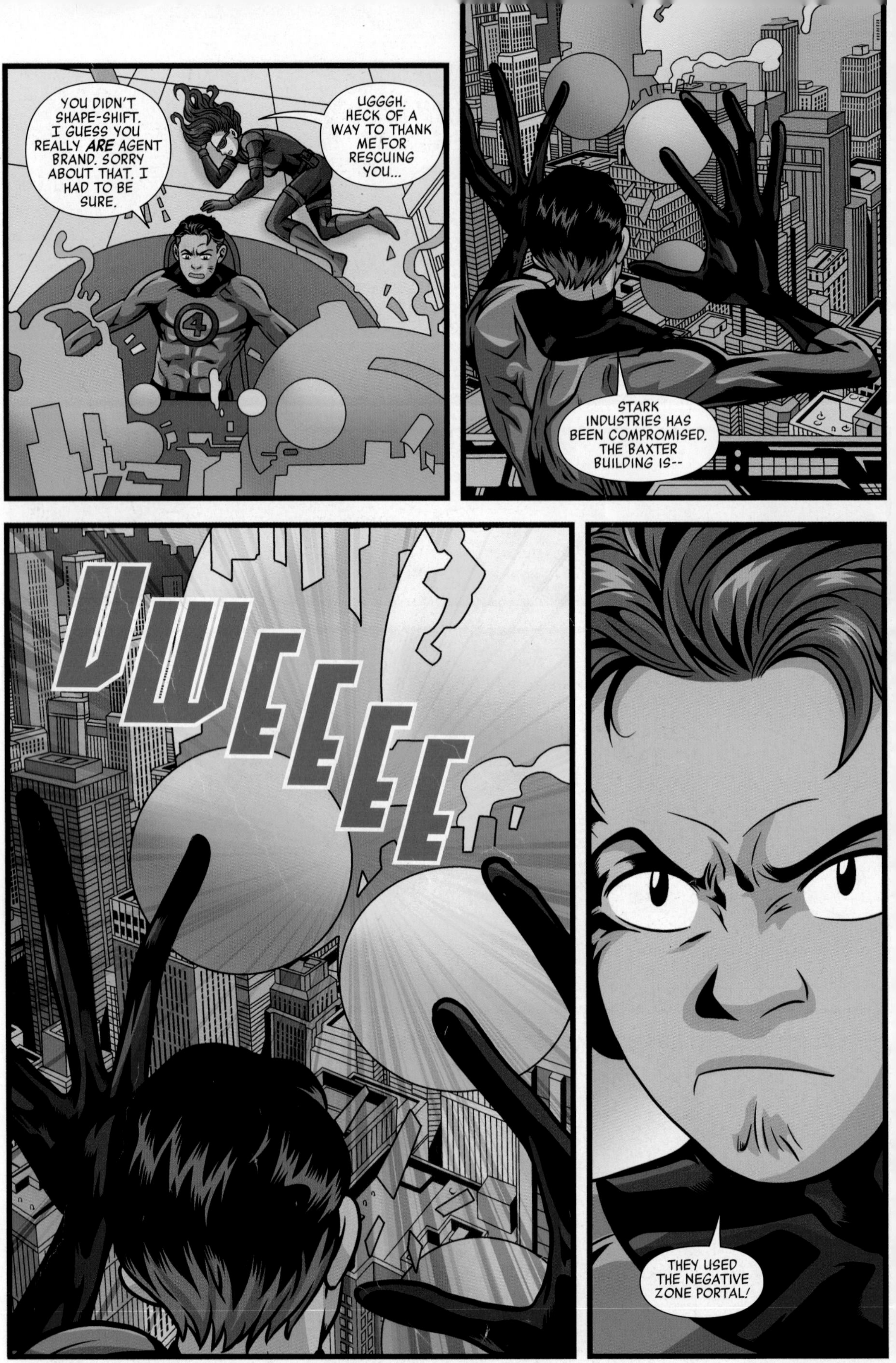
YOU DIDN'T SHAPE-SHIFT. I GUESS YOU REALLY ARE AGENT BRAND. SORRY ABOUT THAT. I HAD TO BE SURE.
UGGGH. HECK OF A WAY TO THANK ME FOR RESCUING YOU...
STARK INDUSTRIES HAS BEEN COMPROMISED. THE BAXTER BUILDING IS--
VWEEEE
THEY USED THE NEGATIVE ZONE PORTAL!

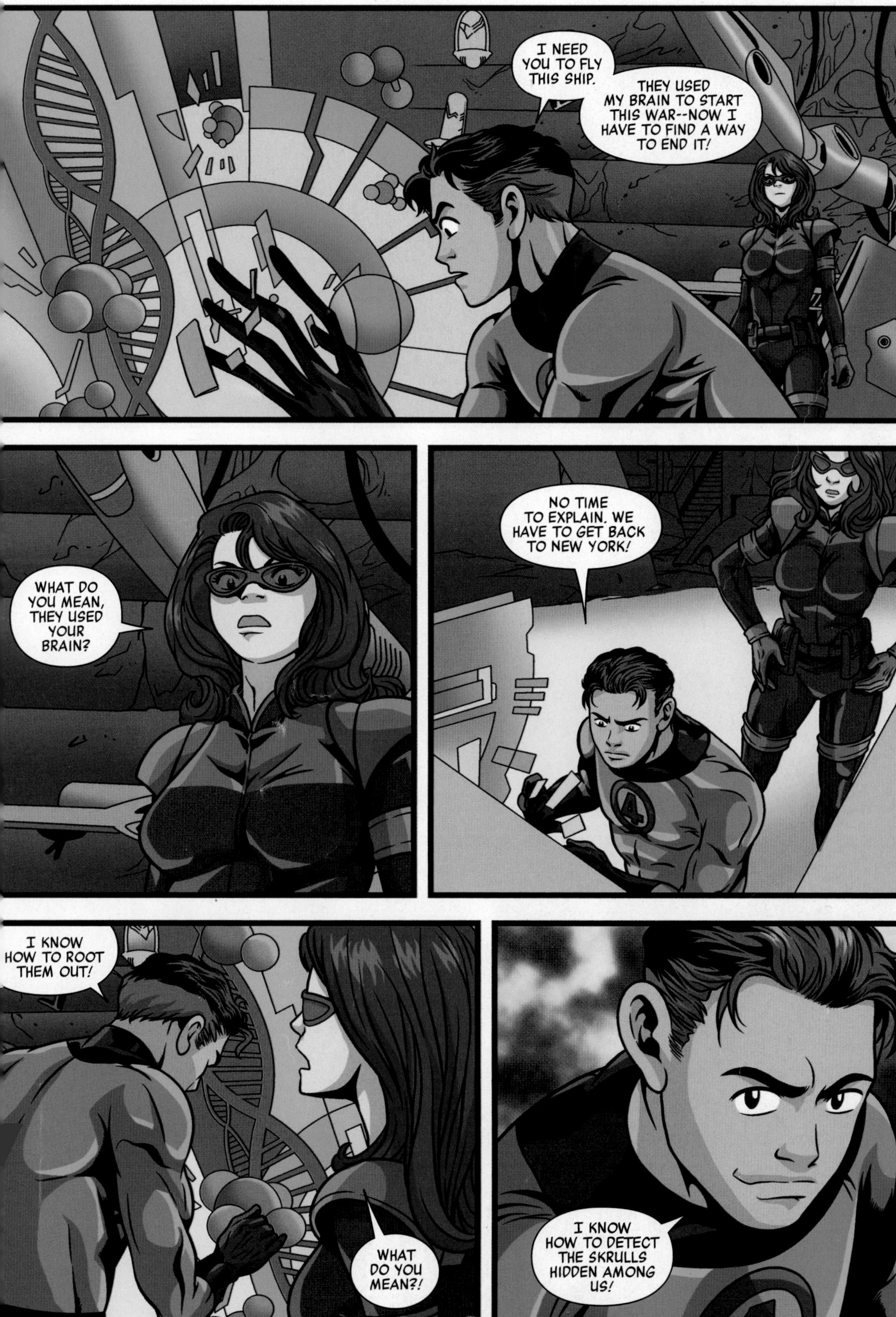
I NEED YOU TO FLY THIS SHIP.
THEY USED MY BRAIN TO START THIS WAR--NOW I HAVE TO FIND A WAY TO END IT!
WHAT DO YOU MEAN, THEY USED YOUR BRAIN?
NO TIME TO EXPLAIN. WE HAVE TO GET BACK TO NEW YORK!
I KNOW HOW TO ROOT THEM OUT!
WHAT DO YOU MEAN?!
I KNOW HOW TO DETECT THE SKRULLS HIDDEN AMONG US!

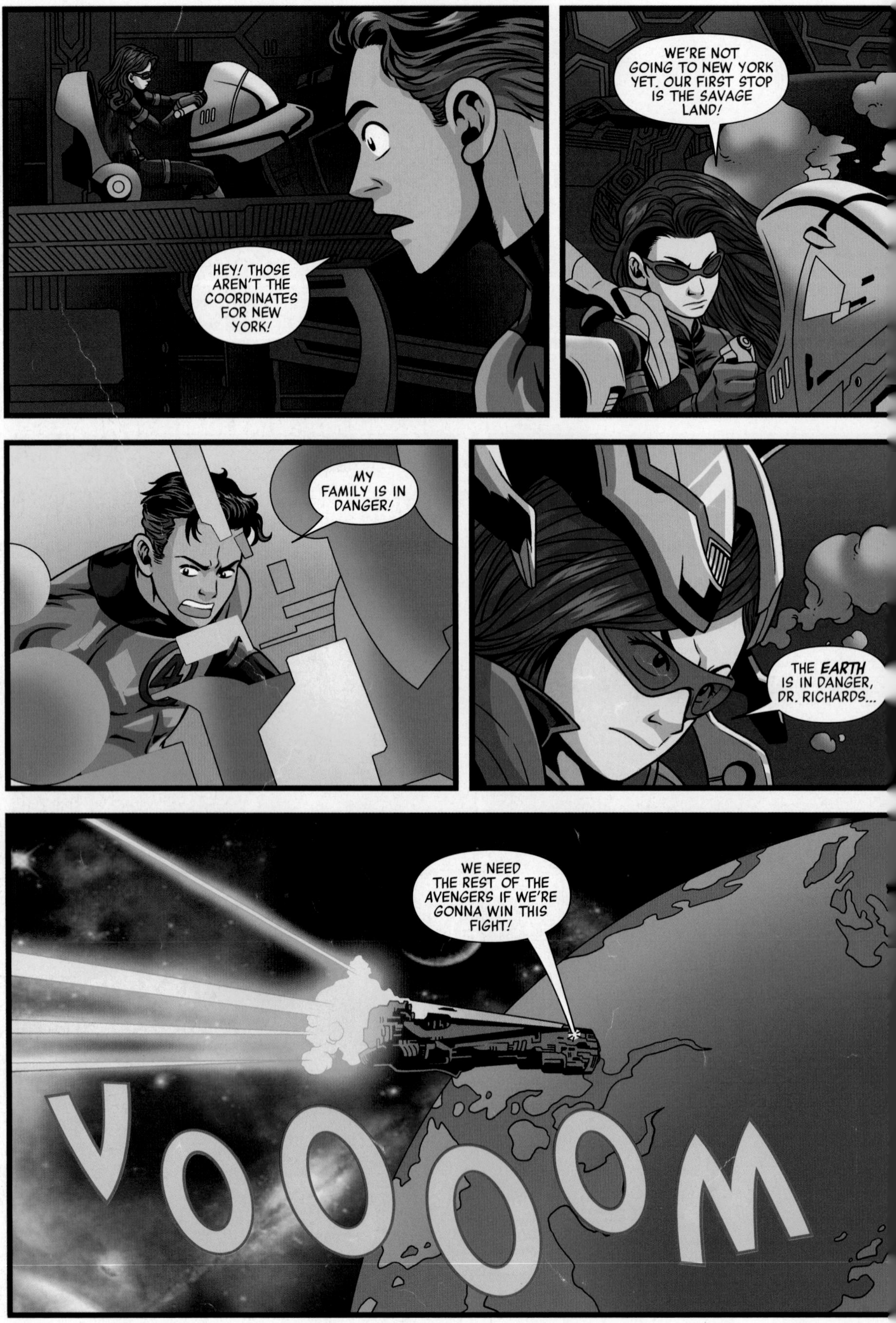
HEY! THOSE AREN'T THE COORDINATES FOR NEW YORK!
WE'RE NOT GOING TO NEW YORK YET. OUR FIRST STOP IS THE SAVAGE LAND!
MY FAMILY IS IN DANGER!
THE EARTH IS IN DANGER, DR. RICHARDS...
WE NEED THE REST OF THE AVENGERS IF WE'RE GONNA WIN THIS FIGHT!
VOOOOM

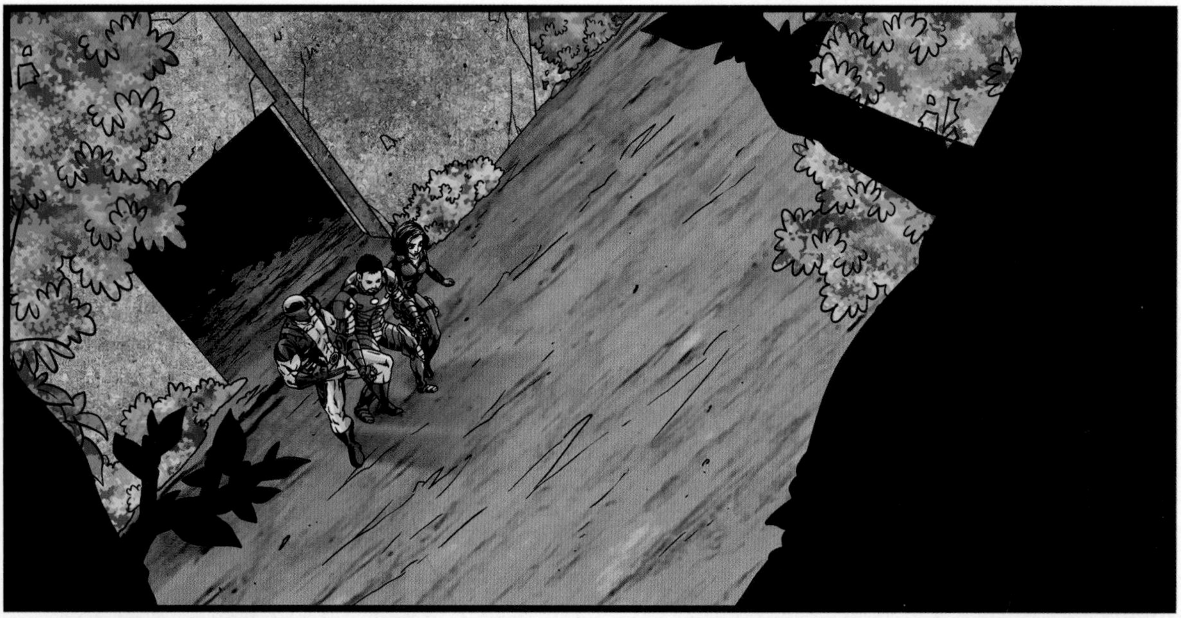

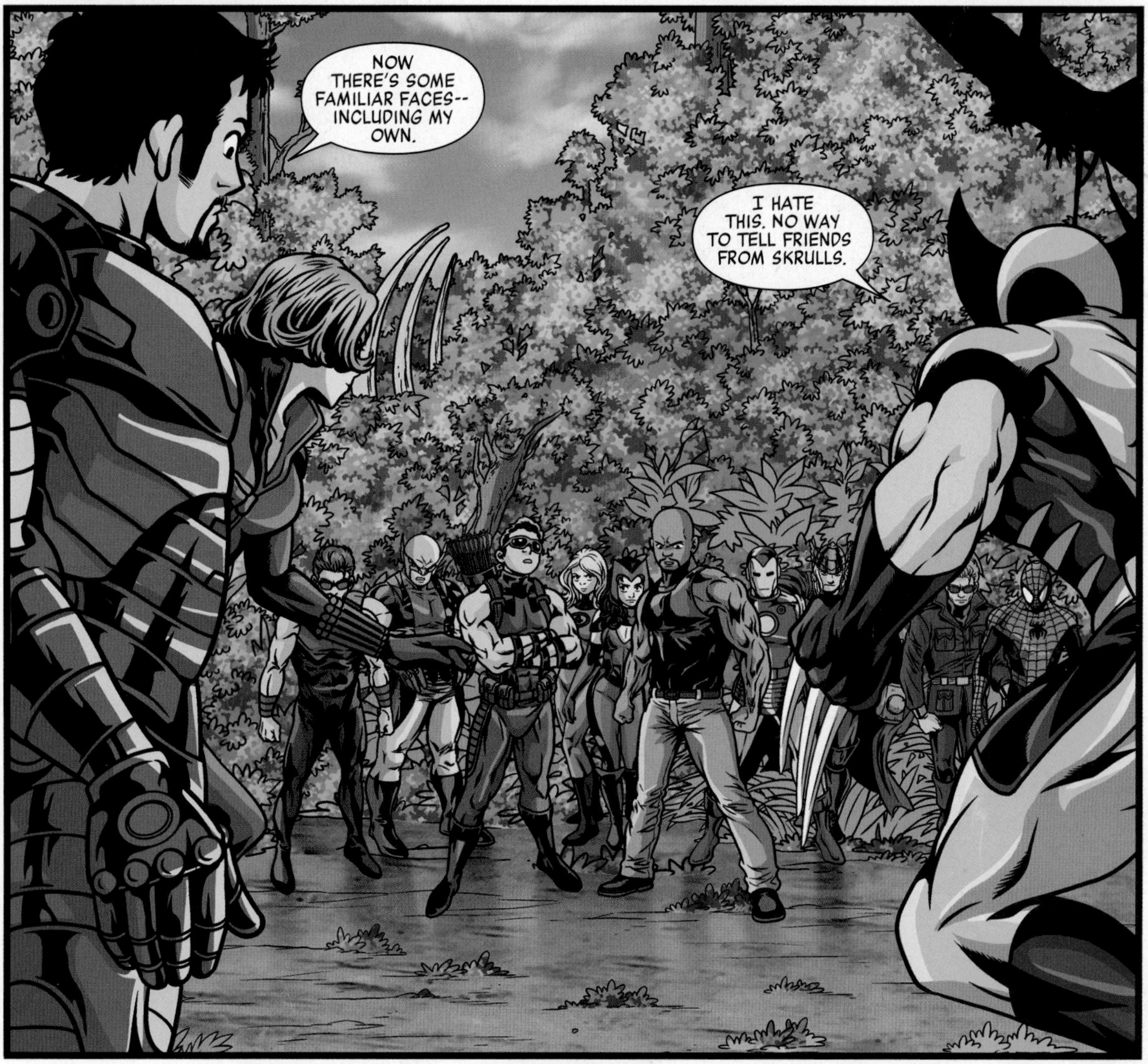
NOW THERE'S SOME FAMILIAR FACES-- INCLUDING MY OWN.
I HATE THIS. NO WAY TO TELL FRIENDS FROM SKRULLS.

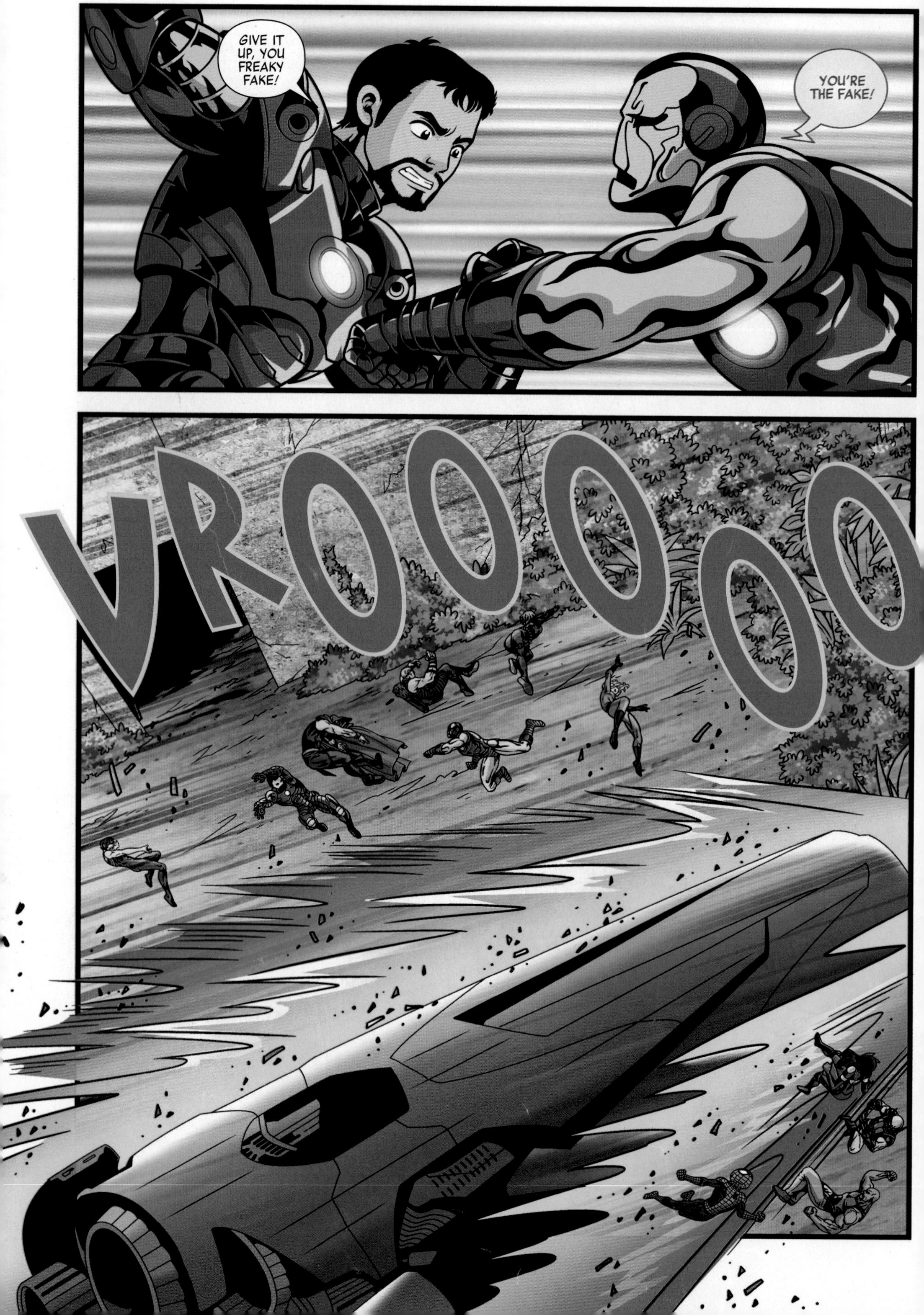
GIVE IT UP, YOU FREAKY FAKE!
YOU'RE THE FAKE!
VROOOOOO

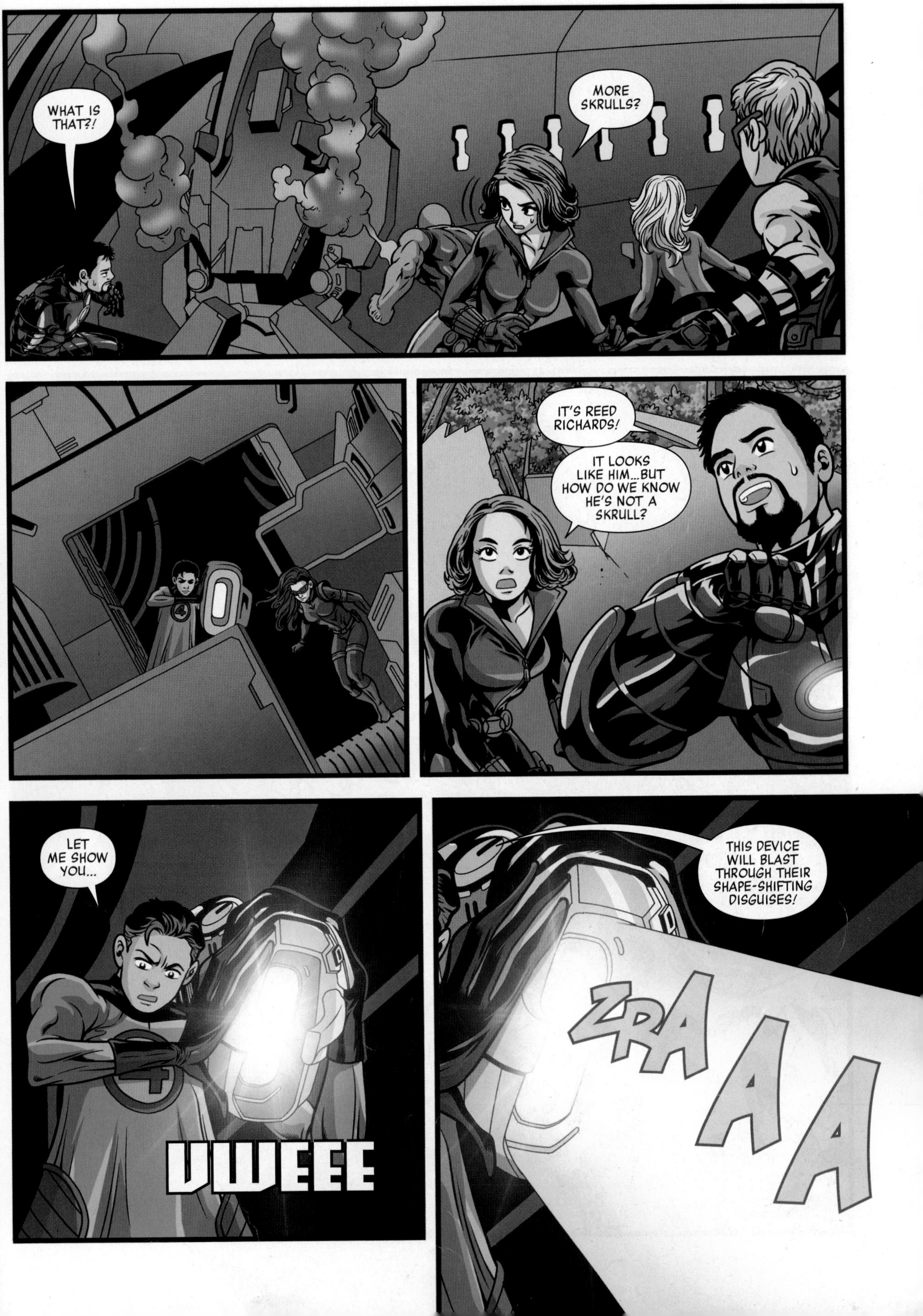

WHAT IS THAT?!
MORE SKRULLS?
IT'S REED RICHARDS!
IT LOOKS LIKE HIM...BUT HOW DO WE KNOW HE'S NOT A SKRULL?
LET ME SHOW YOU...
VWEEE
THIS DEVICE WILL BLAST THROUGH THEIR SHAPE-SHIFTING DISGUISES!
ZRAAAA

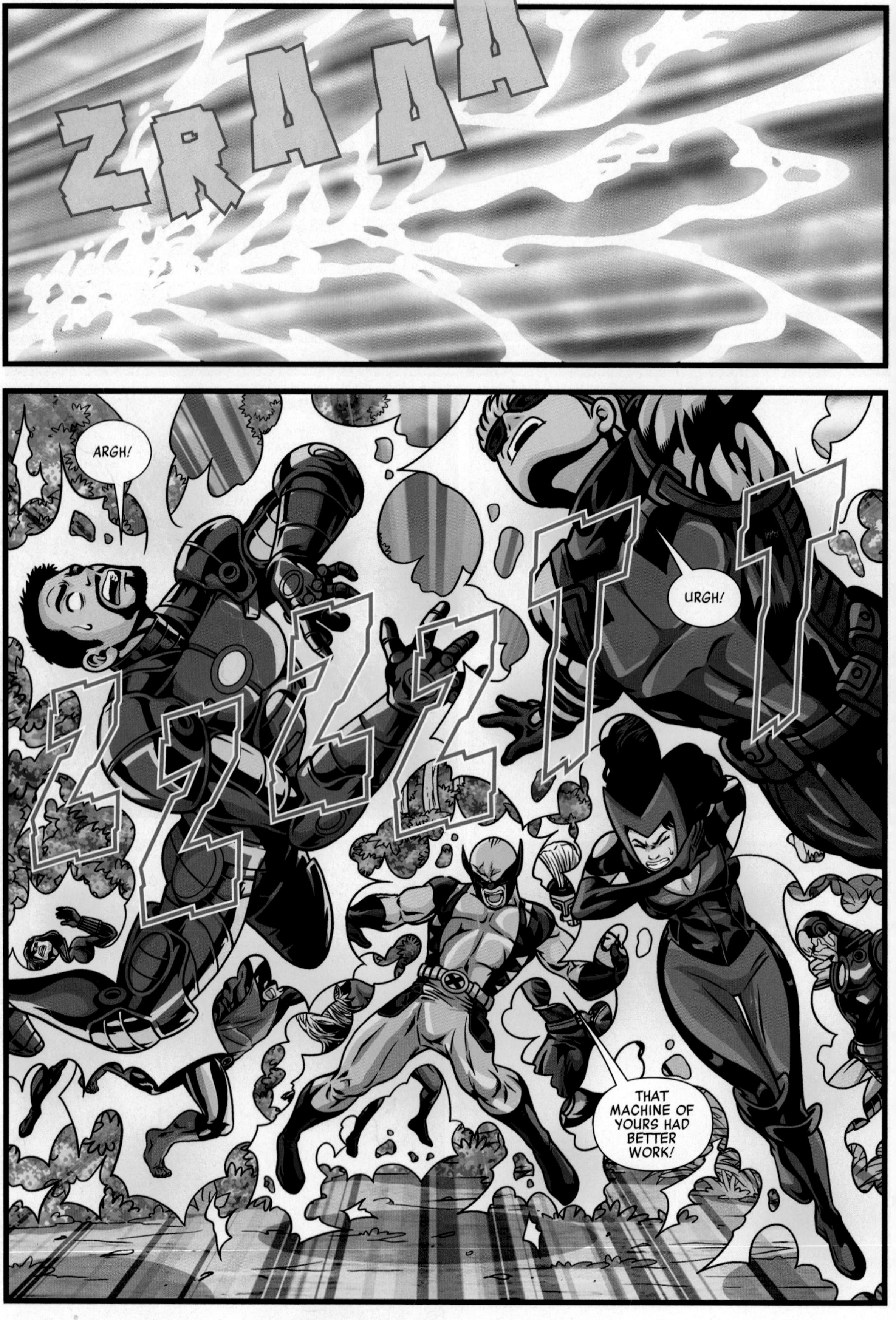
ZRAAAA
ARGH!
ZZZZTT
URGH!
THAT MACHINE OF YOURS HAD BETTER WORK!

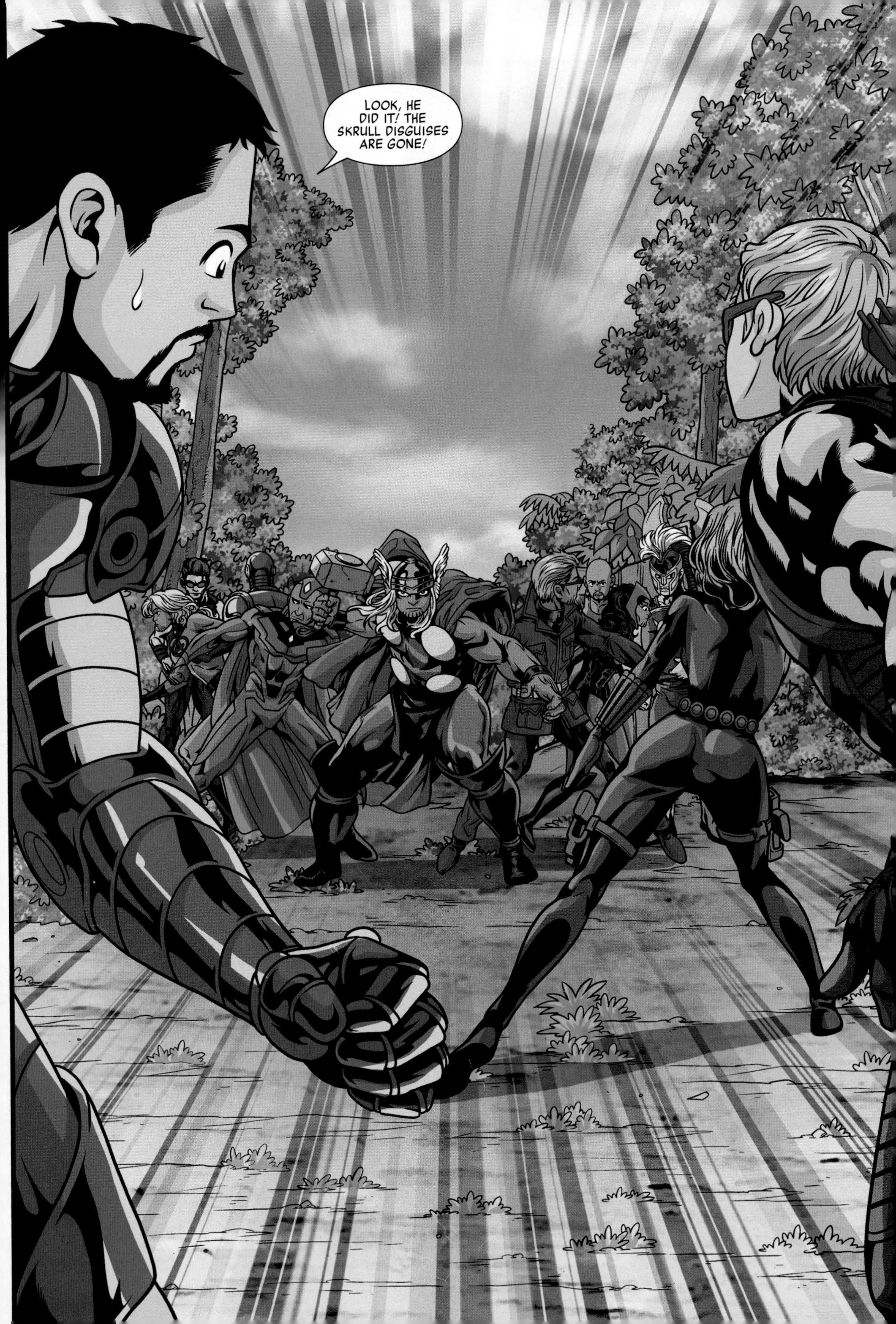
LOOK, HE DID IT! THE SKRULL DISGUISES ARE GONE!

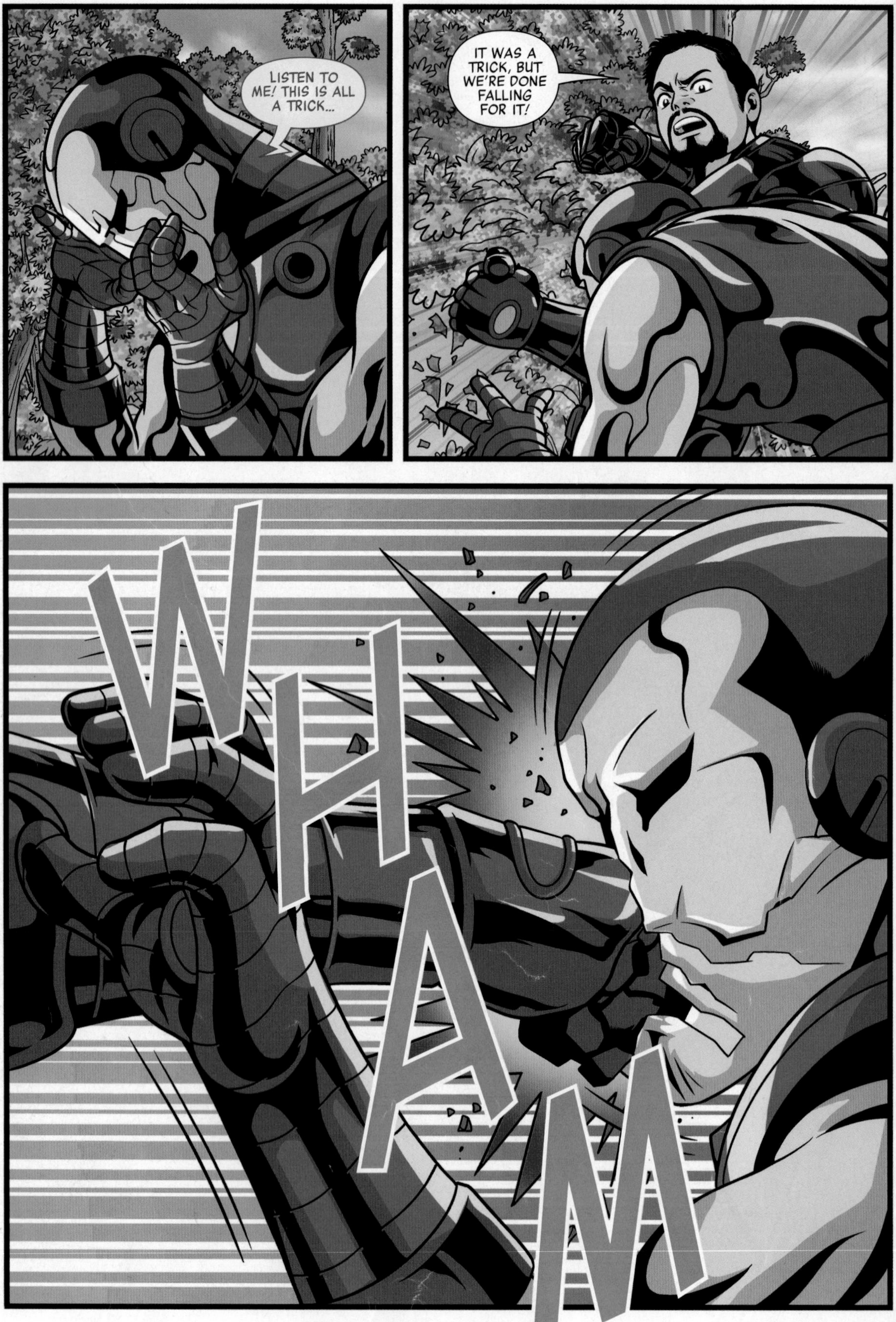
LISTEN TO ME! THIS IS ALL A TRICK...
IT WAS A TRICK, BUT WE'RE DONE FALLING FOR IT!
WHAM

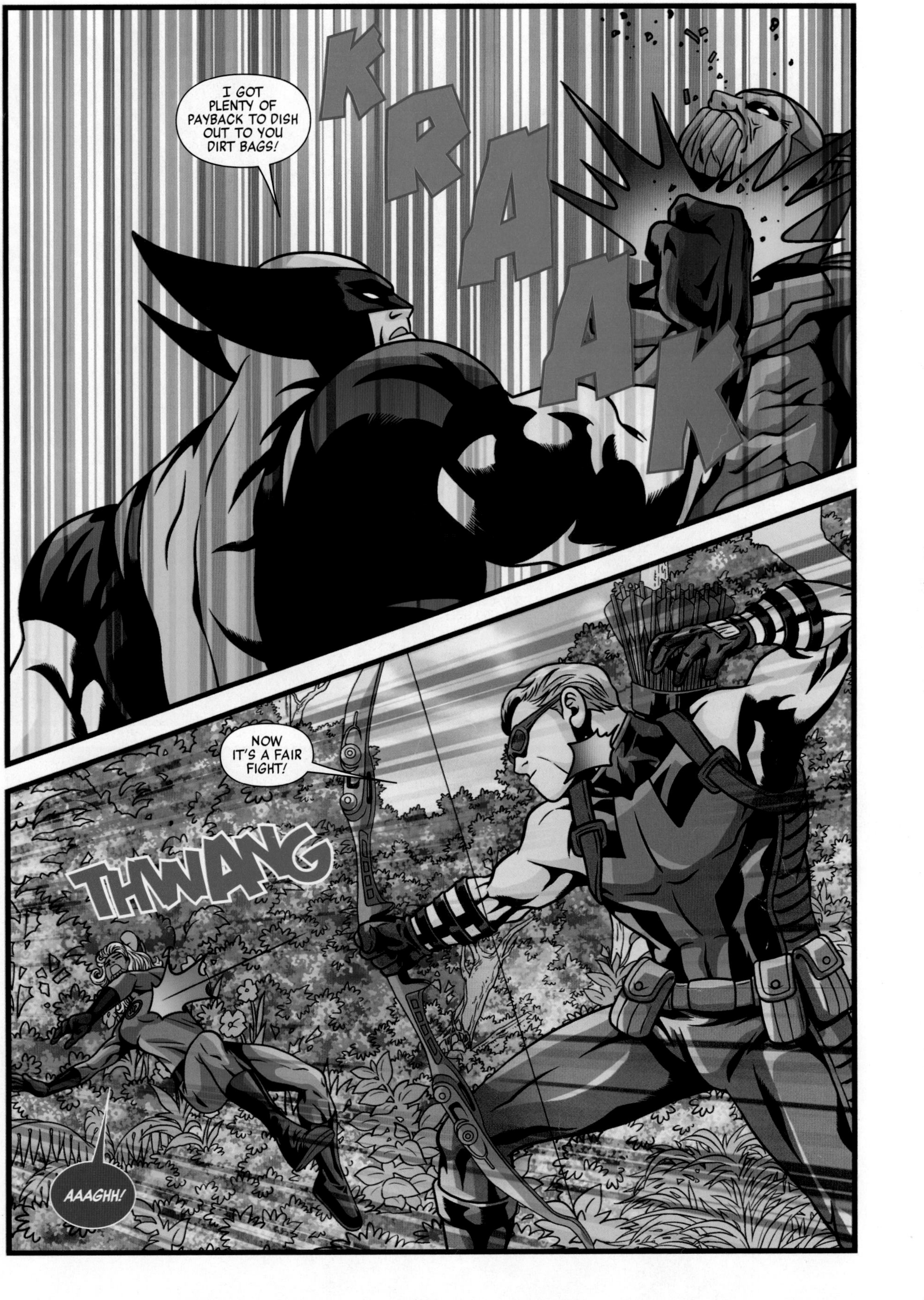
I GOT PLENTY OF PAYBACK TO DISH OUT TO YOU DIRT BAGS!
KRAAAK
NOW IT'S A FAIR FIGHT!
THWANG
AAAGHH!

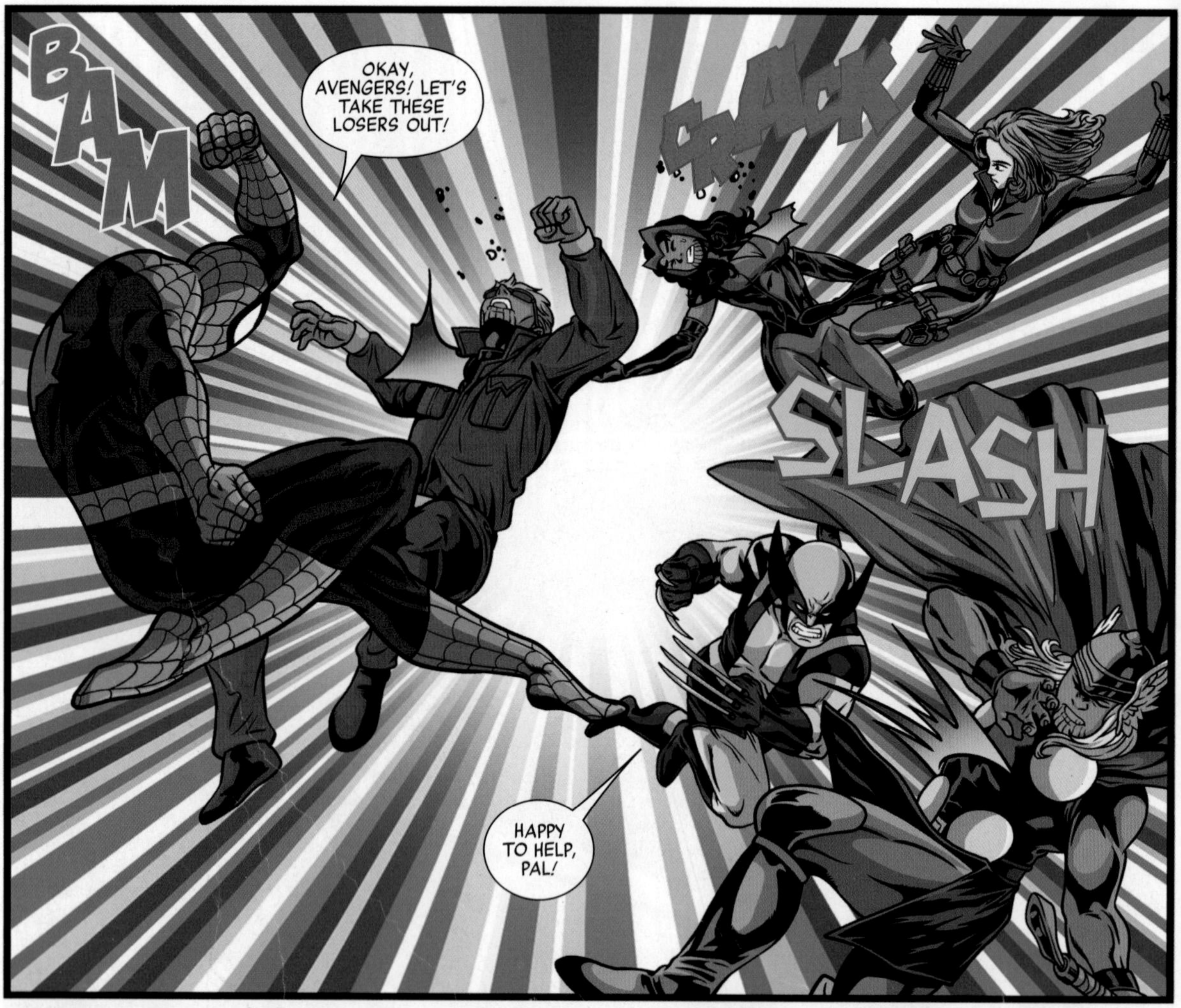
BAM
OKAY, AVENGERS! LET'S TAKE THESE LOSERS OUT!
CRACK
SLASH
HAPPY TO HELP, PAL!

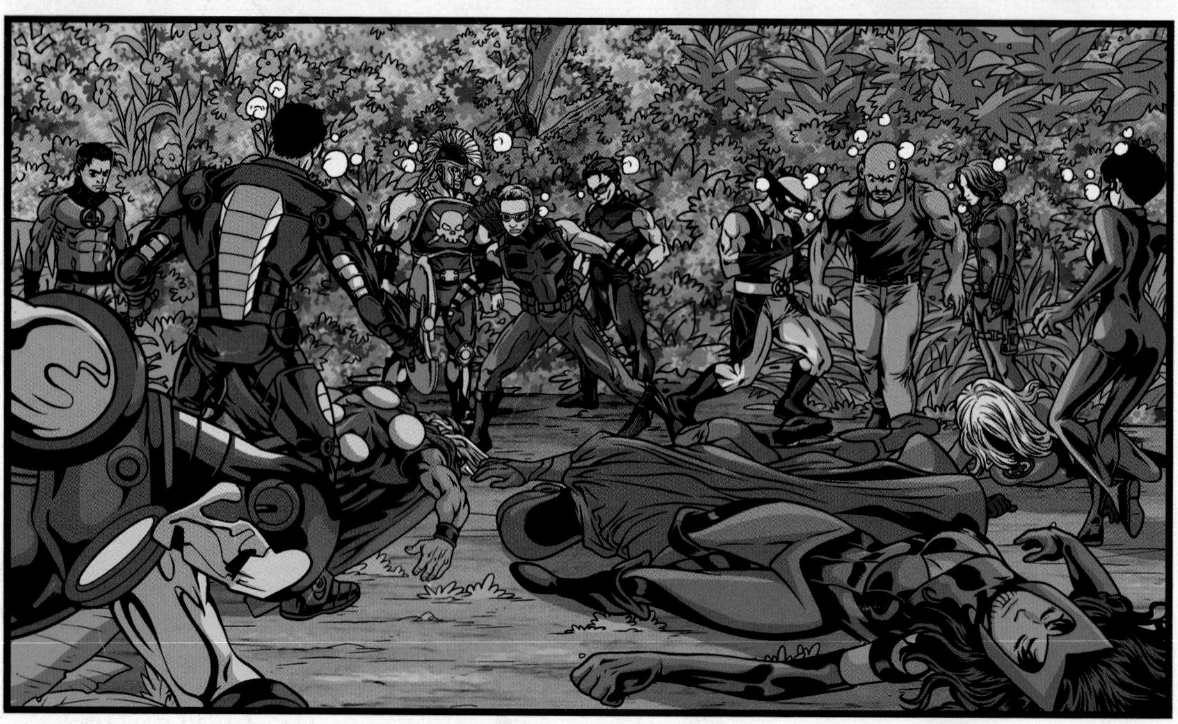

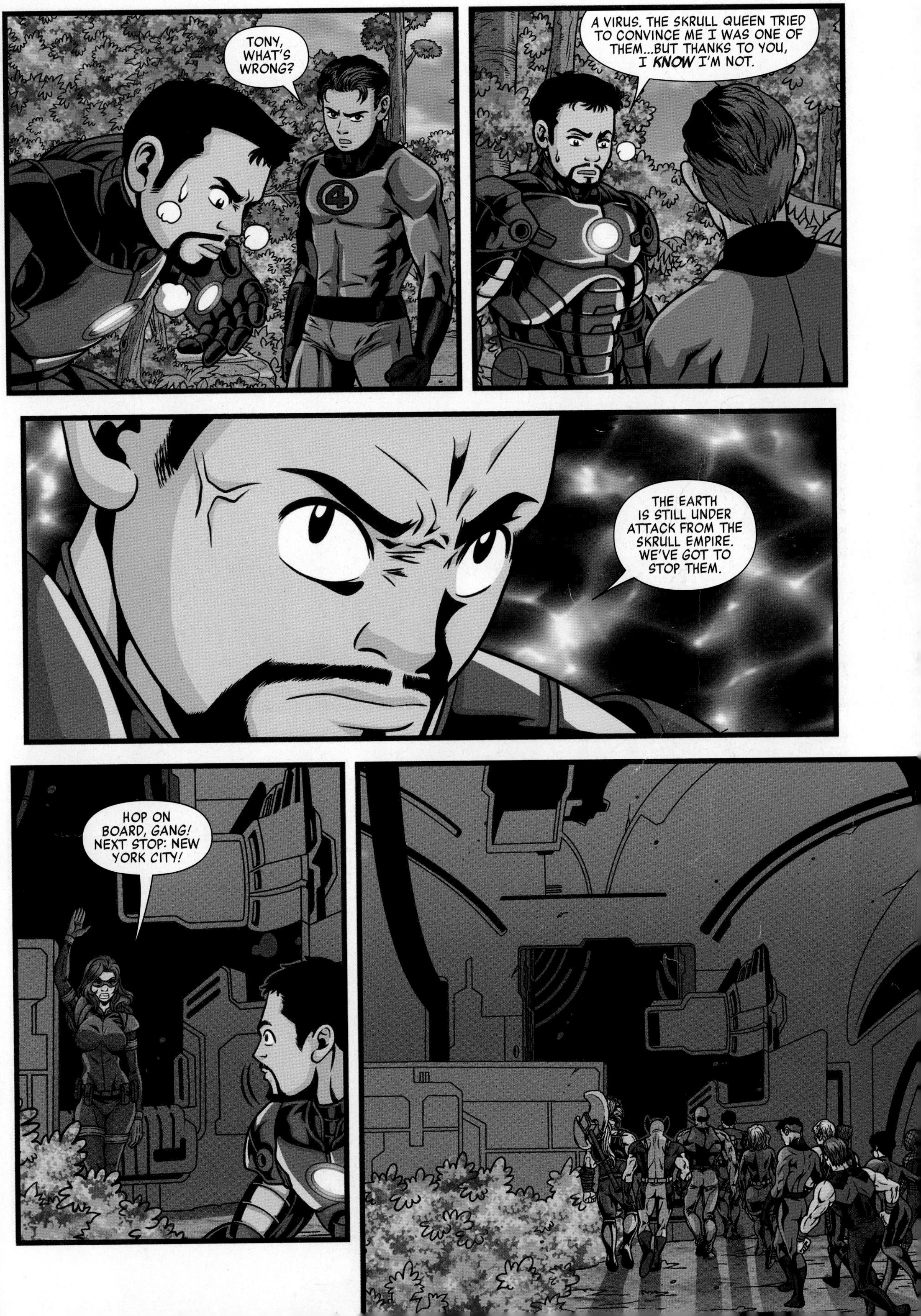
TONY, WHAT'S WRONG?
A VIRUS. THE SKRULL QUEEN TRIED TO CONVINCE ME I WAS ONE OF THEM...BUT THANKS TO YOU, I *KNOW* I'M NOT.
THE EARTH IS STILL UNDER ATTACK FROM THE SKRULL EMPIRE. WE'VE GOT TO STOP THEM.
HOP ON BOARD, GANG! NEXT STOP: NEW YORK CITY!

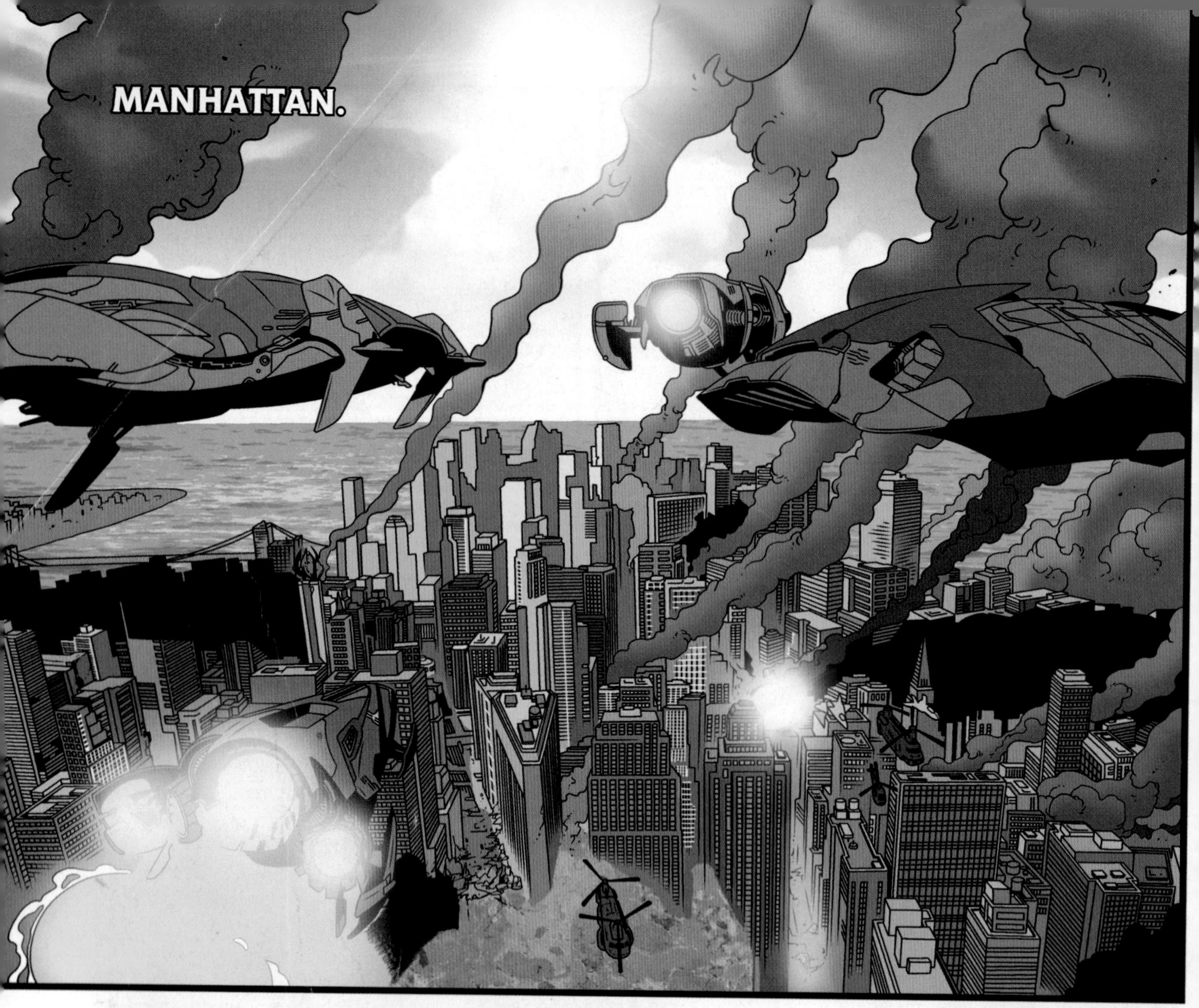
MANHATTAN.

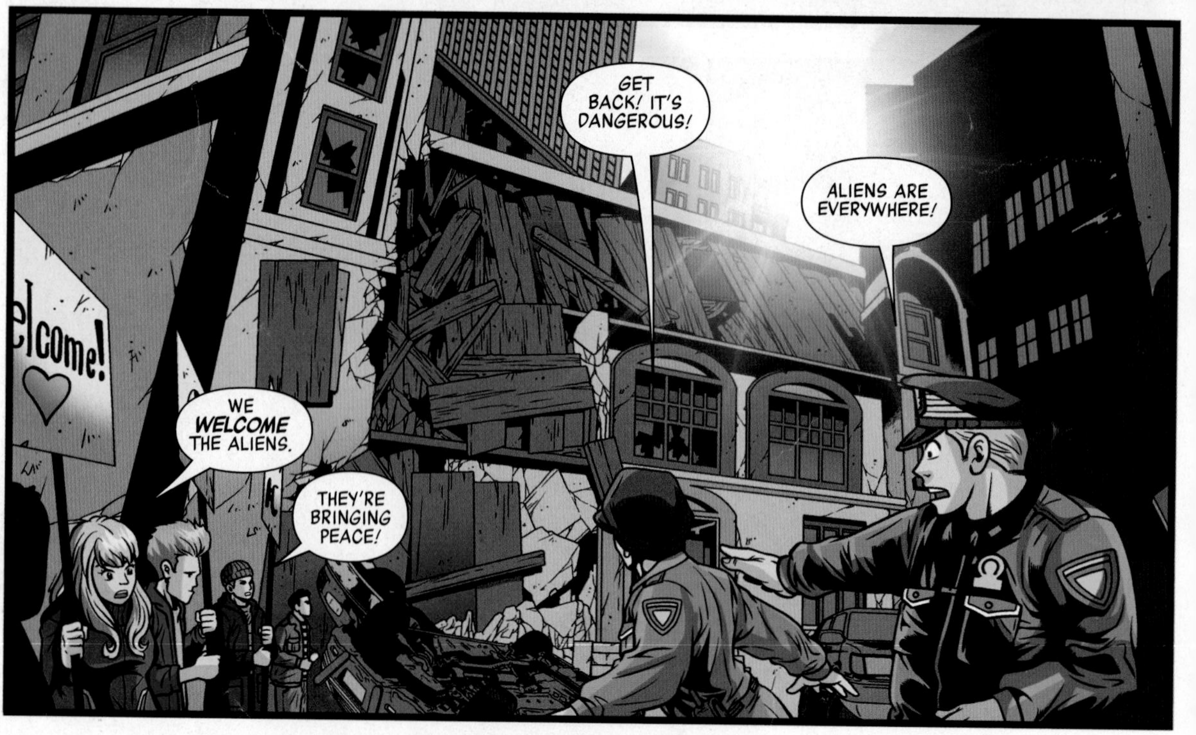
elcome!
WE WELCOME THE ALIENS.
THEY'RE BRINGING PEACE!
GET BACK! IT'S DANGEROUS!
ALIENS ARE EVERYWHERE!

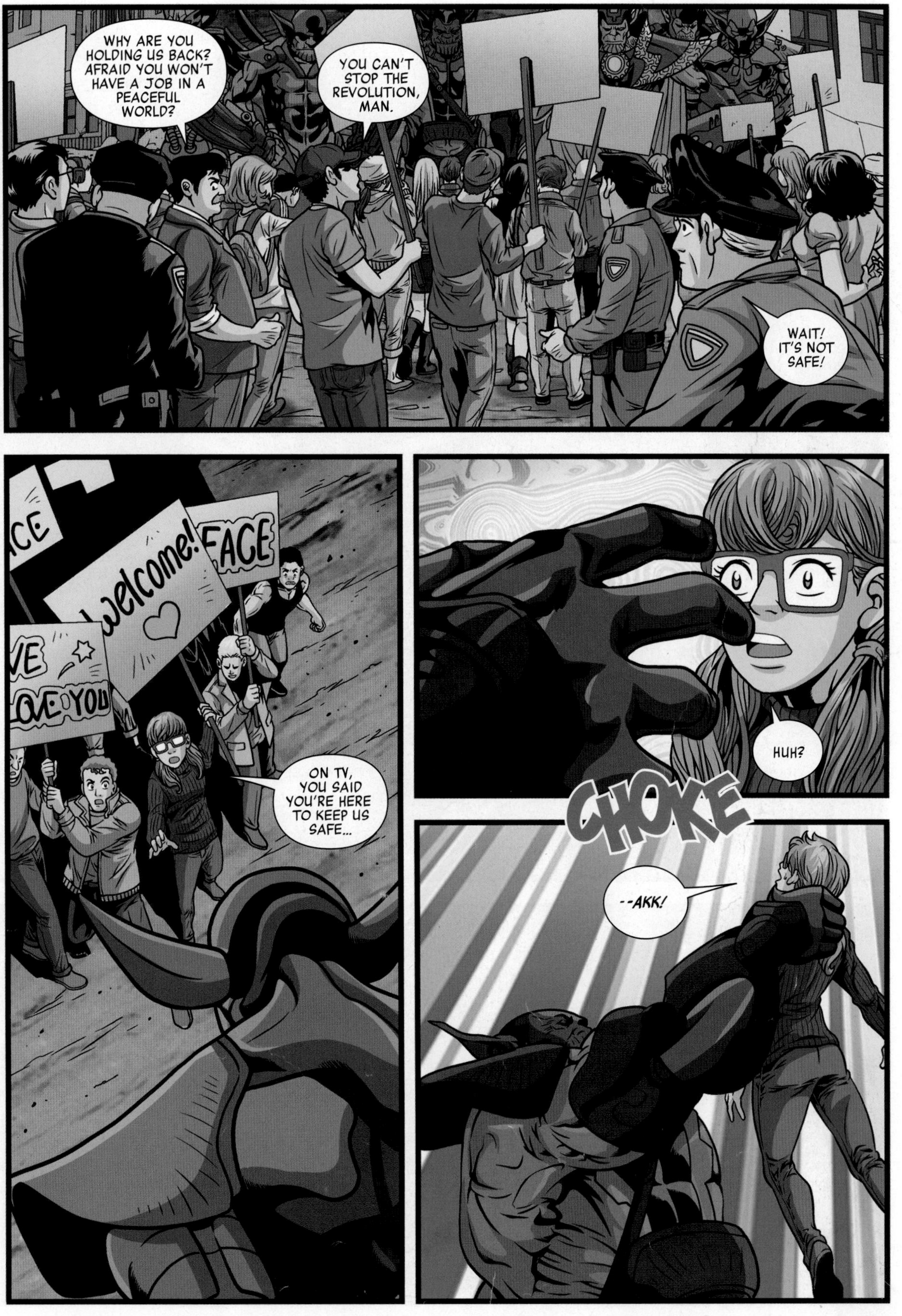
WHY ARE YOU HOLDING US BACK? AFRAID YOU WON'T HAVE A JOB IN A PEACEFUL WORLD?
YOU CAN'T STOP THE REVOLUTION, MAN.
WAIT! IT'S NOT SAFE!
EACE
Welcome!
EACE
VE
LOVE YOU
ON TV, YOU SAID YOU'RE HERE TO KEEP US SAFE...
HUH?
CHOKE
--AKK!

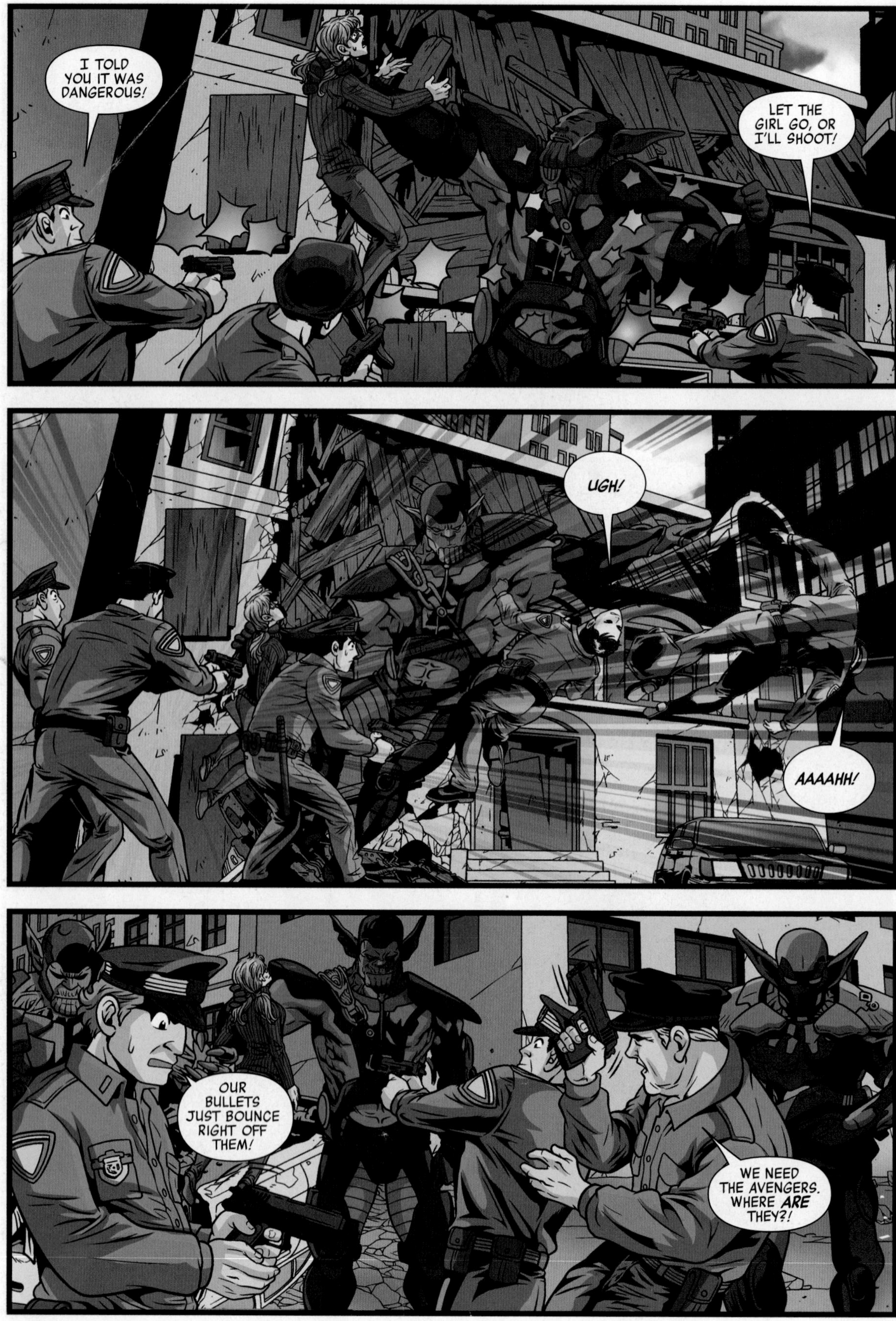
I TOLD YOU IT WAS DANGEROUS!
LET THE GIRL GO, OR I'LL SHOOT!
UGH!
AAAAHH!
OUR BULLETS JUST BOUNCE RIGHT OFF THEM!
WE NEED THE AVENGERS. WHERE ARE THEY?!

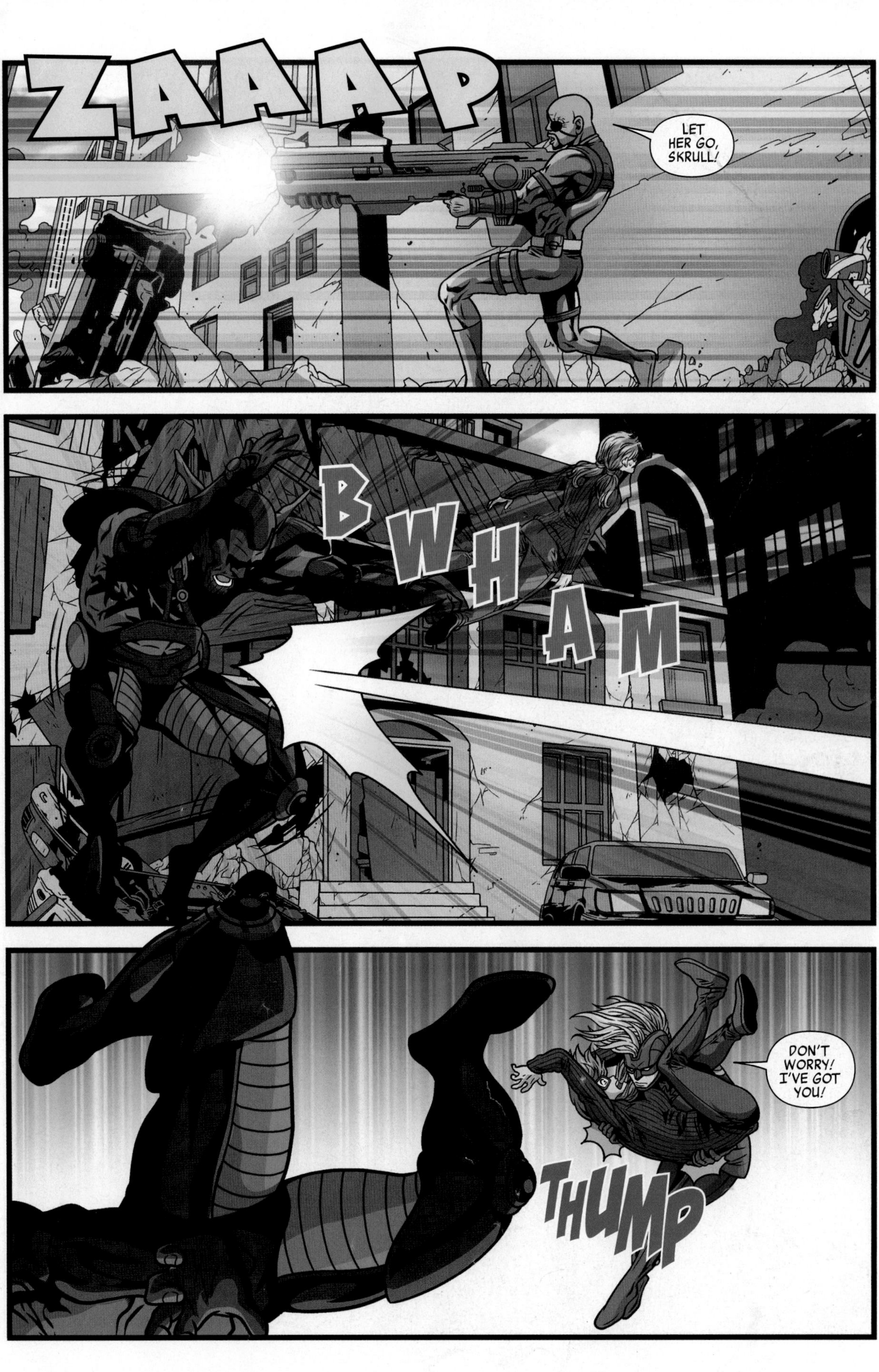
ZAAAP!
LET HER GO, SKRULL!
BWHAM
DON'T WORRY! I'VE GOT YOU!
THUMP

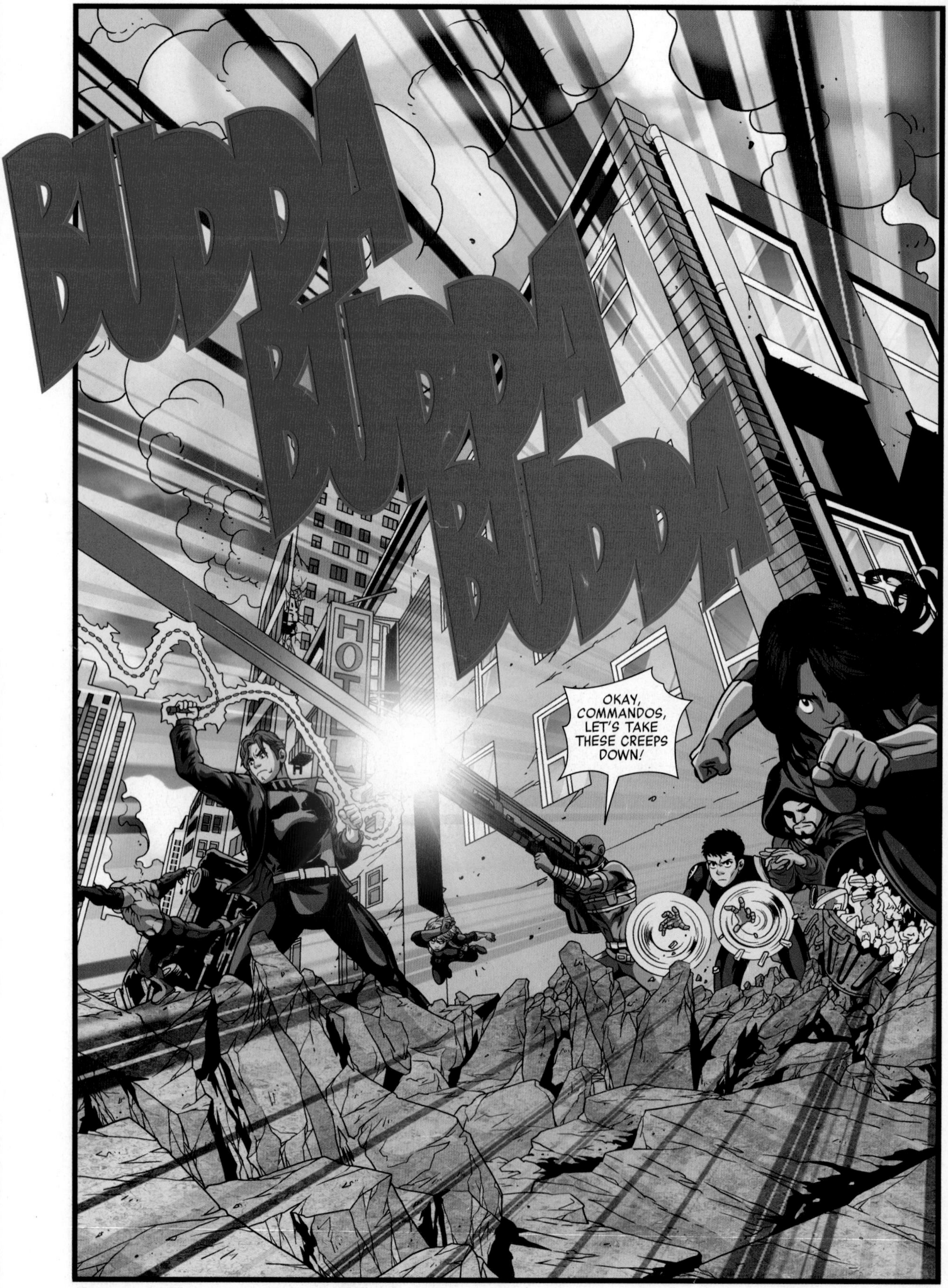
BUDDA
BUDDA
BUDDA
OKAY, COMMANDOS, LET'S TAKE THESE CREEPS DOWN!
HOT

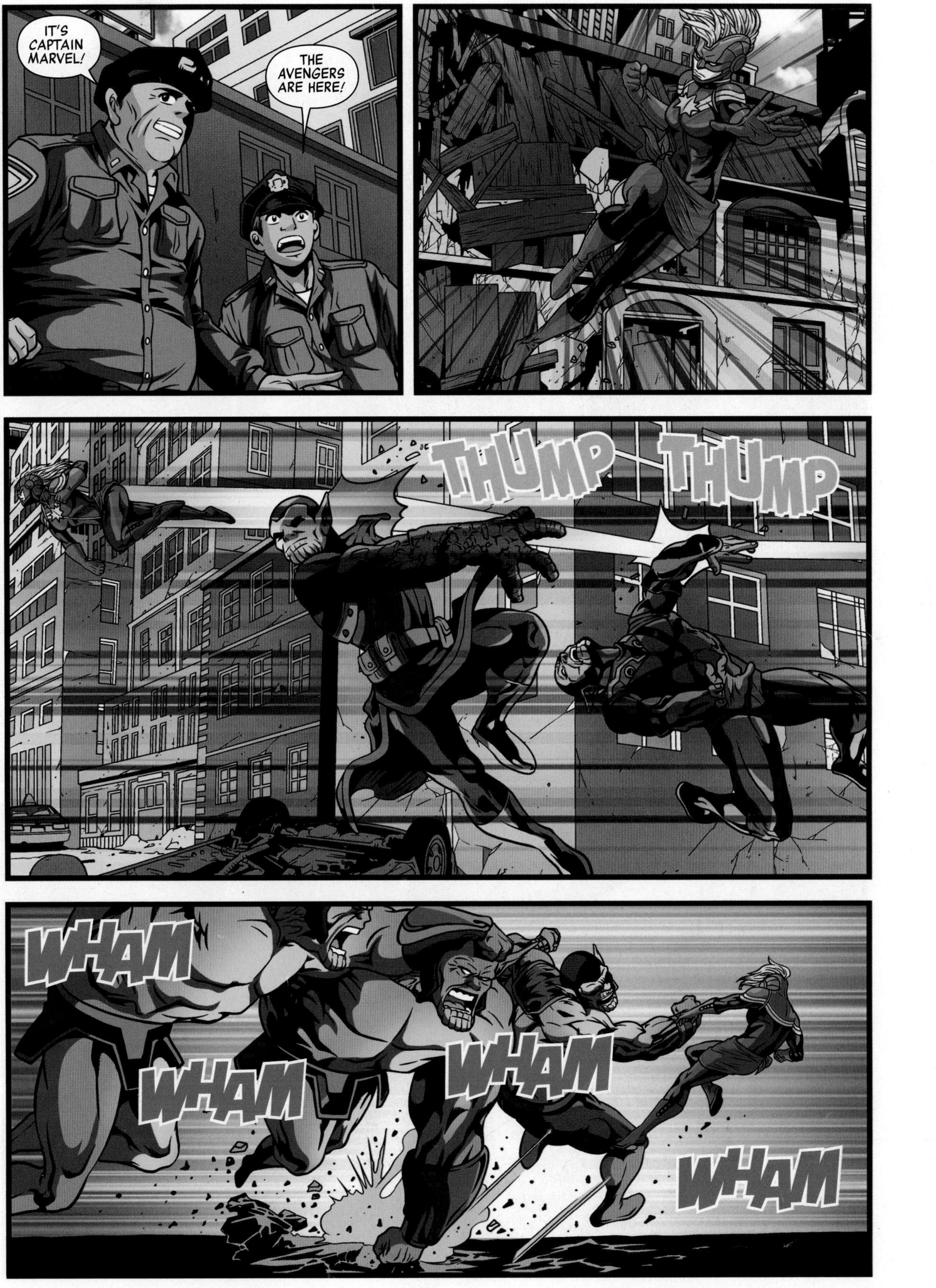
IT'S CAPTAIN MARVEL!
THE AVENGERS ARE HERE!
THUMP
THUMP
WHAM
WHAM
WHAM
WHAM

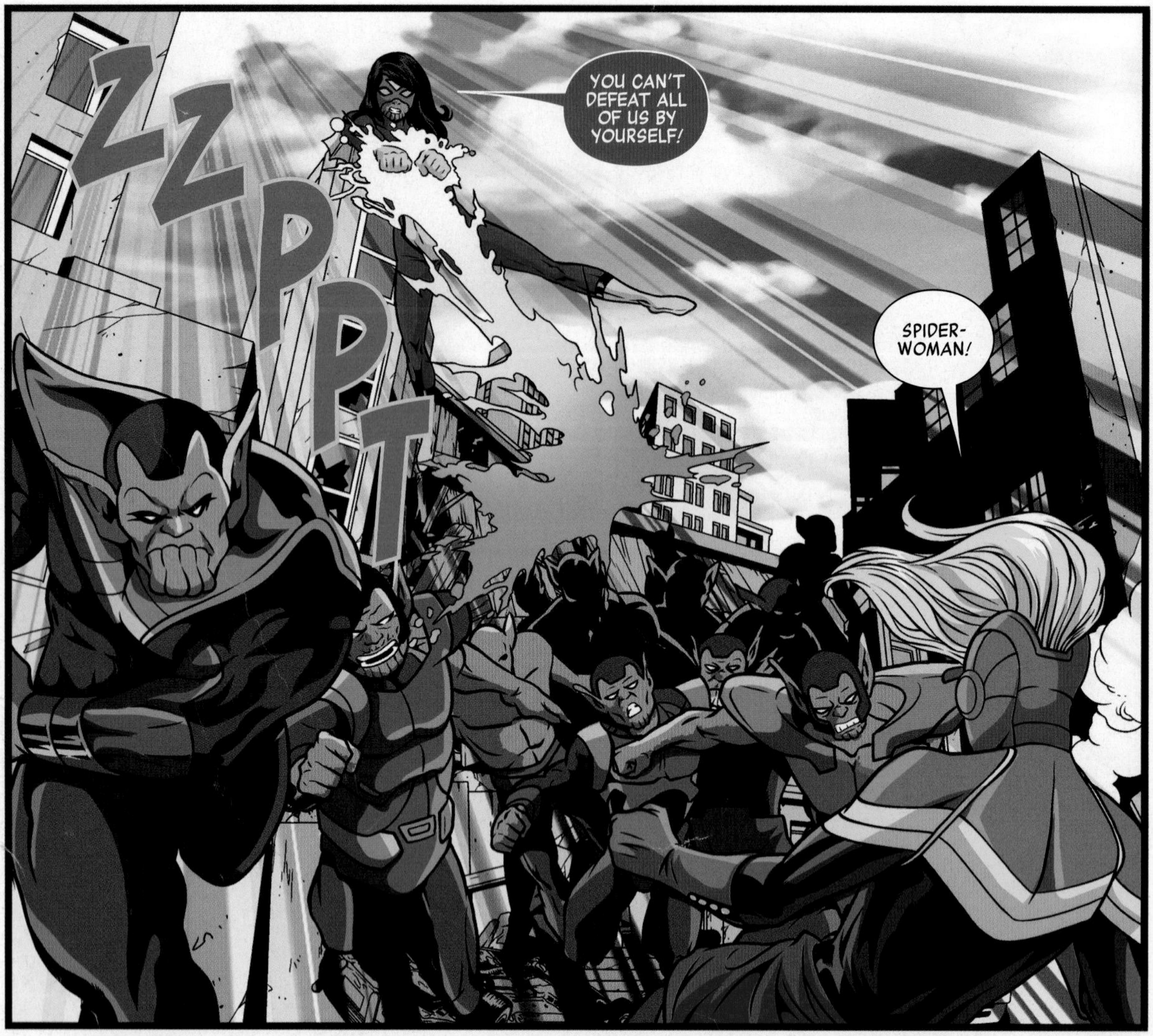
ZZZPPPT
YOU CAN'T DEFEAT ALL OF US BY YOURSELF!
SPIDER-WOMAN!

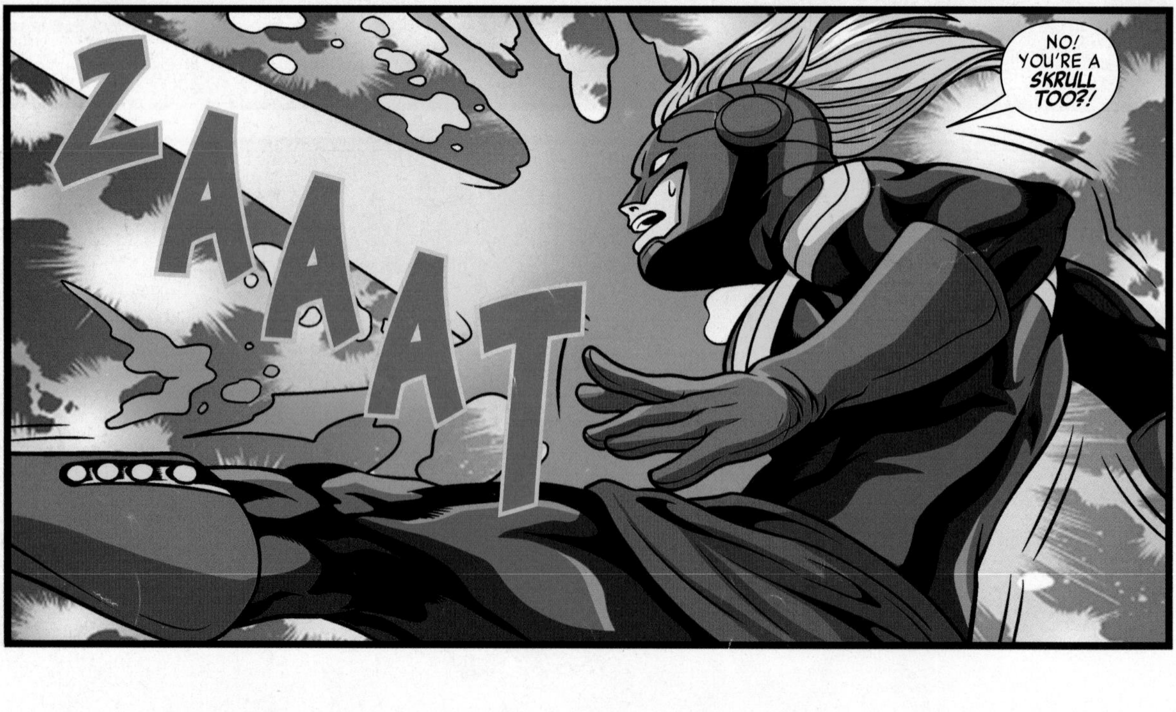
NO! YOU'RE A SKRULL TOO?!
ZAAAAT

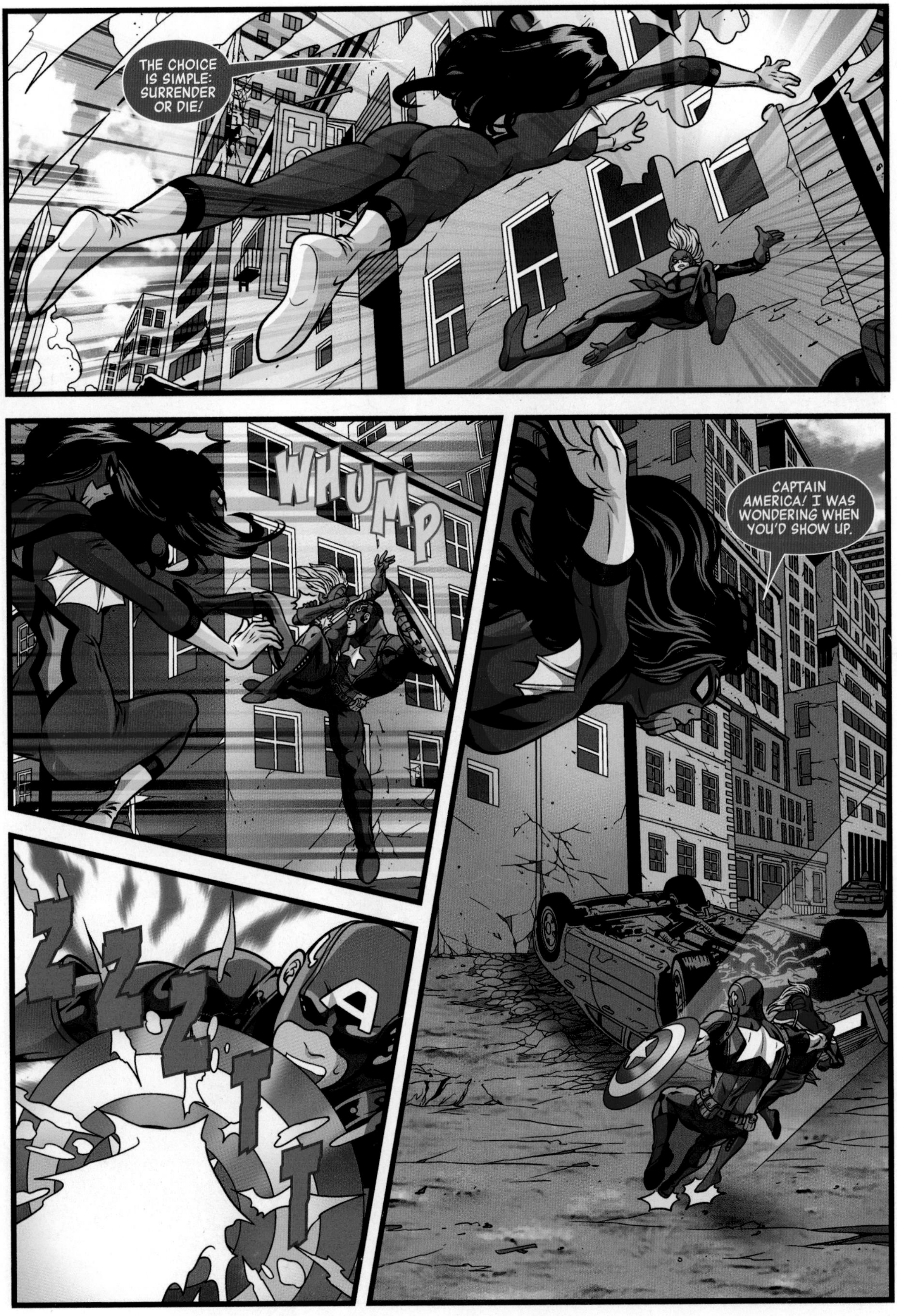

THE CHOICE IS SIMPLE: SURRENDER OR DIE!
WHUMP
CAPTAIN AMERICA! I WAS WONDERING WHEN YOU'D SHOW UP.
ZZZZTTT

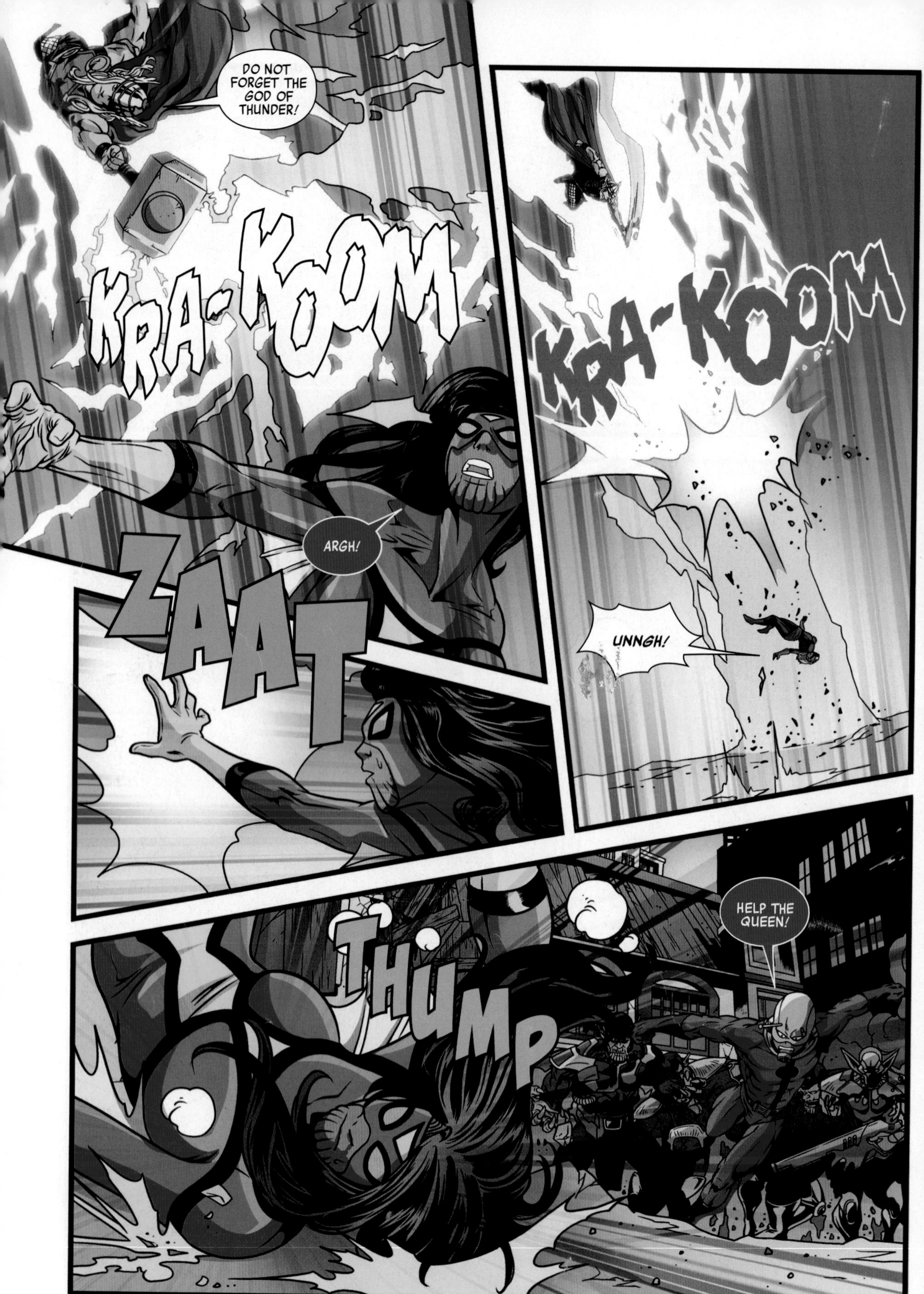

DO NOT FORGET THE GOD OF THUNDER!
KRA-KOOM
ARGH!
KRA-KOOM
UNNGH!
ZAAT
THUMP
HELP THE QUEEN!

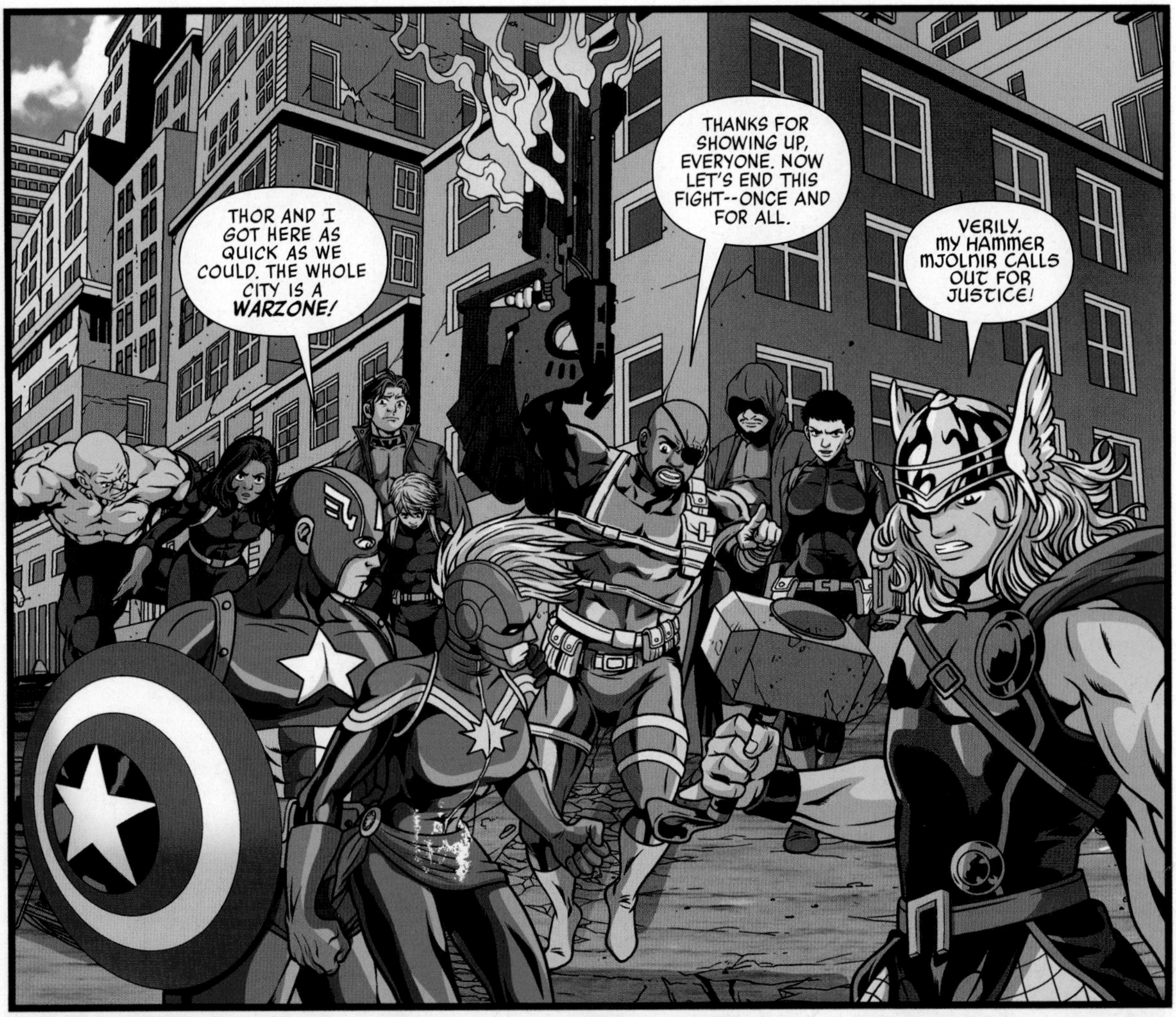
THOR AND I GOT HERE AS QUICK AS WE COULD. THE WHOLE CITY IS A WARZONE!
THANKS FOR SHOWING UP, EVERYONE. NOW LET'S END THIS FIGHT--ONCE AND FOR ALL.
VERILY. MY HAMMER MJOLNIR CALLS OUT FOR JUSTICE!
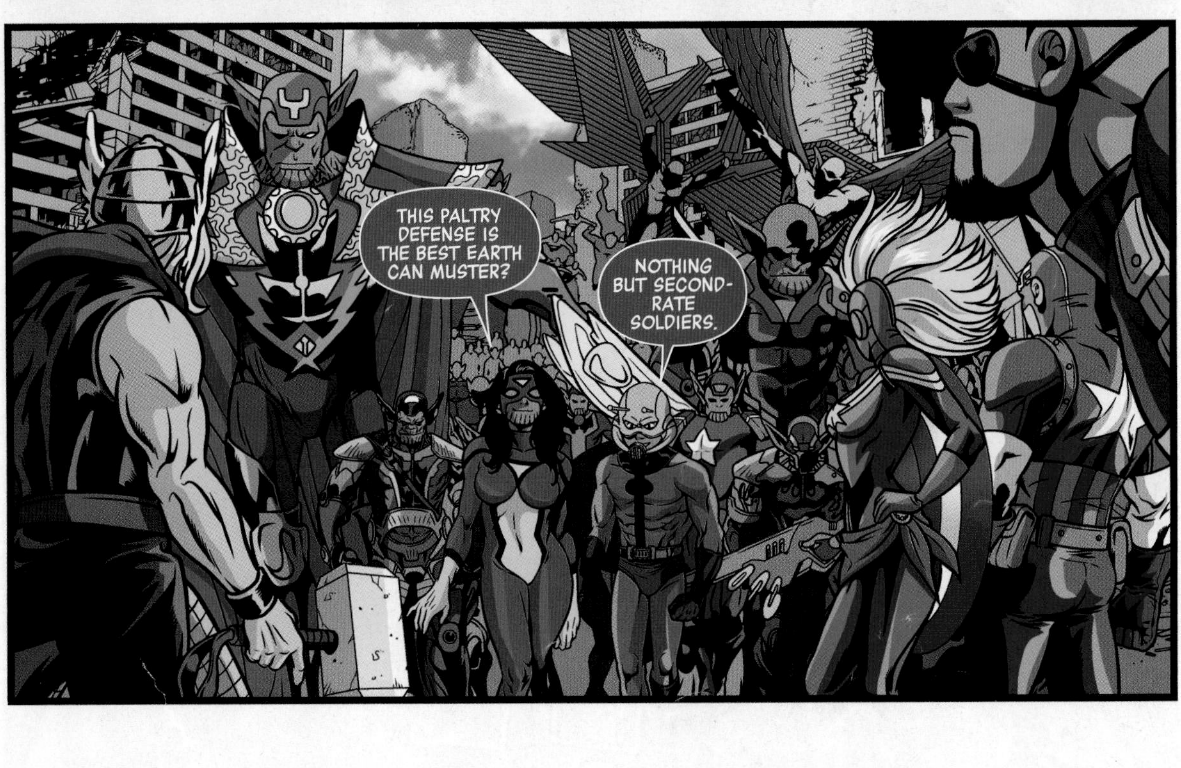
THIS PALTRY DEFENSE IS THE BEST EARTH CAN MUSTER?
NOTHING BUT SECOND-RATE SOLDIERS.

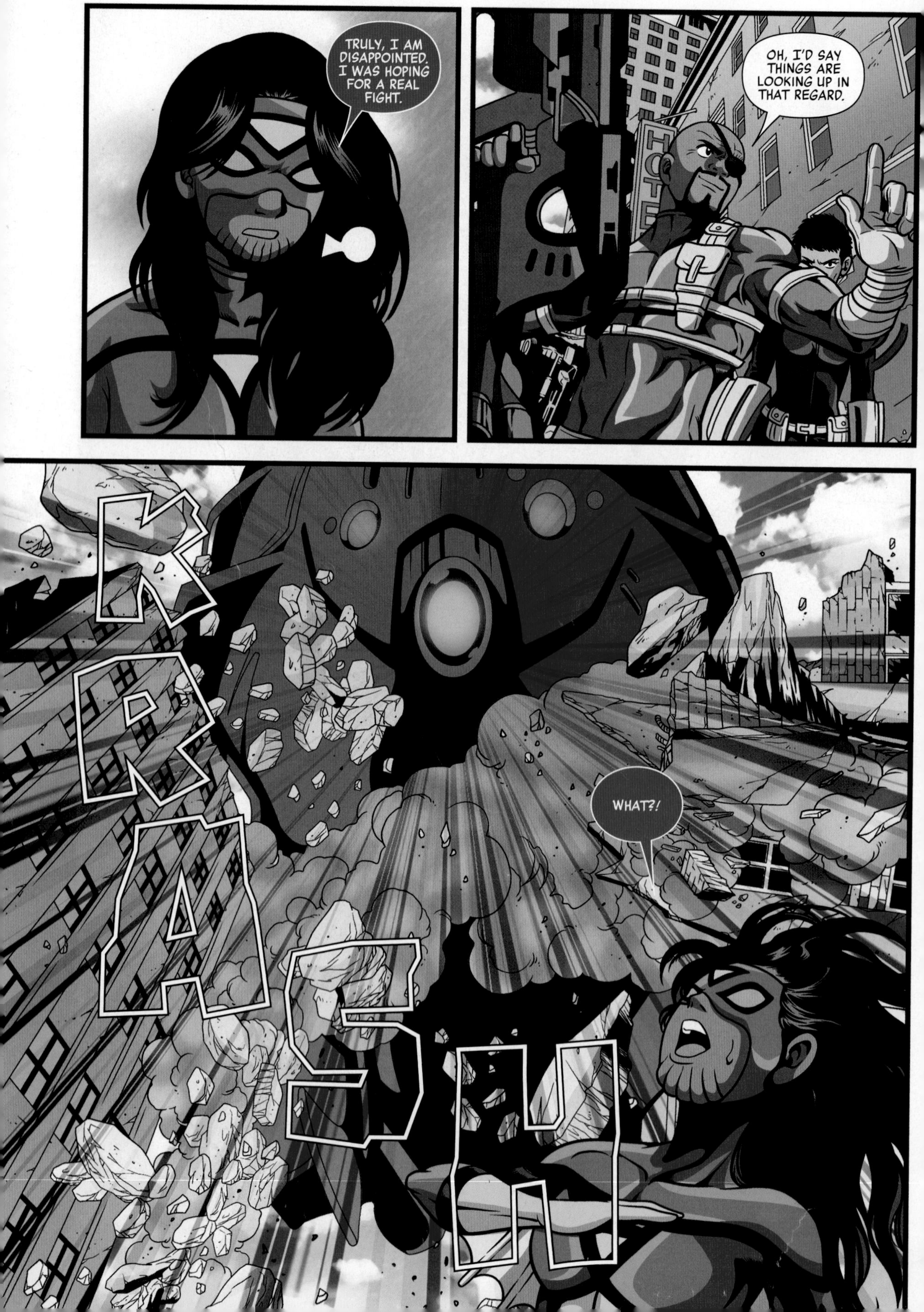
TRULY, I AM DISAPPOINTED. I WAS HOPING FOR A REAL FIGHT.
OH, I'D SAY THINGS ARE LOOKING UP IN THAT REGARD.
KRAASH
WHAT?!

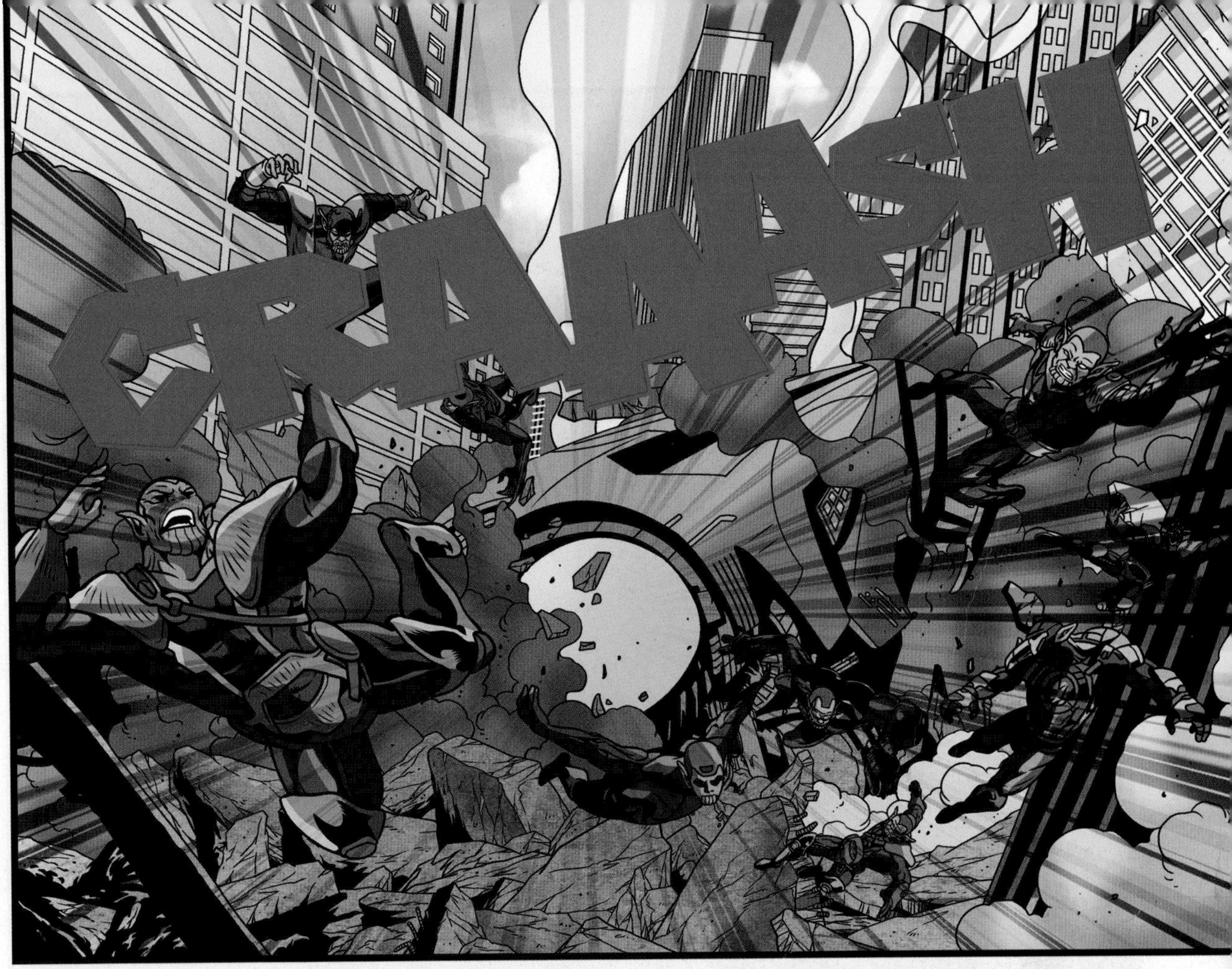
CRAAASH

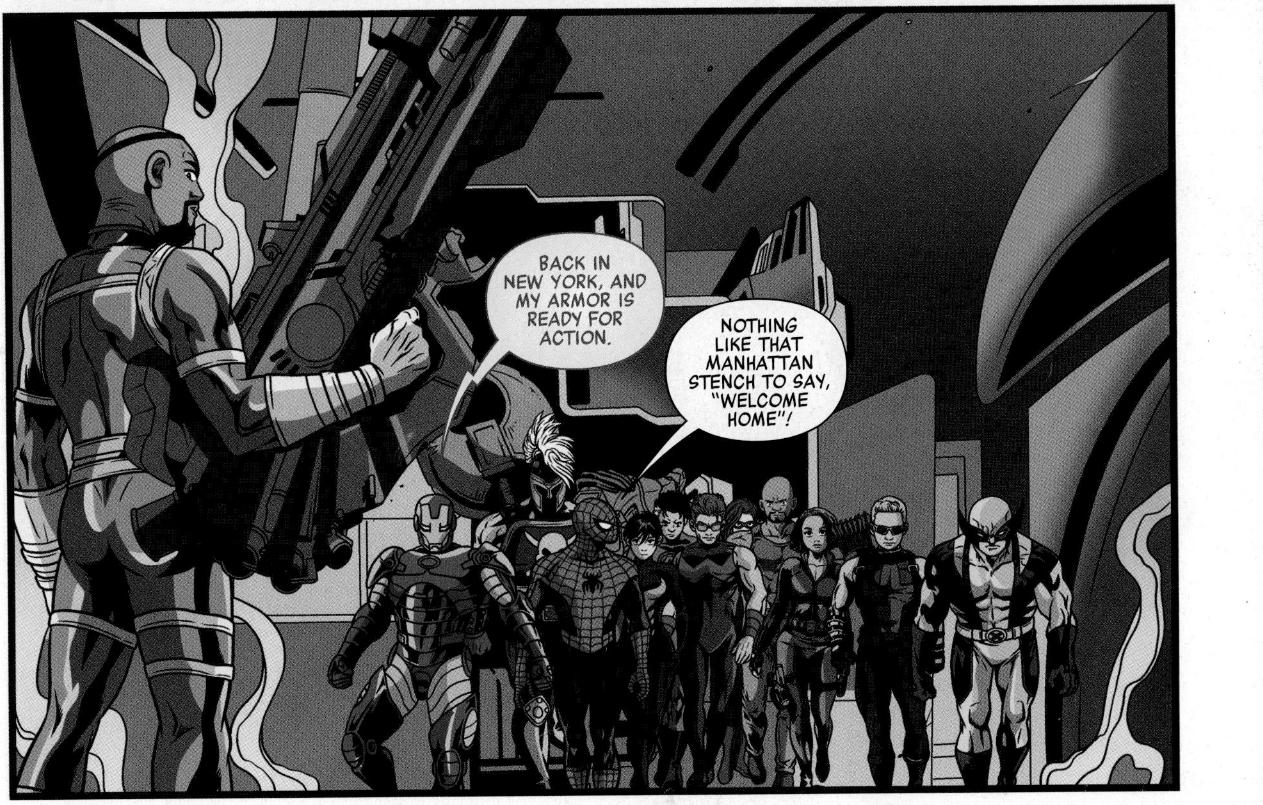
BACK IN NEW YORK, AND MY ARMOR IS READY FOR ACTION.
NOTHING LIKE THAT MANHATTAN STENCH TO SAY, "WELCOME HOME"!

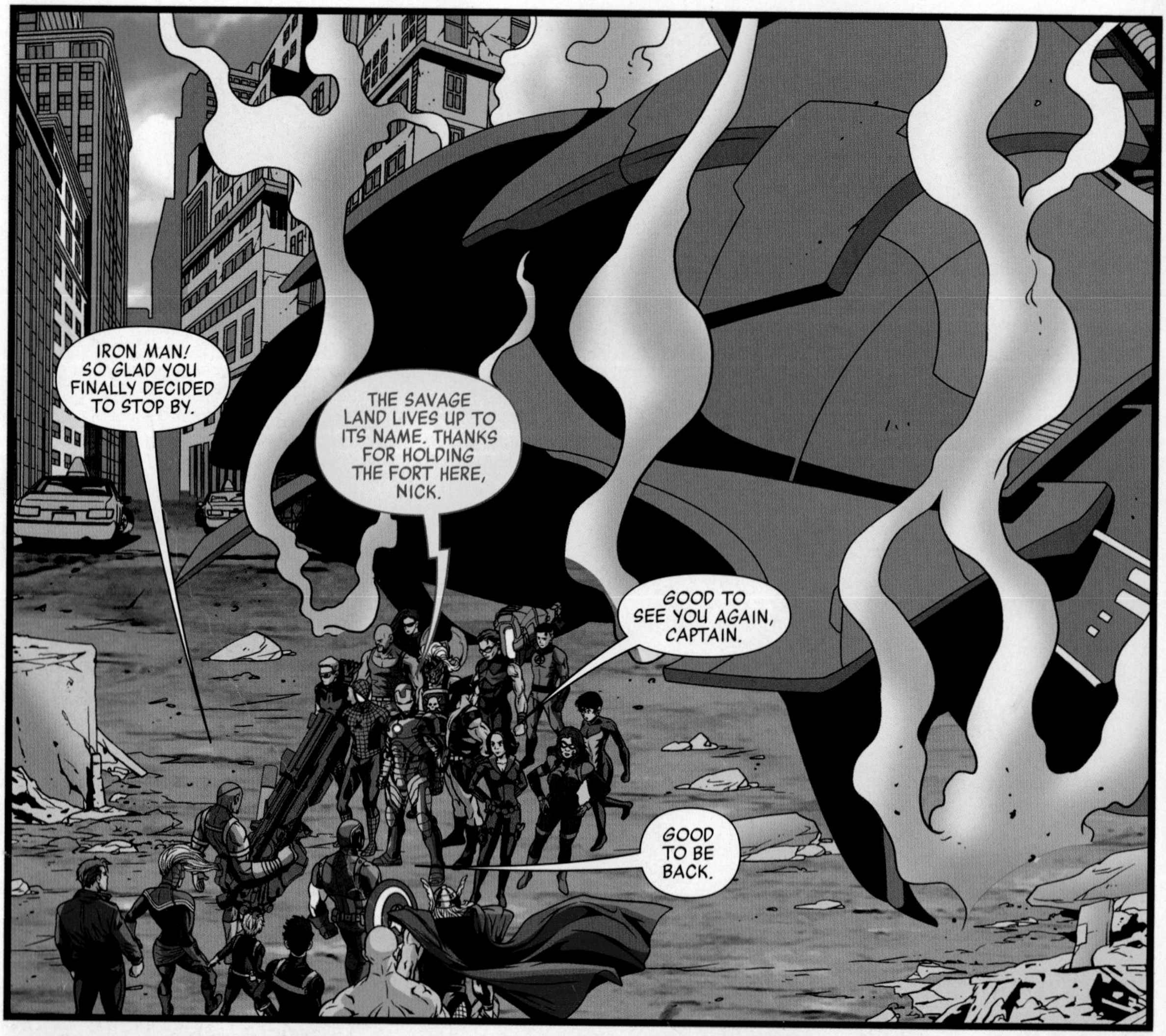
IRON MAN! SO GLAD YOU FINALLY DECIDED TO STOP BY.
THE SAVAGE LAND LIVES UP TO ITS NAME. THANKS FOR HOLDING THE FORT HERE, NICK.
GOOD TO SEE YOU AGAIN, CAPTAIN.
GOOD TO BE BACK.

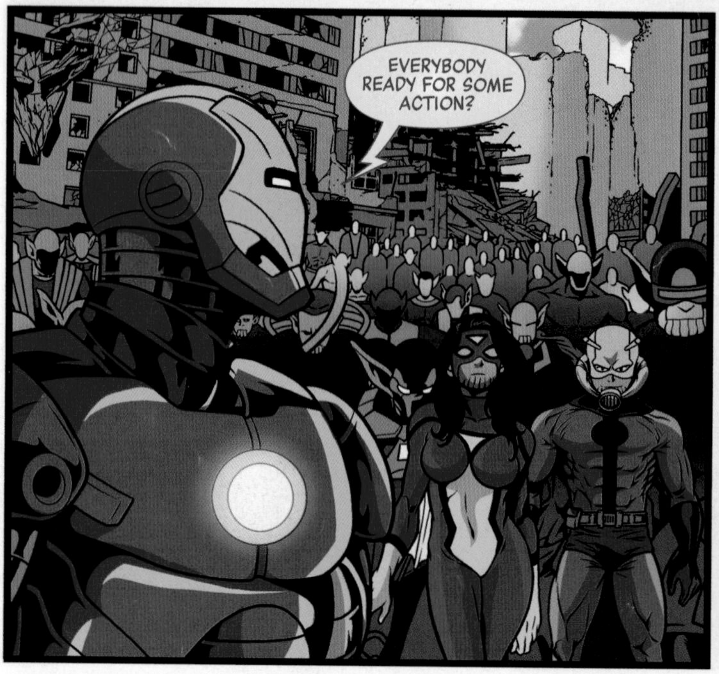
EVERYBODY READY FOR SOME ACTION?

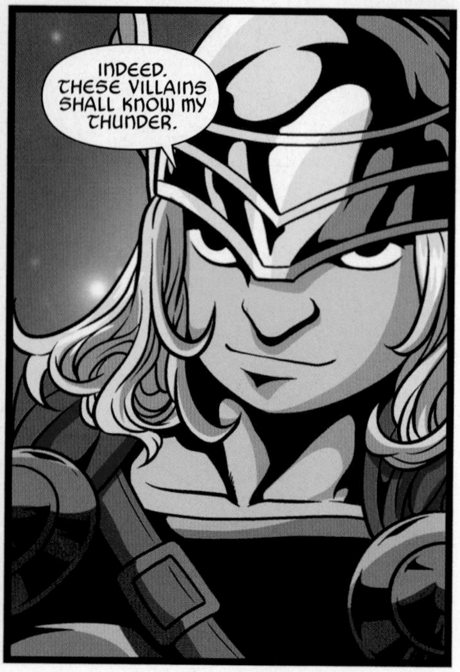
INDEED. THESE VILLAINS SHALL KNOW MY THUNDER.

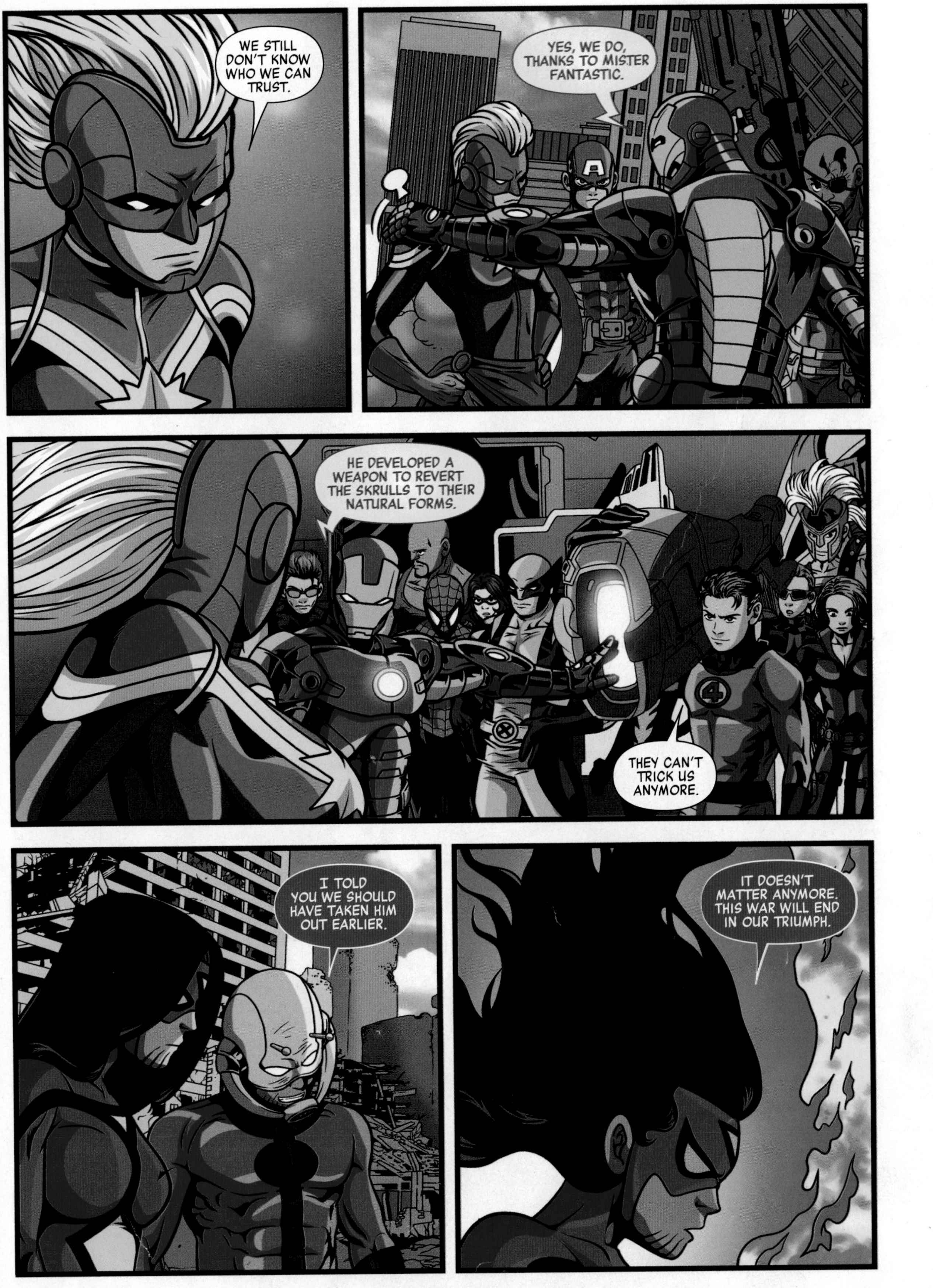
WE STILL DON'T KNOW WHO WE CAN TRUST.
YES, WE DO, THANKS TO MISTER FANTASTIC.
HE DEVELOPED A WEAPON TO REVERT THE SKRULLS TO THEIR NATURAL FORMS.
THEY CAN'T TRICK US ANYMORE.
I TOLD YOU WE SHOULD HAVE TAKEN HIM OUT EARLIER.
IT DOESN'T MATTER ANYMORE. THIS WAR WILL END IN OUR TRIUMPH.

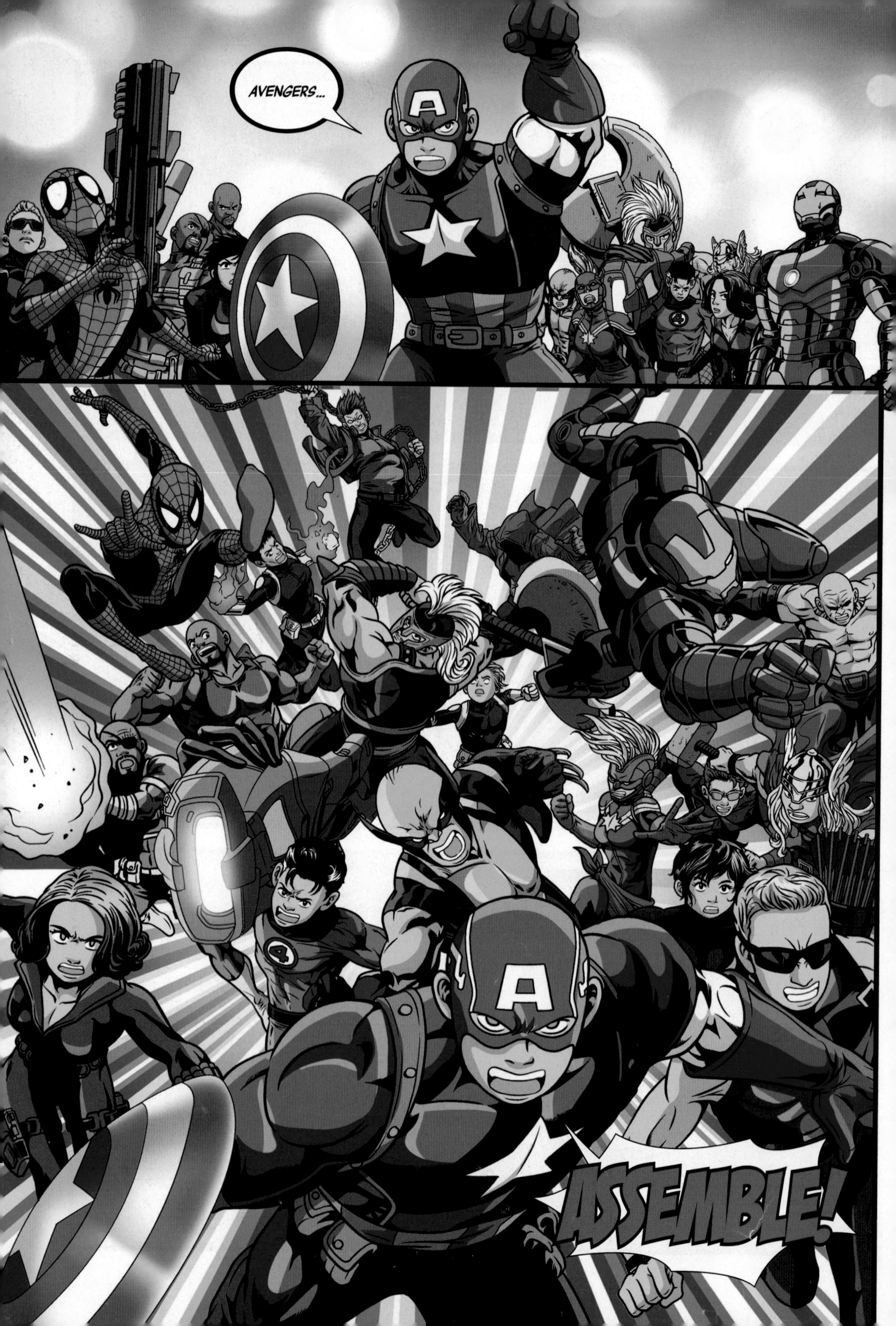
AVENGERS...
ASSEMBLE!

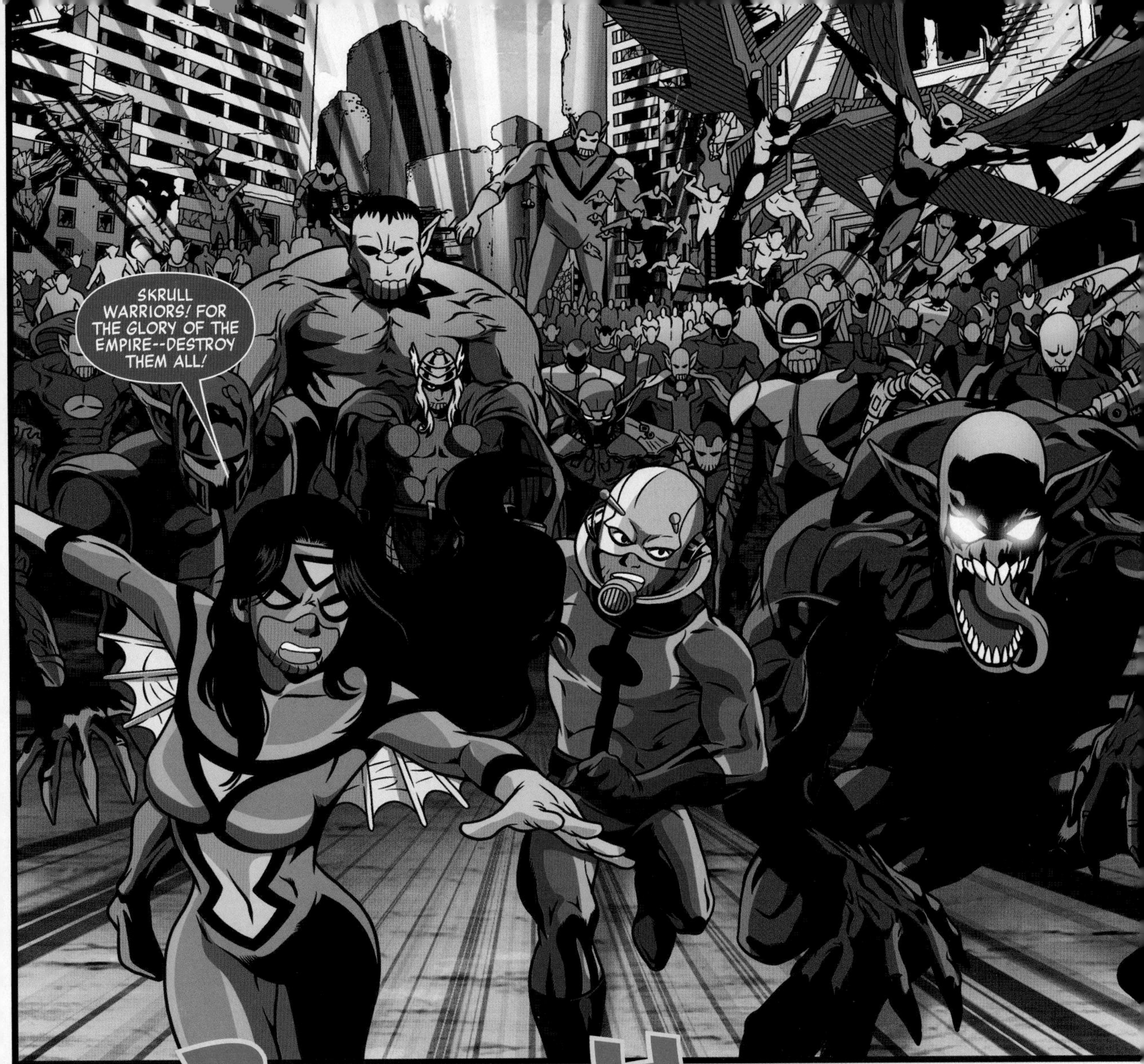
SKRULL WARRIORS! FOR THE GLORY OF THE EMPIRE--DESTROY THEM ALL!

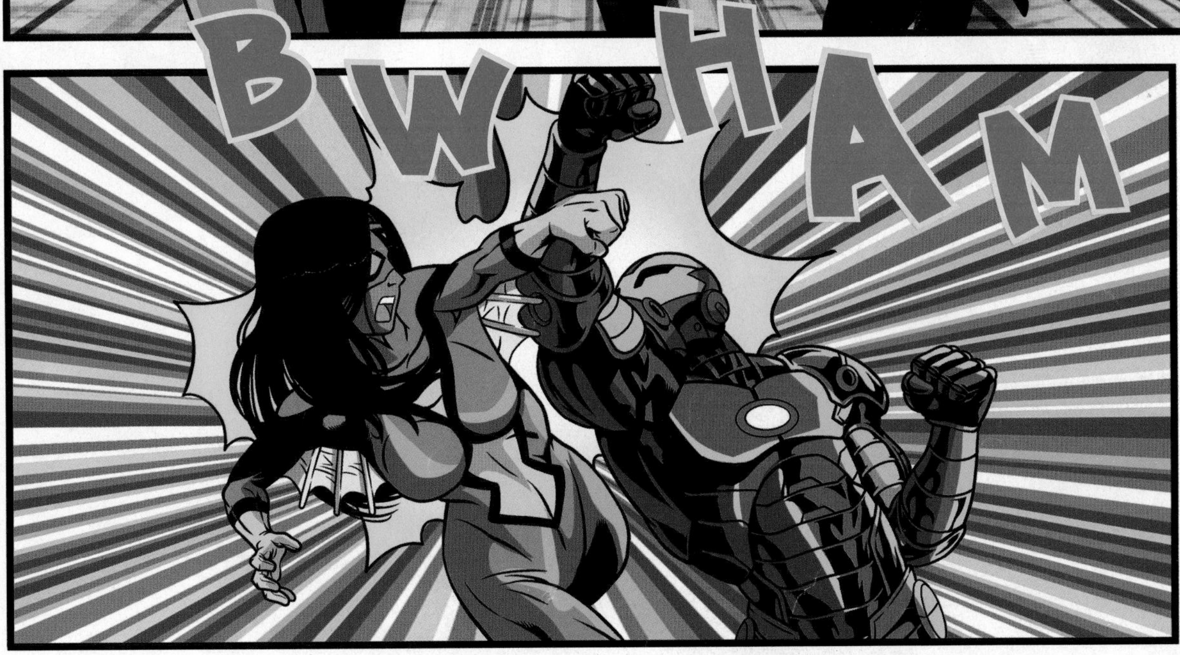
BWHAM

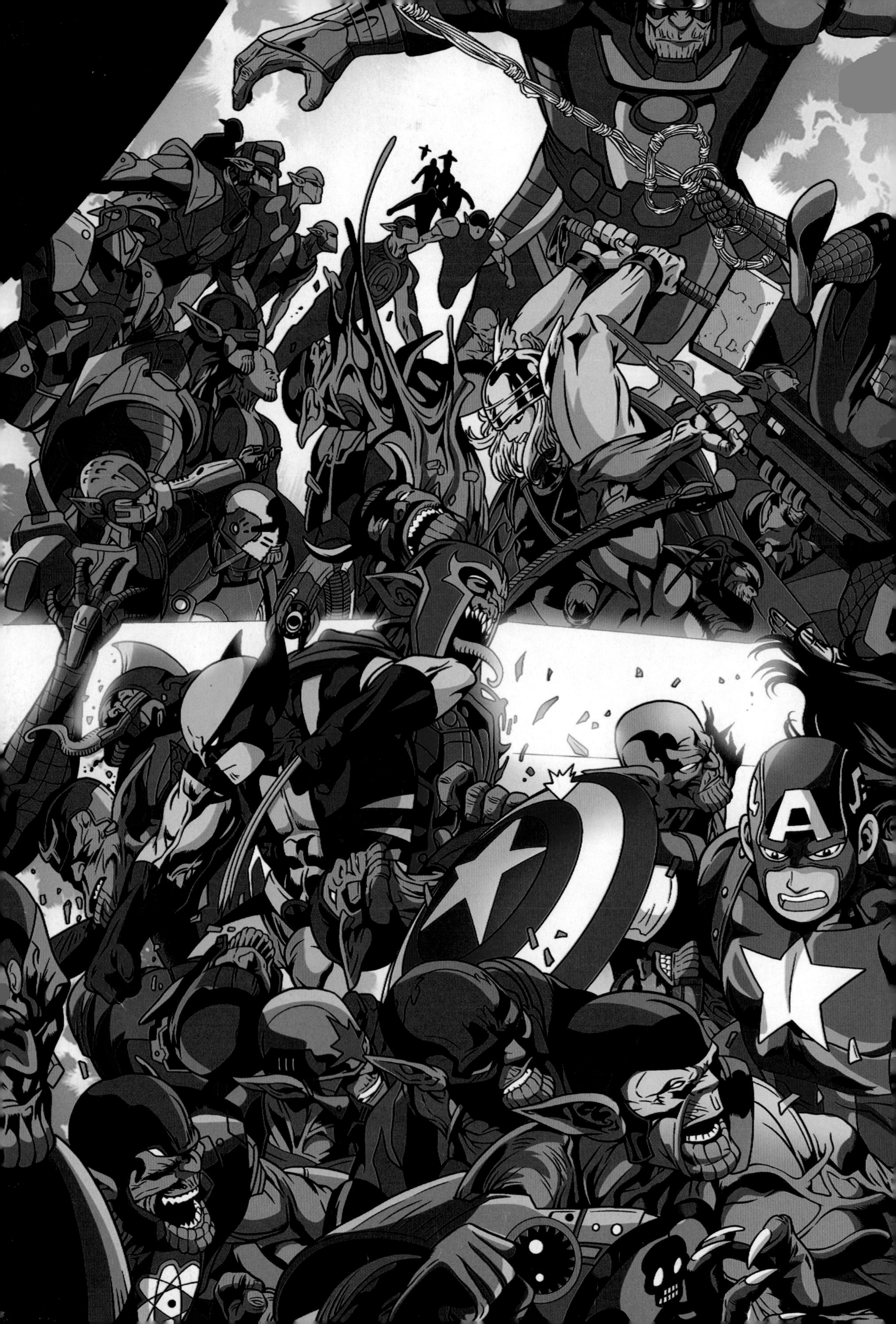

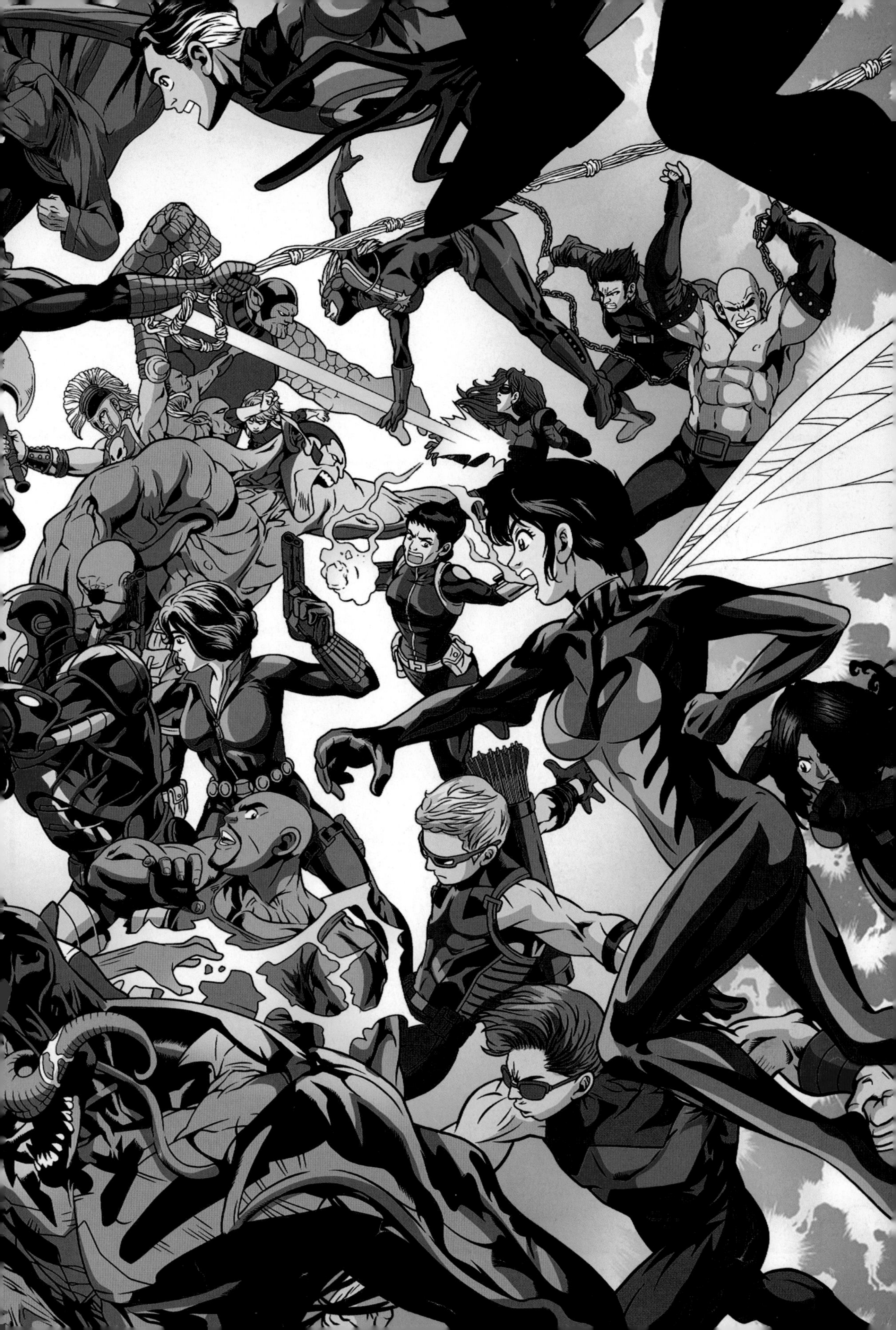

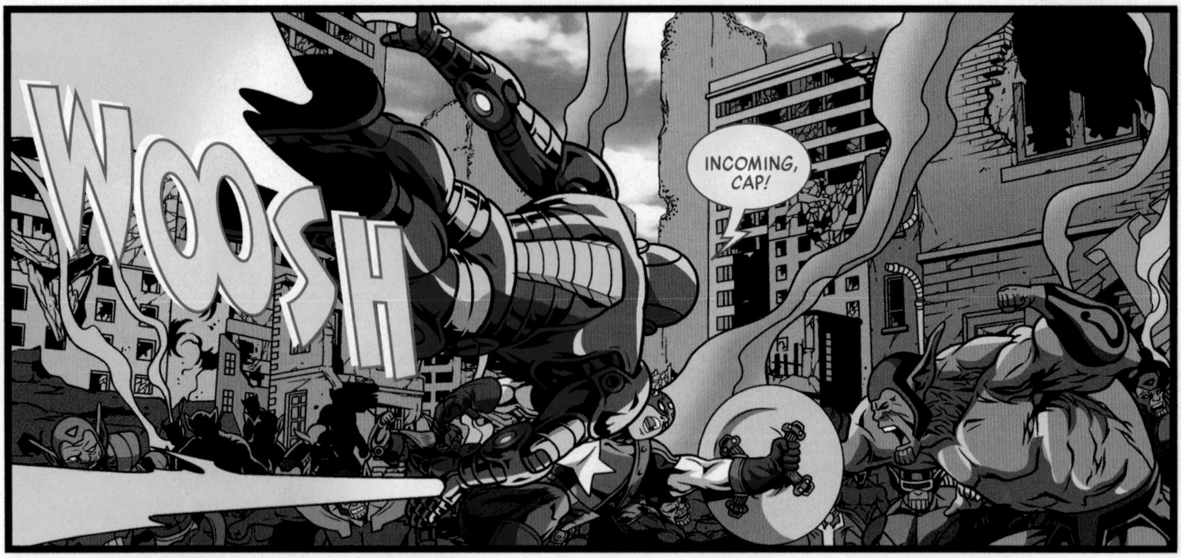
WOOSH
INCOMING, CAP!

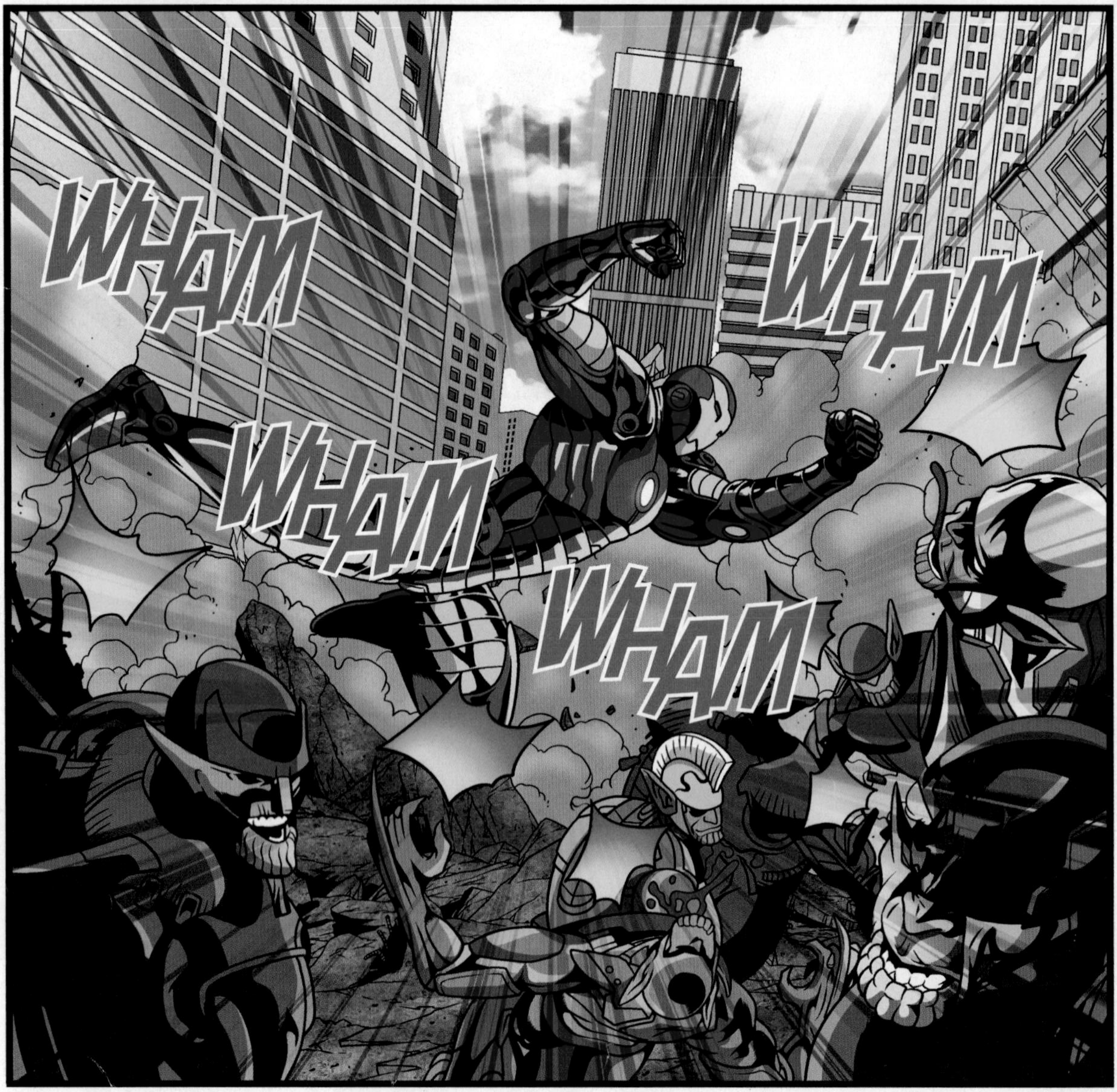
WHAM
WHAM
WHAM
WHAM

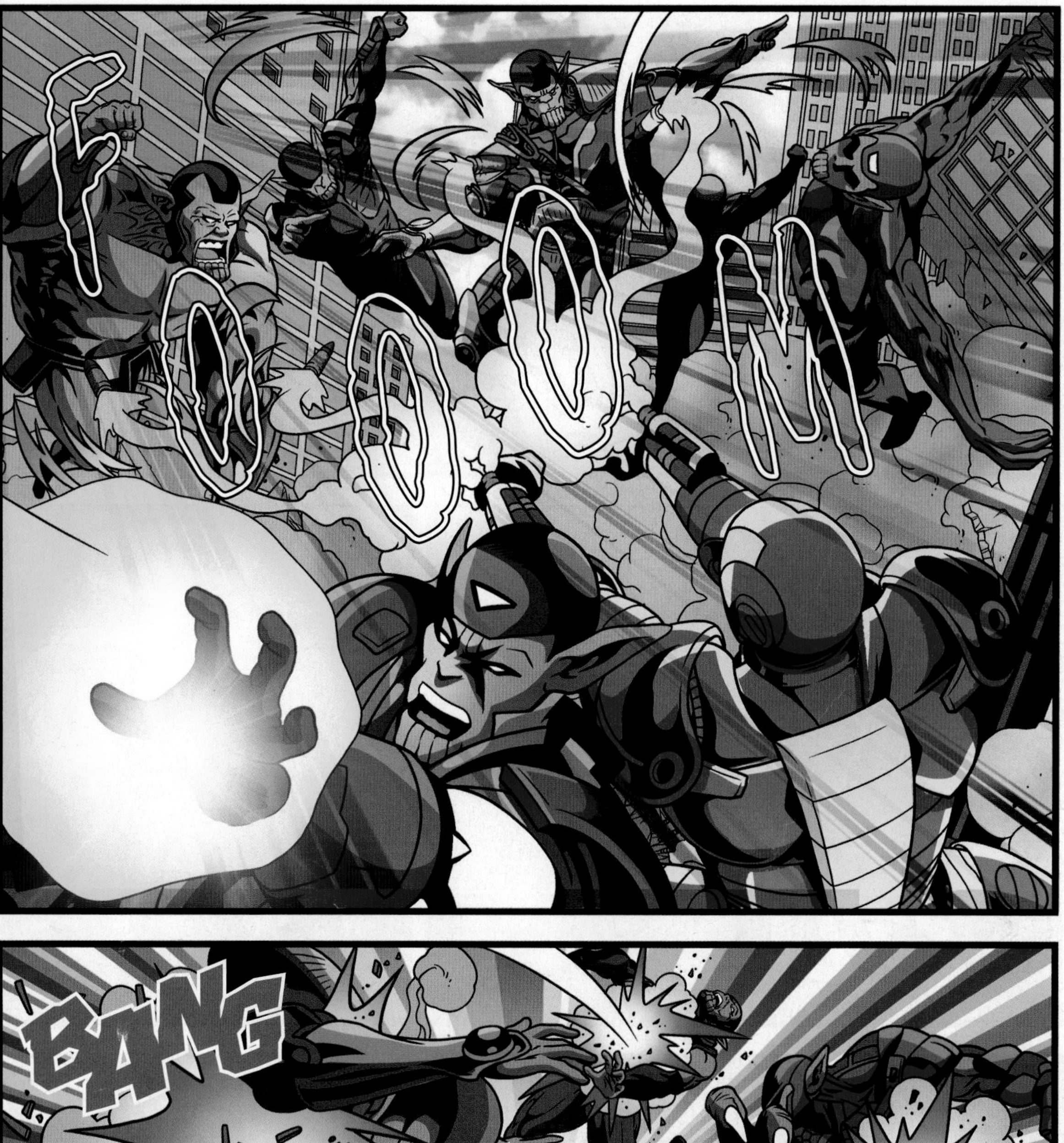
FOOOOM

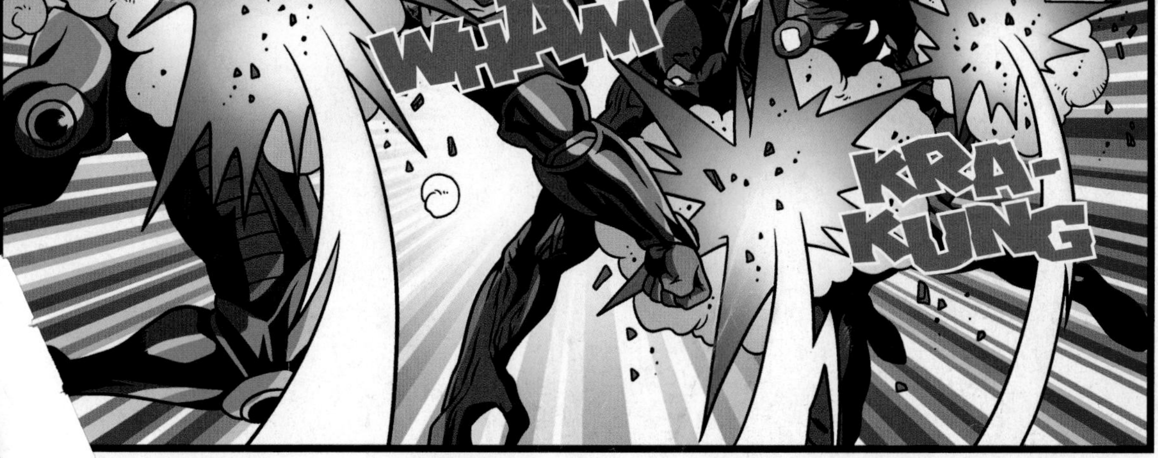
BANG
WHAM
KRA-
KUNG

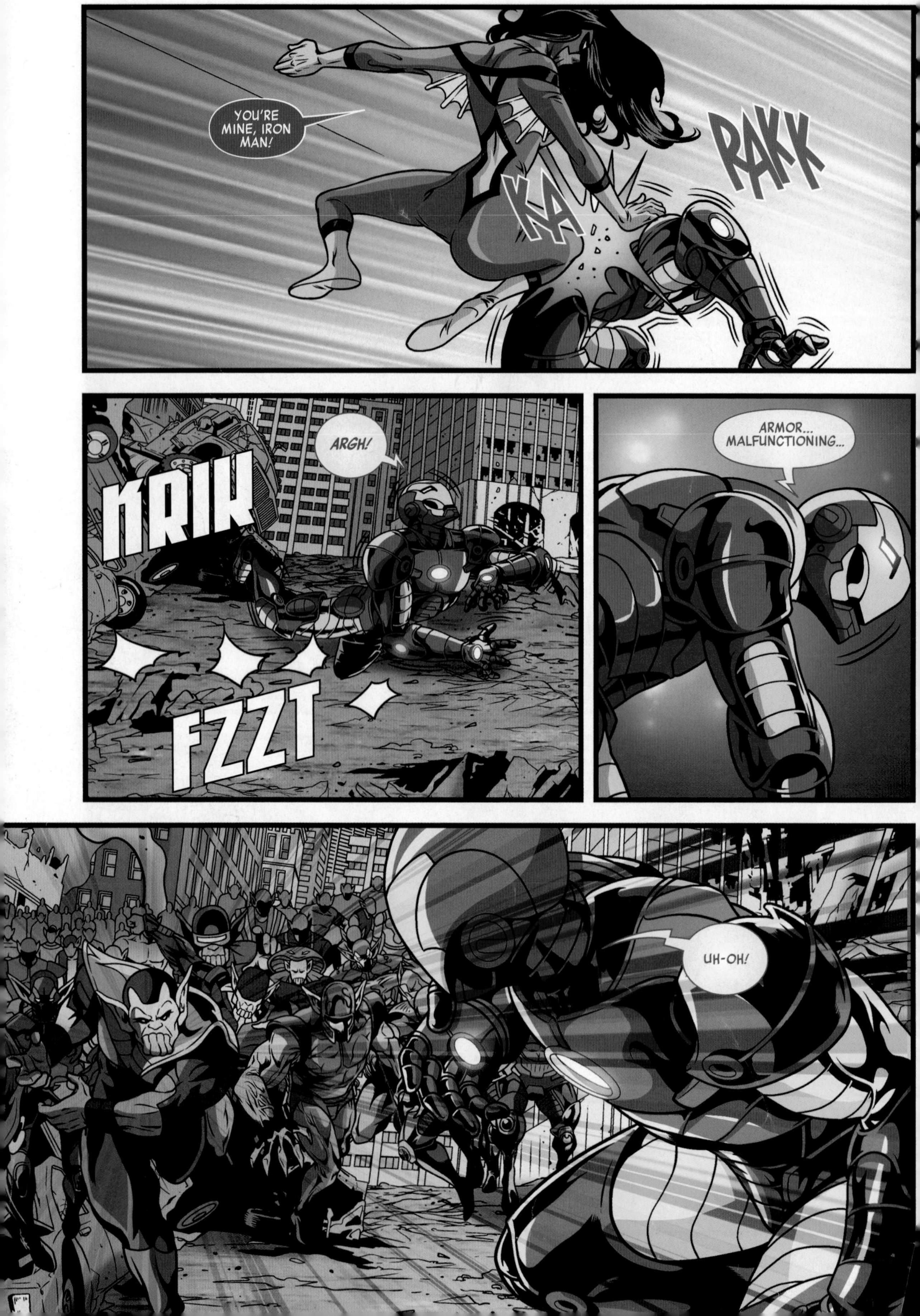
YOU'RE MINE, IRON MAN!
KA
RAKK
KRIK
ARGH!
FZZT
ARMOR... MALFUNCTIONING...
UH-OH!

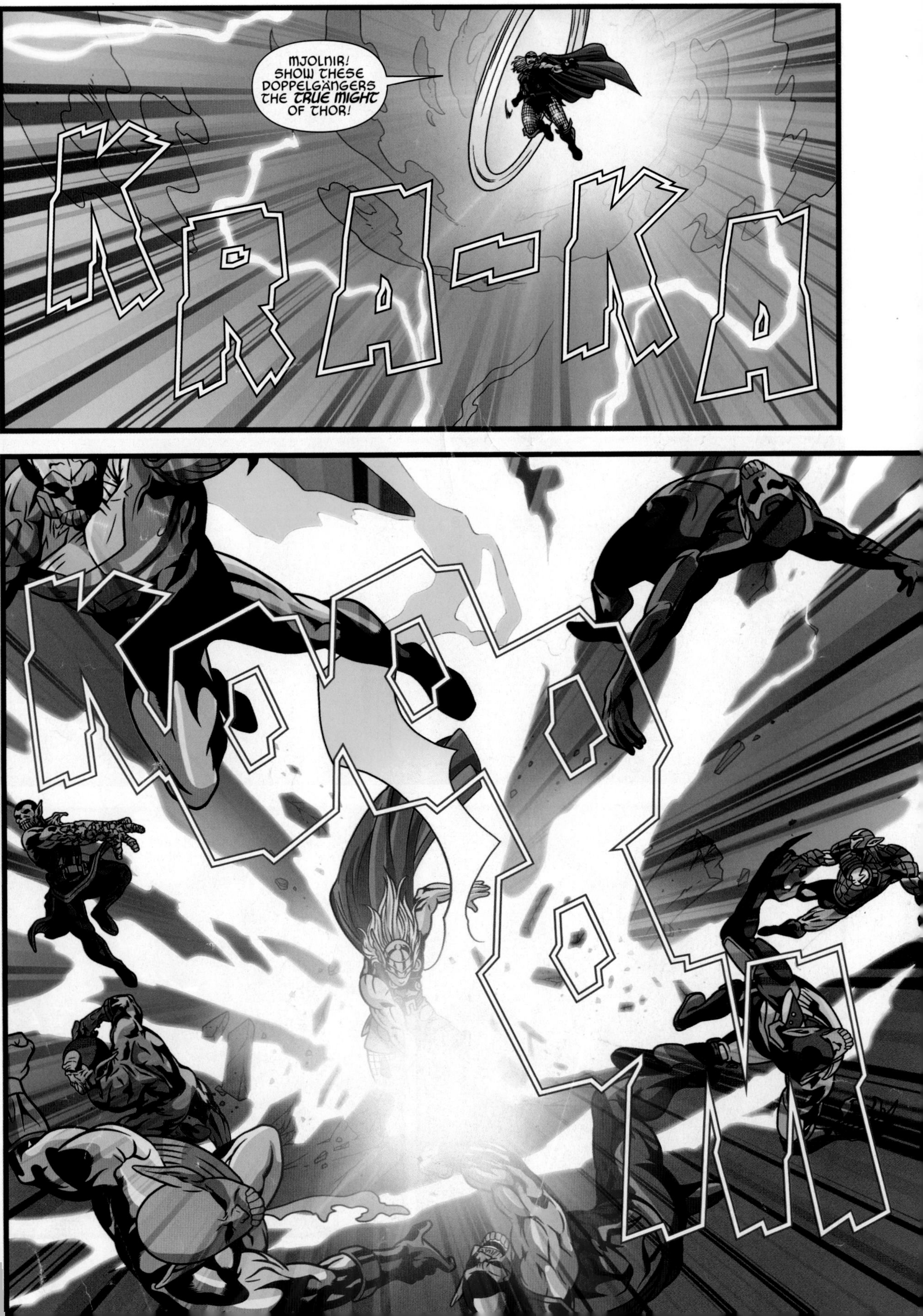
MJOLNIR! SHOW THESE DOPPELGÄNGERS THE TRUE MIGHT OF THOR!
KRA-KA

STOMP
STOMP
IS THERE NO END TO THESE FOUL CREATURES?
THOR! HOLD ON!
TOGETHER WE CAN TURN THE TIDE!
SLAM
KRAK
WHAM
UGH!
KRAK
LEAVE SOME FOR ME, WILL YA, CAP?

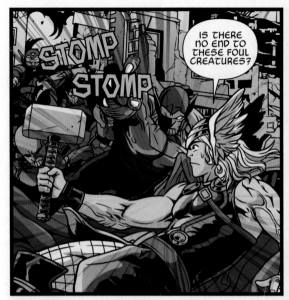

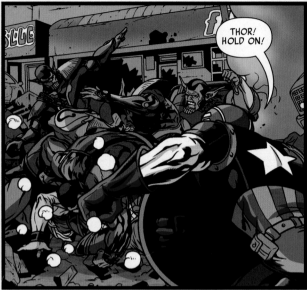

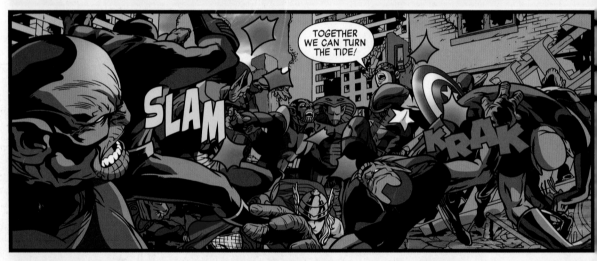

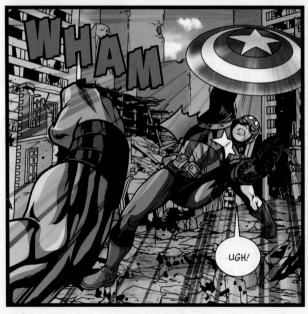

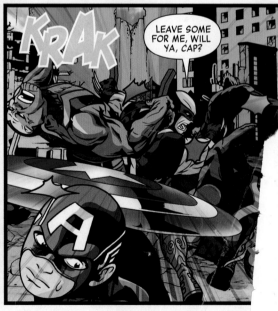

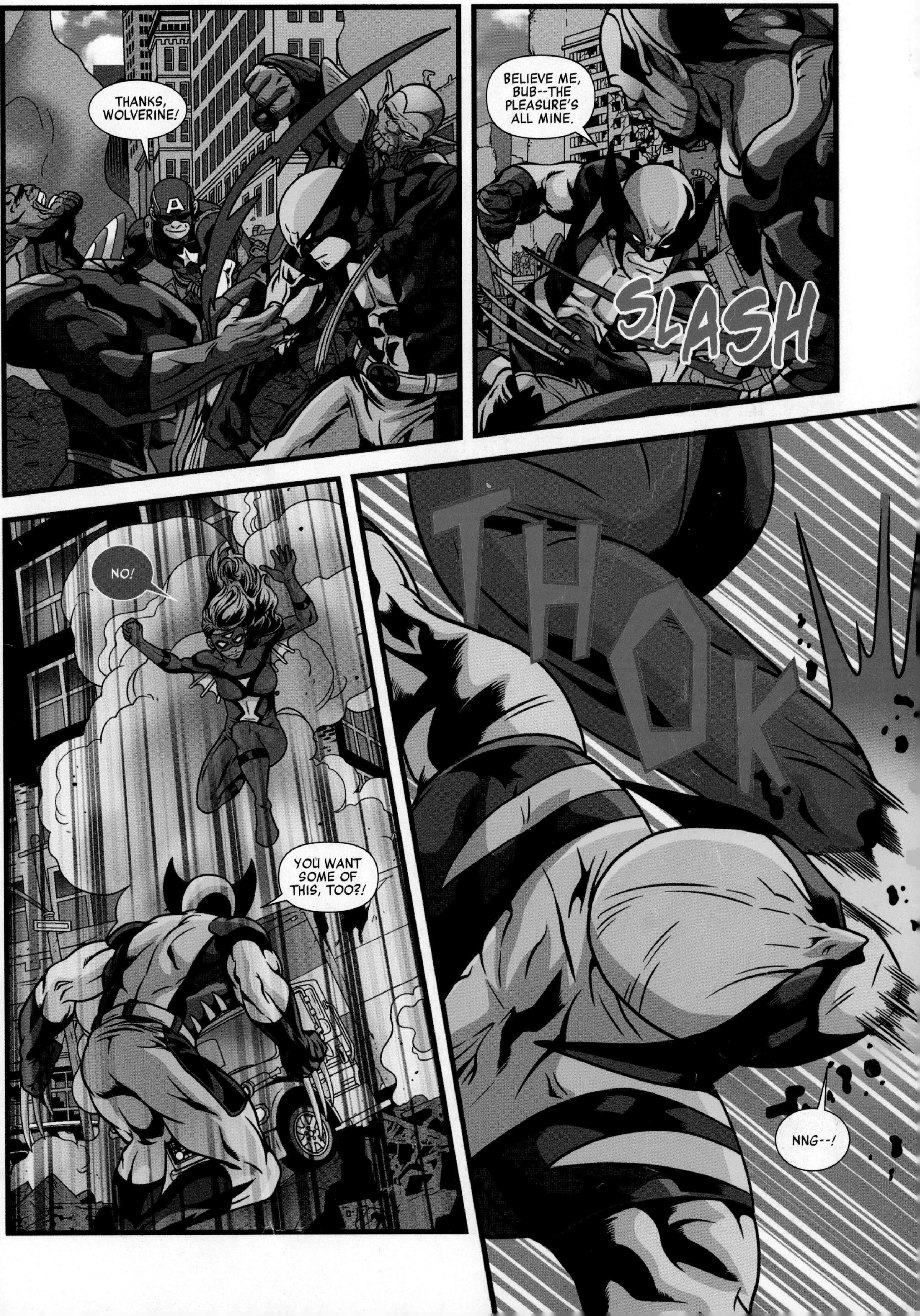
THANKS, WOLVERINE!
BELIEVE ME, BUB--THE PLEASURE'S ALL MINE.
SLASH
NO!
YOU WANT SOME OF THIS, TOO?!
THOK
NNG--!

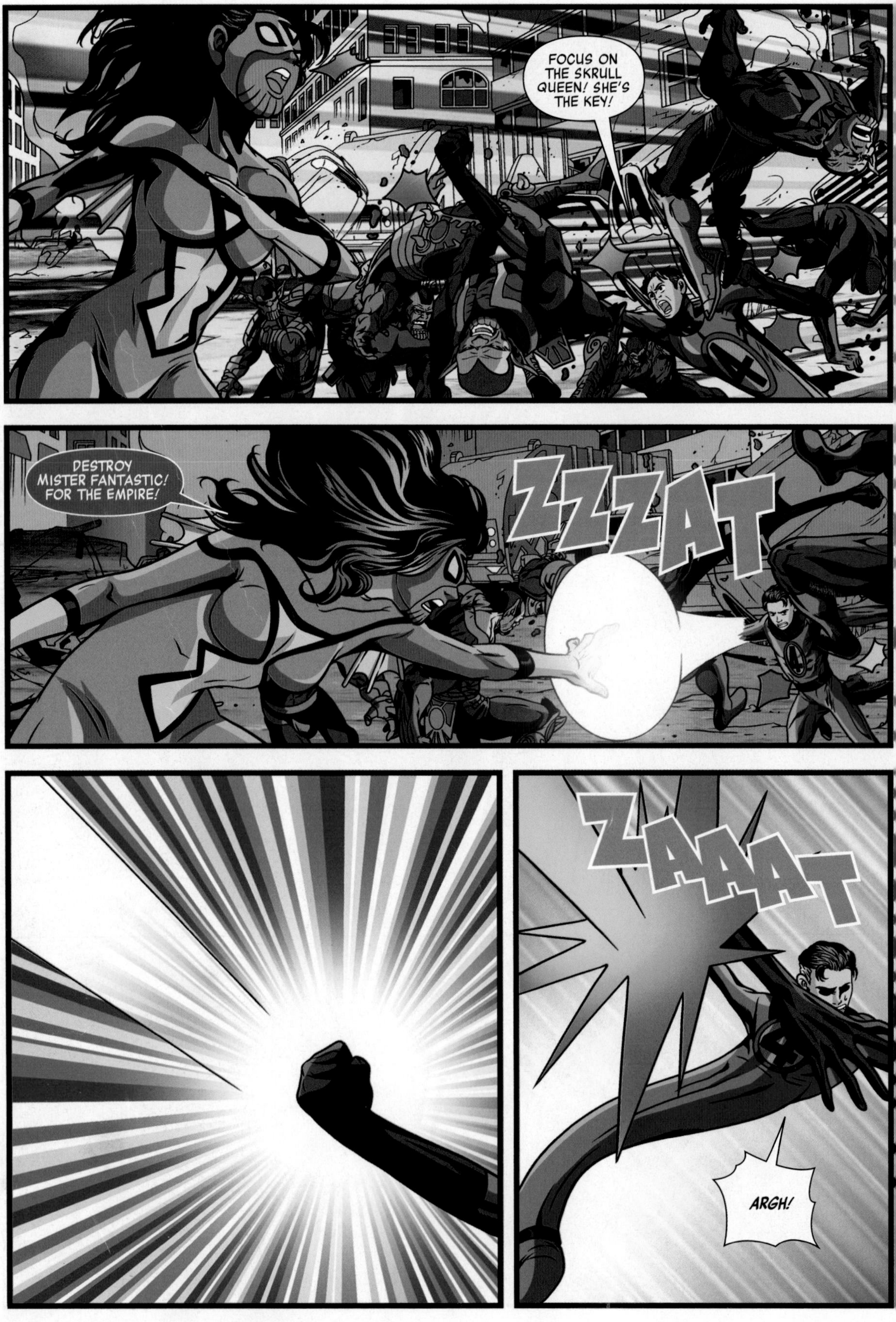
FOCUS ON THE SKRULL QUEEN! SHE'S THE KEY!
DESTROY MISTER FANTASTIC! FOR THE EMPIRE!
ZZZAT
ZAAAT
ARGH!

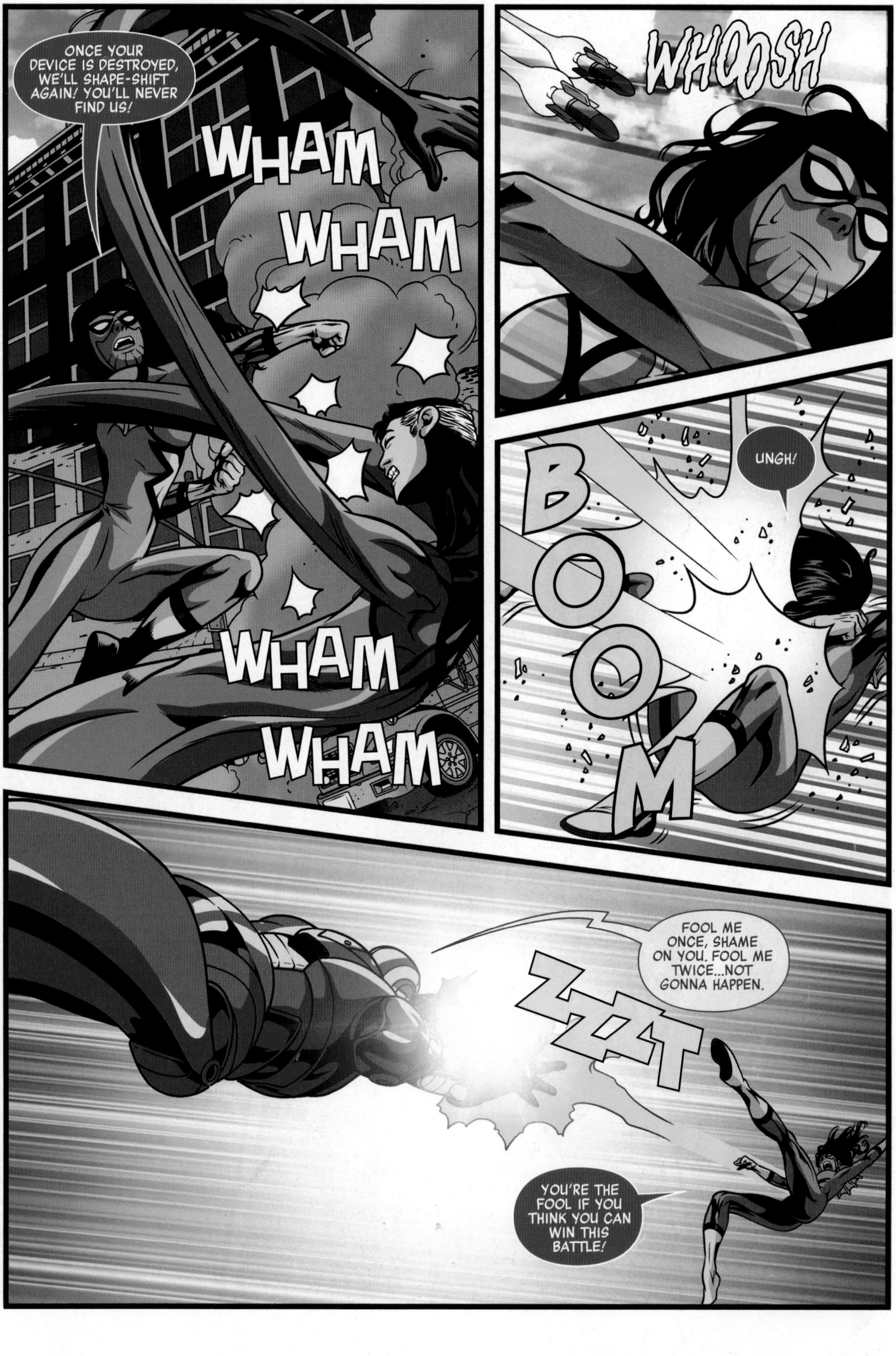
ONCE YOUR DEVICE IS DESTROYED, WE'LL SHAPE-SHIFT AGAIN! YOU'LL NEVER FIND US!
WHAM
WHAM
WHAM
WHAM
WHOOSH
UNGH!
BOOOM
FOOL ME ONCE, SHAME ON YOU. FOOL ME TWICE...NOT GONNA HAPPEN.
ZZZT
YOU'RE THE FOOL IF YOU THINK YOU CAN WIN THIS BATTLE!

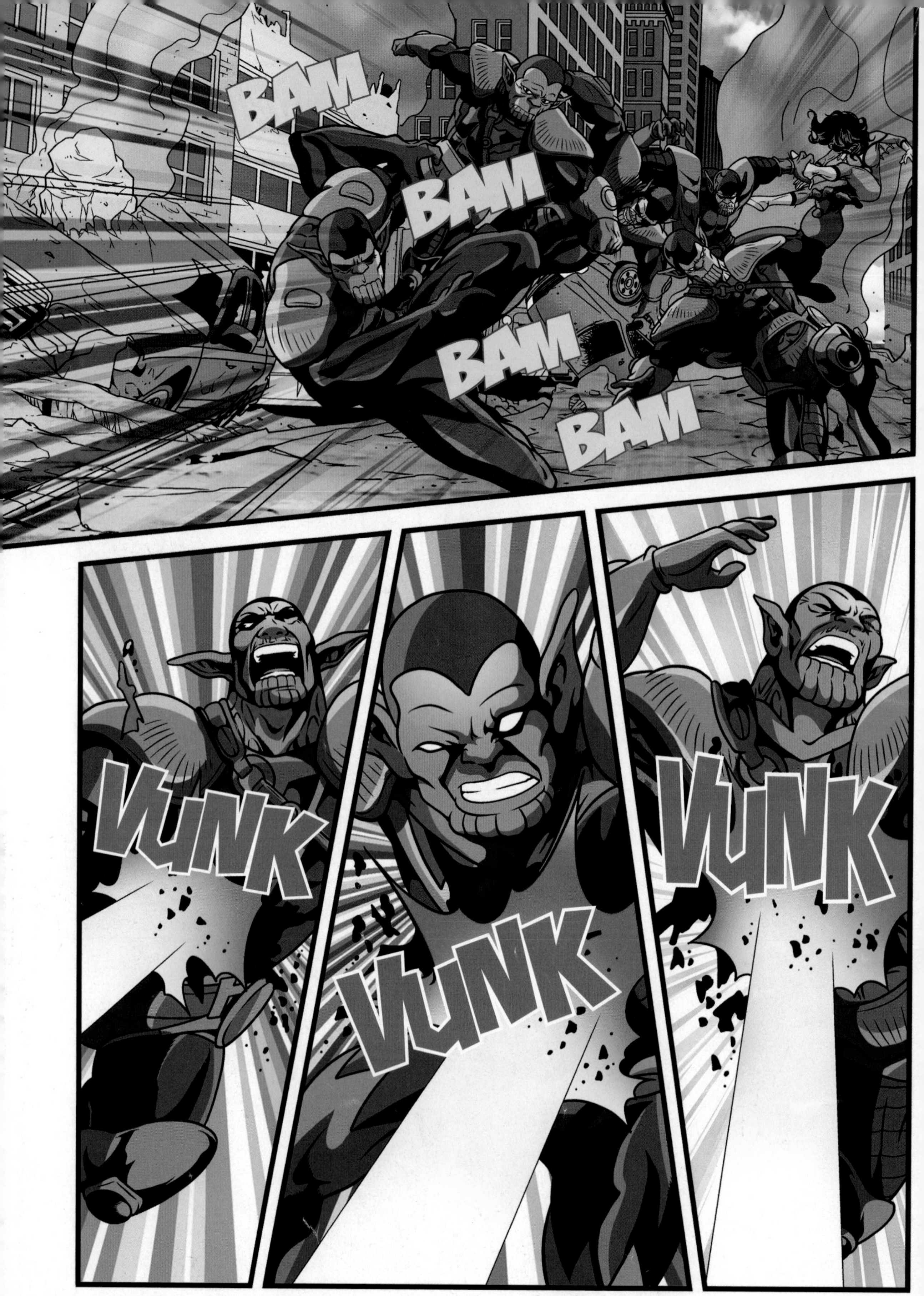
BAM
BAM
BAM
BAM
VUNK
VUNK
VUNK

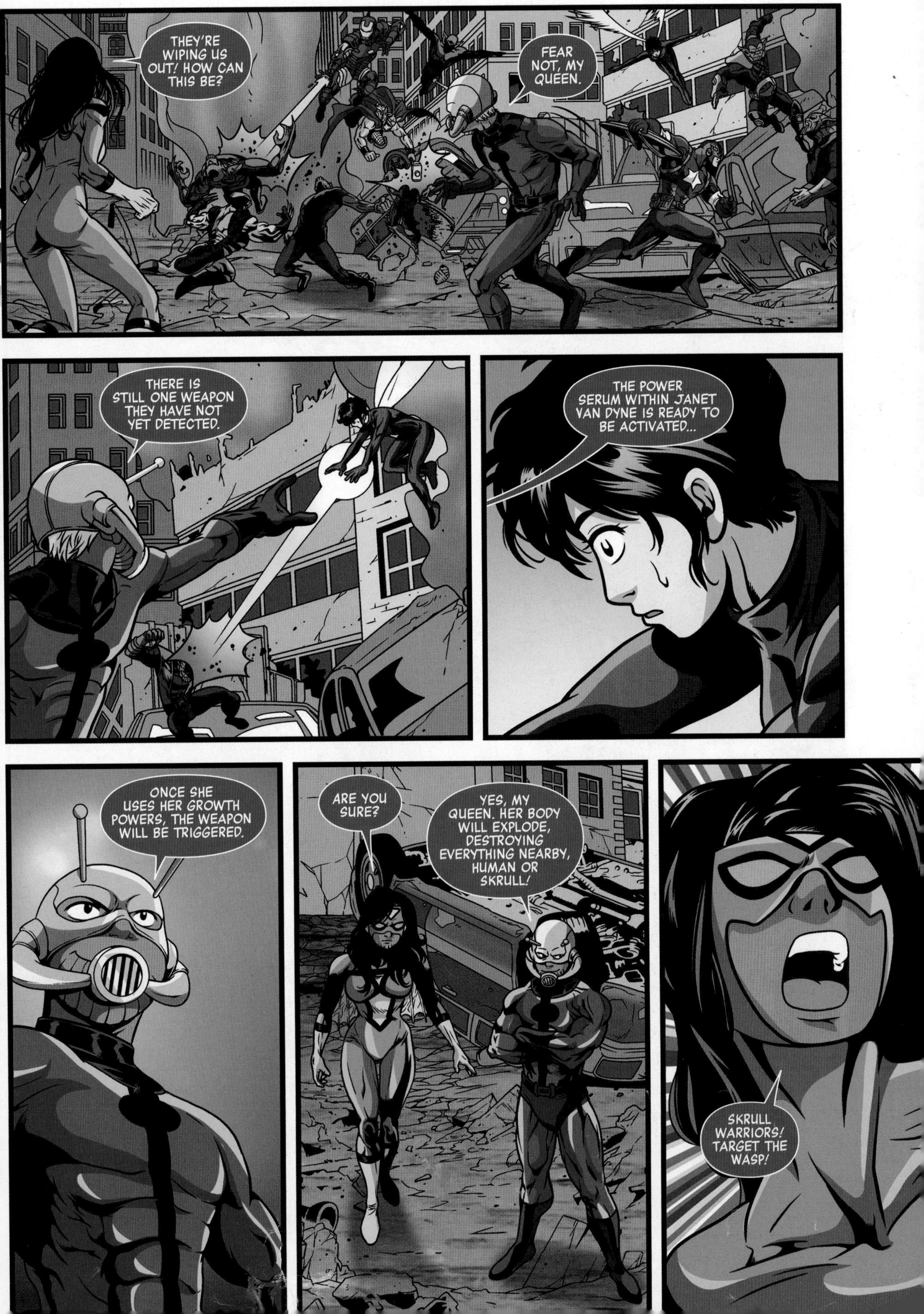
THEY'RE WIPING US OUT! HOW CAN THIS BE?
FEAR NOT, MY QUEEN.
THERE IS STILL ONE WEAPON THEY HAVE NOT YET DETECTED.
THE POWER SERUM WITHIN JANET VAN DYNE IS READY TO BE ACTIVATED...
ONCE SHE USES HER GROWTH POWERS, THE WEAPON WILL BE TRIGGERED.
ARE YOU SURE?
YES, MY QUEEN. HER BODY WILL EXPLODE, DESTROYING EVERYTHING NEARBY, HUMAN OR SKRULL!
SKRULL WARRIORS! TARGET THE WASP!

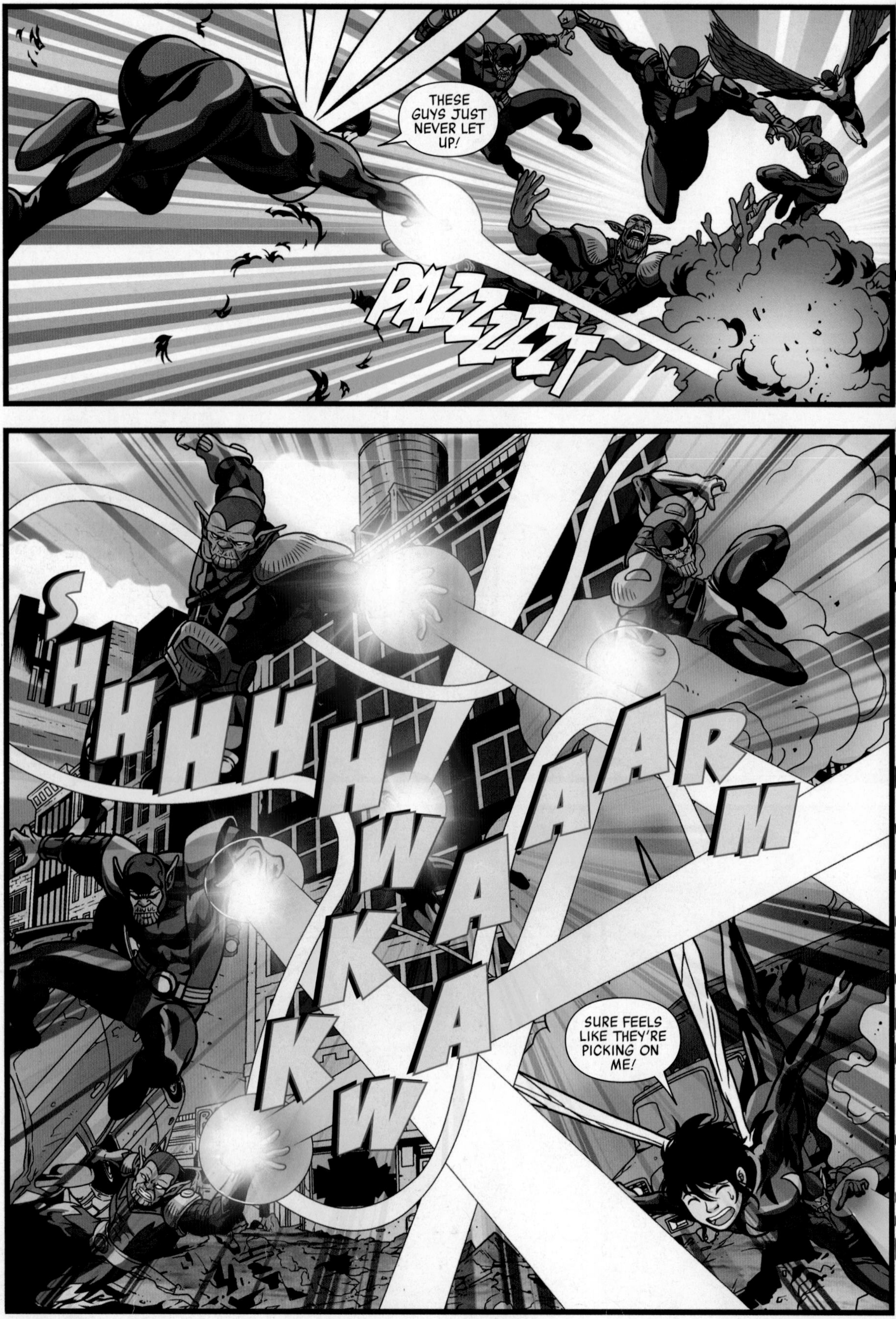
THESE GUYS JUST NEVER LET UP!
PAZZZZZT
SURE FEELS LIKE THEY'RE PICKING ON ME!

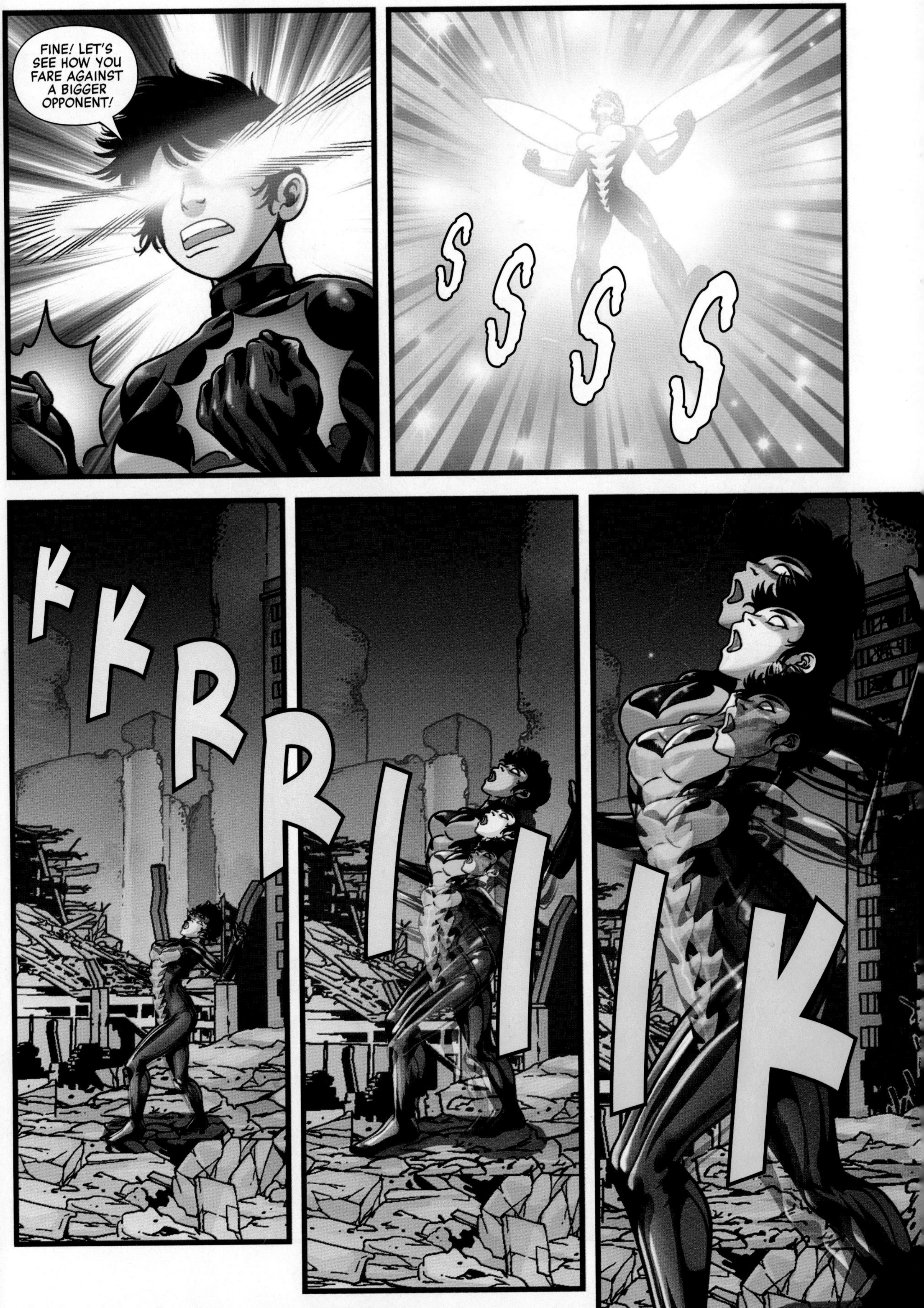
FINE! LET'S SEE HOW YOU FARE AGAINST A BIGGER OPPONENT!
SSSS
KKRRIIIK

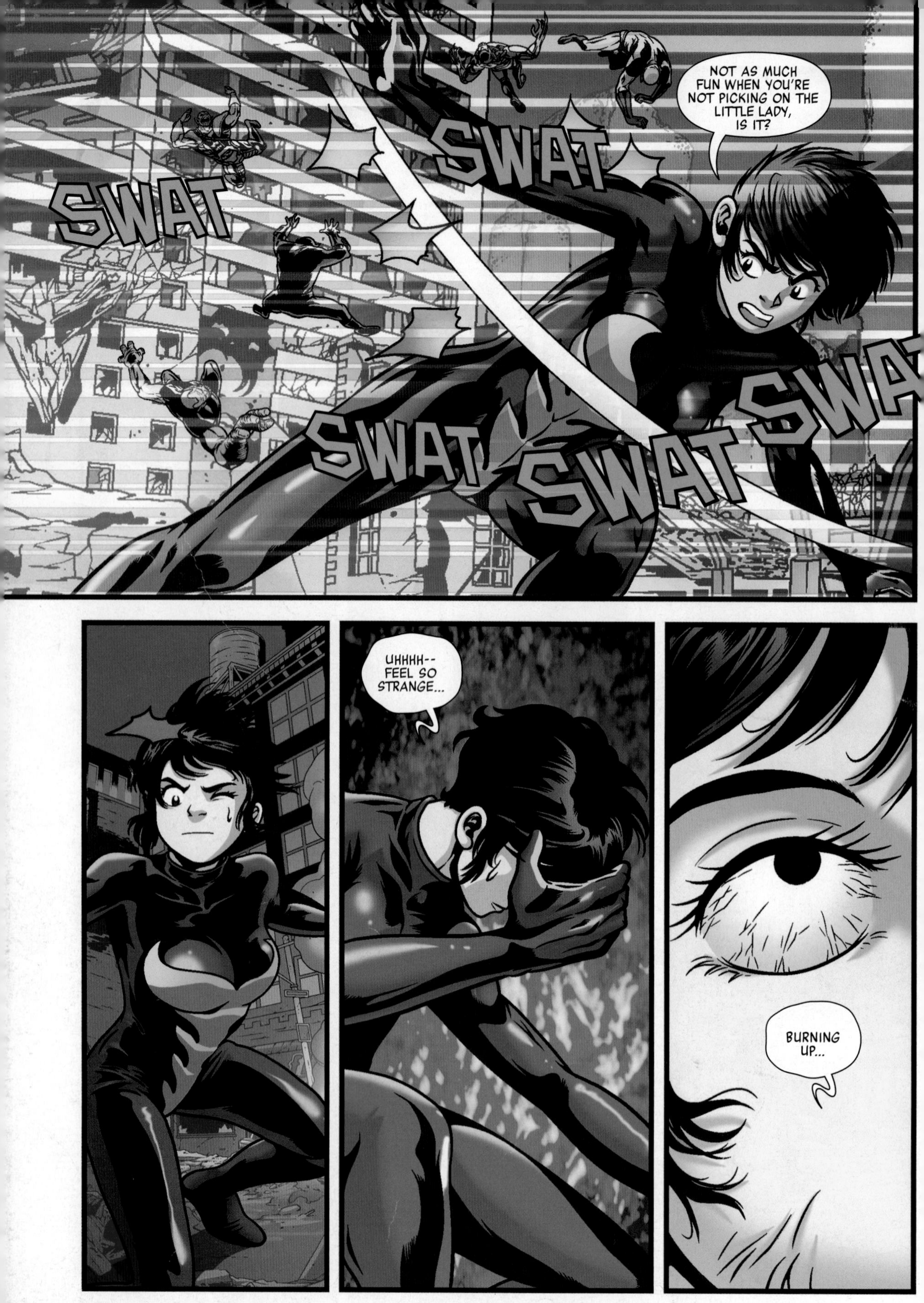
NOT AS MUCH FUN WHEN YOU'RE NOT PICKING ON THE LITTLE LADY, IS IT?
SWAT
SWAT
SWAT
SWAT
SWAT
UHHHH-- FEEL SO STRANGE...
BURNING UP...

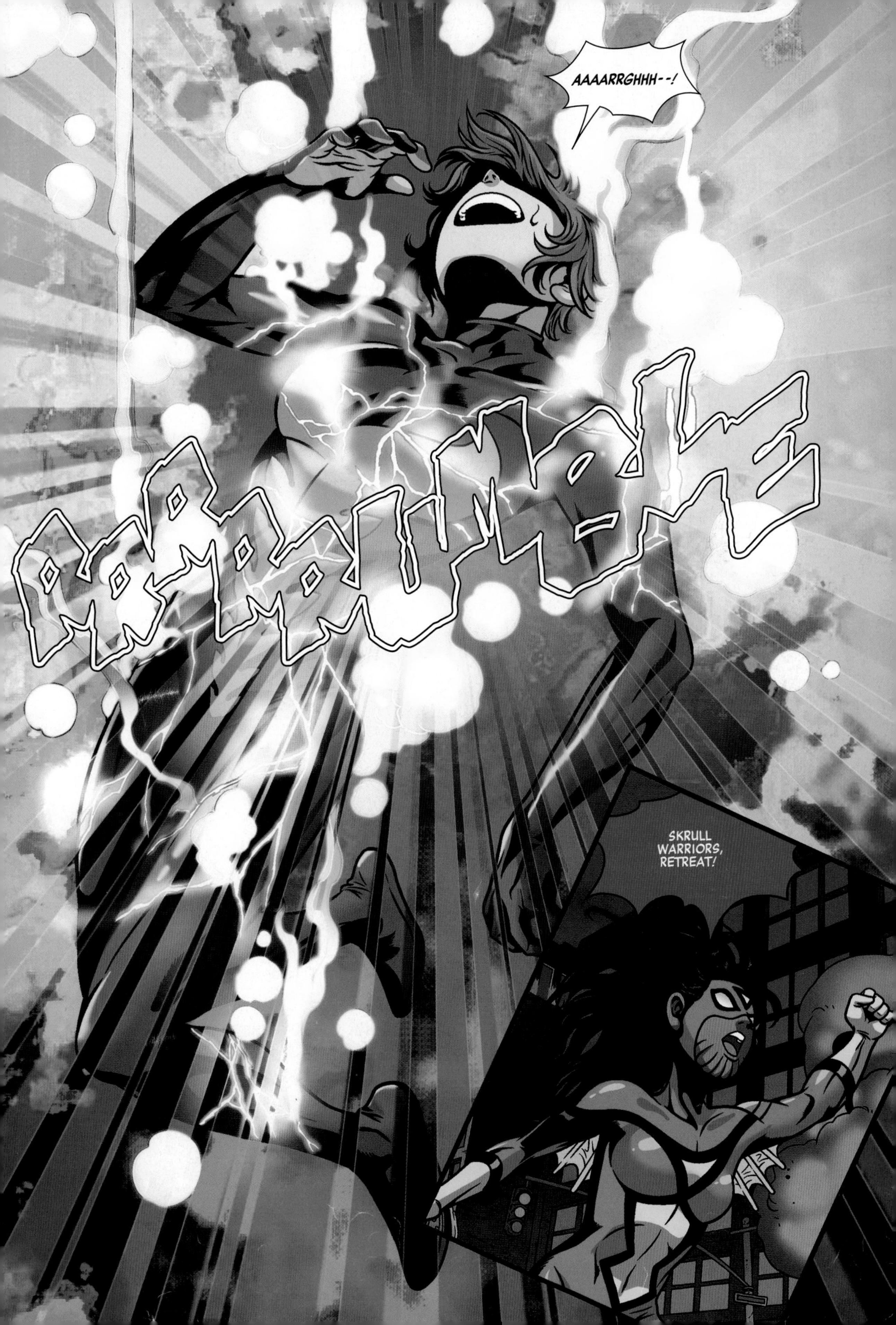
AAAARRGHHH--!
SKRULL WARRIORS, RETREAT!

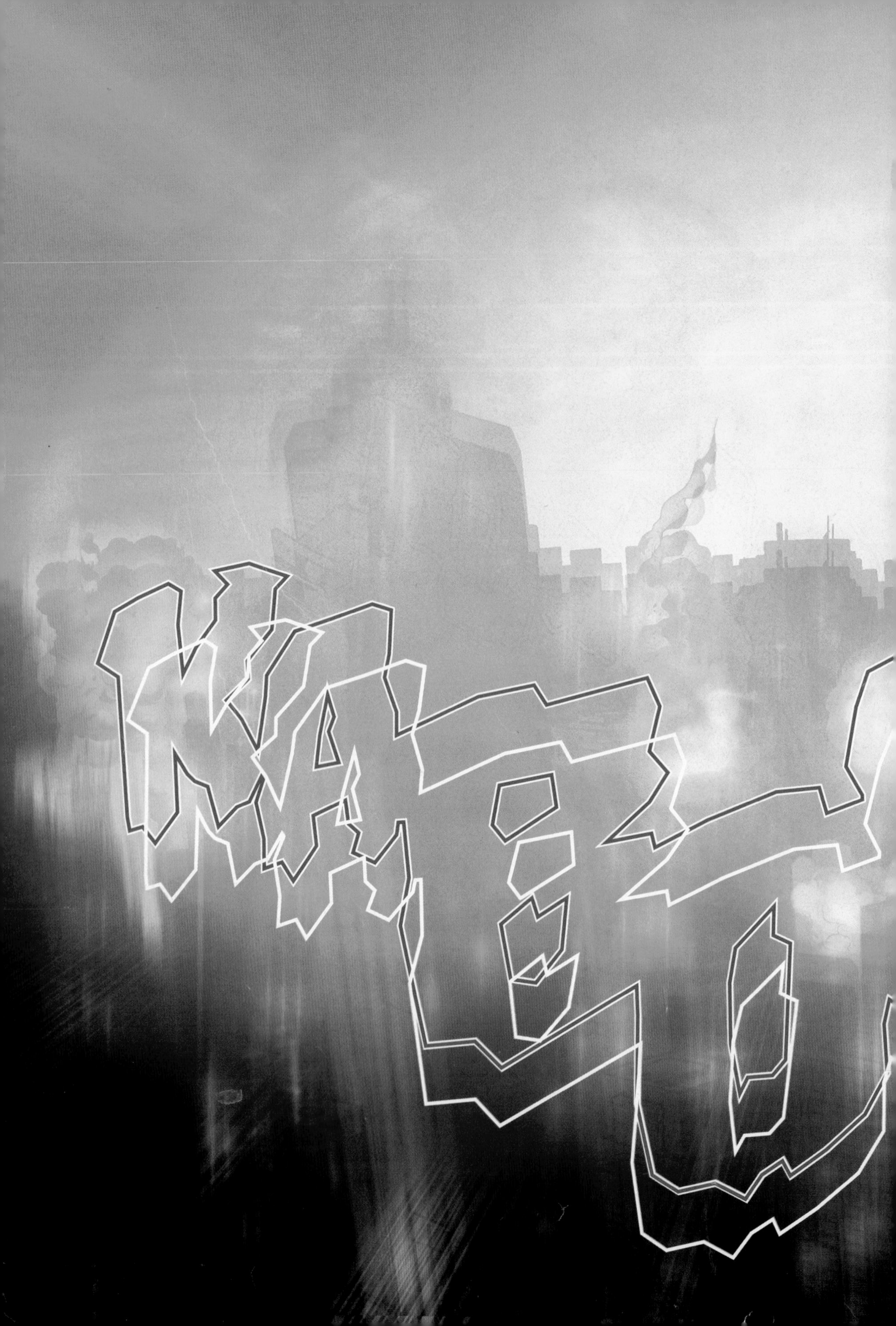

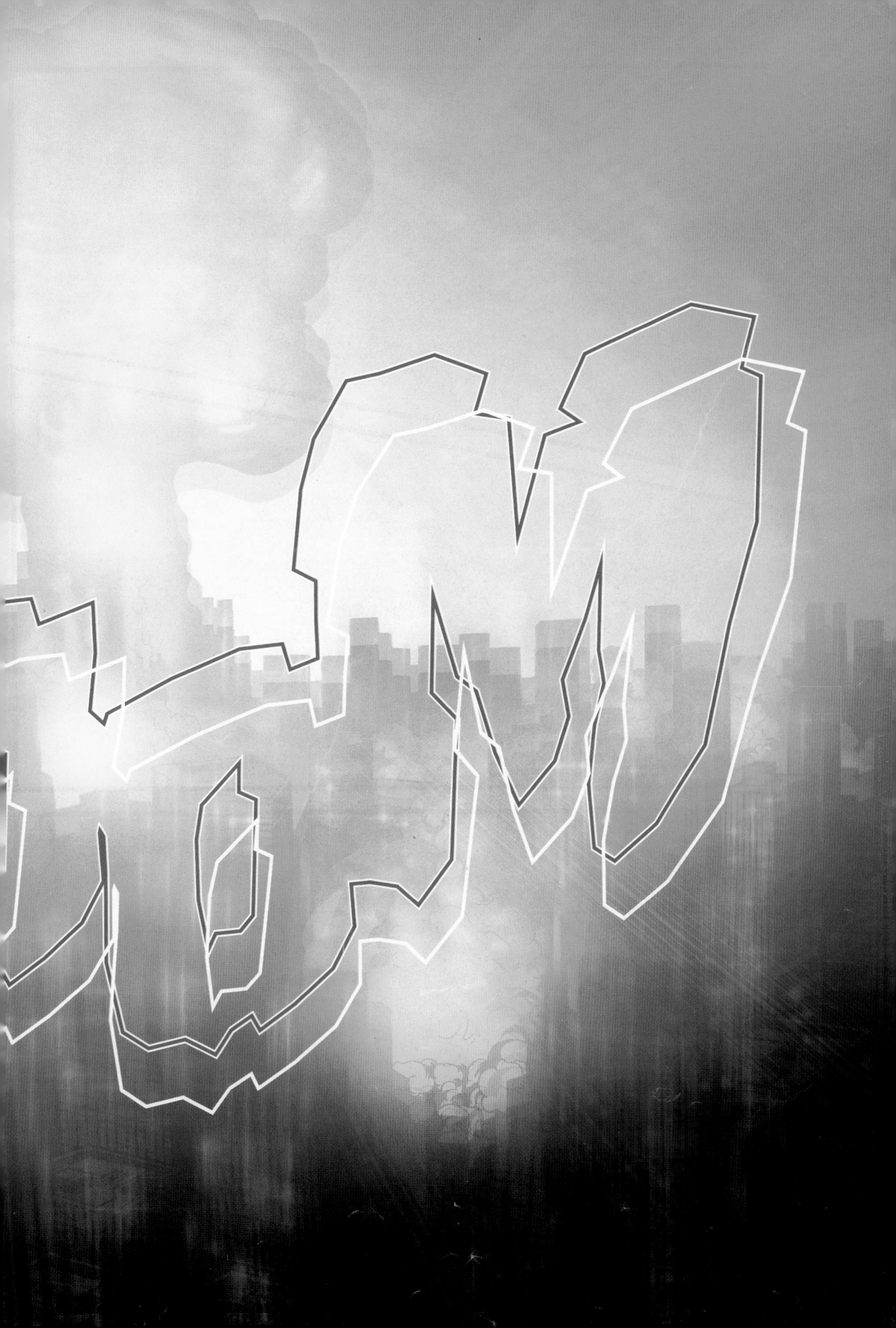

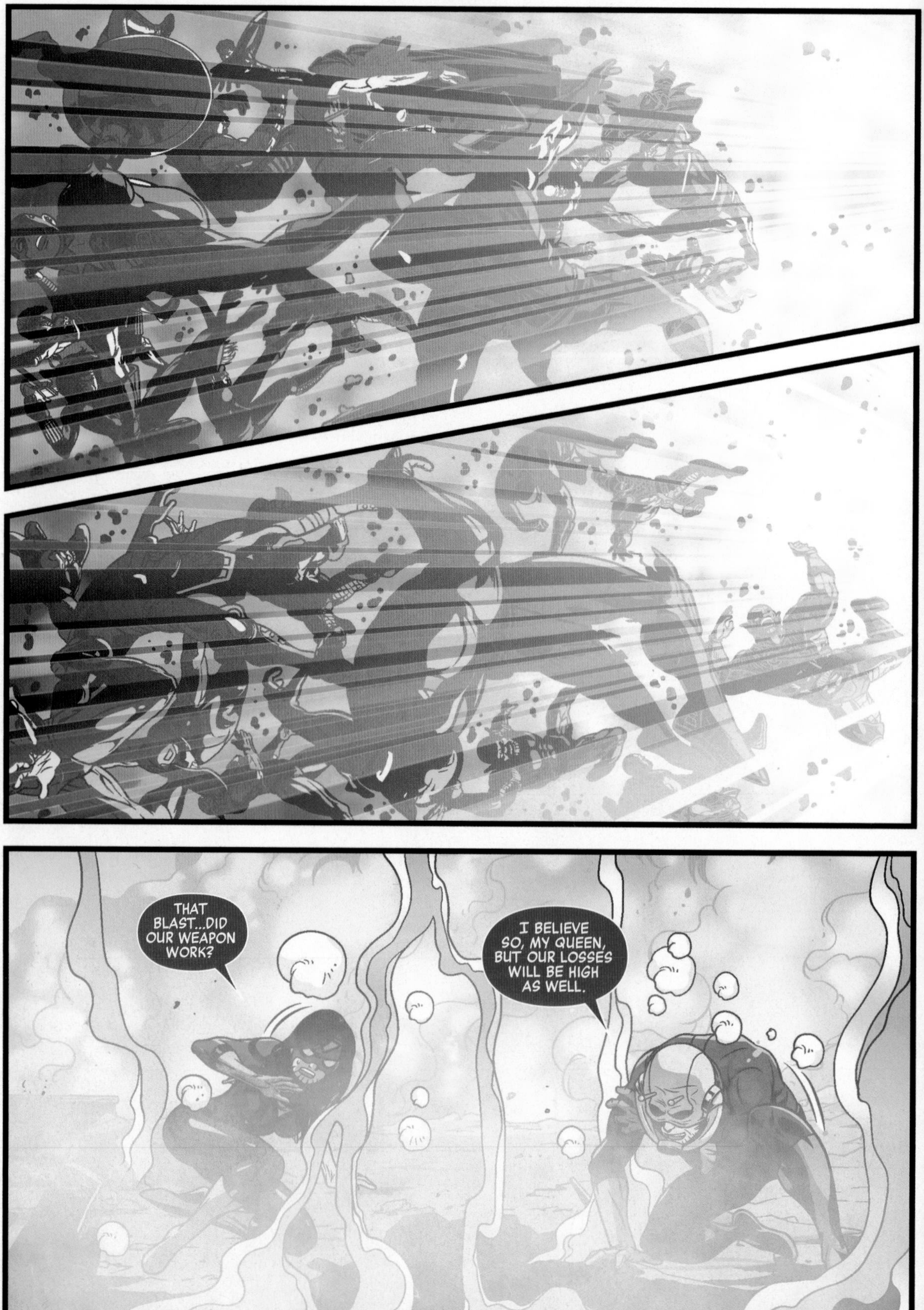
THAT BLAST...DID OUR WEAPON WORK?
I BELIEVE SO, MY QUEEN, BUT OUR LOSSES WILL BE HIGH AS WELL.

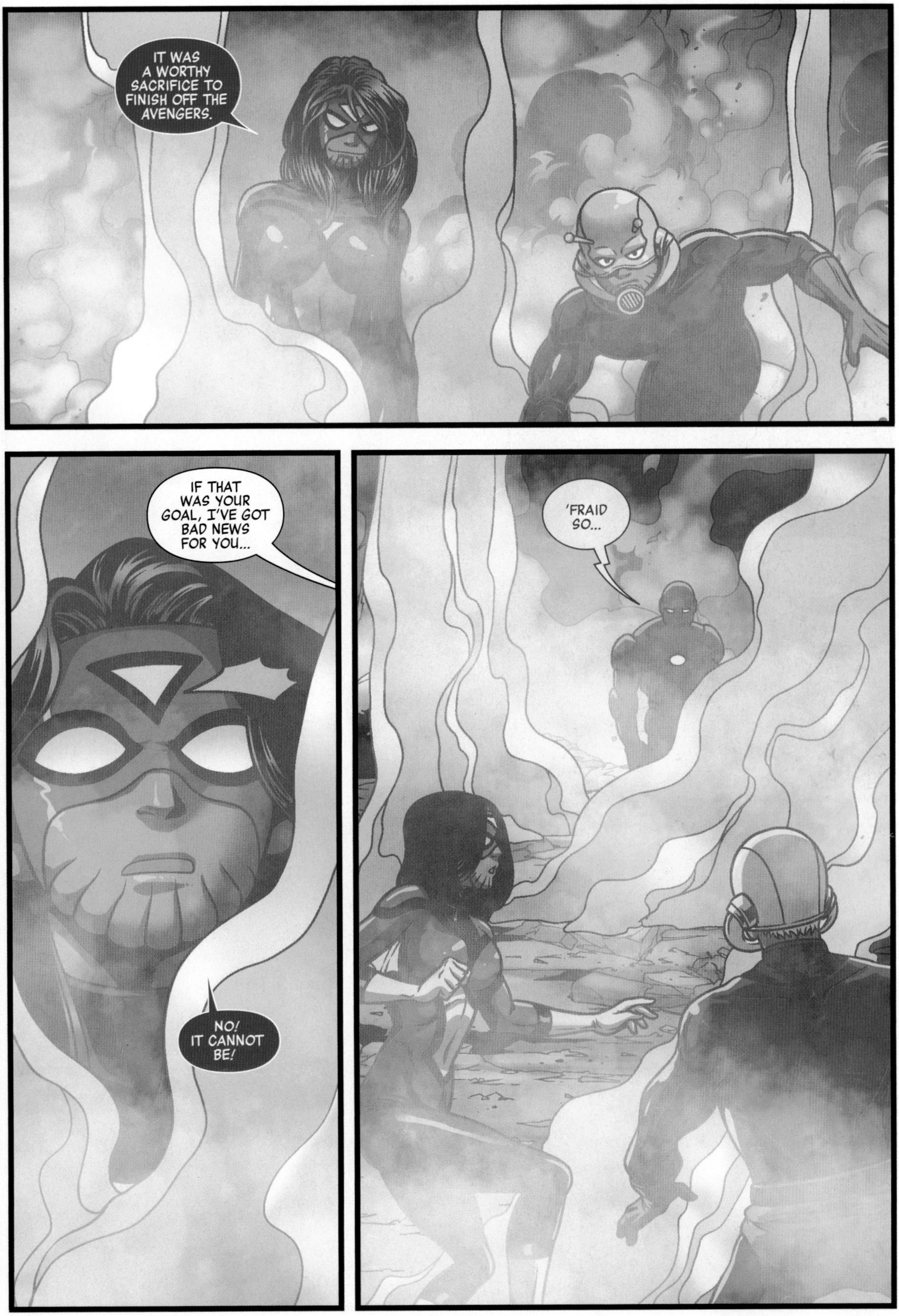
IT WAS A WORTHY SACRIFICE TO FINISH OFF THE AVENGERS.
IF THAT WAS YOUR GOAL, I'VE GOT BAD NEWS FOR YOU...
NO! IT CANNOT BE!
'FRAID SO...

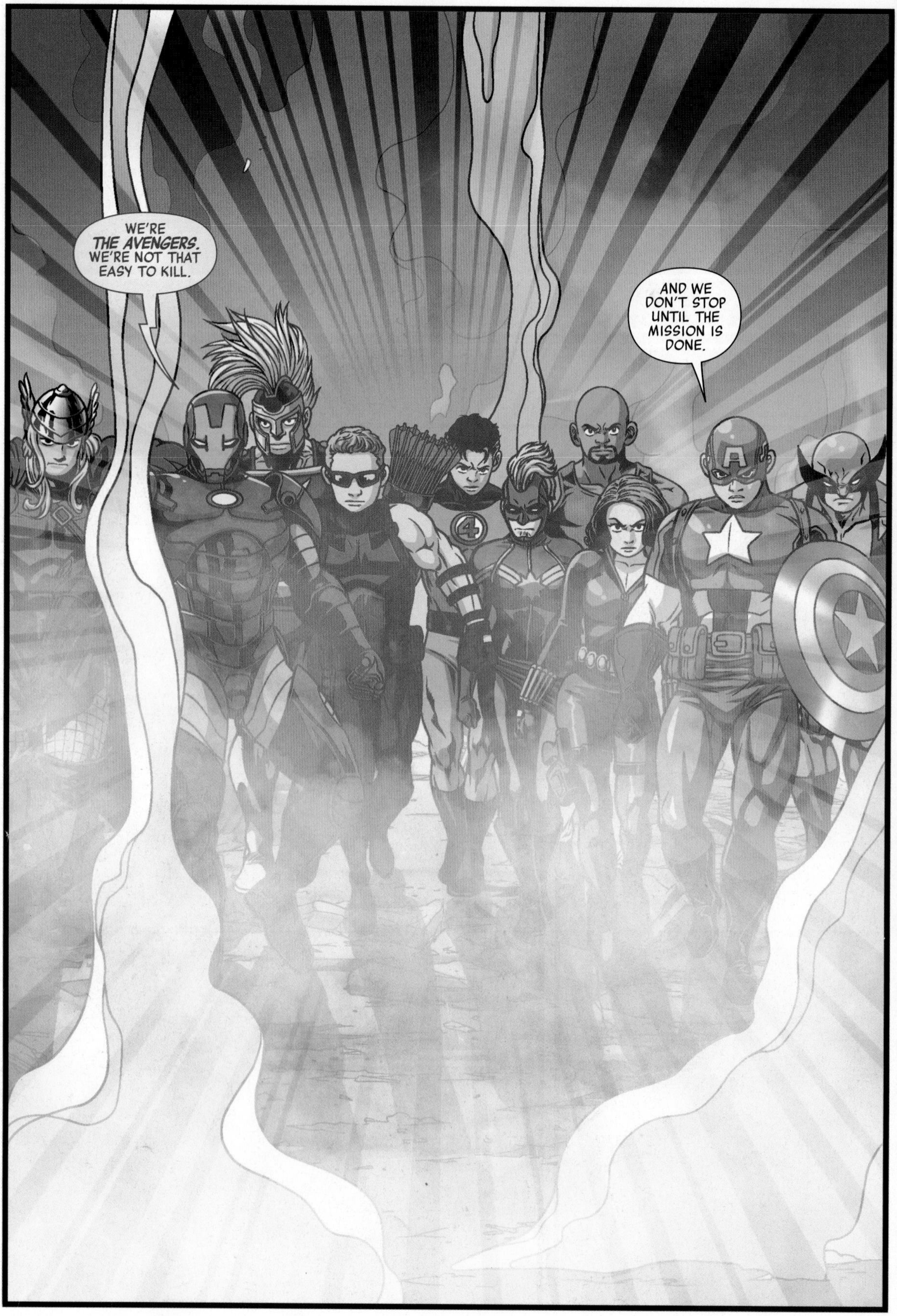
WE'RE *THE AVENGERS.* WE'RE NOT THAT EASY TO KILL.
AND WE DON'T STOP UNTIL THE MISSION IS DONE.

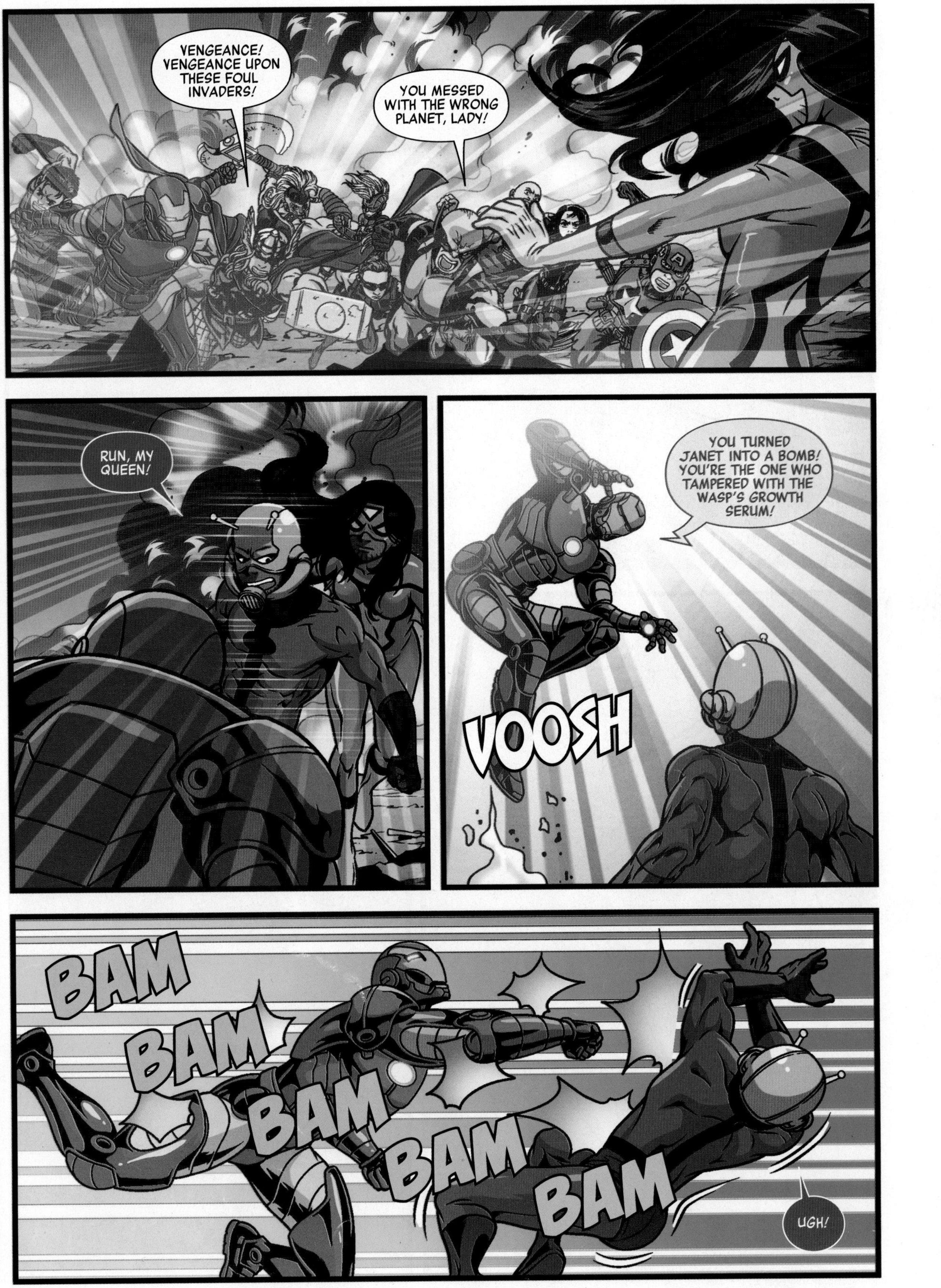
VENGEANCE! VENGEANCE UPON THESE FOUL INVADERS!
YOU MESSED WITH THE WRONG PLANET, LADY!
RUN, MY QUEEN!
YOU TURNED JANET INTO A BOMB! YOU'RE THE ONE WHO TAMPERED WITH THE WASP'S GROWTH SERUM!
VOOSH
BAM
BAM
BAM
BAM
BAM
UGH!

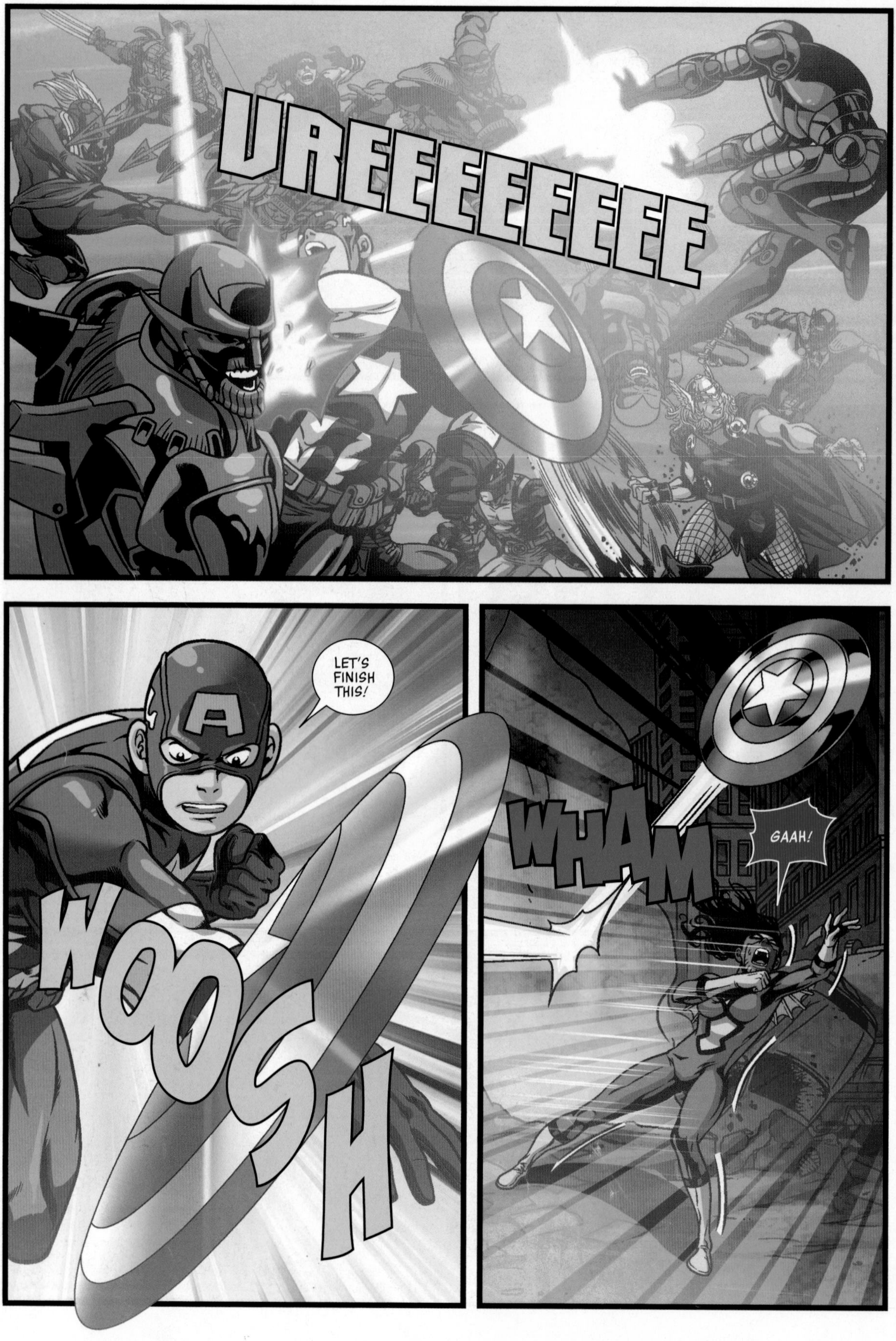
UREEEEEEEEE
LET'S FINISH THIS!
WOOSH
WHAM
GAAH!

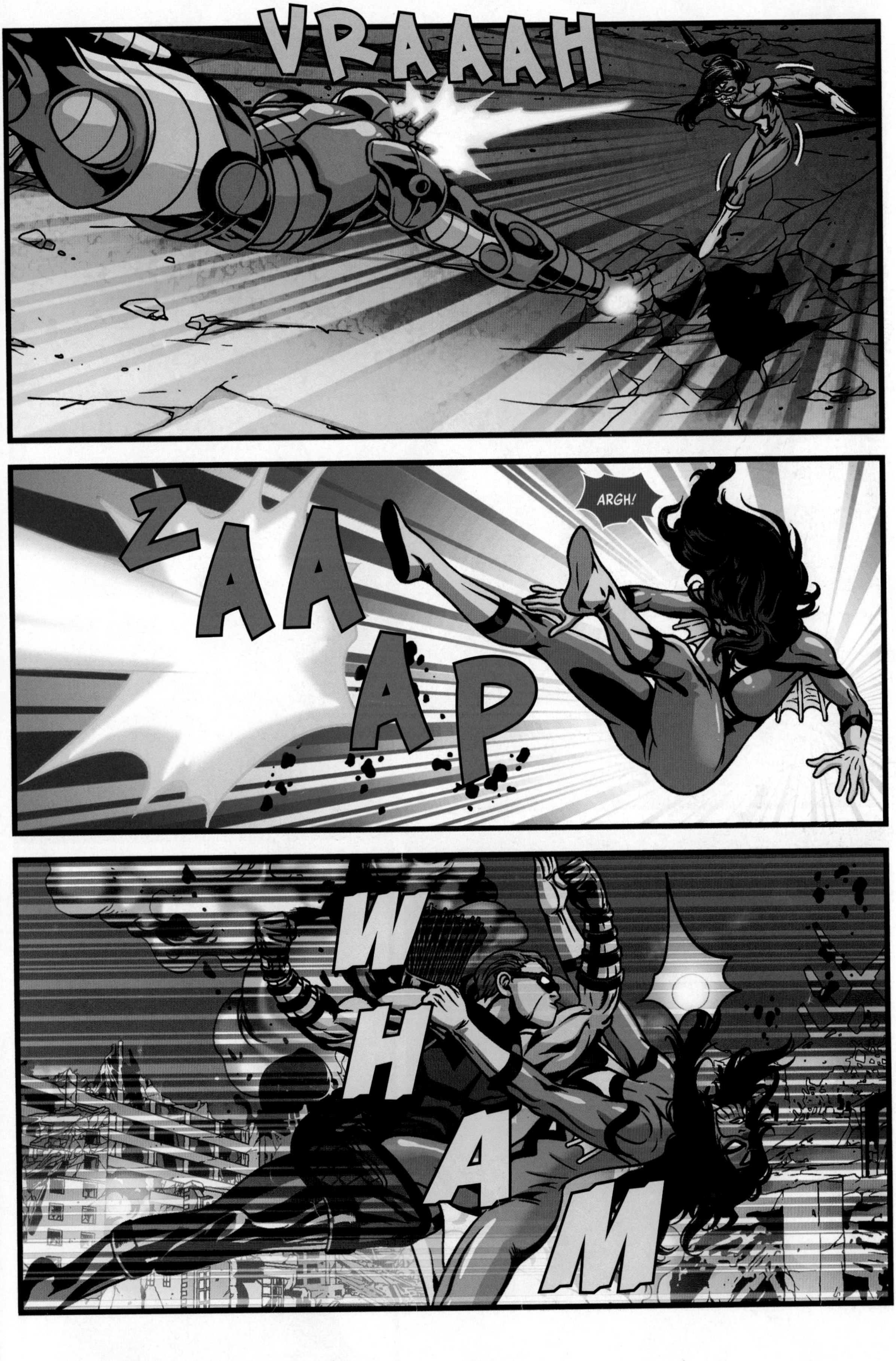
VRAAAH
ZAAAP
ARGH!
WHAM

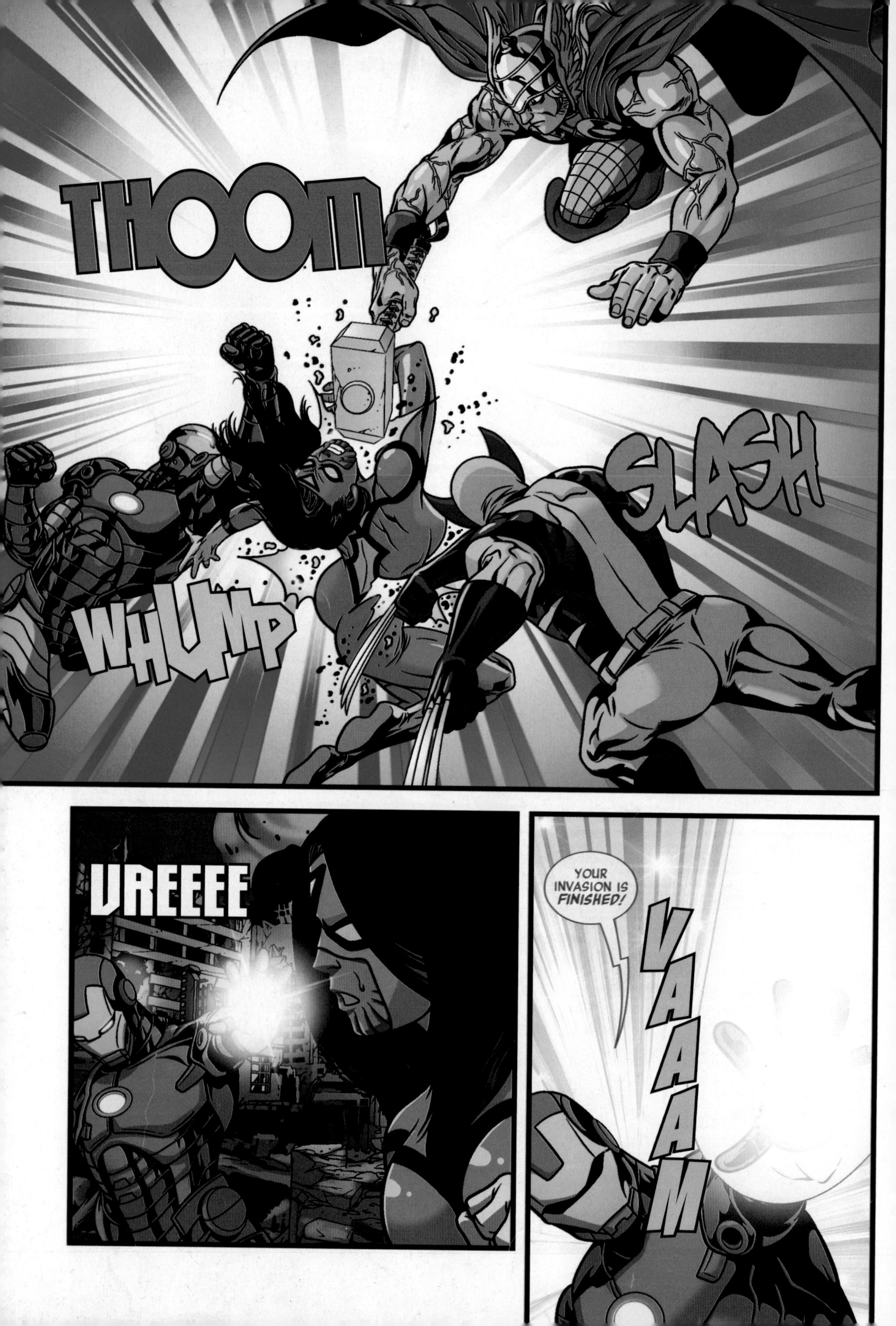
THOOM
SLASH
WHUMP
VREEEE
YOUR INVASION IS FINISHED!
VAAAAM

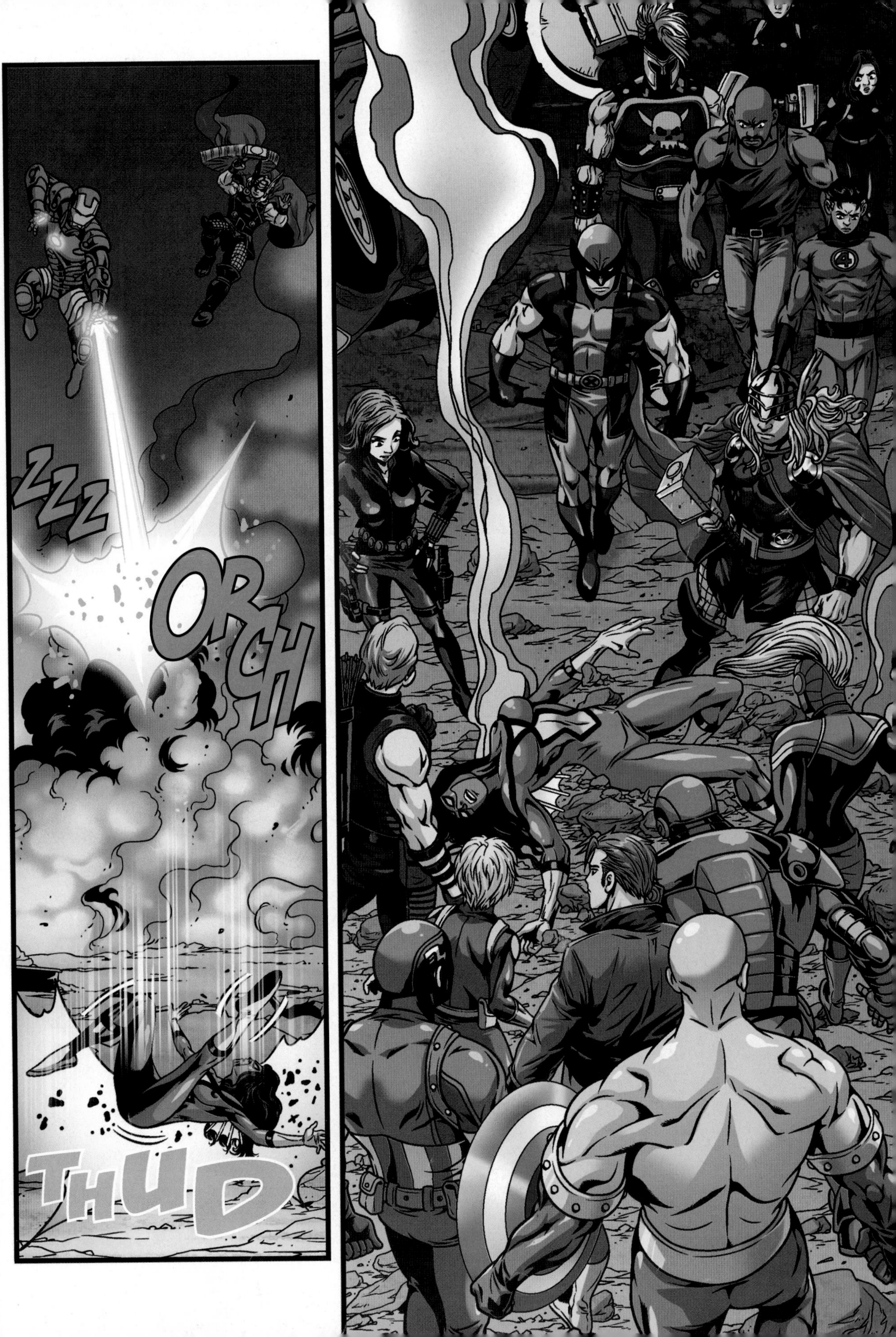
ZZZ
ORCH
THUD

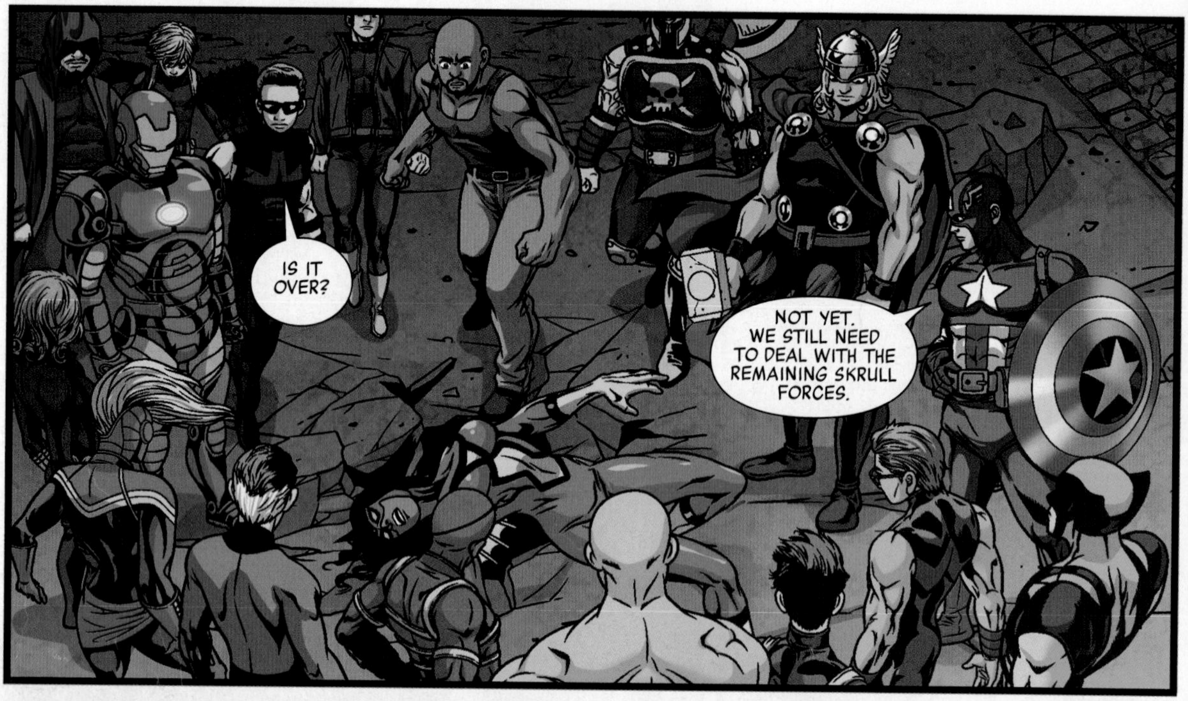
IS IT OVER?
NOT YET. WE STILL NEED TO DEAL WITH THE REMAINING SKRULL FORCES.

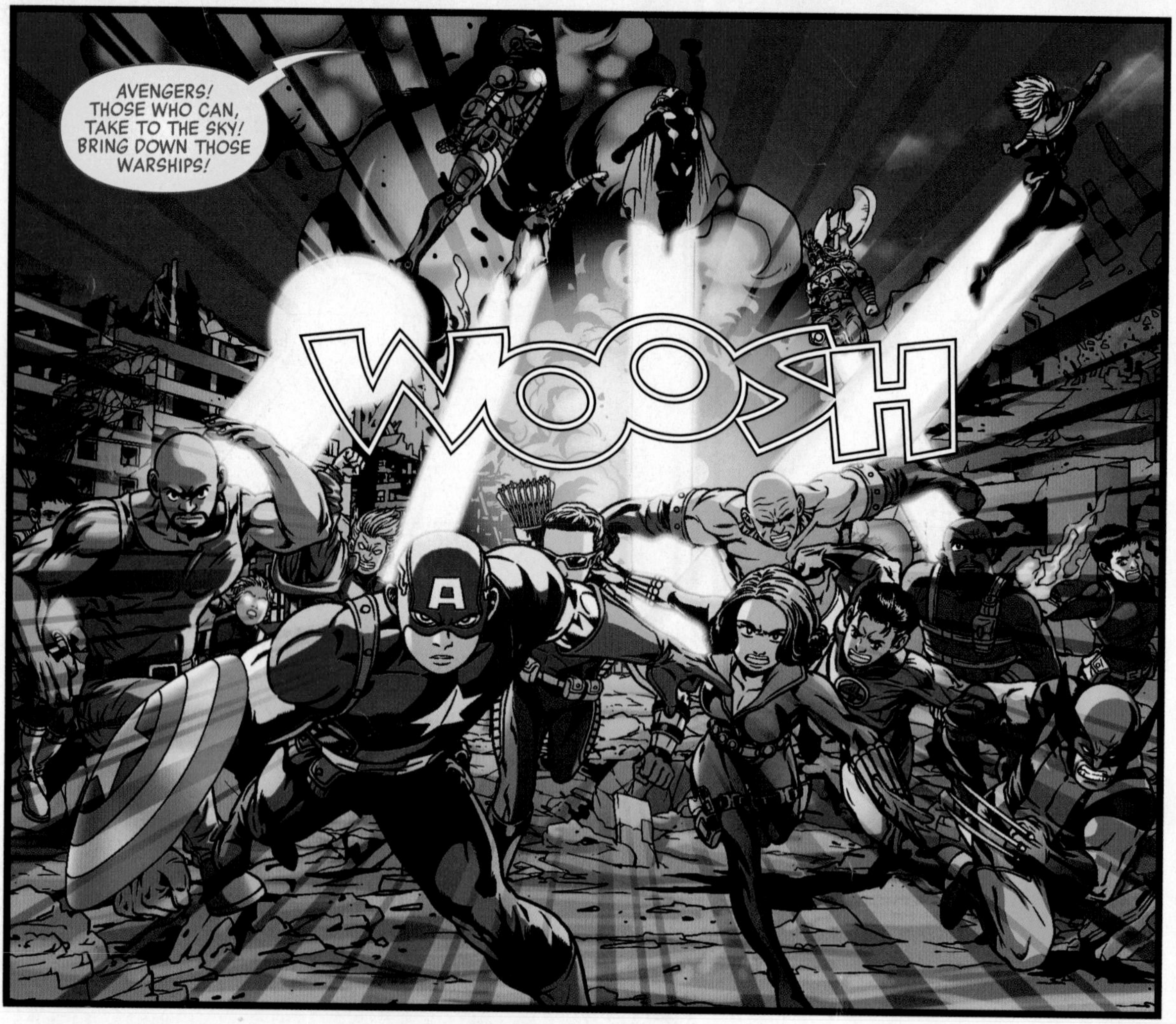
AVENGERS! THOSE WHO CAN, TAKE TO THE SKY! BRING DOWN THOSE WARSHIPS!
WOOSH

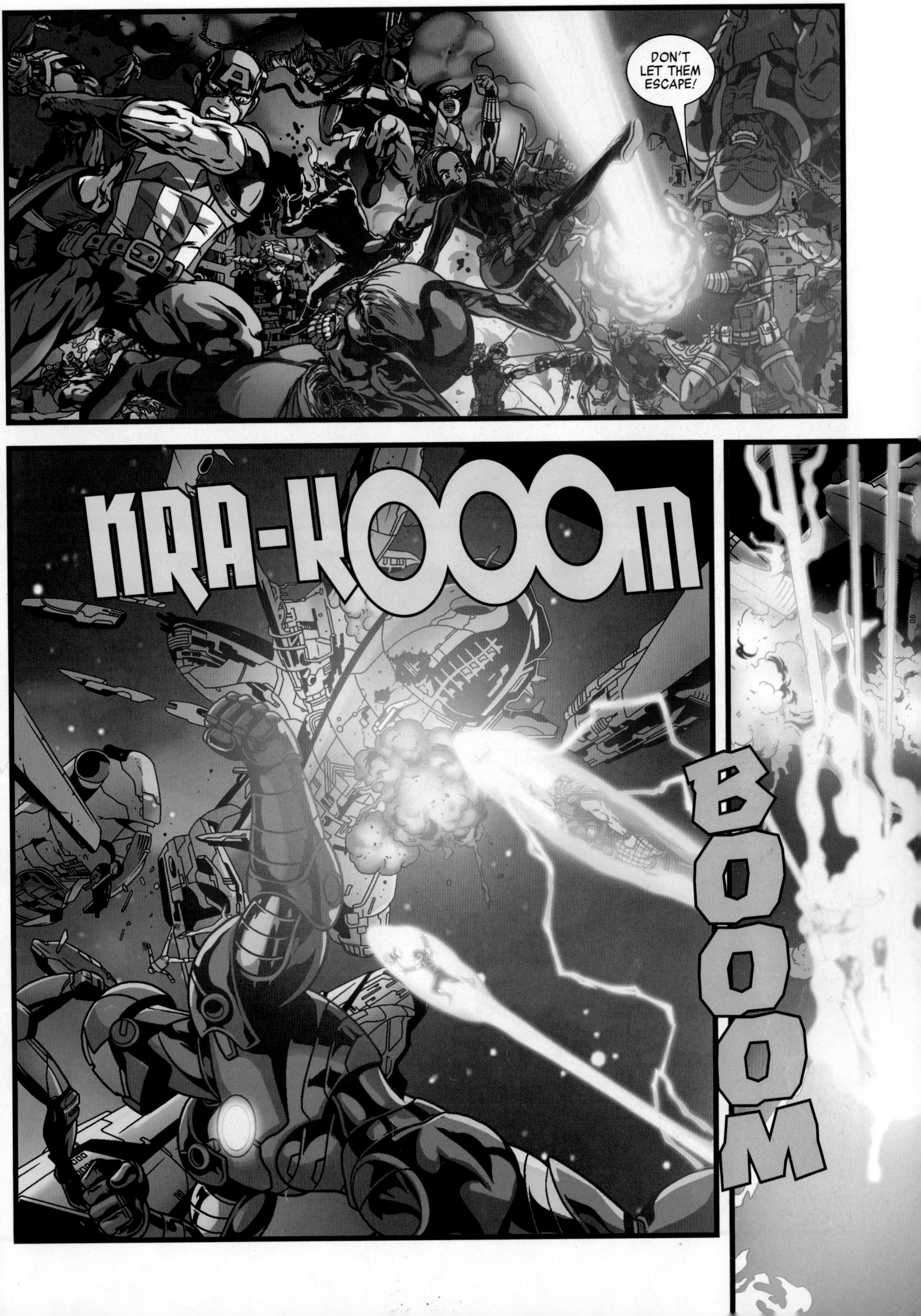
DON'T LET THEM ESCAPE!
KRA-KOOOM
BOOOM

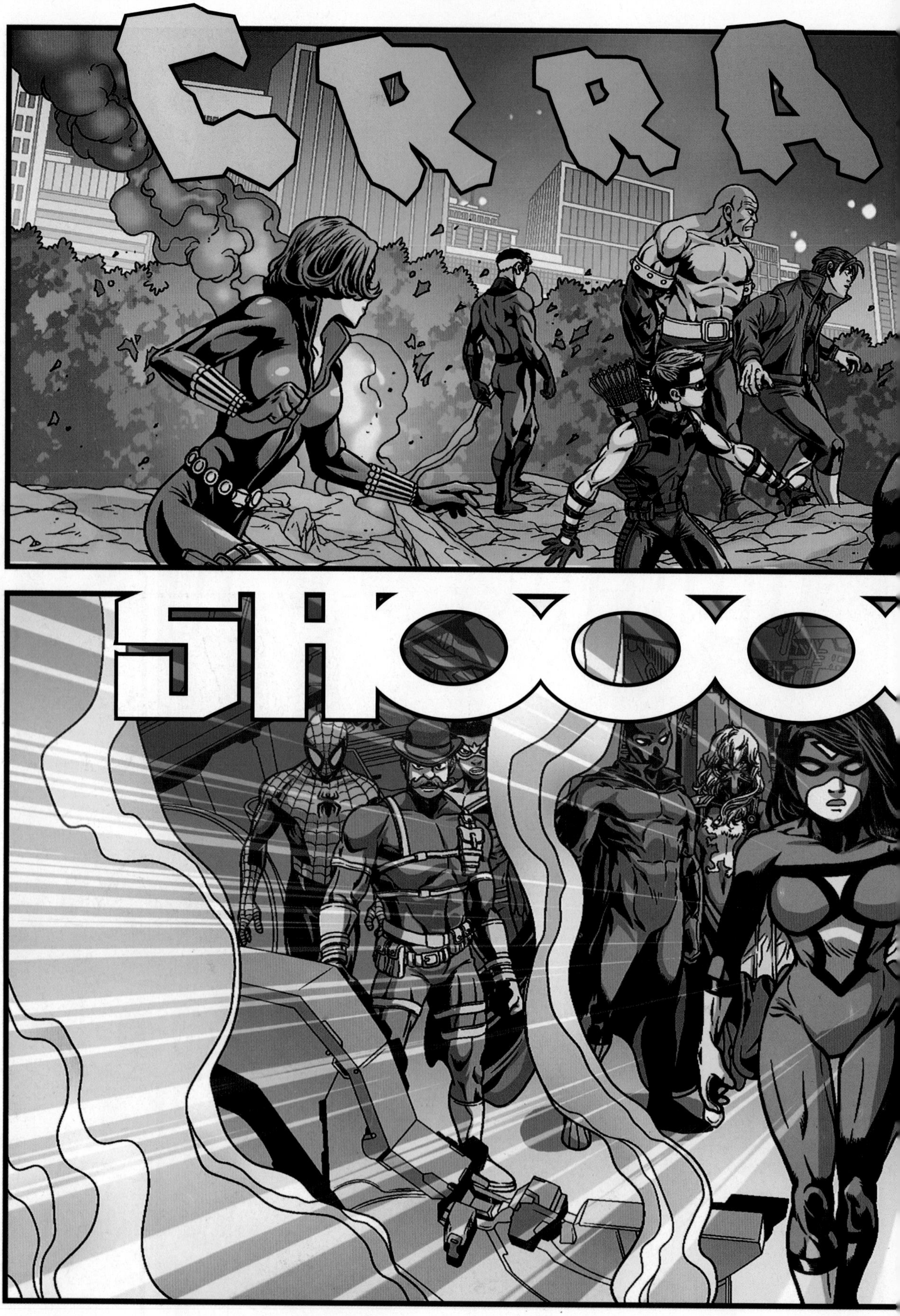
CRRA
SHOOO

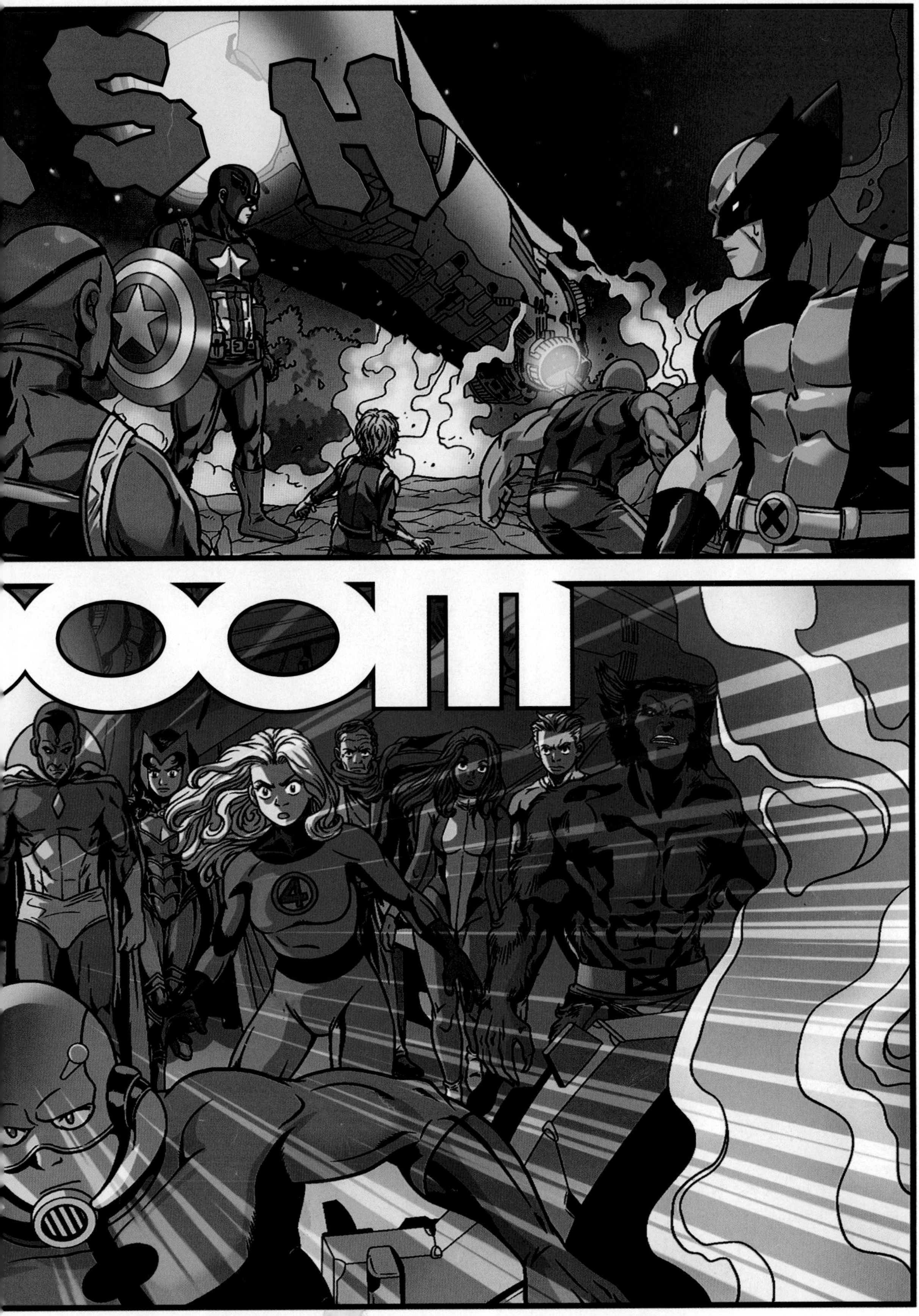
SH

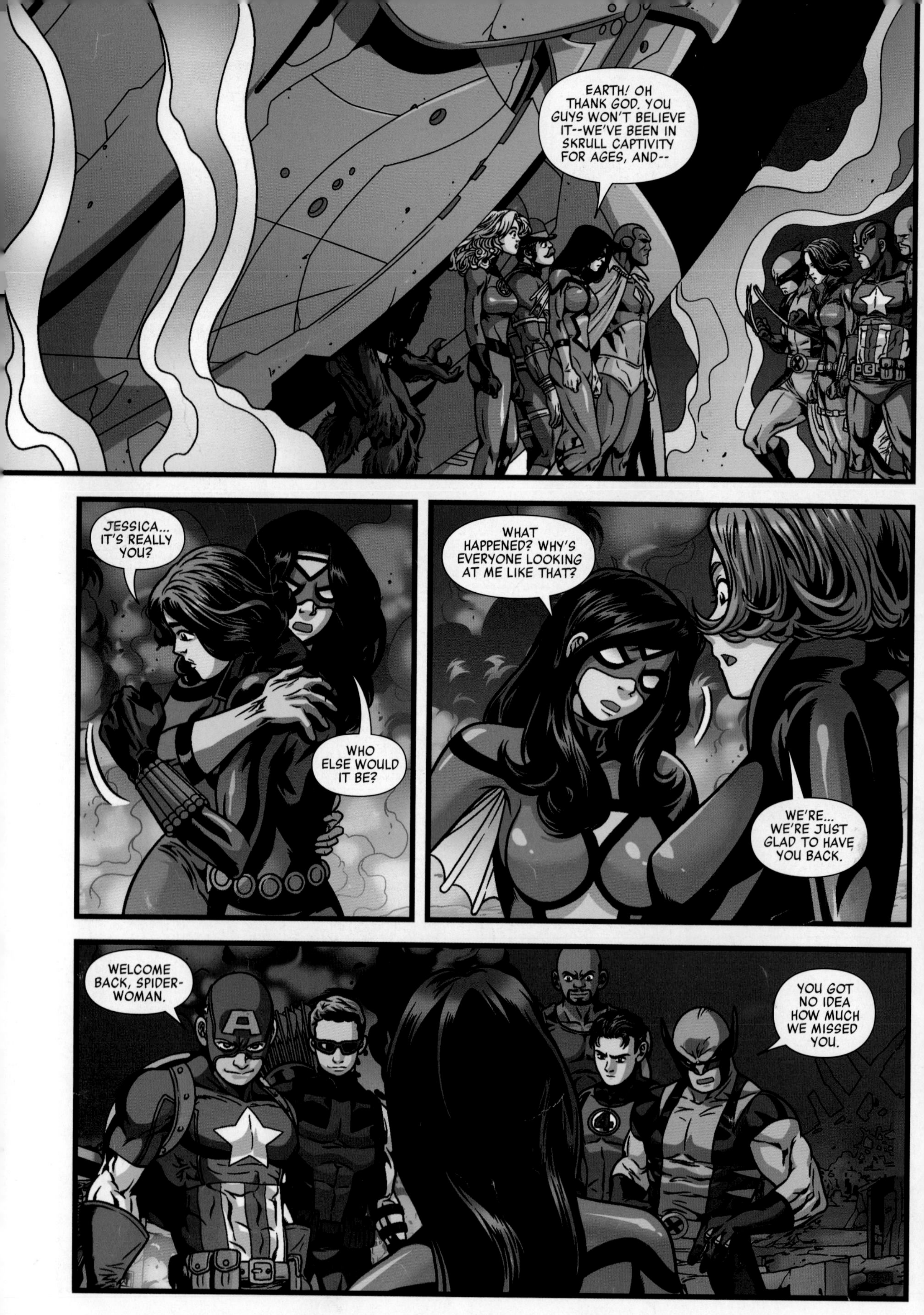
EARTH! OH THANK GOD. YOU GUYS WON'T BELIEVE IT--WE'VE BEEN IN SKRULL CAPTIVITY FOR AGES, AND--
JESSICA... IT'S REALLY YOU?
WHO ELSE WOULD IT BE?
WHAT HAPPENED? WHY'S EVERYONE LOOKING AT ME LIKE THAT?
WE'RE... WE'RE JUST GLAD TO HAVE YOU BACK.
WELCOME BACK, SPIDER-WOMAN.
YOU GOT NO IDEA HOW MUCH WE MISSED YOU.

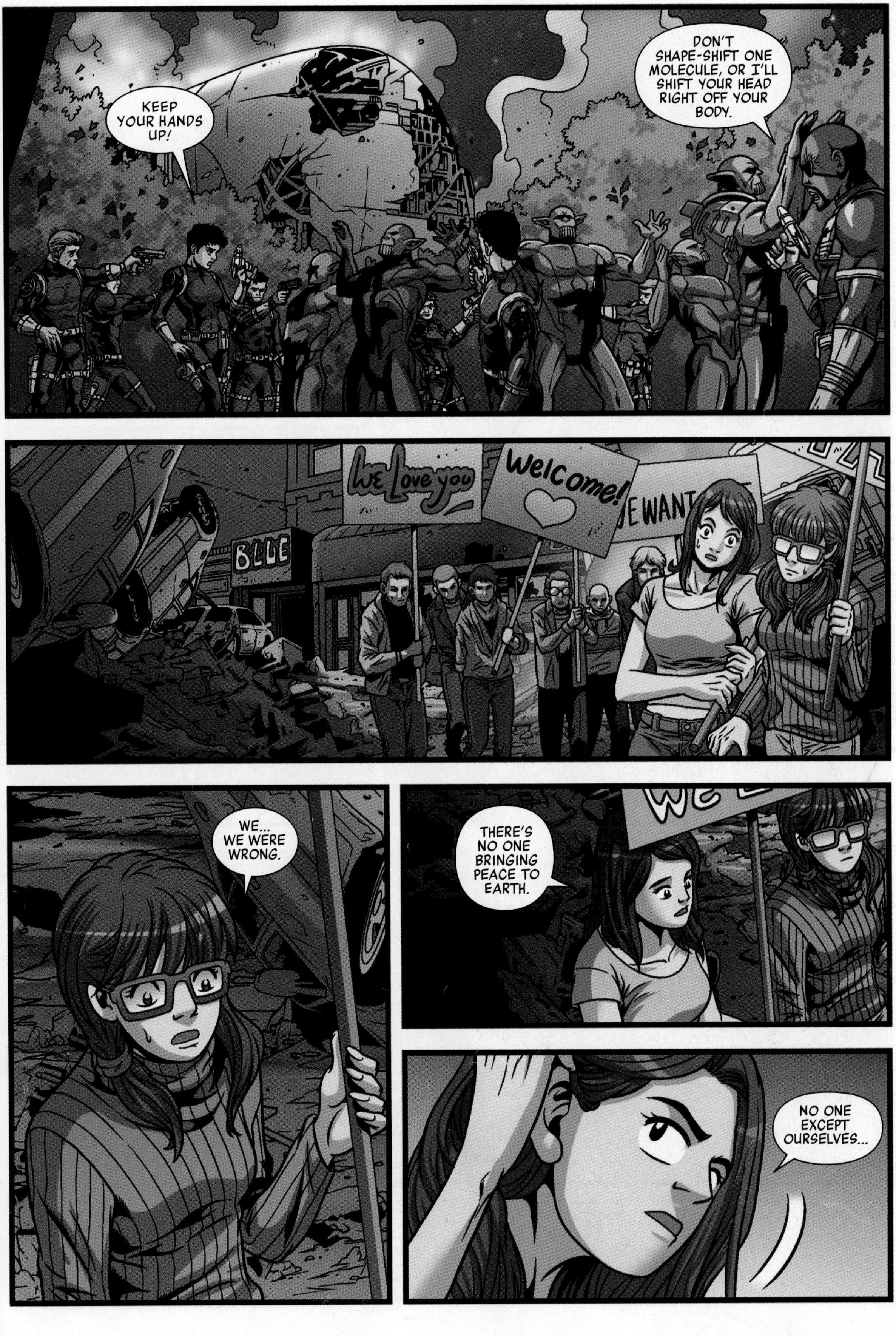
KEEP YOUR HANDS UP!
DON'T SHAPE-SHIFT ONE MOLECULE, OR I'LL SHIFT YOUR HEAD RIGHT OFF YOUR BODY.
WE LOVE YOU
WELCOME!
WE WANT
WE... WE WERE WRONG.
THERE'S NO ONE BRINGING PEACE TO EARTH.
NO ONE EXCEPT OURSELVES...

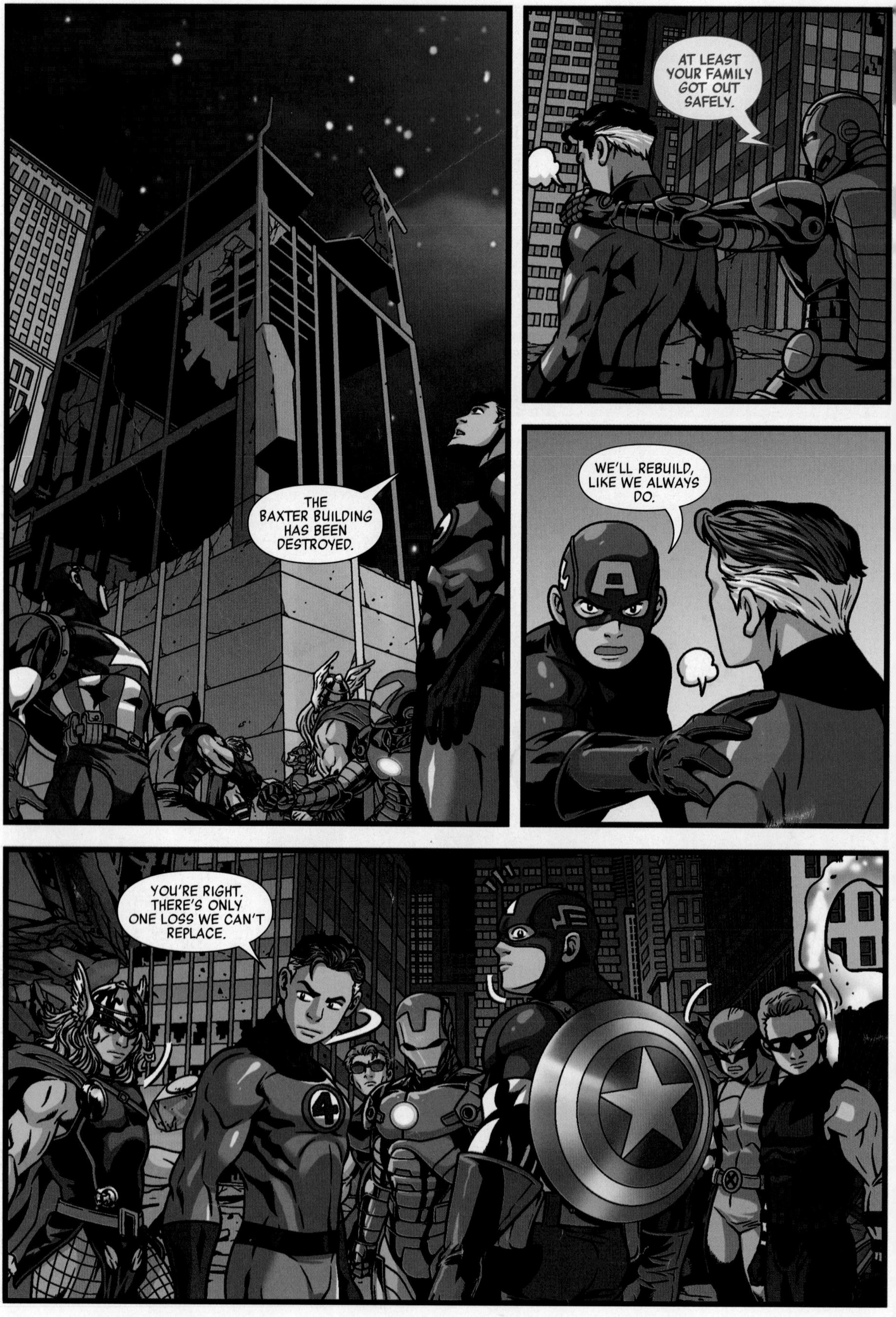
THE BAXTER BUILDING HAS BEEN DESTROYED.
AT LEAST YOUR FAMILY GOT OUT SAFELY.
WE'LL REBUILD, LIKE WE ALWAYS DO.
YOU'RE RIGHT. THERE'S ONLY ONE LOSS WE CAN'T REPLACE.

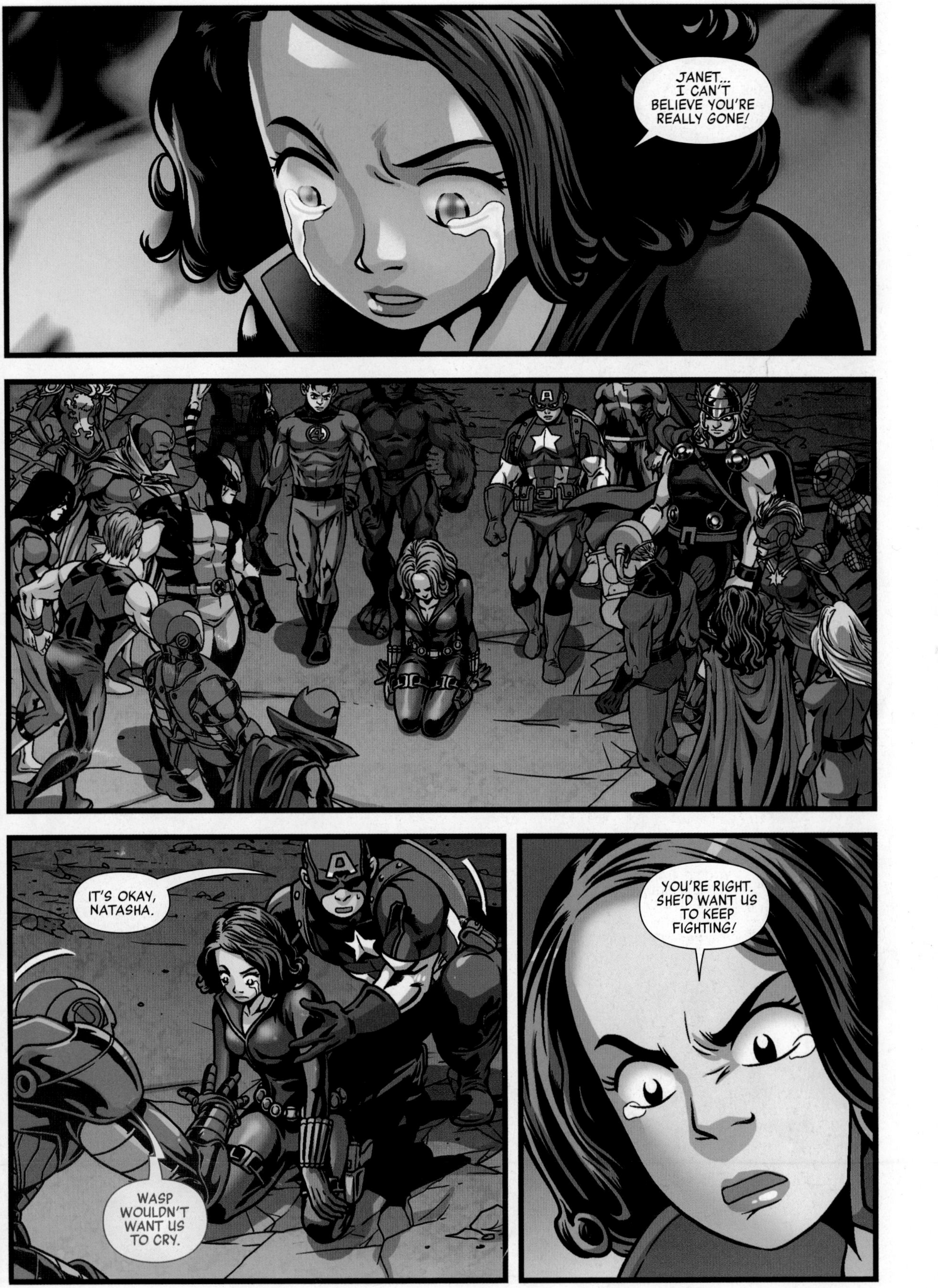
JANET... I CAN'T BELIEVE YOU'RE REALLY GONE!
IT'S OKAY, NATASHA.
WASP WOULDN'T WANT US TO CRY.
YOU'RE RIGHT. SHE'D WANT US TO KEEP FIGHTING!

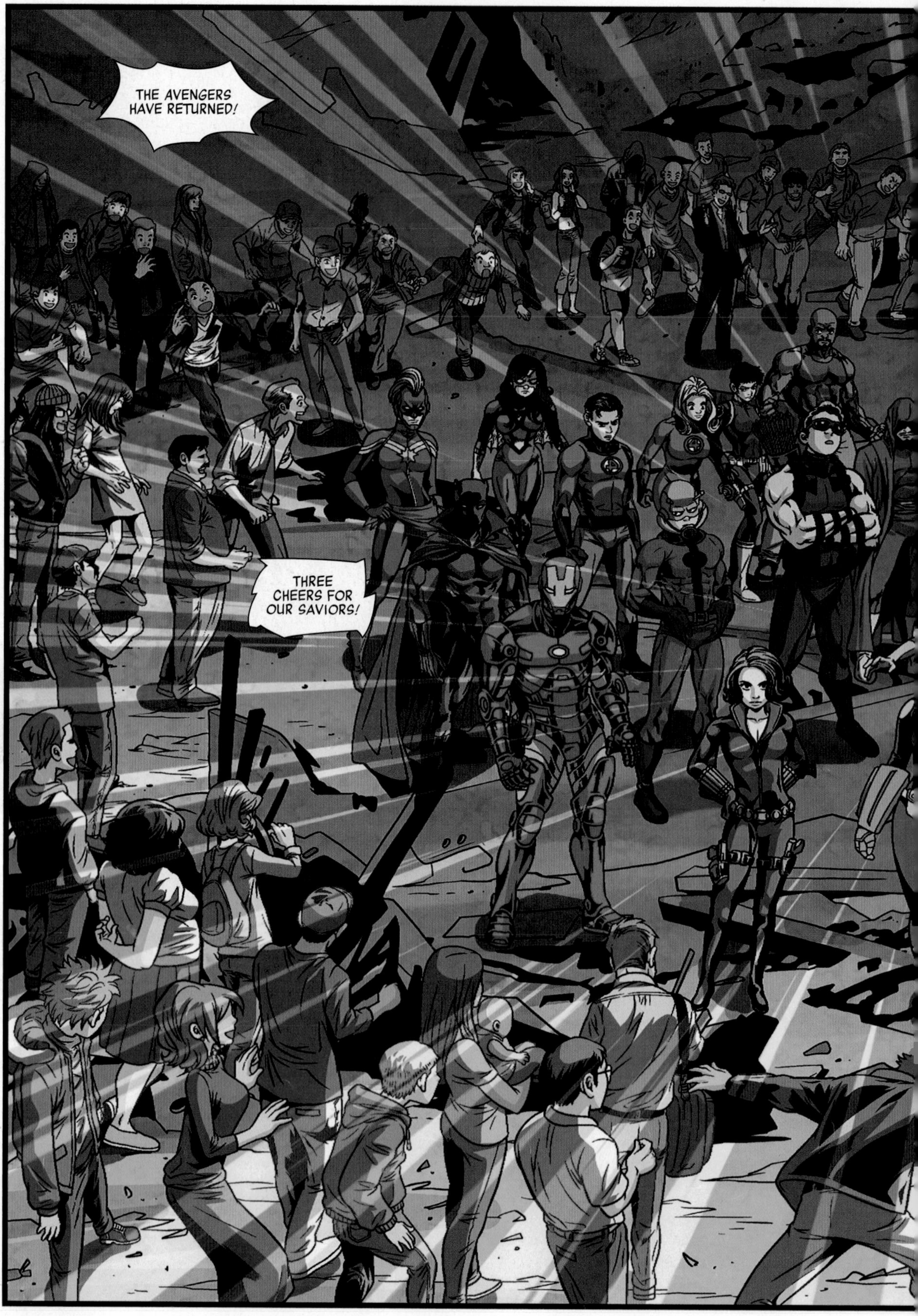
THE AVENGERS HAVE RETURNED!
THREE CHEERS FOR OUR SAVIORS!

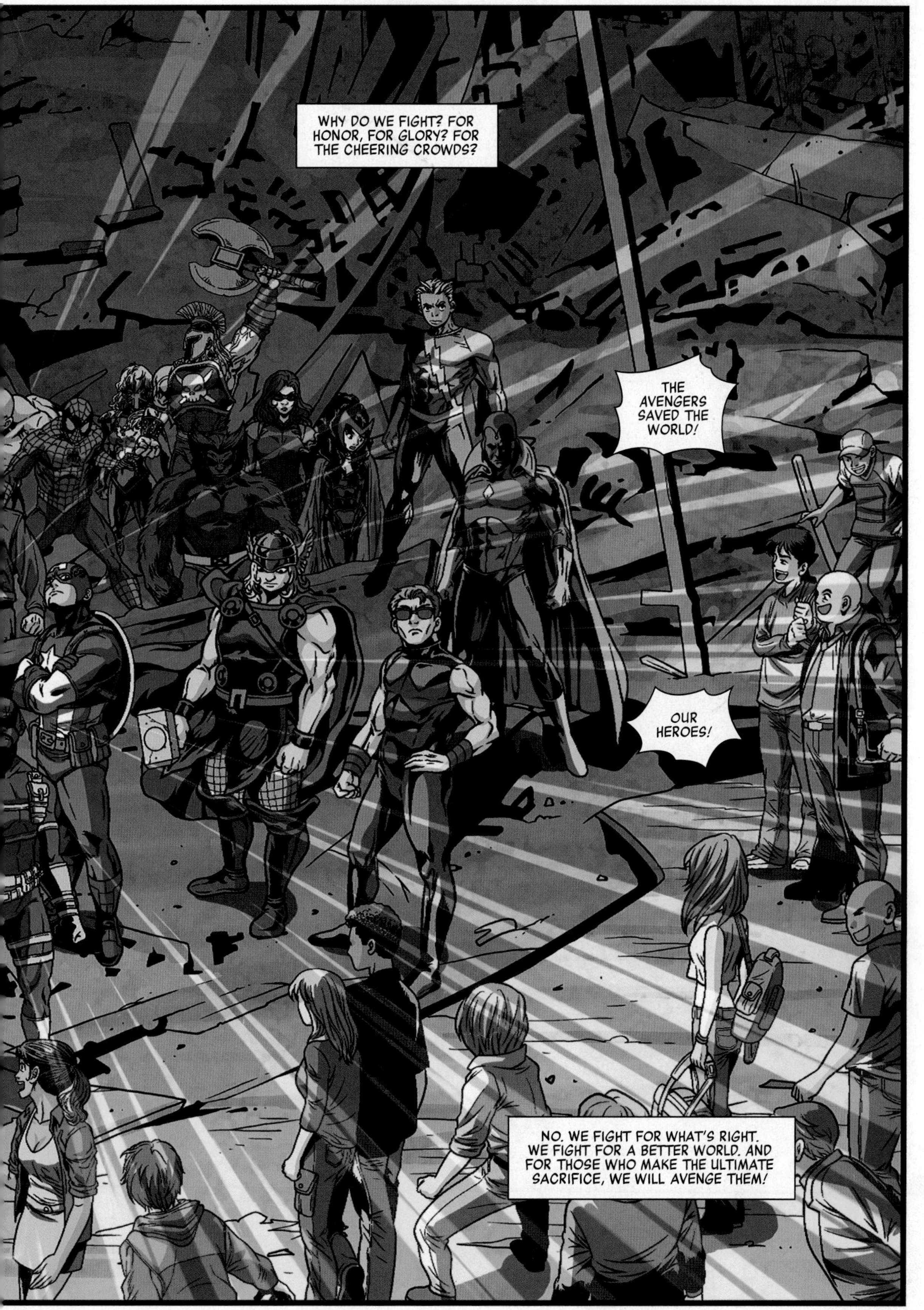
WHY DO WE FIGHT? FOR HONOR, FOR GLORY? FOR THE CHEERING CROWDS?
THE AVENGERS SAVED THE WORLD!
OUR HEROES!
NO. WE FIGHT FOR WHAT'S RIGHT. WE FIGHT FOR A BETTER WORLD. AND FOR THOSE WHO MAKE THE ULTIMATE SACRIFICE, WE WILL AVENGE THEM!

CREATOR PROCESS

TRANSLATOR JI EUN PARK

I am pleased with the publication of the Korean adaptation of the Avengers comics, which are loved throughout the world. Though I had difficulties with some of the older expressions in the original work that aren't used much nowadays, I did my best to show the characteristics of the distinctive characters and the delicate emotional lines as much as possible. It was a wonderful experience for me to read the new English script based on my translation.

WRITER SI YEON PARK

I was happy to join this project, as I myself am a long-time fan of the Avengers, and I have worked with the artist (Woo Bin Choi) several times. I wanted to preserve Marvel's original sentiments, while making the story fun and accessible for Korean readers. The Avengers comics are exciting stories about heroes, and I hope this is the start of a new kind of comic series.

ARTIST WOO BIN CHOI

You wouldn't think so, but it can actually be a more difficult and laborious process to adapt a comic than it is to create an original, especially when you're working with foreign characters. But I was proud to work with Marvel, especially to bring these classic issues to a worldwide audience. This book was my chance to become a different kind of fan of Marvel super heroes. I hope readers have fun!

INKER MIN JU LEE

To ink my colleagues' work, I draw distinct black lines around the sketched figures and shape the backgrounds. I wanted to pay particular attention to the characters' appearance and personalities, and the backgrounds. I'm delighted to be part of the group creating this new Avengers comic, and hope to make better and better work.

COLORIST
JAE WOONG LEE

For the Avengers, color is very important. The original comics used darker, denser colors, so to adapt them for our younger audience, we made the colors brighter and more cheerful. At the same time, each character is symbolized by a specific color, so we tried to respect the original intentions, as well. I was proud to participate in the re-creation of these classic issues.

5